BRAIDING
SWEETGRASS

Also by Robin Wall Kimmerer

Gathering Moss

BRAIDING
SWEETGRASS

Indigenous Wisdom,
Scientific Knowledge, and
the Teachings of Plants

ROBIN WALL
KIMMERER

MILKWEED EDITIONS

Published 2020 by Milkweed Editions
Printed in Canada
Cover design by Mary Austin Speaker
Cover art by Tony Drefahl
Interior art by Nate Christopherson
Author photo by Dale Kakkak
20 21 22 23 24   5 4 3 2 1
Second Hardcover Edition

978-1-57131-177-1

Milkweed Editions, an independent nonprofit publisher, gratefully acknowledges sustaining support from our Board of Directors; the Alan B. Slifka Foundation and its president, Riva Ariella Ritvo-Slifka; the Amazon Literary Partnership; the Ballard Spahr Foundation; *Copper Nickel*; the McKnight Foundation; the National Endowment for the Arts; the National Poetry Series; the Target Foundation; and other generous contributions from foundations, corporations, and individuals. Also, this activity is made possible by the voters of Minnesota through a Minnesota State Arts Board Operating Support grant, thanks to a legislative appropriation from the arts and cultural heritage fund. For a full listing of Milkweed Editions supporters, please visit milkweed.org.

MINNESOTA STATE ARTS BOARD   CLEAN WATER LAND & LEGACY AMENDMENT   TARGET.   NATIONAL ENDOWMENT for the ARTS arts.gov   MCKNIGHT FOUNDATION

Library of Congress Control Number:
2020942641

Milkweed Editions is committed to ecological stewardship. We strive to align our book production practices with this principle, and to reduce the impact of our operations in the environment. We are a member of the Green Press Initiative, a nonprofit coalition of publishers, manufacturers, and authors working to protect the world's endangered forests and conserve natural resources. *Braiding Sweetgrass* was printed on acid-free 100% postconsumer-waste paper by Friesens Corporation.

For all the Keepers of the Fire
my parents
my daughters
and my grandchildren
yet to join us in this beautiful place

Contents

Braiding Sweetgrass

Burning Sweetgrass

Introduction

Sweetgrass has just come into bloom at the edge of my pond, the first grass to flower and so mark its presence in the tangle of winter-brown thatch. The open panicle is a spire spangled with stamens and feathery pistils that quiver in the breeze. Kneeling in the damp soil for a close look, each floret is rimmed with burgundy and copper and gleams with a metallic sheen, far showier than necessity demands for a flower that attracts, not bees but only the wind. It's as if she wants you to notice, raising a flower flag before the great green sward of the meadow engulfs her, so you'll remember this spot when it's time to gather the long shiny blades in mid-summer, with only a whiff of fragrance to guide you.

This stand of Sweetgrass did not volunteer here; I planted it many years ago and I'm gratified to see how far it has spread. Despite the fancy flowers, Sweetgrass does not propagate by windblown seed, but by rhizomes, slender fingers of underground stem that wind their way through the soil unseen until they rise up and bloom. Rarely do they dominate a meadow; rather they come gently, persistently to stand beside the other bigger plants. They delight me with their subversive infiltration of the status quo; all on their own they find their way to new places, where their shine and seductive fragrance beckons, tugging at the edge of consciousness like a memory of something you once knew and want to find again. It stops you, calls you to slow down, and see the meadow with new eyes. Look what was waiting for you; all you needed to do was pay attention. Dropping to your knees, you can't help but sigh in recognition of the gift that was there all along.

Fittingly, this has also been the lifeway of *Braiding Sweetgrass*, as if the stories in the book embody the teachings of their namesake. Slowly, the book moved underground like a network of rhizomes, largely unnoticed at first, until, like the patch at the edge of my pond, you see it blooming everywhere. I'm awash with gratitude for the spread of the message the book carries, with fragrance and shine.

Since time immemorial, we human people have accelerated the movement of *wiingaashk* across Turtle Island, by bringing Sweetgrass to live beside us, to share with a friend. That's how Sweetgrass is best propagated, by carrying the plant with us. And so too, the book has made its way in the world, not by a broadcast of seed, but by loving passage from hand to hand. This beautiful new edition celebrates all those hands.

Milkweed Editions reports that small booksellers offered it to their customers, who then came back for a stack to share. Readers were giving their copies away, saying "I think you need to read this" like a manifesto of love for the world.

I wish I could share all the stories that were shared with me: couples courting by copying out passages for their beloveds, followed by wedding vows inspired by lichens; a daughter reading chapters by phone to her blind father each night on the other side of the country; babies named Hazel; bikes named *wiingaashk*; Thanksgiving Address recitations around the holiday table; protest manifestos; Earth tribunal testimony. Folks have sent me photos of their books as companions: in a dugout down the Amazon, atop a mountain, on a train through Norway, in an ICU bed, on a hay bale in the lambing barn, a touchstone in quarantine. I am bent low by the request of an elder in hospice that the last words she would ever hear carry the scent of wild strawberries. These stories are gifts to the writer's spirit and I thank you.

Everyone has a secret yearning I suppose, a latent desire for some kind of superpower or another life that might have been theirs. I know thou shalt not covet thy neighbor's chloroplasts—and yet I must confess to full-blown chlorophyll envy. What I wrote years ago remains true: "Sometimes I wish I could photosynthesize so that just by being, just by shimmering at the meadow's edge or floating lazily on a pond, I could be doing the work of the world while standing silent in the sun."

In the absence of chloroplasts, writing is as close to that alchemy as I am capable of.

A leaf, bathed in light with stomates wide open to the breath of the air, is not unlike the writer musing in the dark and mind wide open to wisps of thought as amorphous as the atmosphere. We both are sifting and winnowing from the unending flow of materials so ubiquitous as to be invisible, those particular molecules from which life can be built.

I marvel at the glittering green leaf turbines that spin air and water into the building blocks of sugar, like spinning letters into words that can be assembled and reassembled into whatever can be imagined. If only I could turn idea into ink the way they catalyze light into substance, the dross of the ordinary inorganic into the organic word molecules that energize life's unfolding; flowers to seduce, roots to connect, fruits to nourish, seeds to endure, sap to blister skin, and scents to call back memory—all from light and air turned to sugar.

One day, after I'm a daffodil, I will be able to photosynthesize. It's something to look forward to.

On occasions such as this, writers are inevitably asked, Why did you write this book? That question paralyzed me. I was supposed to have an erudite answer, when the truth is I wrote it because I couldn't help myself. There were plant stories wanting to be told and they forced their way up through the ground and down my arm with the motive force of Trillium pushing through soil. I had the honor and responsibility of holding the pen. I'm profoundly grateful for the privilege of carrying a message from the plants, so that they can do their work. I wrote from the belief that since plants are medicines, so too could their stories be healing.

The song leader Laurence Cole crafted songs from *Braiding Sweetgrass*. One is the mesmerizing chant, "A great longing is upon us, to live again in a world made of gifts." It is that longing everywhere I turned that propelled the book. I wrote *Braiding Sweetgrass* in response to longing in Indigenous communities that our philosophy and practices be recognized as guidance to set us back on the path of life. I wrote in response to longing from colonizers, beset with the aftermath of injustice and living on stolen land, to find a path of belonging. I heard longing from the trampled Earth herself to be loved and honored again. Longing from Sandhill cranes and wood thrushes and wild irises just to live.

I wrote from a sense of reciprocity with the Anishinaabe teachings that had been shared with me, by people and by plants. We're told that the reason our ancestors held so tightly to these teachings was that the worldview the settlers tried to obliterate would one day be needed by all beings. Here, at the time of the Seventh Fire, in the age of the Sixth Extinction, of climate chaos, disconnection and dishonor, I think that time is now.

Coupled to the impulse to share is the mandate to protect. Indigenous knowledge has too often been appropriated by its abductors, so the gift of knowledge must be tightly bound to responsibility for that knowledge. If Indigenous wisdom could be medicine for a broken relationship with the Earth, the moral obligation to share the healing must be accompanied by a prescription to avoid misuse. I hoped always to inspire an authentic revitalization of relationship with the land, not by borrowing it from someone else, but by finding your roots and remembering how to grow your own.

I wrote with the intention to provide an antidote for what conservation biologists have termed "plant blindness," the lack of public awareness of the significance of plants to ecosystem function, and the attendant deficiency in policy, scientific knowledge, and conservation funding that follows. Plant blindness and its relative, species loneliness, impedes the recognition of the green world as a garden of gifts. The cycle flows from attention, to gift, to gratitude, to reciprocity. It starts with seeing.

I wrote from a sense of reciprocity, that in return for the privilege of spending my personal and professional life listening to plants, that I might share their teachings with those who didn't even know that they had something to say.

Lewis Hyde, whose book *The Gift* was so important to me, writes how art as a gift behaves like a call-and-response song. One of the elements of traditional Potawatomi songs that quickens my heart is the structure in which a leader raises a song line into the quiet and is met with a surge of voices in return, taking up the line with affirmation and then falling back for the next. Around and around goes the call and response until everyone is singing, the way a storm begins with the first patter and grows into a downpour of everyone wet and dancing in the rain to the beat of thunder. It feels to me like a lone voice that discovers she is not alone. Reader after reader has used the words, "I thought I was alone in loving the earth this way." This is how I have experienced the response to *Braiding Sweetgrass*—that we have found in each other a choir.

I've come to understand the ongoing work of *Braiding Sweetgrass* is this call and response, the call arising from a shared sense of longing and the response building in a chorus of the Great Remembering. Myriad readers have offered their stories of remembering something that was buried by the noise of the world, by the commodification of nature, by the erasure of knowing oneself to be good medicine for the land. People are remembering another way of being in the world, in kinship. They long to remember their gifts and how to give them in the world. Maybe plants help us remember.

Braiding Sweetgrass invites us to hold a *minidewak*, a giveaway for Mother Earth, to spread our blanket and pile it high with gifts of our own making, in return for all we've been given, in compensation for all we've taken. The response to this invitation has been an outpouring of reciprocal gifts of art and music and science on behalf of the land. I could fill pages of praise for these acts of reciprocity; I can mention only a few to inspire you to add your own.

For example, extraordinary music has grown from *Braiding Sweetgrass*: Sarah Fraker's oboe sings in reciprocity for the tree who made it; singers lift Laurence Cole's rounds to the lichens; and in Cheryl L'Hirondelle's Cree round dance anthem, birds, water, and the people all sing together their promise to the plants, to care for them. Such a chorus we make together.

I have been humbled by the unexpected gift of art, posters, mandala, weavings, sculpture, and Tony Drehfal's woodcut that graces the cover of this book. A knitting pattern, a bread recipe, films, podcasts, a dance created for goldenrod and asters, all exemplify the power of gift that grows with every giving, not meant to be held but to be shared.

And a deep bow to the teachers who have written Sweetgrass curricula from forest preschools to university courses and everything in between. A teacher who centers high school biology around the Thanksgiving Address, the MBA course that constructs an Honorable Harvest business plan, the professor of theology who challenges his students to write new liturgies for the Earth. Should your faith in the power of story to change the world ever flag, know that the preserve managers at Cascade Head in Oregon reintroduced healing fire to that high and holy landscape. They acknowledged that their good science of restoration was compelled by the imperative of an ancient story.

This renews my faith in the possibility of lived reciprocity. Together, this is how the world changes. We have braided a Sweetgrass community, awakening for each other the knowing that we are not alone. The strength of that community has the power to activate change, and our collective rhizomes are spreading.

To me, this special edition of *Braiding Sweetgrass* envisioned by Milkweed is a gift to you, in an ongoing circle of gift giving, a giveaway, and the *minidewak*.

I began writing *Braiding Sweetgrass* in what seems, from this moment in the midst of a global pandemic and the upheavals it has generated, a more innocent time, when climate catastrophe was a hot glow on the horizon. We could smell smoke but our home was not yet engulfed in flames. There was guarded optimism for leadership on climate change and justice for land and people, human and otherwise.

A lot has happened since in climate urgency, with the political pain of vile Windigos come to office and all the wounds they have inflicted. I don't need to say more. This evidence might suggest that the medicine of plant stories has not worked very well to heal our relationships with land and each other. The powerful purveyors of destruction are still in power, the skies darkening. But as always, I take my guidance from the forests, who teach us something about change. The forces of creation and destruction are so tightly linked that sometimes we can't tell where one begins and the other leaves off. A long-lived overstory can dominate the forest for generations, setting the ecological conditions for its own thriving while suppressing others by exploiting all the resources with a self-serving dominance. But, all the while it sets the stage for what happens next and something always happens that is more powerful than that overstory: a fire, a windstorm, a disease. Eventually, the old forest is disrupted and replaced by the understory, by the buried seedbank that has been readying itself for this moment of transformation and renewal. A whole new ecosystem rises to replace that which no longer works in a changed world. *Braiding Sweetgrass*, I hope, is part of that understory, seeded by many thinkers and doers, filling the seedbank with diverse species, so that when the canopy falls, as it surely will, a new world is already rising. "New" and ancient, with its origins in the Indigenous worldview of right relation between land and people. What the "overstory" of colonialism tried to suppress is surging. It is the prophesied time of the Seventh Fire, a sacred time when the collective remembering transforms the world. A dark time and a time filled with light. We remember the oft-used words of resistance, "They tried to bury us, but they didn't know we were seeds."

It's as if we can see the world we want to live in just over time's horizon; the question is how do we get there? It's a question familiar to Sweetgrass, unable to leave one place and travel to a better one by seed. Ki* relies on humans to carry rhizomes, the ones who can easily cross distance and boundaries, who know that whatever we wish to see on the other side of the narrows of this ecological and cultural crisis, we must pass lovingly from hand to hand.

The mythic story of Skywoman Falling is the heartbeat of *Braiding*

---

* Ki is a pronoun to signify a living being of the Earth.

Sweetgrass, both an opening and a closing, enfolding the stories between. The version shared in the first edition is the most widely told account of the epic, but it is not the only one. There is always the deep diving Muskrat and the earth on Turtle's back. The rescue by the Geese and the gifts of the animals are a constant, as are the seeds Skywoman brings, initiating the covenant of reciprocity between newcomer humans and our ancient relatives. The detail that varies from one telling to another is just how Skywoman finds herself falling from one world to the next. The common version is that she slips, the earth giving way at the edge of the hole in the sky where the great Tree of Life had fallen. It is an accident, with mythic consequences—and so it begins.

But in other tellings, this was no accident. In one version, she was pushed. In another she was thrown—not from malice but because she was needed for the sacred task and needed "help" in leaving her beloved home for the next. In every version I've ever heard, Skywoman was an accidental and possibly an unwilling traveler to the next world, like a seed on the wind.

As I look around at the strong women I know, Indigenous and new-comer, survivors and thrivers, teachers, artists, farmers, singers, healers, mothers, nokos, aunties, daughters, sisters holding together families and communities and leading the way to a new world, I have a hard time see-ing our Skywoman as an unknowing and passive emissary. No. I see her standing at the edge of the hole in the sky, her belly planted with new life, looking down into the darkness. Guided by the shaft of dazzling light shining through, she catches a glimpse of the world that waits for the seeds she carries, plucked from the Tree of Life. With all humility and respect for the teachings of this sacred story, I cannot help my imagining forward to this moment on the circle of time. What if, with full agency, she spreads her arms, looks over her shoulder, feels her child stir within and then—what if she jumps?

She is a woman with a duty to safeguard life. Just as women have done throughout our painful history, carrying life through times of star-vation and disease, on the long walks of removal, hiding children from the boarding schools and embracing the ones who came back, fighting pipelines, protecting water, saving the seeds, learning the language, holding the ceremonies, honoring the earth... Skywoman's descendants are not women who would step away from the edge, if it meant the protection of life.

As a society we stand at the brink, we know we do. Through the hole that opens at our feet, we can look down and see a glittering blue and green planet, as if from the vantage point of space, vibrating with birdsong and toads and tigers. We could close our eyes, keep breathing poison air, witness the extinction of our relatives and continue to measure our worth by how much we take. We could cover our ears to our own knowing, back away from the edge and retreat to the gray decline.

In this time of transformation, when creation and destruction wrestle like Skywoman's mythic grandsons, gambling with the future of the earth, what would it take for us to follow Skywoman? To jump to the new world, to co-create it? Do we jump because we look over our shoulders at the implacable suffering marching toward us and jump from fear and portent? Or perhaps we look down, drawn toward the glittering green, hear the birdsong, smell the Sweetgrass and yearn to be part of a different story. The story we long for, the story that we are beginning to remember, the story that remembers us.

What does it take to abandon what does not work and take the risks of uncertainty? We'll need courage; we'll need each other's hands to hold and faith in the geese to catch us. It would help to sing. The landing might not be soft, but land holds many medicines. Propelled by love, ready to work, we can jump toward the world we want to co-create, with pockets full of seeds. And rhizomes.

Preface

Hold out your hands and let me lay upon them a sheaf of freshly picked sweetgrass, loose and flowing, like newly washed hair. Golden green and glossy above, the stems are banded with purple and white where they meet the ground. Hold the bundle up to your nose. Find the fragrance of honeyed vanilla over the scent of river water and black earth and you understand its scientific name: *Hierochloe odorata*, meaning the fragrant, holy grass. In our language it is called *wiingaashk*, the sweet-smelling hair of Mother Earth. Breathe it in and you start to remember things you didn't know you'd forgotten.

A sheaf of sweetgrass, bound at the end and divided into thirds, is ready to braid. In braiding sweetgrass—so that it is smooth, glossy, and worthy of the gift—a certain amount of tension is needed. As any little girl with tight braids will tell you, you have to pull a bit. Of course you can do it yourself—by tying one end to a chair, or by holding it in your teeth and braiding backward away from yourself—but the sweetest way is to have someone else hold the end so that you pull gently against each other, all the while leaning in, head to head, chatting and laughing, watching each other's hands, one holding steady while the other shifts the slim bundles over one another, each in its turn. Linked by sweetgrass, there is reciprocity between you, linked by sweetgrass, the holder as vital as the braider. The braid becomes finer and thinner as you near the end, until you're braiding individual blades of grass, and then you tie it off.

Will you hold the end of the bundle while I braid? Hands joined by grass, can we bend our heads together and make a braid to honor the earth? And then I'll hold it for you, while you braid, too.

I could hand you a braid of sweetgrass, as thick and shining as the plait that hung down my grandmother's back. But it is not mine to give, nor yours to take. *Wiingaashk* belongs to herself. So I offer, in its place, a braid of stories meant to heal our relationship with the world. This braid is woven from three strands: Indigenous ways of knowing, scientific knowledge, and the story of an Anishinabekwe scientist trying to bring them together in service to what matters most. It is an intertwining of science, spirit, and story—old stories and new ones that can be medicine for our broken relationship with earth, a pharmacopoeia of healing stories that allow us to imagine a different relationship, in which people and land are good medicine for each other.

BRAIDING

SWEETGRASS

Planting Sweetgrass

Sweetgrass is best planted not by seed, but by
putting roots directly in the ground. Thus the plant
is passed from hand to earth to hand across years
and generations. Its favored habitat is sunny, well-
watered meadows. It thrives along disturbed edges.

Skywoman Falling

In winter, when the green earth lies resting beneath a blanket of snow, this is the time for storytelling. The storytellers begin by calling upon those who came before who passed the stories down to us, for we are only messengers. In the beginning there was the Skyworld.

She fell like a maple seed, pirouetting on an autumn breeze.* A column of light streamed from a hole in the Skyworld, marking her path where only darkness had been before. It took her a long time to fall. In fear, or maybe hope, she clutched a bundle tightly in her hand.

Hurtling downward, she saw only dark water below. But in that emptiness there were many eyes gazing up at the sudden shaft of light. They saw there a small object, a mere dust mote in the beam. As it grew closer, they could see that it was a woman, arms outstretched, long black hair billowing behind as she spiraled toward them.

The geese nodded at one another and rose together from the water in a wave of goose music. She felt the beat of their wings as they flew beneath to break her fall. Far from the only home she'd ever known, she caught her breath at the warm embrace of soft feathers as they gently carried her downward. And so it began.

The geese could not hold the woman above the water for much longer, so they called a council to decide what to do. Resting on their wings,

---

* Adapted from oral tradition and Shenandoah and George, 1988.

3

she saw them all gather: loons, otters, swans, beavers, fish of all kinds. A great turtle floated in their midst and offered his back for her to rest upon. Gratefully, she stepped from the goose wings onto the dome of his shell. The others understood that she needed land for her home and discussed how they might serve her need. The deep divers among them had heard of mud at the bottom of the water and agreed to go find some.

Loon dove first, but the distance was too far and after a long while he surfaced with nothing to show for his efforts. One by one, the other animals offered to help—Otter, Beaver, Sturgeon—but the depth, the darkness, and the pressures were too great for even the strongest of swimmers. They returned gasping for air with their heads ringing. Some did not return at all. Soon only little Muskrat was left, the weakest diver of all. He volunteered to go while the others looked on doubtfully. His small legs flailed as he worked his way downward and he was gone a very long time.

They waited and waited for him to return, fearing the worst for their relative, and, before long, a stream of bubbles rose with the small, limp body of the muskrat. He had given his life to aid this helpless human. But then the others noticed that his paw was tightly clenched and, when they opened it, there was a small handful of mud. Turtle said, "Here, put it on my back and I will hold it."

Skywoman bent and spread the mud with her hands across the shell of the turtle. Moved by the extraordinary gifts of the animals, she sang in thanksgiving and then began to dance, her feet caressing the earth. The land grew and grew as she danced her thanks, from the dab of mud on Turtle's back until the whole earth was made. Not by Skywoman alone, but from the alchemy of all the animals' gifts coupled with her deep gratitude. Together they formed what we know today as Turtle Island, our home.

Like any good guest, Skywoman had not come empty-handed. The bundle was still clutched in her hand. When she toppled from the hole in the Skyworld she had reached out to grab onto the Tree of Life that grew there. In her grasp were branches—fruits and seeds of all kinds of plants. These she scattered onto the new ground and carefully tended each one until the world turned from brown to green. Sunlight streamed through the hole from the Skyworld, allowing the seeds to flourish.

Wild grasses, flowers, trees, and medicines spread everywhere. And now that the animals, too, had plenty to eat, many came to live with her on Turtle Island.

Our stories say that of all the plants, *wiingaashk,* or sweetgrass, was the very first to grow on the earth, its fragrance a sweet memory of Skywoman's hand. Accordingly, it is honored as one of the four sacred plants of my people. Breathe in its scent and you start to remember things you didn't know you'd forgotten. Our elders say that ceremonies are the way we "remember to remember," and so sweetgrass is a power-ful ceremonial plant cherished by many Indigenous nations. It is also used to make beautiful baskets. Both medicine and a relative, its value is both material and spiritual.

There is such tenderness in braiding the hair of someone you love. Kindness and something more flow between the braider and the braided, the two connected by the cord of the plait. *Wiingaashk* waves in strands, long and shining like a woman's freshly washed hair. And so we say it is the flowing hair of Mother Earth. When we braid sweetgrass, we are braiding the hair of Mother Earth, showing her our loving attention, our care for her beauty and well-being, in gratitude for all she has given us. Children hearing the Skywoman story from birth know in their bones the responsibility that flows between humans and the earth.

The story of Skywoman's journey is so rich and glittering it feels to me like a deep bowl of celestial blue from which I could drink again and again. It holds our beliefs, our history, our relationships. Looking into that starry bowl, I see images swirling so fluidly that the past and the present become as one. Images of Skywoman speak not just of where we came from, but also of how we can go forward.

I have Bruce King's portrait of Skywoman, *Moment in Flight,* hanging in my lab. Floating to earth with her handful of seeds and flowers, she looks down on my microscopes and data loggers. It might seem an odd juxtaposition, but to me she belongs there. As a writer, a scientist, and a carrier of Skywoman's story, I sit at the feet of my elder teachers listening for their songs.

On Mondays, Wednesdays, and Fridays at 9:35 a.m., I am usually in a lecture hall at the university, expounding about botany and ecology—trying, in short, to explain to my students how Skywoman's gardens, known by some as "global ecosystems," function. One otherwise unremarkable morning I gave the students in my General Ecology class a survey. Among other things, they were asked to rate their understanding of the negative interactions between humans and the environment. Nearly every one of the two hundred students said confidently that humans and nature are a bad mix. These were third-year students who had selected a career in environmental protection, so the response was, in a way, not very surprising. They were well schooled in the mechanics of climate change, toxins in the land and water, and the crisis of habitat loss. Later in the survey, they were asked to rate their knowledge of positive interactions between people and land. The median response was "none."

I was stunned. How is it possible that in twenty years of education they cannot think of any beneficial relationships between people and the environment? Perhaps the negative examples they see every day—brownfields, factory farms, suburban sprawl—truncated their ability to see some good between humans and the earth. As the land becomes impoverished, so too does the scope of their vision. When we talked about this after class, I realized that they could not even imagine what beneficial relations between their species and others might look like. How can we begin to move toward ecological and cultural sustainability if we cannot even imagine what the path feels like? If we can't imagine the generosity of geese? These students were not raised on the story of Skywoman.

On one side of the world were people whose relationship with the living world was shaped by Skywoman, who created a garden for the well-being of all. On the other side was another woman with a garden and a tree. But for tasting its fruit, she was banished from the garden and the gates clanged shut behind her. That mother of men was made to wander in the wilderness and earn her bread by the sweat of her brow, not by filling her mouth with the sweet juicy fruits that bend the branches low. In order to eat, she was instructed to subdue the wilderness into which she was cast.

Same species, same earth, different stories. Like Creation stories everywhere, cosmologies are a source of identity and orientation to the world. They tell us who we are. We are inevitably shaped by them no matter how distant they may be from our consciousness. One story leads to the generous embrace of the living world, the other to banishment. One woman is our ancestral gardener, a cocreator of the good green world that would be the home of her descendants. The other was an exile, just passing through an alien world on a rough road to her real home in heaven.

And then they met—the offspring of Skywoman and the children of Eve—and the land around us bears the scars of that meeting, the echoes of our stories. They say that hell hath no fury like a woman scorned, and I can only imagine the conversation between Eve and Skywoman: "Sister, you got the short end of the stick . . ."

The Skywoman story, shared by the original peoples throughout the Great Lakes, is a constant star in the constellation of teachings we call the Original Instructions. These are not "instructions" like commandments, though, or rules; rather, they are like a compass: they provide an orientation but not a map. The work of living is creating that map for yourself. How to follow the Original Instructions will be different for each of us and different for every era.

In their time, Skywoman's first people lived by their understanding of the Original Instructions, with ethical prescriptions for respectful hunting, family life, ceremonies that made sense for their world. Those measures for caring might not seem to fit in today's urban world, where "green" means an advertising slogan, not a meadow. The buffalo are gone and the world has moved on. I can't return salmon to the river, and my neighbors would raise the alarm if I set fire to my yard to produce pasture for elk.

The earth was new then, when it welcomed the first human. It's old now, and some suspect that we have worn out our welcome by casting the Original Instructions aside. From the very beginning of the world, the other species were a lifeboat for the people. Now, we must be theirs. But the stories that might guide us, if they are told at all, grow dim in the memory. What meaning would they have today? How can we translate from the stories at the world's beginning to this hour so much closer to its end? The landscape has changed, but the story remains. And as I turn it over again and again, Skywoman seems to look me in the eye and ask, in return for this gift of a world on Turtle's back, what will I give in return?

It is good to remember that the original woman was herself an immigrant. She fell a long way from her home in the Skyworld, leaving behind all who knew her and who held her dear. She could never go back. Since 1492, most here are immigrants as well, perhaps arriving on Ellis Island without even knowing that Turtle Island rested beneath their feet. Some of my ancestors are Skywoman's people, and I belong to them. Some of my ancestors were the newer kind of immigrants, too: a French fur trader, an Irish carpenter, a Welsh farmer. And here we all are, on Turtle Island, trying to make a home. Their stories, of arrivals with empty pockets and nothing but hope, resonate with Skywoman's. She came here with nothing but a handful of seeds and the slimmest of instructions to "use your gifts and dreams for good," the same instructions we all carry. She accepted the gifts from the other beings with open hands and used them honorably. She shared the gifts she brought from Skyworld as she set herself about the business of flourishing, of making a home.

Perhaps the Skywoman story endures because we too are always falling. Our lives, both personal and collective, share her trajectory. Whether we jump or are pushed, or the edge of the known world just crumbles at our feet, we fall, spinning into someplace new and unexpected. Despite our fears of falling, the gifts of the world stand by to catch us.

As we consider these instructions, it is also good to recall that, when Skywoman arrived here, she did not come alone. She was pregnant. Knowing her grandchildren would inherit the world she left behind, she did not work for flourishing in her time only. It was through her actions of reciprocity, the give and take with the land, that the original immigrant became Indigenous. For all of us, becoming Indigenous to a place means living as if your children's future mattered, to take care of the land as if our lives, both material and spiritual, depended on it.

In the public arena, I've heard the Skywoman story told as a bauble of colorful "folklore." But, even when it is misunderstood, there is power in the telling. Most of my students have never heard the origin story of this land where they were born, but when I tell them, something begins to kindle behind their eyes. Can they, can we all, understand the Skywoman story not as an artifact from the past but as instructions for the future? Can a nation of immigrants once again follow her example to become native, to make a home?

Look at the legacy of poor Eve's exile from Eden: the land shows the bruises of an abusive relationship. It's not just land that is broken, but more importantly, our relationship to land. As Gary Nabhan has written, we can't meaningfully proceed with healing, with restoration, without "re-story-ation." In other words, our relationship with land cannot heal until we hear its stories. But who will tell them?

In the Western tradition there is a recognized hierarchy of beings, with, of course, the human being on top—the pinnacle of evolution, the darling of Creation—and the plants at the bottom. But in Native ways of knowing, human people are often referred to as "the younger brothers of Creation." We say that humans have the least experience with how to live and thus the most to learn—we must look to our teachers among the other species for guidance. Their wisdom is apparent in the way that they live. They teach us by example. They've been on the earth far longer than we have been, and have had time to figure things out. They live both above and below ground, joining Skyworld to the earth. Plants know how to make food and medicine from light and water, and then they give it away.

I like to imagine that when Skywoman scattered her handful of seeds across Turtle Island, she was sowing sustenance for the body and also for the mind, emotion, and spirit: she was leaving us teachers. The plants can tell us her story; we need to learn to listen.

The Council of Pecans

Heat waves shimmer above the grasses, the air heavy and white and ringing with the buzz of cicadas. They've been shoeless all summer long, but even so the dry September stubble of 1895 pricks their feet as they trot across the sunburned prairie, lifting their heels like grass dancers. Just young willow whips in faded dungarees and nothing else, their ribs showing beneath narrow brown chests as they run. They veer off toward the shady grove where the grass is soft and cool underfoot, flopping in the tall grass with the loose-limbed abandon of boys. They rest for a few moments in the shade and then spring to their feet, palming grasshoppers for bait.

The fishing poles are right where they left them, leaning up against an old cottonwood. They hook the grasshoppers through the back and throw out a line while the silt of the creek bottom oozes up cool between their toes. But the water hardly moves in the paltry channel left by drought. Nothing's biting but a few mosquitoes. After a bit, the prospect of a fish dinner seem as thin as their bellies, beneath faded denim pants held up with twine. Looks like nothing but biscuits and redeye gravy for supper tonight. Again. They hate to go home empty-handed and disappoint Mama, but even a dry biscuit fills the belly.

The land here, along the Canadian River, smack in the middle of Indian Territory, is a rolling savanna of grass with groves of trees in the bottomlands. Much of it has never been plow broke, as no one has a plow. The boys follow the stream from grove to grove back up toward the home place on the allotment, hoping for a deep pool somewhere, finding nothing. Until one boy stubs his toe on something hard and round hidden in the long grass.

There's one and then another, and then another—so many he can hardly walk. He takes up a hard green ball from the ground and whips it through the trees at his brother like a fastball as he yells, *"Piganek!* Let's bring 'em home!"* The nuts have just begun to ripen and fall and blanket the grass. The boys fill their pockets in no time and then pile up a great heap more. Pecans are good eating but hard to carry, like trying to carry a bushel of tennis balls: the more you pick up, the more end up on the ground. They hate to go home empty-handed, and Mama would be glad for these—but you can't carry more than a handful . . .

The heat eases a little as the sun sinks low and evening air settles in the bottomland, cool enough for them to run home for supper. Mama hollers for them and the boys come running, their skinny legs pumping and their underpants flashing white in the fading light. It looks like they're each carrying a big forked log, hung like a yoke over their shoulders. They throw them down at her feet with grins of triumph: two pairs of worn-out pants, tied shut with twine at the ankles and bulging with nuts.

One of those skinny little boys was my grandpa, hungry enough to gather up food whenever he found it, living in a shanty on the Oklahoma prairie when it was still "Indian Territory," just before it all blew away. As unpredictable as life may be, we have even less control over the stories they tell about us after we're gone. He'd laugh so hard to hear that his great-grandchildren know him not as a decorated World War I veteran, not as a skilled mechanic for newfangled automobiles, but as a barefoot boy on the reservation running home in his underwear with his pants stuffed with pecans.

The word *pecan*—the fruit of the tree known as the pecan hickory *(Carya illinoensis)*—comes to English from Indigenous languages. *Pigan* is a nut, any nut. The hickories, black walnuts, and butternuts of our northern homelands have their own specific names. But those trees, like the homelands, were lost to my people. Our lands around Lake Michigan were wanted by settlers, so in long lines, surrounded by soldiers, we were marched at gunpoint along what became known as the Trail of Death. They took us to a new place, far from our lakes and forests. But someone wanted that land too, so the bedrolls were packed again, thinner this time. In the span of a single generation my ancestors were "removed" three times—Wisconsin to Kansas, points in between, and then to Oklahoma. I wonder if they looked back for a last glimpse of the lakes, glimmering like a mirage. Did they touch the trees in remembrance as they became fewer and fewer, until there was only grass?

So much was scattered and left along that trail. Graves of half the people. Language. Knowledge. Names. My great-grandmother Sha-note, "wind blowing through," was renamed Charlotte. Names the soldiers or the missionaries could not pronounce were not permitted.

When they got to Kansas they must have been relieved to find groves of nut trees along the rivers—a type unknown to them, but delicious and plentiful. Without a name for this new food they just called them nuts—*pigan*—which became *pecan* in English.

I only make pecan pie at Thanksgiving, when there are plenty around to eat it all. I don't even like it especially, but I want to honor that tree. Feeding guests its fruit around the big table recalls the trees' welcome to our ancestors when they were lonesome and tired and so far from home.

The boys may have come home fishless, but they brought back nearly as much protein as if they'd had a stringer of catfish. Nuts are like the pan fish of the forest, full of protein and especially fat—"poor man's meat," and they were poor. Today we eat them daintily, shelled and toasted, but in the old times they'd boil them up in a porridge. The fat floated to the top like a chicken soup and they skimmed it and stored it as nut butter: good winter food. High in calories and vitamins—everything you needed to sustain life. After all, that's the whole point of nuts: to provide the embryo with all that is needed to start a new life.

Butternuts, black walnuts, hickories, and pecans are all closely related members of the same family *(Juglandaceae)*. Our people carried them wherever they migrated, more often in baskets than in pants, though. Pecans today trace the rivers through the prairies, populating fertile bottomlands where people settled. My Haudenosaunee neighbors say that their ancestors were so fond of butternuts that they are a good marker of old village sites today. Sure enough, there is a grove of butternuts, uncommon in "wild" forests, on the hill above the spring at my house. I clear the weeds around the young ones every year and slosh a bucket of water on them when the rains are late. Remembering.

The old family home place on the allotment in Oklahoma has a pecan tree shading what remains of the house. I imagine Grammy pouring nuts out to prepare them and one rolling away to a welcoming spot at the edge of the dooryard. Or maybe she paid her debt to the trees by planting a handful in her garden right then and there.

Thinking back to that old story again, it strikes me that the boys in the pecan grove were very wise to carry home all that they could: nut trees don't make a crop every year, but rather produce at unpredictable intervals. Some years a feast, most years a famine, a boom and bust cycle known as mast fruiting. Unlike juicy fruits and berries, which invite you to eat them right away before they spoil, nuts protect themselves with a hard, almost stony shell and a green, leathery husk. The tree does not mean for you to eat them right away with juice dripping down your chin. They are designed to be food for winter, when you need fat and protein, heavy calories to keep you warm. They are safety for hard times, the embryo of survival. So rich is the reward that the contents are protected in a vault, double locked, a box inside a box. This protects the embryo within and its food supply, but it also virtually guarantees that the nut will be squirreled away someplace safe.

The only way through the shell is a lot of work, and a squirrel would be unwise to sit gnawing it in the open where a hawk would gladly take advantage of its preoccupation. Nuts are designed to be brought inside, to save for later in a chipmunk's cache, or in the root cellar of an Oklahoma cabin. In the way of all hoards, some will surely be forgotten—and then a tree is born.

For mast fruiting to succeed in generating new forests, each tree has to make lots and lots of nuts—so many that it overwhelms the would-be seed predators. If a tree just plodded along making a few nuts every year, they'd all get eaten and there would be no next generation of pecans. But given the high caloric value of nuts, the trees can't afford this outpouring every year—they have to save up for it, as a family saves up for a special event. Mast-fruiting trees spend years making sugar, and rather than spending it little by little, they stick it under the proverbial mattress, banking calories as starch in their roots. When the account has a surplus, only then could my Grandpa bring home pounds of nuts.

This boom and bust cycle remains a playground of hypotheses for tree physiologists and evolutionary biologists. Forest ecologists hypothesize that mast fruiting is the simple outcome of this energetic equation: make fruit only when you can afford it. That makes sense. But trees grow and accumulate calories at different rates depending on their habitats. So, like the settlers who got the fertile farmland, the fortunate ones would get rich quickly and fruit often, while their shaded neighbors would struggle and only rarely have an abundance, waiting for years to reproduce. If this were true, each tree would fruit on its own schedule, predictable by the size of its reserves of stored starch. But they don't. If one tree fruits, they all fruit—there are no soloists. Not one tree in a grove, but the whole grove; not one grove in the forest, but every grove; all across the county and all across the state. The trees act not as individuals, but somehow as a collective. Exactly how they do this, we don't yet know. But what we see is the power of unity. What happens to one happens to us all. We can starve together or feast together. All flourishing is mutual.

In the summer of 1895, the root cellars throughout Indian Territory were full of pecans, and so were the bellies of boys and squirrels. For people, the pulse of abundance felt like a gift, a profusion of food to be simply picked up from the ground. That is, if you got there before the squirrels. And if you didn't, at least there would be lots of squirrel stew that winter. The pecan groves give, and give again. Such communal generosity might seem incompatible with the process of evolution, which invokes the imperative of individual survival. But we make a grave error if we try to separate individual well-being from the health of the whole. The gift of abundance from pecans is also a gift to themselves. By sating squirrels and people, the trees are ensuring their own survival. The genes that translate to mast fruiting flow on evolutionary currents into the next generations, while those that lack the ability to participate will be eaten and reach an evolutionary dead end. Just so, people who know how to read the land for nuts and carry them home to safety will survive the February blizzards and pass on that behavior to their progeny, not by genetic transmission but by cultural practice.

Forest scientists describe the generosity of mast fruiting with the predator-satiation hypothesis. The story seems to go like this: When the trees produce more than the squirrels can eat, some nuts escape predation. Likewise, when the squirrel larders are packed with nuts, the plump pregnant mamas have more babies in each litter and the squirrel population skyrockets. Which means that the hawk mamas have more babies, and fox dens are full too. But when the next fall comes, the happy days are over, because the trees have shut off nut production. There's little to fill the squirrels' larders now—they come home empty-handed—so they go out looking, harder and harder, exposing themselves to the increased population of watchful hawks and hungry foxes. The predator-prey ratio is not in their favor, and through starvation and predation the squirrel population plummets and the woods grow quiet without their chattering. You can imagine the trees whispering to each other at this point, "There are just a few squirrels left. Wouldn't this be a good time to make some nuts?" All across the landscape, out come the pecan flowers poised to become a bumper crop again. Together, the trees survive, and thrive.

The federal government's Indian Removal policies wrenched many Native peoples from our homelands. It separated us from our traditional knowledge and lifeways, the bones of our ancestors, our sustaining plants—but even this did not extinguish identity. So the government tried a new tool, separating children from their families and cultures, sending them far away to school, long enough, they hoped, to make them forget who they were.

Throughout Indian Territory there are records of Indian agents being paid a bounty for rounding up kids to ship to the government boarding schools. Later, in a pretense of choice, the parents had to sign papers to let their children go "legally." Parents who refused could go to jail. Some may have hoped it would give their children a better future than a dust-bowl farm. Sometimes federal rations—weevilly flour and rancid lard that were supposed to replace the buffalo—would be withheld until the children were signed over. Maybe it was a good pecan year that staved off the agents for one more season. The threat of being sent away would surely make a small boy run home half naked, his pants stuffed with food. Maybe it was a low year for pecans when the Indian agent came again, looking for skinny brown kids who had no prospect of supper—maybe that was the year Grammy signed the papers.

Children, language, lands: almost everything was stripped away, stolen when you weren't looking because you were trying to stay alive. In the face of such loss, one thing our people could not surrender was the meaning of land. In the settler mind, land was property, real estate, capital, or natural resources. But to our people, it was everything: identity, the connection to our ancestors, the home of our nonhuman kinfolk, our pharmacy, our library, the source of all that sustained us. Our lands were where our responsibility to the world was enacted, sacred ground. It belonged to itself; it was a gift, not a commodity, so it could never be bought or sold. These are the meanings people took with them when they were forced from their ancient homelands to new places. Whether it was their homeland or the new land forced upon them, land held in common gave people strength; it gave them something to fight for. And so—in the eyes of the federal government—that belief was a threat.

So after thousands of miles of forced moves and loss and finally settling us in Kansas, the federal government came once again to my people and offered another move, this time to a place that would be theirs forever, a move to end all moves. And what's more, the people were offered a chance to become United States citizens, to be part of the great country that surrounded them and to be protected by its power. Our leaders, my grandpa's grandpa among them, studied and counciled and sent delegations to Washington to consult. The U.S. Constitution apparently had no power to protect the homelands of Indigenous peoples. Removal had made that abundantly clear. But the Constitution did explicitly protect the land rights of citizens who were individual property owners. Perhaps that was the route to a permanent home for the people.

The leaders were offered the American Dream, the right to own their own property as individuals, inviolate from the vagaries of shifting Indian policy. They'd never be forced off their lands again. There would be no more graves along a dusty road. All they had to do was agree to surrender their allegiance to land held in common and agree to private property. With heavy hearts, they sat in council all summer, struggling to decide and weighing the options, which were few. Families were divided against families. Stay in Kansas on communal land and run the risk of losing it all, or go to Indian Territory as individual landowners with a legal guarantee. This historic council met all that hot summer in a shady place that came to be known as the Pecan Grove.

We have always known that the plants and animals have their own councils, and a common language. The trees, especially, we recognize as our teachers. But it seems no one listened that summer when the Pecans counseled: Stick together, act as one. We Pecans have learned that there is strength in unity, that the lone individual can be picked off as easily as the tree that has fruited out of season. The teachings of Pecans were not heard, or heeded.

And so our families packed the wagon one more time and moved west to Indian Territory, to the promised land, to become the Citizen Potawatomi. Tired and dusty but hopeful for their future, they found an old friend their first night on the new lands: a pecan grove. They rolled their wagons beneath the shelter of its branches and began again. Every tribal member, even my grandpa, a baby in arms, was given title to an allotment of land the federal government deemed sufficient for making a living as a farmer. By accepting citizenship, they ensured that their allotments could not be taken from them. Unless, of course, a citizen could not pay his taxes. Or a rancher offered a keg of whiskey and a lot of money, "fair and square." Any unallocated parcels were snapped up by non-Indian settlers just as hungry squirrels snap up pecans. During the allotment era, more than two-thirds of the reservation lands were lost. Barely a generation after land was "guaranteed" through the sacrifice of common land converted to private property, most of it was gone.

The pecan trees and their kin show a capacity for concerted action, for unity of purpose that transcends the individual trees. They ensure somehow that all stand together and thus survive. How they do so is still elusive. There is some evidence that certain cues from the environment may trigger fruiting, like a particularly wet spring or a long growing season. These favorable physical conditions help all the trees achieve an energy surplus that they can spend on nuts. But, given the individual differences in habitat, it seems unlikely that environment alone could be the key to synchrony.

In the old times, our elders say, the trees talked to each other. They'd stand in their own council and craft a plan. But scientists decided long ago that plants were deaf and mute, locked in isolation without communication. The possibility of conversation was summarily dismissed. Science pretends to be purely rational, completely neutral, a system of knowledge-making in which the observation is independent of the observer. And yet the conclusion was drawn that plants cannot communicate because they lack the mechanisms that *animals* use to speak. The potentials for plants were seen purely through the lens of animal capacity. Until quite recently no one seriously explored the possibility that plants might "speak" to one another. But pollen has been carried reliably on the wind for eons, communicated by males to receptive females to make those very nuts. If the wind can be trusted with that fecund responsibility, why not with messages?

There is now compelling evidence that our elders were right—the trees *are* talking to one another. They communicate via pheromones, hormonelike compounds that are wafted on the breeze, laden with meaning. Scientists have identified specific compounds that one tree will release when it is under the stress of insect attack—gypsy moths gorging on its leaves or bark beetles under its skin. The tree sends out a distress call: "Hey, you guys over there? I'm under attack here. You might want to raise the drawbridge and arm yourselves for what is coming your way." The downwind trees catch the drift, sensing those few molecules of alarm, the whiff of danger. This gives them time to manufacture defensive chemicals. Forewarned is forearmed. The trees warn each other and the invaders are repelled. The individual benefits, and so does the entire grove. Trees appear to be talking about mutual defense. Could they also communicate to synchronize masting? There is so much we cannot yet sense with our limited human capacity. Tree conversations are still far above our heads.

Some studies of mast fruiting have suggested that the mechanism for synchrony comes not through the air, but underground. The trees in a forest are often interconnected by subterranean networks of mycorrhizae, fungal strands that inhabit tree roots. The mycorrhizal symbiosis enables the fungi to forage for mineral nutrients in the soil and deliver them to the tree in exchange for carbohydrates. The mycorrhizae may form fungal bridges between individual trees, so that all the trees in a forest are connected. These fungal networks appear to redistribute the wealth of carbohydrates from tree to tree. A kind of Robin Hood, they take from the rich and give to the poor so that all the trees arrive at the same carbon surplus at the same time. They weave a web of reciprocity, of giving and taking. In this way, the trees all act as one because the fungi have connected them. Through unity, survival. All flourishing is mutual. Soil, fungus, tree, squirrel, boy—all are the beneficiaries of reciprocity.

How generously they shower us with food, literally giving themselves so that we can live. But in the giving their lives are also ensured. Our taking returns benefit to them in the circle of life making life, the chain of reciprocity. Living by the precepts of the Honorable Harvest—to take only what is given, to use it well, to be grateful for the gift, and to reciprocate the gift—is easy in a pecan grove. We reciprocate the gift by taking care of the grove, protecting it from harm, planting seeds so that new groves will shade the prairie and feed the squirrels.

Now, two generations later, after removal, after allotment, after the boarding schools, after diaspora, my family returns to Oklahoma, to what is left of my grandfather's allotment. From the hilltop you can still see pecan groves along the river. At night we dance on the old powwow grounds. The ancient ceremonies greet the sunrise. The smell of corn soup and the sound of drums fill the air as the nine bands of Potawatomi, scattered across the country by this history of removal, come together again for a few days each year in a search for belonging. The Potawatomi Gathering of Nations reunites the people, an antidote to the divide-and-conquer strategy that was used to separate our people from each other and from our homelands. The synchrony of our Gathering is determined by our leaders, but more importantly, there is something like a mycorrhizal network that unites us, an unseen connection of history and family and responsibility to both our ancestors and our children. As a nation, we are beginning to follow the guidance of our elders the pecans by standing together for the benefit of all. We are remembering what they said, that all flourishing is mutual.

This is a mast year for my family; we are all here at the Gathering, thick on the ground, like seeds for the future. Like an embryo provisioned and protected inside layers of stony shell, we have survived the lean years and flower together. I go walking in the pecan grove, perhaps the very place where my grandfather stuffed his pant legs full. He would be surprised to find us all here, dancing the circle, remembering pecans.

The Gift of Strawberries

I once heard Evon Peter—a Gwich'in man, a father, a husband, an environmental activist, and Chief of Arctic Village, a small village in northeastern Alaska—introduce himself simply as "a boy who was raised by a river." A description as smooth and slippery as a river rock. Did he mean only that he grew up near its banks? Or was the river responsible for rearing him, for teaching him the things he needed to live? Did it feed him, body and soul? Raised by a river: I suppose both meanings are true—you can hardly have one without the other.

In a way, I was raised by strawberries, fields of them. Not to exclude the maples, hemlocks, white pines, goldenrod, asters, violets, and mosses of upstate New York, but it was the wild strawberries, beneath dewy leaves on an almost-summer morning, who gave me my sense of the world, my place in it. Behind our house were miles of old hay fields divided by stone walls, long abandoned from farming but not yet grown up to forest. After the school bus chugged up our hill, I'd throw down my red plaid book bag, change my clothes before my mother could think of a chore, and jump across the crick to go wandering in the goldenrod. Our mental maps had all the landmarks we kids needed: the fort under the sumacs, the rock pile, the river, the big pine with branches so evenly spaced you could climb to the top as if it were a ladder—and the strawberry patches.

White petals with a yellow center—like a little wild rose—they dotted the acres of curl grass in May during the Flower Moon, *waabigwani-giizis*. We kept good track of them, peeking under the trifoliate leaves to check their progress as we ran through on our way to catch frogs. After the flower finally dropped its petals, a tiny green nub appeared in its place, and as the days got longer and warmer it swelled to a small white berry. These were sour but we ate them anyway, impatient for the real thing.

You could smell ripe strawberries before you saw them, the fragrance mingling with the smell of sun on damp ground. It was the smell of June, the last day of school, when we were set free, and the Strawberry Moon, *ode'mini-giizis*. I'd lie on my stomach in my favorite patches, watching the berries grow sweeter and bigger under the leaves. Each tiny wild berry was scarcely bigger than a raindrop, dimpled with seeds under the cap of leaves. From that vantage point I could pick only the reddest of the red, leaving the pink ones for tomorrow.

Even now, after more than fifty Strawberry Moons, finding a patch of wild strawberries still touches me with a sensation of surprise, a feeling of unworthiness and gratitude for the generosity and kindness that comes with an unexpected gift all wrapped in red and green. "Really? For me? Oh, you shouldn't have." After fifty years they still raise the question of how to respond to their generosity. Sometimes it feels like a silly question with a very simple answer: eat them.

But I know that someone else has wondered these same things. In our Creation stories the origin of strawberries is important. Skywoman's beautiful daughter, whom she carried in her womb from Skyworld, grew on the good green earth, loving and loved by all the other beings. But tragedy befell her when she died giving birth to her twins, Flint and Sapling. Heartbroken, Skywoman buried her beloved daughter in the earth. Her final gifts, our most revered plants, grew from her body. The strawberry arose from her heart. In Potawatomi, the strawberry is *ode min*, the heart berry. We recognize them as the leaders of the berries, the first to bear fruit.

Strawberries first shaped my view of a world full of gifts simply scattered at your feet. A gift comes to you through no action of your own, free, having moved toward you without your beckoning. It is not a reward; you cannot earn it, or call it to you, or even deserve it. And yet it appears. Your only role is to be open-eyed and present. Gifts exist in a realm of humility and mystery—as with random acts of kindness, we do not know their source.

Those fields of my childhood showered us with strawberries, raspberries, blackberries, hickory nuts in the fall, bouquets of wildflowers brought to my mom, and family walks on Sunday afternoon. They were our playground, retreat, wildlife sanctuary, ecology classroom, and the place where we learned to shoot tin cans off the stone wall. All for free. Or so I thought.

I experienced the world in that time as a gift economy, "goods and services" not purchased but received as gifts from the earth. Of course I was blissfully unaware of how my parents must have struggled to make ends meet in the wage economy raging far from this field.

In our family, the presents we gave one another were almost always homemade. I thought that was the definition of a gift: something you made for someone else. We made all our Christmas gifts: piggy banks from old Clorox bottles, hot pads from broken clothespins, and puppets from retired socks. My mother says it was because we had no money for store-bought presents. It didn't seem like a hardship to me; it was something special.

My father loves wild strawberries, so for Father's Day my mother would almost always make him strawberry shortcake. She baked the crusty shortcakes and whipped the heavy cream, but we kids were responsible for the berries. We each got an old jar or two and spent the Saturday before the celebration out in the fields, taking forever to fill them as more and more berries ended up in our mouths. Finally, we returned home and poured them out on the kitchen table to sort out the bugs. I'm sure we missed some, but Dad never mentioned the extra protein.

In fact, he thought wild strawberry shortcake was the best possible present, or so he had us convinced. It was a gift that could never be bought. As children raised by strawberries, we were probably unaware that the gift of berries was from the fields themselves, not from us. Our gift was time and attention and care and red-stained fingers. Heart berries, indeed.

Gifts from the earth or from each other establish a particular relationship, an obligation of sorts to give, to receive, and to reciprocate. The field
gave to us, we gave to my dad, and we tried to give back to the strawberries. When the berry season was done, the plants would send out
slender red runners to make new plants. Because I was fascinated by the
way they would travel over the ground looking for good places to take
root, I would weed out little patches of bare ground where the runners
touched down. Sure enough, tiny little roots would emerge from the run-
ner and by the end of the season there were even more plants, ready to
bloom under the next Strawberry Moon. No person taught us this—the
strawberries showed us. Because they had given us a gift, an ongoing
relationship opened between us.

Farmers around us grew a lot of strawberries and frequently hired
kids to pick for them. My siblings and I would ride our bikes a long way
to Crandall's farm to pick berries to earn spending money. A dime for
every quart we picked. But Mrs. Crandall was a persnickety overseer.
She stood at the edge of the field in her bib apron and instructed us how
to pick and warned us not to crush any berries. She had other rules, too.
"These berries belong to me," she said, "not to you. I don't want to see
you kids eating my berries." I knew the difference: In the fields behind
my house, the berries belonged to themselves. At this lady's roadside
stand, she sold them for sixty cents a quart.

It was quite a lesson in economics. We'd have to spend most of our
wages if we wanted to ride home with berries in our bike baskets. Of
course those berries were ten times bigger than our wild ones, but not
nearly so good. I don't believe we ever put those farm berries in Dad's
shortcake. It wouldn't have felt right.

It's funny how the nature of an object—let's say a strawberry or a pair of
socks—is so changed by the way it has come into your hands, as a gift
or as a commodity. The pair of wool socks that I buy at the store, red and
gray striped, are warm and cozy. I might feel grateful for the sheep that
made the wool and the worker who ran the knitting machine. I hope so.

But I have no *inherent* obligation to those socks as a commodity, as private property. There is no bond beyond the politely exchanged "thank yous" with the clerk. I have paid for them and our reciprocity ended the minute I handed her the money. The exchange ends once parity has been established, an equal exchange. They become my property. I don't write a thank-you note to JCPenney.

But what if those very same socks, red and gray striped, were knitted by my grandmother and given to me as a gift? That changes everything. A gift creates ongoing relationship. I will write a thank-you note. I will take good care of them and if I am a very gracious grandchild I'll wear them when she visits even if I don't like them. When it's her birthday, I will surely make her a gift in return. As the scholar and writer Lewis Hyde notes, "It is the cardinal difference between gift and commodity exchange that a gift establishes a feeling-bond between two people."

Wild strawberries fit the definition of gift, but grocery store berries do not. It's the relationship between producer and consumer that changes everything. As a gift-thinker, I would be deeply offended if I saw wild strawberries in the grocery store. I would want to kidnap them all. They were not meant to be sold, only to be given. Hyde reminds us that in a gift economy, one's freely given gifts cannot be made into someone else's capital. I can see the headline now: "Woman Arrested for Shoplifting Produce. Strawberry Liberation Front Claims Responsibility."

This is the same reason we do not sell sweetgrass. Because it is given to us, it should only be given to others. My dear friend Wally "Bear" Meshigaud is a ceremonial firekeeper for our people and uses a lot of sweetgrass on our behalf. There are folks who pick for him in a good way, to keep him supplied, but even so, at a big gathering sometimes he runs out. At powwows and fairs you can see our own people selling sweetgrass for ten bucks a braid. When Wally really needs *wiingashk* for a ceremony, he may visit one of those booths among the stalls selling frybread or hanks of beads. He introduces himself to the seller, explains his need, just as he would in a meadow, asking permission of the sweetgrass. He *cannot* pay for it, not because he doesn't have the money, but because it cannot be bought or sold and still retain its essence for ceremony. He expects sellers to graciously give him what he needs, but sometimes they don't. The guy at the booth thinks he's being shaken down by an elder. "Hey, you can't get something for nothin'," he says. But that is exactly the point. A gift *is* something for nothing, except that certain obligations are attached. For the plant to be sacred, it cannot be sold. Reluctant entrepreneurs will get a teaching from Wally, but they'll never get his money.

Sweetgrass belongs to Mother Earth. Sweetgrass pickers collect properly and respectfully, for their own use and the needs of their community. They return a gift to the earth and tend to the well-being of the *wiingashk*. The braids are given as gifts, to honor, to say thank you, to heal and to strengthen. The sweetgrass is kept in motion. When Wally gives sweetgrass to the fire, it is a gift that has passed from hand to hand, growing richer as it is honored in every exchange.

That is the fundamental nature of gifts: they move, and their value increases with their passage. The fields made a gift of berries to us and we made a gift of them to our father. The more something is shared, the greater its value becomes. This is hard to grasp for societies steeped in notions of private property, where others are, by definition, excluded from sharing. Practices such as posting land against trespass, for example, are expected and accepted in a property economy but are unacceptable in an economy where land is seen as a gift to all.

Lewis Hyde wonderfully illustrates this dissonance in his exploration of the "Indian giver." This expression, used negatively today as a pejorative for someone who gives something and then wants to have it back, actually derives from a fascinating cross-cultural misinterpretation between an Indigenous culture operating in a gift economy and a colonial culture predicated on the concept of private property. When gifts were given to the settlers by the Native inhabitants, the recipients understood that they were valuable and were intended to be retained. Giving them away would have been an affront. But the Indigenous people understood the value of the gift to be based in reciprocity and would be affronted if the gifts did not circulate back to them. Many of our ancient teachings counsel that whatever we have been given is supposed to be given away again.

From the viewpoint of a private property economy, the "gift" is deemed to be "free" because we obtain it free of charge, at no cost. But in the gift economy, gifts are not free. The essence of the gift is that it creates a set of relationships. The currency of a gift economy is, at its root, reciprocity. In Western thinking, private land is understood to be a "bundle of rights," whereas in a gift economy property has a "bundle of responsibilities" attached.

I was once lucky enough to spend time doing ecological research in the Andes. My favorite part was market day in the local village, when the square filled with vendors. There were tables loaded with *platanos*, carts of fresh papaya, stalls in bright colors with pyramids of tomatoes, and buckets of hairy yucca roots. Other vendors spread blankets on the ground, with everything you could need, from flip-flops to woven palm hats. Squatting behind her red blanket, a woman in a striped shawl and navy blue bowler spread out medicinal roots as beautifully wrinkled as she was. The colors, the smells of corn roasting on a wood fire and sharp limes, and the sounds of all the voices mingle wonderfully in my memory. I had a favorite stall where the owner, Edita, looked for me each day. She'd kindly explain how to cook unfamiliar items and pull out the sweetest pineapple she'd been saving under the table. Once she even had strawberries. I know that I paid the *gringa* prices but the experience of abundance and goodwill were worth every peso.

I dreamed not long ago of that market with all its vivid textures. I walked through the stalls with a basket over my arm as always and went right to Edita for a bunch of fresh cilantro. We chatted and laughed and when I held out my coins she waved them off, patting my arm and sending me away. A gift, she said. *Muchas gracias, señora,* I replied. There was my favorite *panadera*, with clean cloths laid over the round loaves. I chose a few rolls, opened my purse, and this vendor too gestured away my money as if I were impolite to suggest paying. I looked around in bewilderment; this was my familiar market and yet everything had changed. It wasn't just for me—no shopper was paying. I floated through the market with a sense of euphoria. Gratitude was the only currency accepted here.

It was all a gift. It was like picking strawberries in my field: the merchants were just intermediaries passing on gifts from the earth.

I looked in my basket: two zucchinis, an onion, tomatoes, bread, and a bunch of cilantro. It was still half empty, but it felt full. I had everything I needed. I glanced over at the cheese stall, thinking to get some, but knowing it would be given, not sold, I decided I could do without. It's funny: Had all the things in the market merely been a very low price, I probably would have scooped up as much as I could. But when everything became a gift, I felt self-restraint. I didn't want to take too much. And I began thinking of what small presents I might bring to the vendors tomorrow.

The dream faded, of course, but the feelings first of euphoria and then of self-restraint remain. I've thought of it often and recognize now that I was witness there to the conversion of a market economy to a gift economy, from private goods to common wealth. And in that transformation the relationships became as nourishing as the food I was getting. Across the market stalls and blankets, warmth and compassion were changing hands. There was a shared celebration of abundance for all we'd been given. And since every market basket contained a meal, there was justice.

I'm a plant scientist and I want to be clear, but I am also a poet and the world speaks to me in metaphor. When I speak of the gift of berries, I do not mean that *Fragaria virginiana* has been up all night making a present just for me, strategizing to find exactly what I'd like on a summer morning. So far as we know, that does not happen, but as a scientist I am well aware of how little we do know. The plant has in fact been up all night assembling little packets of sugar and seeds and fragrance and color, because when it does so its evolutionary fitness is increased. When it is successful in enticing an animal such as me to disperse its fruit, its genes for making yumminess are passed on to ensuing generations with a higher frequency than those of the plant whose berries were inferior. The berries made by the plant shape the behaviors of the dispersers and have adaptive consequences.

What I mean of course is that our human relationship with strawberries is transformed by our choice of perspective. It is human perception that makes the world a gift. When we view the world this way, strawberries and humans alike are transformed. The relationship of gratitude and reciprocity thus developed can increase the evolutionary fitness of both plant and animal. A species and a culture that treat the natural world with respect and reciprocity will surely pass on genes to ensuing generations with a higher frequency than the people who destroy it. The stories we choose to shape our behaviors have adaptive consequences.

Lewis Hyde has made extensive studies of gift economies. He finds that "objects . . . will remain plentiful *because* they are treated as gifts." A gift relationship with nature is a "formal give-and-take that acknowledges our participation in, and dependence upon, natural increase. We tend to respond to nature as a part of ourselves, not a stranger or alien available for exploitation. Gift exchange is the commerce of choice, for it is commerce that harmonizes with, or participates in, the process of [nature's] increase."

In the old times, when people's lives were so directly tied to the land, it was easy to know the world as gift. When fall came, the skies would darken with flocks of geese, honking "Here we are." It reminds the people of the Creation story, when the geese came to save Skywoman. The people are hungry, winter is coming, and the geese fill the marshes with food. It is a gift and the people receive it with thanksgiving, love, and respect.

But when the food does not come from a flock in the sky, when you don't feel the warm feathers cool in your hand and know that a life has been given for yours, when there is no gratitude in return—that food may not satisfy. It may leave the spirit hungry while the belly is full. Something is broken when the food comes on a Styrofoam tray wrapped in slippery plastic, a carcass of a being whose only chance at life was a cramped cage. That is not a gift of life; it is a theft.

How, in our modern world, can we find our way to understand the earth as a gift again, to make our relations with the world sacred again? I know we cannot all become hunter-gatherers—the living world could not bear our weight—but even in a market economy, can we behave "as if" the living world were a gift?

We could start by listening to Wally. There are those who will try to sell the gifts, but, as Wally says of sweetgrass for sale, "Don't buy it."

Refusal to participate is a moral choice. Water is a gift for all, not meant to be bought and sold. Don't buy it. When food has been wrenched from the earth, depleting the soil and poisoning our relatives in the name of higher yields, don't buy it.

In material fact, Strawberries belong only to themselves. The exchange relationships we choose determine whether we share them as a common gift or sell them as a private commodity. A great deal rests on that choice. For the greater part of human history, and in places in the world today, common resources were the rule. But some invented a different story, a social construct in which everything is a commodity to be bought and sold. The market economy story has spread like wildfire, with uneven results for human well-being and devastation for the natural world. But it is just a story we have told ourselves and we are free to tell another, to reclaim the old one.

One of these stories sustains the living systems on which we depend. One of these stories opens the way to living in gratitude and amazement at the richness and generosity of the world. One of these stories asks us to bestow our own gifts in kind, to celebrate our kinship with the world. We can choose. If all the world is a commodity, how poor we grow. When all the world is a gift in motion, how wealthy we become.

In those childhood fields, waiting for strawberries to ripen, I used to eat the sour white ones, sometimes out of hunger but mostly from impatience. I knew the long-term results of my short-term greed, but I took them anyway. Fortunately, our capacity for self-restraint grows and develops like the berries beneath the leaves, so I learned to wait. A little. I remember lying on my back in the fields watching the clouds go by and rolling over to check the berries every few minutes. When I was young, I thought the change might happen that fast. Now I am old and I know that transformation is slow. The commodity economy has been here on Turtle Island for four hundred years, eating up the white strawberries and everything else. But people have grown weary of the sour taste in their mouths. A great longing is upon us, to live again in a world made of gifts. I can scent it coming, like the fragrance of ripening strawberries rising on the breeze.

An Offering

Our people were canoe people. Until they made us walk. Until our lakeshore lodges were signed away for shanties and dust. Our people were a circle, until we were dispersed. Our people shared a language with which to thank the day, until they made us forget. But we didn't forget. Not quite.

Most summer mornings of childhood I woke to the sound of the outhouse door—the squeak of the hinge followed by the hollow *thunk* as it shut. I rose to consciousness through the hazy songs of vireos and thrushes, the lapping of the lake, and finally the sound of my father pumping the tank on the Coleman stove. By the time my brother and sisters and I emerged from our sleeping bags the sun would just be topping the eastern shore, pulling mist off the lake in long white coils. The small four-cup coffeepot of battered aluminum, blackened with the smoke of many fires, would already be thumping. Our family spent summers canoe camping in the Adirondacks and every day began this way.

I can picture my father, in his red-checked wool shirt, standing atop the rocks above the lake. When he lifts the coffeepot from the stove the morning bustle stops; we know without being told that it's time to pay attention. He stands at the edge of camp with the coffeepot in his hands, holding the top in place with a folded pot holder. He pours coffee out on the ground in a thick brown stream.

The sunlight catches the flow, striping it amber and brown and black as it falls to the earth and steams in the cool morning air. With his face to the morning sun, he pours and speaks into the stillness, "Here's to the gods of Tahawus." The stream runs down over smooth granite to merge with the lake water, as clear and brown as the coffee. I watch it trickle, picking up bits of pale lichen and soaking a tiny clump of moss as it follows a crack to the water's edge. The moss swells with the liquid and unfurls its leaves to the sun. Then and only then does he pour out steaming cups of coffee for himself and my mother, who stands at the stove making pancakes. So begins each morning in the north woods: the words that come before all else.

I was pretty sure that no other family I knew began their day like this, but I never questioned the source of those words and my father never explained. They were just part of our life among the lakes. But their rhythm made me feel at home and the ceremony drew a circle around our family. By those words we said "Here we are," and I imagined that the land heard us—murmured to itself, "Ohh, *here* are the ones who know how to say thank you."

Tahawus is the Algonquin name for Mount Marcy, the highest peak in the Adirondacks. It's called Mount Marcy to commemorate a governor who never set foot on those wild slopes. Tahawus, "the Cloud Splitter," is its true name, invoking its essential nature. Among our Potawatomi people, there are public names and true names. True names are used only by intimates and in ceremony. My father had been on Tahawus's summit many times and knew it well enough to call it by name, speaking with intimate knowledge of the place and the people who came before. When we call a place by name it is transformed from wilderness to homeland. I imagined that this beloved place knew my true name as well, even when I myself did not.

Sometimes my father would name the gods of Forked Lake or South Pond or Brandy Brook Flow, wherever our tents were settled for the night. I came to know that each place was inspirited, was home to others before we arrived and long after we left. As he called out the names and offered a gift, the first coffee, he quietly taught us the respect we owed these other beings and how to show our thanks for summer mornings.

I knew that in the long-ago times our people raised their thanks in morning songs, in prayer, and the offering of sacred tobacco. But at that time in our family history we didn't have sacred tobacco and we didn't know the songs—they'd been taken away from my grandfather at the doors of the boarding school. But history moves in a circle and here we were, the next generation, back to the loon-filled lakes of our ancestors, back to canoes.

My mother had her own more pragmatic ritual of respect: the translation of reverence and intention into action. Before we paddled away from any camping place she made us kids scour the place to be sure that it was spotless. No burnt matchstick, no scrap of paper escaped her notice. "Leave this place better than you found it," she admonished. And so we did. We also had to leave wood for the next person's fire, with tinder and kindling carefully sheltered from rain by a sheet of birch bark. I liked to imagine their pleasure, those other paddlers, arriving after dark to find a ready pile of fuel to warm their evening meal. My mother's ceremony connected us to them, too.

The offering was made only under an open sky and never back in town where we lived. On Sundays, when other kids would go to church, my folks would take us out along the river to look for herons and muskrats, to the woods to hunt for spring flowers, or on picnics. The words came along. For our winter picnics, we would walk all morning on snowshoes and then build a fire in the center of a circle stomped down with our webbed feet. This time the pot was full of bubbling tomato soup, and the first draught poured was for the snow. "Here's to the gods of Tahawus"—only then would we wrap mittened hands around our steaming cups.

And yet, as I grew to adolescence, the offering began to leave me angry or sad. The circle that had brought me a sense of belonging turned inside out. I heard in the words a message that we did not belong because we spoke in the language of exiles. It was a secondhand ceremony. Somewhere there were people who knew the right ceremony, who knew the lost language and spoke the true names, including my own.

But, still, every morning I watched the coffee disappear into the crumbly brown humus, as if returning to itself. In the same way that the flow of coffee down the rock opened the leaves of the moss, ceremony brought the quiescent back to life, opened my mind and heart to what I knew, but had forgotten. The words and the coffee called us to remember that these woods and lakes were a gift. Ceremonies large and small have the power to focus attention to a way of living awake in the world. The visible became invisible, merging with the soil. It may have been a secondhand ceremony, but even through my confusion I recognized that the earth drank it up as if it were right. The land knows you, even when you are lost.

A people's story moves along like a canoe caught in the current, being carried closer and closer to where we had begun. As I grew up, my family found again the tribal connections that had been frayed, but never broken, by history. We found the people who knew our true names. And when I first heard in Oklahoma the sending of thanks to the four directions at the sunrise lodge—the offering in the old language of the sacred tobacco—I heard it as if in my father's voice. The language was different but the heart was the same.

Ours was a solitary ceremony, but fed from the same bond with the land, founded on respect and gratitude. Now the circle drawn around us is bigger, encompassing a whole people to which we again belong. But still the offering says, "Here we are," and still I hear at the end of the words the land murmuring to itself, "Ohh, *here* are the ones who know how to say thank you." Today, my father can speak his prayer in our language. But it was "Here's to the gods of Tahawus" that came first, in the voice that I will always hear.

It was in the presence of the ancient ceremonies that I understood that our coffee offering was not secondhand, it was ours.

Much of who I am and what I do is wrapped up in my father's offering by the lakeshore. Each day still begins with a version of "Here's to the gods of Tahawus," a thanksgiving for the day. My work as an ecologist, a writer, a mother, as a traveler between scientific and traditional ways of knowing, grows from the power of those words. It reminds me of who we are; it reminds me of our gifts and our responsibility to those gifts. Ceremony is a vehicle for belonging—to a family, to a people, and to the land.

At last, I thought that I understood the offering to the gods of Tahawus. It was, for me, the *one* thing that was not forgotten, that which could not be taken by history: the knowing that we belonged to the land, that we were the people who knew how to say thank you. It welled up from a deep blood memory that the land, the lakes, and the spirit had held for us. But years later, with my own answer already in place, I asked my father, "Where did the ceremony come from—did you learn it from your father, and he from his? Did it stretch all the way back to the time of the canoes?"

He thought for a long time. "No, I don't think so. It's just what we did. It seemed right." That was all.

Some weeks went by, though, and when we spoke again he said, "I've been thinking about the coffee and how we started giving it to the ground. You know, it was boiled coffee. There's no filter and if it boils too hard the grounds foam up and get stuck in the spout. So the first cup you pour would get that plug of grounds and be spoiled. I think we first did it to clear the spout." It was as if he'd told me that the water didn't change to wine—the whole web of gratitude, the whole story of remembrance, was nothing more than the *dumping* of the grounds?

"But, you know," he said, "there weren't always grounds to clear. It started out that way, but it became something else. A thought. It was a kind of respect, a kind of thanks. On a beautiful summer morning, I suppose you could call it joy."

That, I think, is the power of ceremony: it marries the mundane to the sacred. The water turns to wine, the coffee to a prayer. The material and the spiritual mingle like grounds mingled with humus, transformed like steam rising from a mug into the morning mist.

What else can you offer the earth, which has everything? What else can you give but something of yourself? A homemade ceremony, a ceremony that makes a home.

Asters and Goldenrod

The girl in the picture holds a slate with her name and "class of '75" chalked in, a girl the color of deerskin with long dark hair and inky unreadable eyes that meet yours and won't look away. I remember that day. I was wearing the new plaid shirt that my parents had given me, an outfit I thought to be the hallmark of all foresters. When I looked back at the photo later in life, it was a puzzle to me. I recall being elated to be going to college, but there is no trace of that in the girl's face.

Even before I arrived at school, I had all of my answers prepared for the freshman intake interview. I wanted to make a good first impression. There were hardly any women at the forestry school in those days and certainly none who looked like me. The adviser peered at me over his glasses and said, "So, why do you want to major in botany?" His pencil was poised over the registrar's form.

How could I answer, how could I tell him that I was born a botanist, that I had shoeboxes of seeds and piles of pressed leaves under my bed, that I'd stop my bike along the road to identify a new species, that plants colored my dreams, that the plants had chosen me? So I told him the truth. I was proud of my well-planned answer, its freshman sophistication apparent to anyone, the way it showed that I already knew some plants and their habitats, that I had thought deeply about their nature and was clearly well prepared for college work. I told him that I chose botany because I wanted to learn about why asters and goldenrod looked so beautiful together. I'm sure I was smiling then, in my red plaid shirt.

But he was not. He laid down his pencil as if there was no need to record what I had said. "Miss Wall," he said, fixing me with a disappointed smile, "I must tell you that *that* is not science. That is not at all the sort of thing with which botanists concern themselves." But he promised to put me right. "I'll enroll you in General Botany so you can learn what it is." And so it began.

I like to imagine that they were the first flowers I saw, over my mother's shoulder, as the pink blanket slipped away from my face and their colors flooded my consciousness. I've heard that early experience can attune the brain to certain stimuli, so that they are processed with greater speed and certainty, so that they can be used again and again, so that we remember. Love at first sight. Through cloudy newborn eyes their radiance formed the first botanical synapses in my wide-awake, newborn brain, which until then had encountered only the blurry gentleness of pink faces. I'm guessing all eyes were on me, a little round baby all swaddled in bunting, but mine were on Goldenrod and Asters. I was born to these flowers and they came back for my birthday every year, weaving me into our mutual celebration.

People flock to our hills for the fiery suite of October but they often miss the sublime prelude of September fields. As if harvest time were not enough—peaches, grapes, sweet corn, squash—the fields are also embroidered with drifts of golden yellow and pools of deepest purple, a masterpiece.

If a fountain could jet bouquets of chrome yellow in dazzling arches of chrysanthemum fireworks, that would be Canada Goldenrod. Each three-foot stem is a geyser of tiny gold daisies, ladylike in miniature, exuberant en masse. Where the soil is damp enough, they stand side by side with their perfect counterpart, New England Asters. Not the pale domesticates of the perennial border, the weak sauce of lavender or sky blue, but full-on royal purple that would make a violet shrink. The daisylike fringe of purple petals surrounds a disc as bright as the sun at high noon, a golden-orange pool, just a tantalizing shade darker than the surrounding goldenrod. Alone, each is a botanical superlative. Together, the visual effect is stunning. Purple and gold, the heraldic colors of the king and queen of the meadow, a regal procession in complementary colors. I just wanted to know why.

Why do they stand beside each other when they could grow alone? Why this particular pair? There are plenty of pinks and whites and blues dotting the fields, so is it only happenstance that the magnificence of purple and gold end up side by side? Einstein himself said that "God doesn't play dice with the universe." What is the source of this pattern? Why is the world so beautiful? It could so easily be otherwise: flowers could be ugly to us and still fulfill their own purpose. But they're not. It seemed like a good question to me.

But my adviser said, "It's not science," not what botany was about. I wanted to know why certain stems bent easily for baskets and some would break, why the biggest berries grew in the shade and why they made us medicines, which plants are edible, why those little pink orchids only grow under pines. "Not science," he said, and he ought to know, sitting in his laboratory, a learned professor of botany. "And if you want to study beauty, you should go to art school." He reminded me of my deliberations over choosing a college, when I had vacillated between training as a botanist or as a poet. Since everyone told me I couldn't do both, I'd chosen plants. He told me that science was not about beauty, not about the embrace between plants and humans.

I had no rejoinder; I had made a mistake. There was no fight in me, only embarrassment at my error. I did not have the words for resistance. He signed me up for my classes and I was dismissed to go get my photo taken for registration. I didn't think about it at the time, but it was happening all over again, an echo of my grandfather's first day at school, when he was ordered to leave everything—language, culture, family— behind. The professor made me doubt where I came from, what I knew, and claimed that his was the *right* way to think. Only he didn't cut my hair off.

In moving from a childhood in the woods to the university I had unknowingly shifted between worldviews, from a natural history of experience, in which I knew plants as teachers and companions to whom I was linked with mutual responsibility, into the realm of science. The questions scientists raised were not "Who are you?" but "What is it?" No one asked plants, "What can you tell us?" The primary question was "How does it work?" The botany I was taught was reductionist, mechanistic, and strictly objective. Plants were reduced to objects; they were not subjects. The way botany was conceived and taught didn't seem to leave much room for a person who thought the way I did. The only way I could make sense of it was to conclude that the things I had always believed about plants must not be true after all.

That first plant science class was a disaster. I barely scraped by with a C and could not muster much enthusiasm for memorizing the concentrations of essential plant nutrients. There were times when I wanted to quit, but the more I learned, the more fascinated I became with the intricate structures that made up a leaf and the alchemy of photosynthesis. Companionship between asters and goldenrod was never mentioned, but I memorized botanical Latin as if it was poetry, eagerly tossing aside the name "goldenrod" for *Solidago canadensis*. I was mesmerized by plant ecology, evolution, taxonomy, physiology, soils, and fungi. All around me were my good teachers, the plants. I found good mentors, too, warm and kind professors who were doing heart-driven science, whether they could admit it or not. They too were my teachers. And yet there was always something tapping at my shoulder, willing me to turn around. When I did, I did not know how to recognize what stood behind me.

My natural inclination was to see relationships, to seek the threads that connect the world, to join instead of divide. But science is rigorous in separating the observer from the observed, and the observed from the observer. Why two flowers are beautiful together would violate the division necessary for objectivity.

I scarcely doubted the primacy of scientific thought. Following the path of science trained me to separate, to distinguish perception from physical reality, to atomize complexity into its smallest components, to honor the chain of evidence and logic, to discern one thing from another, to savor the pleasure of precision. The more I did this, the better I got at it, and I was accepted to do graduate work in one of the world's finest botany programs, no doubt on the strength of the letter of recommendation from my adviser, which read, "She's done remarkably well for an Indian girl."

A master's degree, a PhD, and a faculty position followed. I am grateful for the knowledge that was shared with me and deeply privileged to carry the powerful tools of science as a way of engaging the world. It took me to other plant communities, far from the asters and goldenrod. I remember feeling, as a new faculty member, as if I finally understood plants. I too began to teach the mechanics of botany, emulating the approach that I had been taught.

It reminds me of a story told by my friend Holly Youngbear Tibbetts. A plant scientist, armed with his notebooks and equipment, is exploring the rainforests for new botanical discoveries, and he has hired an Indigenous guide to lead him. Knowing the scientist's interests, the young guide takes care to point out the interesting species. The botanist looks at him appraisingly, surprised by his capacity. "Well, well, young man, you certainly know the names of a lot of these plants." The guide nods and replies with downcast eyes. "Yes, I have learned the names of all the bushes, but I have yet to learn their songs."

I was teaching the names and ignoring the songs.

When I was in graduate school in Wisconsin, my then husband and I had the good fortune to land jobs as caretakers at the university arboretum. In return for a little house at the edge of the prairie, we had only to make the nighttime rounds, checking that doors and gates were secure before we left the darkness to the crickets. There was just one time that a light was left burning, a door left ajar, in the horticulture garage. There was no mischief, but as my husband checked around, I stood and idly scanned the bulletin board. There was a news clipping there with a photo of a magnificent American elm, which had just been named the champion for its species, the largest of its kind. It had a name: The Louis Vieux Elm.

My heart began to pound and I knew my world was about to change, for I'd known the name Louis Vieux all my life and here was his face looking at me from a news clipping. He was our Potawatomi grandfather, one who had walked all the way from the Wisconsin forests to the Kansas prairie with my grandma Sha-note. He was a leader, one who took care of the people in their hardship. That garage door was left ajar, that light was left burning, and it shone on the path back home for me. It was the beginning of a long, slow journey back to my people, called out to me by the tree that stood above their bones.

To walk the science path I had stepped off the path of Indigenous knowledge. But the world has a way of guiding your steps. Seemingly out of the blue came an invitation to a small gathering of Native elders, to talk about traditional knowledge of plants. One I will never forget—a Navajo woman without a day of university botany training in her life—spoke for hours and I hung on every word. One by one, name by name, she told of the plants in her valley. Where each one lived, when it bloomed, who it liked to live near and all its relationships, who ate it, who lined their nests with its fibers, what kind of medicine it offered. She also shared the stories held by those plants, their origin myths, how they got their names, and what they have to tell us. She spoke of beauty.

Her words were like smelling salts waking me to what I had known back when I was picking strawberries. I realized how shallow my understanding was. Her knowledge was so much deeper and wider and engaged all the human ways of understanding. She could have explained asters and goldenrod. To a new PhD, this was humbling. It was the beginning of my reclaiming that other way of knowing that I had helplessly let science supplant. I felt like a malnourished refugee invited to a feast, the dishes scented with the herbs of home.

I circled right back to where I had begun, to the question of beauty. Back to the questions that science does not ask, not because they aren't important, but because science as a way of knowing is too narrow for the task. Had my adviser been a better scholar, he would have celebrated my questions, not dismissed them. He offered me only the cliché that beauty is in the eye of the beholder, and since science separates the observer and the observed, by definition beauty could not be a valid scientific question. I should have been told that my questions were bigger than science could touch.

He *was* right about beauty being in the eye of the beholder, especially when it comes to purple and yellow. Color perception in humans relies on banks of specialized receptor cells, the rods and cones in the retina. The job of the cone cells is to absorb light of different wavelengths and pass it on to the brain's visual cortex, where it can be interpreted. The visible light spectrum, the rainbow of colors, is broad, so the most effective means of discerning color is not one generalized jack-of-all-trades cone cell, but rather an array of specialists, each perfectly tuned to absorb certain wavelengths. The human eye has three kinds. One type excels at detecting red and associated wavelengths. One is tuned to blue. The other optimally perceives light of two colors: purple and yellow.

The human eye is superbly equipped to detect these colors and send a signal pulsing to the brain. This doesn't explain why I perceive them as beautiful, but it does explain why that combination gets my undivided attention. I asked my artist buddies about the power of purple and gold, and they sent me right to the color wheel: these two are complementary colors, as different in nature as could be. In composing a palette, putting them together makes each more vivid; just a touch of one will bring out the other. In an 1890 treatise on color perception, Goethe, who was both a scientist and a poet, wrote that "the colors diametrically opposed to each other . . . are those which *reciprocally* evoke each other in the eye." Purple and yellow are a reciprocal pair.

Our eyes are so sensitive to these wavelengths that the cones can get oversaturated and the stimulus pours over onto the other cells. A printmaker I know showed me that if you stare for a long time at a block of yellow and then shift your gaze to a white sheet of paper, you will see it, for a moment, as violet. This phenomenon—the colored afterimage—occurs because there is energetic reciprocity between purple and yellow pigments, which goldenrod and asters knew well before we did.

If my adviser was correct, the visual effect that so delights a human like me may be irrelevant to the flowers. The real beholder whose eye they hope to catch is a bee bent on pollination. Bees perceive many flowers differently than humans do due to their perception of additional spectra such as ultraviolet radiation. As it turns out, though, goldenrod and asters appear very similarly to bee eyes and human eyes. We both think they're beautiful. Their striking contrast when they grow together makes them the most attractive target in the whole meadow, a beacon for bees. Growing together, both receive more pollinator visits than they would if they were growing alone. It's a testable hypothesis; it's a question of science, a question of art, and a question of beauty.

Why are they beautiful together? It is a phenomenon simultaneously material and spiritual, for which we need all wavelengths, for which we need depth perception. When I stare too long at the world with science eyes, I see an afterimage of traditional knowledge. Might science and traditional knowledge be purple and yellow to one another, might they be goldenrod and asters? We see the world more fully when we use both.

The question of goldenrod and asters was of course just emblematic of what I really wanted to know. It was an architecture of relationships, of connections that I yearned to understand. I wanted to see the shimmering threads that hold it all together. And I wanted to know why we love the world, why the most ordinary scrap of meadow can rock us back on our heels in awe.

When botanists go walking the forests and fields looking for plants, we say we are going on a *foray*. When writers do the same, we should call it a *metaphoray*, and the land is rich in both. We need them both; scientist and poet Jeffrey Burton Russell writes that "as the sign of a deeper truth, metaphor was close to sacrament. Because the vastness and richness of reality cannot be expressed by the overt sense of a statement alone."

Native scholar Greg Cajete has written that in Indigenous ways of knowing, we understand a thing only when we understand it with all four aspects of our being: mind, body, emotion, and spirit. I came to understand quite sharply when I began my training as a scientist that science privileges only one, possibly two, of those ways of knowing: mind and body. As a young person wanting to know everything about plants, I did not question this. But it is a whole human being who finds the beautiful path.

There was a time when I teetered precariously with an awkward foot in each of two worlds—the scientific and the Indigenous. But then I learned to fly. Or at least try. It was the bees that showed me how to move between different flowers—to drink the nectar and gather pollen from both. It is this dance of cross-pollination that can produce a new species of knowledge, a new way of being in the world. After all, there aren't two worlds, there is just this one good green earth.

That September pairing of purple and gold is lived reciprocity; its wisdom is that the beauty of one is illuminated by the radiance of the other. Science and art, matter and spirit, Indigenous knowledge and Western science—can they be goldenrod and asters for each other? When I am in their presence, their beauty asks me for reciprocity, to be the complementary color, to make something beautiful in response.

Learning the Grammar of Animacy

To be native to a place we must learn to speak its language.

I come here to listen, to nestle in the curve of the roots in a soft hollow of pine needles, to lean my bones against the column of white pine, to turn off the voice in my head until I can hear the voices outside it: the *shhh* of wind in needles, water trickling over rock, nuthatch tapping, chipmunks digging, beechnut falling, mosquito in my ear, and something more—something that is not me, for which we have no language, the wordless being of others in which we are never alone. After the drumbeat of my mother's heart, *this* was my first language.

I could spend a whole day listening. And a whole night. And in the morning, without my hearing it, there might be a mushroom that was not there the night before, creamy white, pushed up from the pine needle duff, out of darkness to light, still glistening with the fluid of its passage. *Puhpowee.*

Listening in wild places, we are audience to conversations in a language not our own. I think now that it was a longing to comprehend this language I hear in the woods that led me to science, to learn over the years to speak fluent botany. A tongue that should not, by the way, be mistaken for the language of plants. I did learn another language in science, though, one of careful observation, an intimate vocabulary that names each little part. To name and describe you must first see, and science polishes the gift of seeing. I honor the strength of the language that has become a second tongue to me. But beneath the richness of its vocabulary and its descriptive power, something is missing, the same something that swells around you and in you when you listen to the world. Science can be a language of distance which reduces a being to its working parts; it is a language of objects. The language scientists speak, however precise, is based on a profound error in grammar, an omission, a grave loss in translation from the native languages of these shores.

My first taste of the missing language was the word *Puhpowee* on my tongue. I stumbled upon it in a book by the Anishinaabe ethno-botanist Keewaydinoquay, in a treatise on the traditional uses of fungi by our people. *Puhpowee*, she explained, translates as "the force which causes mushrooms to push up from the earth overnight." As a biologist, I was stunned that such a word existed. In all its technical vocabulary, Western science has no such term, no words to hold this mystery. You'd think that biologists, of all people, would have words for life. But in scientific language our terminology is used to define the boundaries of our knowing. What lies beyond our grasp remains unnamed.

In the three syllables of this new word I could see an entire process of close observation in the damp morning woods, the formulation of a theory for which English has no equivalent. The makers of this word understood a world of being, full of unseen energies that animate everything. I've cherished it for many years, as a talisman, and longed for the people who gave a name to the life force of mushrooms. The language that holds *Puhpowee* is one that I wanted to speak. So when I learned that the word for rising, for emergence, belonged to the language of my ancestors, it became a signpost for me.

Had history been different, I would likely speak Bodewadmimwin, or Potawatomi, an Anishinaabe language. But, like many of the three hundred and fifty Indigenous languages of the Americas, Potawatomi is threatened, and I speak the language you read. The powers of assimilation did their work as my chance of hearing that language, and yours too, was washed from the mouths of Indian children in government boarding schools where speaking your native tongue was forbidden. Children like my grandfather, who was taken from his family when he was just a little boy of nine years old. This history scattered not only our words but also our people. Today I live far from our reservation, so even if I could speak the language, I would have no one to talk to. But a few summers ago, at our yearly tribal gathering, a language class was held and I slipped into the tent to listen.

There was a great deal of excitement about the class because, for the first time, every single fluent speaker in our tribe would be there as a teacher. When the speakers were called forward to the circle of folding chairs, they moved slowly—with canes, walkers, and wheelchairs, only a few entirely under their own power. I counted them as they filled the chairs. Nine. Nine fluent speakers. In the whole world. Our language, millennia in the making, sits in those nine chairs. The words that praised creation, told the old stories, lulled my ancestors to sleep, rests today in the tongues of nine very mortal men and women. Each in turn addresses the small group of would-be students.

A man with long gray braids tells how his mother hid him away when the Indian agents came to take the children. He escaped boarding school by hiding under an overhung bank where the sound of the stream covered his crying. The others were all taken and had their mouths washed out with soap, or worse, for "talking that dirty Indian language." Because he alone stayed home and was raised up calling the plants and animals by the name Creator gave them, he is here today, a carrier of the language. The engines of assimilation worked well. The speaker's eyes blaze as he tells us, "We're the end of the road. We are all that is left. If you young people do not learn, the language will die. The missionaries and the U.S. government will have their victory at last."

A great-grandmother from the circle pushes her walker up close to the microphone. "It's not just the words that will be lost," she says. "The language is the heart of our culture; it holds our thoughts, our way of seeing the world. It's too beautiful for English to explain." *Puhpowee*.

Jim Thunder, at seventy-five the youngest of the speakers, is a round brown man of serious demeanor who spoke only in Potawatomi. He began solemnly, but as he warmed to his subject his voice lifted like a breeze in the birch trees and his hands began to tell the story. He became more and more animated, rising to his feet, holding us rapt and silent although almost no one understood a single word. He paused as if reaching the climax of his story and looked out at the audience with a twinkle of expectation. One of the grandmothers behind him covered her mouth in a giggle and his stern face suddenly broke into a smile as big and sweet as a cracked watermelon. He bent over laughing and the grandmas dabbed away tears of laughter, holding their sides, while the rest of us looked on in wonderment. When the laughter subsided, he spoke at last in English: "What will happen to a joke when no one can hear it anymore? How lonely those words will be, when their power is gone. Where will they go? Off to join the stories that can never be told again."

So now my house is spangled with Post-it notes in another language, as if I were studying for a trip abroad. But I'm not going away, I'm coming home.

Ni pi je ezhyayen? asks the little yellow sticky note on my back door. My hands are full and the car is running, but I switch my bag to the other hip and pause long enough to respond. *Odanek nde zhya,* I'm going to town. And so I do, to work, to class, to meetings, to the bank, to the grocery store. I talk all day and sometimes write all evening in the beautiful language I was born to, the same one used by 70 percent of the world's people, a tongue viewed as the most useful, with the richest vocabulary in the modern world. English. When I get home at night to my quiet house, there is a faithful Post-it note on the closet door. *Gisken I gbiskewagen!* And so I take off my coat.

I cook dinner, pulling utensils from cupboards labeled *emkwanen, nagen.* I have become a woman who speaks Potawatomi to household objects. When the phone rings I barely glance at the Post-it there as I *dopnen* the *giktogan.* And whether it is a solicitor or a friend, they speak

English. Once a week or so, it is my sister from the West Coast who says *Bozho. Moktthewenkwe nda*—as if she needed to identify herself: who else speaks Potawatomi? To call it speaking is a stretch. Really, all we do is blurt garbled phrases to each other in a parody of conversation: How are you? I am fine. Go to town. See bird. Red. Frybread good. We sound like Tonto's side of the Hollywood dialogue with the Lone Ranger. "Me try talk good Injun way." On the rare occasion when we actually can string together a halfway coherent thought, we freely insert high school Spanish words to fill in the gaps, making a language we call Spanawatomi.

Tuesdays and Thursdays at 12:15 Oklahoma time, I join the Potawatomi lunchtime language class, streaming from tribal headquarters via the Internet. There are usually about ten of us, from all over the country. Together we learn to count and to say *pass the salt*. Someone asks, "How do you say *please* pass the salt?" Our teacher, Justin Neely, a young man devoted to language revival, explains that while there are several words for *thank you*, there is no word for *please*. Food was meant to be shared, no added politeness needed; it was simply a cultural given that one was asking respectfully. The missionaries took this absence as further evidence of crude manners.

Many nights, when I should be grading papers or paying bills, I'm at the computer running through Potawatomi language drills. After months, I have mastered the kindergarten vocabulary and can confidently match the pictures of animals to their Indigenous names. It reminds me of reading picture books to my children: "Can you point to the squirrel? Where is the bunny?" All the while I'm telling myself that I really don't have time for this, and what's more, little need to know the words for *bass* and *fox* anyway. Since our tribal diaspora left us scattered to the four winds, who would I talk to?

The simple phrases I'm learning are perfect for my dog. Sit! Eat! Come here! Be quiet! But since she scarcely responds to these commands in English, I'm reluctant to train her to be bilingual. An admiring student once asked me if I spoke my native language. I was tempted to say, "Oh yes, we speak Potawatomi at home"—me, the dog, and the Post-it notes. Our teacher tells us not to be discouraged and thanks us every time a word is spoken—thanks us for breathing life into the language, even if we only speak a single word. "But I have no one to talk to," I complain. "None of us do," he reassures me, "but someday we will."

So I dutifully learn the vocabulary but find it hard to see the "heart of our culture" in translating *bed* and *sink* into Potawatomi. Learning nouns was pretty easy; after all, I'd learned thousands of botanical Latin names and scientific terms. I reasoned that this could not be too much different—just a one-for-one substitution, memorization. At least on paper, where you can see the letters, this is true. Hearing the language is a different story. There are fewer letters in our alphabet, so the distinction among words for a beginner is often subtle. With the beautiful clusters of consonants of *zh* and *mb* and *shwe* and *kwe* and *mshk,* our language sounds like wind in the pines and water over rocks, sounds our ears may have been more delicately attuned to in the past, but no longer. To learn again, you really have to listen.

To actually *speak,* of course, requires verbs, and here is where my kindergarten proficiency at naming things leaves off. English is a noun-based language, somehow appropriate to a culture so obsessed with things. Only 30 percent of English words are verbs, but in Potawatomi that proportion is 70 percent. Which means that 70 percent of the words have to be conjugated, and 70 percent have different tenses and cases to be mastered.

European languages often assign gender to nouns, but Potawatomi does not divide the world into masculine and feminine. Nouns and verbs both are animate and inanimate. You hear a person with a word that is completely different from the one with which you hear an airplane. Pronouns, articles, plurals, demonstratives, verbs—all those syntactical bits I never could keep straight in high school English are all aligned in Potawatomi to provide different ways to speak of the living world and the lifeless one. Different verb forms, different plurals, different everything apply depending on whether what you are speaking of is alive.

No wonder there are only nine speakers left! I try, but the complexity makes my head hurt and my ear can barely distinguish between words that mean completely different things. One teacher reassures us that this will come with practice, but another elder concedes that these close similarities are inherent in the language. As Stewart King, a knowledge keeper and great teacher, reminds us, the Creator meant for us to laugh, so humor is deliberately built into the syntax. Even a small slip of the tongue can convert "We need more firewood" to "Take off your clothes." In fact, I learned that the mystical word *Puhpowee* is used not only for mushrooms, but also for certain other shafts that rise mysteriously in the night.

My sister's gift to me one Christmas was a set of magnetic tiles for the refrigerator in Ojibwe, or Anishinabemowin, a language closely related to Potawatomi. I spread them out on my kitchen table looking for familiar words, but the more I looked, the more worried I got. Among the hundred or more tiles, there was but a single word that I recognized: *megwech*, thank you. The small feeling of accomplishment from months of study evaporated in a moment.

I remember paging through the Ojibwe dictionary she sent, trying to decipher the tiles, but the spellings didn't always match and the print was too small and there are way too many variations on a single word and I was feeling that this was just way too hard. The threads in my brain knotted and the harder I tried, the tighter they became. Pages blurred and my eyes settled on a word—a verb, of course: "to be a Saturday." *Pfft!* I threw down the book. Since when is *Saturday* a verb? Everyone knows it's a noun. I grabbed the dictionary and flipped more pages and all kinds of things seemed to be verbs: "to be a hill," "to be red," "to be a long sandy stretch of beach," and then my finger rested on *wiikwegamaa*: "to be a bay." "Ridiculous!" I ranted in my head. "There is no reason to make it so complicated. No wonder no one speaks it. A cumbersome language, impossible to learn, and more than that, it's all wrong. A bay is most definitely a person, place, or thing—a noun and not a verb." I was ready to give up. I'd learned a few words, done my duty to the language that was taken from my grandfather. Oh, the ghosts of the missionaries in the boarding schools must have been rubbing their hands in glee at my frustration. "She's going to surrender," they said.

And then I swear I heard the zap of synapses firing. An electric current sizzled down my arm and through my finger, and practically scorched the page where that one word lay. In that moment I could smell the water of the bay, watch it rock against the shore and hear it sift onto the sand. A bay is a noun only if water is *dead*. When *bay* is a noun, it is defined by humans, trapped between its shores and contained by the word. But the verb *wiikwegamaa*—to *be* a bay— releases the water from bondage and lets it live. "To be a bay" holds the wonder that, for this moment, the living water has decided to shelter itself between these shores, conversing with cedar roots and a flock of baby mergansers. Because it could do otherwise—become a stream or an ocean or a waterfall, and there are verbs for that, too. To be a hill, to be a sandy beach, to be a Saturday, all are possible verbs in a world where everything is alive. Water, land, and even a day, the language a mirror for seeing the animacy of the world, the life that pulses through all things, through pines and nuthatches and mushrooms. *This* is the language I hear in the woods; this is the language that lets us speak of what wells up all around us. And the vestiges of boarding schools, the soap-wielding missionary wraiths, hang their heads in defeat.

This is the grammar of animacy. Imagine seeing your grandmother standing at the stove in her apron and then saying of her, "Look, it is making soup. It has gray hair." We might snicker at such a mistake, but we also recoil from it. In English, we never refer to a member of our family, or indeed to any person, as *it*. That would be a profound act of disrespect. *It* robs a person of selfhood and kinship, reducing a person to a mere thing. So it is that in Potawatomi and most other Indigenous languages, we use the same words to address the living world as we use for our family. Because they are our family.

To whom does our language extend the grammar of animacy? Naturally, plants and animals are animate, but as I learn, I am discovering that the Potawatomi understanding of what it means to be animate diverges from the list of attributes of living beings we all learned in Biology 101. In Potawatomi 101, rocks are animate, as are mountains and water and fire and places. Beings that are imbued with spirit, our sacred medicines, our songs, drums, and even stories, are all animate. The list of the inanimate seems to be smaller, filled with objects that are made by people. Of an inanimate being, like a table, we say, "*What* is it?" And we answer *Dopwen yewe*. Table it is. But of apple, we must say, "*Who* is that being?" And reply *Mshimin yawe*. Apple that being is.

Yawe—the animate *to be*. I am, you are, s/he is. To speak of those possessed with life and spirit we must say *yawe*. By what linguistic confluence do Yahweh of the Old Testament and *yawe* of the New World both fall from the mouths of the reverent? Isn't this just what it means, to be, to have the breath of life within, to be the offspring of Creation? The language reminds us, in every sentence, of our kinship with all of the animate world.

English doesn't give us many tools for incorporating respect for animacy. In English, you are either a human or a thing. Our grammar boxes us in by the choice of reducing a nonhuman being to an *it*, or it must be gendered, inappropriately, as a *he* or a *she*. Where are our words for the simple existence of another living being? Where is our *yawe?* My friend Michael Nelson, an ethicist who thinks a great deal about moral inclusion, told me about a woman he knows, a field biologist whose work is among other-than-humans. Most of her companions are not two-legged, and so her language has shifted to accommodate her relationships. She kneels along the trail to inspect a set of moose tracks, saying, "Someone's already been this way this morning." "Someone is in my hat," she says, shaking out a deerfly. Someone, not something.

When I am in the woods with my students, teaching them the gifts of plants and how to call them by name, I try to be mindful of my language, to be bilingual between the lexicon of science and the grammar of animacy. Although they still have to learn scientific roles and Latin names, I hope I am also teaching them to know the world as a neighborhood of nonhuman residents, to know that, as ecotheologian Thomas

Berry has written, "we must say of the universe that it is a communion of subjects, not a collection of objects."

One afternoon, I sat with my field ecology students by a *wiikwega-maa* and shared this idea of animate language. One young man, Andy, splashing his feet in the clear water, asked the big question. "Wait a second," he said as he wrapped his mind around this linguistic distinction, "doesn't this mean that speaking English, thinking in English, somehow gives us permission to disrespect nature? By denying everyone else the right to be persons? Wouldn't things be different if nothing was an *it?*"

Swept away with the idea, he said it felt like an awakening to him. More like a remembering, I think. The animacy of the world is something we already know, but the language of animacy teeters on extinction—not just for Native peoples, but for everyone. Our toddlers speak of plants and animals as if they were people, extending to them self and intention and compassion—until we teach them not to. We quickly retrain them and make them forget. When we tell them that the tree is not a *who*, but an *it,* we make that maple an object; we put a barrier between us, absolving ourselves of moral responsibility and opening the door to exploitation. Saying *it* makes a living land into "natural resources." If a maple is an *it,* we can take up the chain saw. If a maple is a *her,* we think twice.

Another student countered Andy's argument. "But we can't say *he* or *she*. That would be anthropomorphism." They are well-schooled biologists who have been instructed, in no uncertain terms, never to ascribe human characteristics to a study object, to another species. It's a cardinal sin that leads to a loss of objectivity. Carla pointed out that "it's also disrespectful to the animals. We shouldn't project our perceptions onto them. They have their own ways—they're not just people in furry costumes." Andy countered, "But just because we don't think of them as humans doesn't mean they aren't beings. Isn't it even more disrespectful to assume that we're the only species that counts as 'persons'?" The arrogance of English is that the only way to be animate, to be worthy of respect and moral concern, is to be a human.

A language teacher I know explained that grammar is just the way we chart relationships in language. Maybe it also reflects our relationships with each other. Maybe a grammar of animacy could lead us to whole new ways of living in the world, other species a sovereign people, a world with a democracy of species, not a tyranny of one—with moral responsibility to water and wolves, and with a legal system that recognizes the standing of other species. It's all in the pronouns.

Andy is right. Learning the grammar of animacy could well be a restraint on our mindless exploitation of land. But there is more to it. I have heard our elders give advice like "You should go among the standing people" or "Go spend some time with those Beaver people." They remind us of the capacity of others as our teachers, as holders of knowledge, as guides. Imagine walking through a richly inhabited world of Birch people, Bear people, Rock people, beings we think of and therefore speak of as persons worthy of our respect, of inclusion in a peopled world. We Americans are reluctant to learn a foreign language of our own species, let alone another species. But imagine the possibilities. Imagine the access we would have to different perspectives, the things we might see through other eyes, the wisdom that surrounds us. We don't have to figure out everything by ourselves: there are intelligences other than our own, teachers all around us. Imagine how much less lonely the world would be.

Every word I learn comes with a breath of gratitude for our elders who have kept this language alive and passed along its poetry. I still struggle mightily with verbs, can hardly speak at all, and I'm still most adept with only kindergarten vocabulary. But I like that in the morning I can go for my walk around the meadow greeting neighbors by name. When Crow caws at me from the hedgerow, I can call back *Mno gizhget andushukwe!* I can brush my hand over the soft grasses and murmur *Bozho mishkos.* It's a small thing, but it makes me happy.

I'm not advocating that we all learn Potawatomi or Hopi or Seminole, even if we could. Immigrants came to these shores bearing a legacy of languages, all to be cherished. But to become native to this place, if we are to survive here, and our neighbors too, our work is to learn to speak the grammar of animacy, so that we might truly be at home.

I remember the words of Bill Tall Bull, a Cheyenne elder. As a young person, I spoke to him with a heavy heart, lamenting that I had no native language with which to speak to the plants and the places that I love. "They love to hear the old language," he said, "it's true." "But," he said, with fingers on his lips, "You don't have to speak it here." "If you speak it here," he said, patting his chest, "They will hear you."

Tending Sweetgrass

Wild meadow sweetgrass grows long and fragrant when it
is looked after by humans. Weeding and care for the habitat
and neighboring plants strengthens its growth.

Maple Sugar Moon

*When Nanabozho, the Anishinaabe Original Man, our teacher, part man, part manido, walked through the world, he took note of who was flourishing and who was not, of who was mindful of the Original Instructions and who was not. He was dismayed when he came upon villages where the gardens were not being tended, where the fishnets were not repaired and the children were not being taught the way to live. Instead of seeing piles of firewood and caches of corn, he found the people lying beneath maple trees with their mouths wide open, catching the thick, sweet syrup of the generous trees. They had become lazy and took for granted the gifts of the Creator. They did not do their ceremonies or care for one another. He knew his responsibility, so he went to the river and dipped up many buckets of water. He poured the water straight into the maple trees to dilute the syrup. Today, maple sap flows like a stream of water with only a trace of sweetness to remind the people both of possibility and of responsibility. And so it is that it takes forty gallons of sap to make a gallon of syrup.**

Plink. On an afternoon in March, when the late winter sun is starting to strengthen and moving north a degree or so each day, the sap runs strong. *Plink.* The yard of our old farmhouse in Fabius, New York, is graced with seven Maples, big ones, planted almost two hundred years ago to shade the house. The largest tree is as wide at its base as our picnic table is long.

---

* Adapted from oral tradition and Ritzenthaler and Ritzenthaler, 1983.

When we first moved here my daughters reveled in rooting through the loft above the old stable, a space full of the flotsam of almost two centuries of families before us. One day I found them playing with an entire village of little metal pup tents set up under the trees. "They're going camping," they said of their various dolls and stuffed animals, who were peeking out from under their shelter. The loft was full of such "tents" that fit over old-time sap buckets to keep out the rain and snow during sugaring season. When the girls discovered what these little tents were for, of course they wanted to make maple syrup. We scrubbed out the mouse droppings and readied the buckets for spring.

During that first winter I read up on the whole process. We had buckets and covers, but no spiles—the spouts you need to drive into the tree to allow the sap out. But we live in Maple Nation and a nearby hardware store carried all things maple sugaring. *All* things: molds for forming maple sugar leaves, evaporators of every size, miles of rubber tubing, hydrometers, kettles, filters, and jars—none of which I could afford. But tucked away in the back they had old-fashioned spiles, which hardly anyone wants anymore. I got a whole box for seventy-five cents each.

Sugaring has changed over the years. Gone are the days of emptying buckets and sledging barrels of sap through the snowy woods. In many sugaring operations, plastic tubing runs right from the trees to the sugar house. But there are still purists out there who cherish the *plink* of sap into a metal bucket, and that requires a spile. One end is formed into a tube like a drinking straw, which you tap into a hole drilled in the tree. The tube then opens into a trough about four inches long. And at the base there is a handy hook on which to hang the bucket. I bought a big clean garbage can to store the sap and we were ready. I didn't think we'd need all that storage space, but better to be prepared.

In a climate where winter lasts six months, we always search assiduously for signs of spring, but never more eagerly than after we decided to make syrup. The girls ask every day, "Can we start yet?" But our beginning was entirely determined by the season. For the sap to run you need a combination of warm days and freezing nights. *Warm* is a relative term, of course, thirty-five to forty-two degrees, so that the sun thaws the trunk

and starts the flow of sap inside. We watch the calendar and the thermometer, and Larkin asks, "How do the trees know it's time if they can't see the
thermometer?" Indeed, how does a being without eyes or nose or nerves
of any kind know what to do and when to do it? There are not even leaves
out to detect the sun; every bit of the tree, except the buds, is swathed in
thick, dead bark. And yet the trees are not fooled by a midwinter thaw.

The fact is, Maples have a far more sophisticated system for detecting
spring than we do. There are photosensors by the hundreds in every single
bud, packed with light-absorbing pigments called phytochromes. Their
job is to take the measure of light every day. Tightly furled, covered in
red-brown scales, each bud holds an embryonic copy of a maple branch,
and each bud wants desperately to someday be a full-fledged branch,
leaves rustling in the wind and soaking up sun. But if the buds come out
too soon they'll be killed by freezing. Too late and they'll miss the spring.
So the buds keep the calendar. But those baby buds need energy for their
growth into branches—like all newborns, they are hungry.

We who lack such sophisticated sensors look for other signs. When
hollows appear in the snow around the tree bases, I start to think it's tapping time. The dark bark absorbs the growing heat of the sun and then
radiates it back to slowly melt the snow that has lain there all winter.
When those circles of bare ground appear, that's when the first drops of
sap will plop onto your head from a broken branch in the canopy.

And so with drill in hand we circle our trees searching out just the
right spot, three feet up, on a smooth face. Lo and behold, there are scars
of past taps long healed over, made by whoever had left those sap buckets in our loft. We don't know their names or their faces, but our fingers
rest right where theirs had been and we know what they too were doing
one morning in April long ago. And we know what they had on their
pancakes. Our stories are linked in this run of sap; our trees knew them
as they know us today.

The spiles begin to drip almost as soon as we tap them into place.
The first drops splat onto the bottom of the bucket. The girls slide the
tented covers on, which makes the sound echo even more. Trees of this
diameter could accept six taps without damage, but we don't want to be

greedy and only place three. By the time we're done setting them up, the first bucket is already singing a different tune, the *plink* of another drop into the half inch of sap. All day long they change pitch as the buckets fill, like water glasses of different pitch. *Plink, ploink, plonk*— the tin buckets and their tented tops reverberate with every drop and the yard is singing. This is spring music as surely as the cardinal's insistent whistle.

My girls watch in fascination. Each drop is as clear as water but somehow thicker, catching the light and hanging for a second at the end of the spile, growing invitingly into a larger and larger drop. The girls stretch out their tongues and slurp with a look of bliss, and unaccountably I am moved to tears. It reminds me of when I alone fed them. Now, on sturdy young legs, they are nursed by a maple—as close as they can come to being suckled by Mother Earth.

All day long the buckets fill and by evening they are brimming. The girls and I haul all twenty-one to the big garbage can and pour until it is almost full. I had no idea there would be so much. The girls rehang the buckets while I build the fire. Our evaporator is just my old canning kettle, set on an oven rack, spanning stacks of cinder blocks scavenged from the barn. It takes a long time to heat up a kettle of sap and the girls lose interest pretty quickly. I am in and out of the house, keeping fires going in both places. When I tuck them into bed that night, they are full of anticipation of syrup by morning.

I set up a lawn chair on the packed-down snow next to the fire, feeding it constantly to keep up a good boil in the now-freezing night. Steam billows from the pot, covering and uncovering the moon in the dry, cold sky.

I taste the sap as it boils down, and with every passing hour it is discernibly sweeter, but the yield from this four-gallon kettle will be nothing more than a skin of syrup on the bottom of the pan, scarcely enough for one pancake. So as it boils down I add more fresh sap from the garbage can, hoping to have just one cup of syrup by morning. I add wood, then wrap myself back in blankets, dozing until I can add more logs or sap.

I don't know what time I woke, but I was cold and stiff in my lawn chair, and the fire was burnt to embers, leaving the sap lukewarm. Beaten, I went inside to bed.

When I returned in the morning, I found the sap in the garbage can frozen hard. As I got the fire going again, I remembered something I had heard about how our ancestors made maple sugar. The ice on the surface was pure water, so I cracked it and threw it on the ground like a broken window.

People of the Maple Nation made sugar long before they possessed trade kettles for boiling. Instead, they collected sap in birch bark pails and poured it into log troughs hollowed from basswood trees. The large surface area and shallow depth of the troughs was ideal for ice formation. Every morning, ice was removed, leaving a more concentrated sugar solution behind. The concentrated solution could then be boiled to sugar with far less energy required. The freezing nights did the work of many cords of firewood, a reminder of elegant connections: maple sap runs at the one time of year when this method is possible.

Wooden evaporating dishes were placed on flat stones over the coals of a fire that burned night and day. In the old times, families would all move together to "sugar camp," where firewood and equipment had been stored the year before. Grandmothers and the youngest babies would be pulled on toboggans through the softening snow so that all could attend to the process—it took all the knowledge and all the arms to make sugar. Most of the time was spent stirring, good storytelling time when folks from the dispersed winter camps came together. But there were also pulses of furious activity: when the syrup reached just the right consistency, it was beaten so that it would solidify in the desired way, into soft cakes, hard candy, and granulated sugar. The women stored it in birch bark boxes called *makaks*, sewn tight with spruce root. Given birch bark's natural antifungal preservatives, the sugars would keep for years.

It is said that our people learned to make sugar from the squirrels. In late winter, the hungry time, when caches of nuts are depleted, squirrels take to the treetops and gnaw on the branches of sugar maples. Scraping the bark allows sap to exude from the twig, and the squirrels drink it. But the real goods come the next morning, when they follow the same circuit they made the day before, licking up the sugar crystals that formed on the bark overnight. Freezing temperatures cause the water in the sap to sublimate, leaving a sweet crystalline crust like rock candy behind, enough to tide them over through the hungriest time of year.

Our people call this time the Maple Sugar Moon, *Ziibaskwet Giizis*, The month before is known as the Hard Crust on Snow Moon. People living a subsistence lifestyle also know it as the Hunger Moon, when stored food has dwindled and game is scarce. But the maples carried the people through, provided food just when they needed it most. They had to trust that Mother Earth would find a way to feed them even in the depths of winter. But mothers are like that. In return, ceremonies of thanksgiving are held at the start of the sap run.

The Maples each year carry out their part of the Original Instructions, to care for the people. But they care for their own survival at the same time. The buds that sensed the incipient turn of the season are hungry. For shoots that are only one millimeter long to become full-fledged leaves, they need food. So when the buds sense spring, they send a hormonal signal down the trunk to the roots, a wake-up call, telegraphed from the light world to the underworld. The hormone triggers the formation of amylase, the enzyme responsible for cleaving large molecules of starch stored in the roots into small molecules of sugar. When the concentration of sugar in the roots begins to grow, it creates an osmotic gradient that draws water in from the soil. Dissolved in this water from the spring-wet earth, the sugar streams upward as rising sap to feed the buds. It takes a lot of sugar to feed people and buds, so the tree uses its sapwood, the xylem, as the conduit. Sugar transport is usually restricted to the thin layer of phloem tissue under the bark. But in spring, before there are leaves to make their own sugar, the need is so great that xylem is called into duty as well. At no other time of year does sugar move this way, only now when it is needed. Sugar flows upstream for a few weeks in the spring. But when the buds break and leaves emerge, they start making sugar on their own and the sapwood returns to its work as the water conduit.

Because the mature leaves make more sugar than they can use right away, the sugar stream starts to flow in the opposite direction, from leaves back to roots, through the phloem. And so the roots, which fed the buds, are now fed in return by the leaves all summer long. The sugar is converted back to starch, stored in the original "root cellar." The syrup we pour over pancakes on a winter morning is summer sunshine flowing in golden streams to pool on our plates.

Night after night I stayed up tending the fire, boiling our little kettle of sap. All day long the *plink plink plink* of sap filled the buckets and the girls and I gathered them after school to pour into the collecting can. The trees gave sap much faster than I could boil it so we bought another garbage can to hold the excess. And then another. Eventually we pulled the spiles from the trees to stop the flow and avoid wasting the sugars. The end result was terrible bronchitis from sleeping in a lawn chair in the driveway in March and three quarts of syrup, a little bit gray with wood ash.

When my daughters remember our sugaring adventure now, they roll their eyes and groan, "That was *so* much work." They remember hauling branches to feed the fire and slopping sap on their jackets as they carried heavy buckets. They tease me about being a wretched mother who wove their connection to the land through forced labor. They *were* awfully little to be doing the work of a sugaring crew. But they also remember the wonder of drinking sap straight from the tree. Sap, but not syrup. Nanabozho made certain that the work would never be too easy. His teachings remind us that one half of the truth is that the earth endows us with great gifts, the other half is that the gift is not enough. The responsibility does not lie with the maples alone. The other half belongs to us; we participate in its transformation. It is our work, and our gratitude, that distills the sweetness.

Night after night I sat by the fire, the girls tucked safely in bed, the rustle of the fire and the bubbling sap a lullaby. Transfixed by the fire, I hardly noticed the sky silver as the Maple Sugar Moon rose in the east. So bright on a clear freezing night, it threw tree shadows against the house—bold black embroidery around the windows where the girls lay sleeping, the shadows of the twin trees. These two, perfectly matched in girth and form, stand centered in front of the house by the edge of the road, their shadows framing the front door like dark columns of a maple portico. They rise in unison without a branch until they reach the roofline, where they spread like an umbrella. They grew up with this house, shaped by its protection.

There was a custom in the mid-eighteen hundreds of planting twin trees to celebrate a marriage and the starting of a home. The stance of these two, just ten feet apart, recalls a couple standing together on the porch steps, holding hands. The reach of their shade links the front porch with the barn across the road, creating a shady path of back and forth for that young family.

I realize that those first homesteaders were not the beneficiaries of that shade, at least not as a young couple. They must have meant for their people to stay here. Surely those two were sleeping up on Cemetery Road long before the shade arched across the road. I am living today in the shady future they imagined, drinking sap from trees planted with their wedding vows. They could not have imagined me, many generations later, and yet I live in the gift of their care. Could they have imagined that when my daughter Linden was married, she would choose leaves of maple sugar for the wedding giveaway?

Such a responsibility I have to these people and these trees, left to me, an unknown come to live under the guardianship of the twins, with a bond physical, emotional, and spiritual. I have no way to pay them back. Their gift to me is far greater than I have ability to reciprocate. They're so huge as to be nearly beyond my care, although I do scatter granules of fertilizer at their feet and turn the hose on them in summer drought. Perhaps all I can do is love them. All I know to do is to leave another gift, for them and for the future, those next unknowns who will live here. I heard once that Maori people make beautiful wood sculptures that they carry long distances into the forest and leave there as a gift to the trees. And so I plant Daffodils, hundreds of them, in sunny flocks beneath the Maples, in homage to their beauty and in reciprocity for their gift.

Even now, as the sap rises, so too the Daffodils rise underfoot.

Witch Hazel

As told through the eyes of my daughter.

November is not a time for flowers, the days short and cold. Heavy clouds drag at my mood, and sleet like a muttered curse propels me indoors—I am reluctant to venture out again. So when the sun breaks through for that rare yellow day, maybe the last before the snow falls, I have to go. Because the woods are quiet this time of year without leaves or birds, the buzz of a bee seems inordinately loud. Intrigued, I follow her path—what could bring her out in November? She makes directly for bare branches, which, when I look more closely, are strewn with yellow flowers—Witch Hazel. The flowers are a ragged affair: five long petals, each like a scrap of fading yellow cloth that snagged on the branch, torn strips that wave in the breeze. But, *oh* are they welcome, a spot of color when months of gray lie ahead. A last hurrah before winter that suddenly reminds me of a November long ago.

The house had stood empty since she left. The cardboard Santas she had pasted on the tall windows were faded from shafts of summer sun and plastic poinsettias on the table were draped in cobwebs. You could smell that the mice ransacked the pantry while the Christmas ham turned to mounds of mold in the icebox after the power was shut off. Outside on the porch a wren built its nest in the lunch box again, awaiting her return. Asters bloomed in profusion under the sagging clothesline, where a gray cardigan was still pinned.

I first met Hazel Barnett when I was walking the fields in Kentucky, looking for wild blackberries with my mother. We were bent to our picking when I heard a high voice from the hedgerow call, "Howdy-do. Howdy-do." There at the fence stood the oldest woman I'd ever seen. Slightly afraid, I took my mother's hand as we walked over to greet her. She supported herself by leaning against the fence among the pink and burgundy hollyhocks. Her iron-gray hair was drawn into a bun at the back of her neck with a corona of white wisps standing out like sun rays around her toothless face.

"I like to see yer light at night," she said. "It feels real neighborly. I seen y'all out walkin' and come to say hi-dee." My mother introduced herself, explained we'd moved in a few months ago. "And who is this lil' bundle of joy?" she asked, leaning over the barbed wire to pinch my cheek. The fence pressed into the loose breast of her housedress, where pink and purple flowers like the hollyhocks were fading from many washings. She wore bedroom slippers outside in the garden, something my mother would never allow. She stuck her wrinkled old hand over the fence, veiny and crooked with a wire-thin band of gold loose on her ring finger. I'd never heard of a person named Hazel, but I'd heard of Witch Hazel and was quite certain that this must be the witch herself. I held my mother's hand even tighter.

I suppose, given the way she is with plants, there was a time when some might have called her "witch." And there *is* something eerie about a tree that flowers so far out of season and then spits its seeds—shiny pearls as black as midnight—twenty feet into the quiet fall woods, with a sound like an elfin footfall.

She and my mother became unlikely friends, trading recipes and garden tips. By day my mother was a professor at the college in town, sitting at her microscope, writing scientific articles. But spring twilight found her barefoot in the garden, planting beans and helping me fill my pail with earthworms that were severed by her shovel. I thought I could nurse them back to health in the worm hospital I constructed beneath the irises. She encouraged me in this, always saying, "There is no hurt that can't be healed by love."

Before dark many evenings, we would wander across the pasture to the fence and meet Hazel. "I do like to see your light in the window," she said. "There ain't nothing better than a good neighbor." I listened while they discussed putting stove ash at the base of tomato plants to keep off cutworms or Mama bragged on how fast I was learning to read. "Lord, she's a quick study, ain't you, my little honeybee?" Hazel said. Sometimes she had a wrapped peppermint in her dress pocket for me, the cellophane old and soft around it.

The visits progressed from the fence line to the front porch. When we baked, we would take over a plate of cookies and sip lemonade on her sagging stoop. I never liked to go in the house, an overwhelming jumble of old junk, trash bags, cigarette smoke, and what I now know as the smell of poverty. Hazel lived in the little shotgun house with her son Sam and daughter Janie. Janie was, as her mother explained, "simple," on account of she came late in life, her mother's last child. She was kind and loving and always wanting to smother my sister and me in her deep, soft arms.

Sam was disabled, couldn't work but received some veteran's benefits and pension from the coal company that they all lived on. Barely. When he was well enough to go fishing, he would bring us big catfish from the river. He coughed like crazy but had twinkling blue eyes and a world of stories, having been overseas in the war. Once he brought us a whole bucket of blackberries he'd picked along the railroad track. My mom tried to refuse that big pail as too generous a gift. "Why, don't talk nonsense," Hazel said. "They aren't my berries. The Lord done made these things for us to share."

My mother loved to work. For her, a good time was building stone walls or clearing brush. On occasion, Hazel would come over and sit in a lawn chair under the oaks while Mama stacked stones or split kindling. They would just talk about this and that, Hazel telling about how she liked a good woodpile, especially when she used to take in washing to earn a little extra. She needed a goodly pile to fuel her washtubs. She had worked as a cook in a place down by the river and she shook her head at the number of platters she could carry at one time. Mama would tell about her students or a trip she had taken and Hazel would wonder at the very idea of flying in an airplane.

And Hazel would tell about the time she was called out to deliver a baby in a snowstorm, or how people would come to her door for healing herbs. She said how some other lady professor had once come with a tape recorder to talk to her and was going to put her in a book, on account of all the old ways she knew. But the professor had never come back and Hazel had never seen the book. I half listened to talk about gathering hickory nuts under the big trees or carrying a lunch pail to her daddy, who worked making barrels at the distillery down by the river, but my mother was charmed by Hazel's stories.

I know my mother loved being a scientist, but she always said that she was born too late. Her real calling, she was sure, was to be a nineteenth-century farmwife. She sang while she canned tomatoes, stewed peaches, punched down the dough for bread, and was insistent that I learn how, too. When I think back on her friendship with Hazel, I suppose that the deep respect they had for each other was rooted in such things: both were women with feet planted deep in the earth who took pride in a back strong enough to carry a load for others.

Mostly I heard their talk as a drone of grown-up chatter, but one time, when my mother was coming across the yard with a big armload of wood, I saw Hazel drop her head in her hands and cry. "When I lived at home," she said, "I could carry a load like that. Why, I could carry a bushel of peaches on one hip and a baby on the other without hardly trying. But now it's all gone, gone with the wind."

Hazel was born and raised over in Jessamine County, Kentucky, just down the road. To hear her talk, though, it might have been hundreds of miles away. She couldn't drive, nor could Janie or Sam, so her old house was as lost to her as if it lay across the Great Divide.

She had come here to live with Sam when he had a heart attack on Christmas Eve. She loved Christmas—all the folks coming by, cooking a big dinner—but she dropped everything that Christmas, locked her door, and came to live with her son and look after him. She hadn't been back home since, but you could see that her heart achèd for the place—she would get a faraway look in her eyes when she spoke of it.

My mother understood this, the longing for home. She was a northern girl, born in the shadow of the Adirondacks. She had lived lots of places for graduate school and research, but always thought she'd go back home. I remember the fall she cried for missing the blaze of red maple. She was transplanted to Kentucky by dint of a good job and my father's career, but I know she missed her own folks and the woods of home. The taste of exile was as much in her mouth as it was in Hazel's.

As Hazel grew older, she got sadder and would talk more and more about the old times, the things she would never see again: how tall and handsome her husband, Rowley, had been, how beautiful her gardens were. My mother once offered to take her back to see her old place, but she shook her head. "That's mighty nice of you, but I couldn't be beholden like that. Anyway, it's gone with the wind," she would say, "all gone." But one fall afternoon when the light was long and gold, she phoned up.

"Now, honey, I know yer hands and heart are full, but if there was any way you could see fit to drive me back to the old place, I'd be right thankful. I need to see to that roof before the snow flies." My mother and I picked her up and drove up the Nicholasville Road toward the river. It's all four-lane now, with a big span across the Kentucky River, so high you hardly know it's flowing, muddy, below you. At the old distillery, boarded up and empty now, we left the highway and drove down a little dirt road that angles back away from the river. Hazel began to cry in the backseat the minute we made the turn.

"Oh, my dear old road," she cried, and I patted her hand. I knew what to do, for I'd seen my mother cry just like this when she took me past the house where she had grown up. Hazel directed Mama past the ramshackle little houses, a few stove-in trailers, and remnants of barns. We stopped before a grassy swale under a thick grove of black locust trees. "Here it is," she said, "my home sweet home." She talked like that, like it was right out of a book. Before us was an old schoolhouse with long chapel windows set all around and two doors at the front, one for boys and one for girls. It was silvery gray with just a few swipes of whitewash blurred across the clapboard.

Hazel was eager to get out and I had to hurry to get her walker to her before she stumbled in the tall grass. Pointing all the way at the spring house, the old chicken coop, she led Mama and me to the side door and up onto the porch. She fumbled in her big purse for the keys, but her hands were shaking so badly she asked me if I would unlock the door. I opened the tattered old screen door and the key slid easily into the padlock. I held the door back for her and she clumped inside and stopped. Just stopped and looked. It was quiet as a church. The air was cold inside and flowed out past me into the warm November afternoon. I started to go in, but my mother's hand on my arm stopped me. "Just let her be," her look said.

The room before us was like a picture book about the olden days. A big old woodstove sat along the back wall, cast iron frying pans hung alongside. Dishtowels were neatly hung on dowels over the dry sink, and once-white curtains framed the view of the grove outside. The ceilings were high, as befits an old schoolhouse, and festooned with garlands of tinsel, blue and silver, flickering in the breeze from the open door. Christmas cards outlined the doorframes, fixed with yellowing tape. The whole kitchen was decked out for Christmas, an oilcloth of a holiday print covered the table and plastic poinsettias swathed in cobwebs sat in jam jars as a centerpiece. The table was set for six places and there was still food on the plates, the chairs pushed back just as they were when dinner had been interrupted by the call from the hospital.

"What a sight," she said. "Let's put this all to rights." Suddenly Hazel became as businesslike as if she'd just walked into her house after supper and found it below her housewifely standards. She set her walker aside and began gathering up the dishes from the long kitchen table and carrying them over to the sink. My mother tried to slow her down by asking for a tour of the place and saying we could get to tidying another time. Hazel took us into the parlor, where the skeleton of a Christmas tree stood with a pile of needles on the floor below. The ornaments hung like orphans on the bare branches. There was a little red drum and silver plastic birds with paint worn off and stubs where their tails should be. It had been a cozy room; there were rocking chairs and a couch, a little spindle-leg table and gas lamps. An old oak sideboard held a china pitcher and basin painted with roses. A hand-embroidered scarf, cross-stitched in pink and blue, ran the length of the sideboard. "My goodness," she said, wiping the corner of her housedress over the thick layer of dust. "I've got to get after my dustin' in here."

While she and Mama looked at the pretty dishes in the sideboard, I wandered off to explore. I pushed one door open to a big unmade bed heaped with blankets thrown back. Beside it was what looked like a potty chair, only grown-up size. It didn't smell very good in there and I quickly retreated, not wanting to be caught snooping around. Another door gave way to a bedroom with a beautiful patchwork quilt and more tinsel garlands draped over the mirror above the dresser where a hurricane lamp sat, all caked in soot.

Hazel leaned on my mother's arm as we circled around the clearing outside, pointing out trees she had planted and flowerbeds long overgrown. At the back of the house, under the oaks, was a clump of bare gray branches erupting with a froth of stringy yellow blossoms. "Why lookee here, it's my old medicine come to greet me," she said and reached out to take the branch as if she was going to shake its hand. "I made me many a batch of this old witch hazel and folks would come to me for it, special. I'd cook up that bark in the fall and have it all winter to rub on aches and pains, burns and rashes—everybody wanted it. There ain't hardly no hurt the woods don't have medicine for."

"That witch hazel," she said, "it's not just good for you outside, but inside too. Land sakes, flowers in November. The good Lord gave us witch hazel to remind us that there's always somethin' good even when it seems like there ain't. It just lightens your heavy heart, is what it does."

After that first visit, Hazel would often call on a Sunday afternoon and ask, "Would y'all like to go for a ride?" My mother thought it important that we girls go along. It was like her insistence that we learn to bake bread and plant beans—things that didn't seem important then, but now I know differently. We got to pick hickory nuts from behind the old house, wrinkle our noses at the tilting outhouse, and root around in the barn for treasures while Mama and Hazel sat on the porch and talked. Hung on a nail right beside her door was an old, black metal lunch box, open and lined with what looked like shelf paper. There were remnants of a bird's nest within. Hazel had brought along a small plastic bag filled with cracker crumbs, which she scattered on the porch rail.

"This little Jenny Wren has made her home here every year since Rowley passed on. This here was his lunch pail. Now she counts on me for house and home and I cain't let her down." A lot of people must have counted on Hazel when she was young and strong. She took us driving down her road and we stopped at nearly every house but one. "Them are no count folks," she said, and looked away. The others seemed overjoyed to see Hazel again. My sister and I would follow the chickens around or pet the hound dogs while Mama and Hazel would visit with the neighbors.

These folks were very different from the ones we met at school or at parties at the college. One lady reached out to tap my teeth. "Those are mighty purty teeth you got," she said. I'd never thought that teeth were worthy of a compliment, but then I hadn't met people before who had so few. I mostly remember their kindness, though. They were ladies Hazel had sung with in the choir of the little white church under the pines. Ladies she had known since girlhood, and they cackled together about dances by the river and shook their heads sadly over the fate of kids who up and moved away. We'd go home in the afternoon with a basket of fresh eggs or a slice of cake for each of us and Hazel just beaming.

When winter began, our visits were fewer and the light seemed to go out of Hazel's eyes. She sat at our kitchen table one day and said, "I know I shouldn't ask the good Lord for nuthin more'n what I already got, but how I wish I could have just one more Christmas in my dear old home. But those days are gone. Gone with the wind." This was an ache for which the woods had no medicine.

We were not going north to my grandma and grandpa's for Christmas that year and my mother was taking it hard. It was still weeks until Christmas but already she was baking up a fury while we girls strung popcorn and cranberries for the tree. She talked about how she would miss the snow, the smell of balsam, and her family. And then she got an idea.

It was to be a complete surprise. She got the house key from Sam and went to the old schoolhouse to see what she could do. She got on the phone to the Rural Electric Co-op and arranged to have Hazel's power reconnected, just for those few days. As soon as the lights came on, it became clear how dirty it all was. There was no running water, so we had to bring jugs of water from home to sponge things down. The job was bigger than us, so Mama enlisted the help of some fraternity boys from her classes at the college who needed a community service project. They sure got one: cleaning out that refrigerator rivaled any microbiology experiment.

We drove up and down Hazel's road, where I ran in to houses with handmade invitations for all her old friends. There weren't too many, so Mama invited the college boys and her friends, too. The house still had its Christmas decorations, but we made more, paper chains and candles, out of paper towel tubes. My dad cut a tree and set it up in the parlor with a box of lights stripped from the skeleton tree that had stood there before. We brought armloads of prickly red cedar boughs to decorate the tables and hung candy canes on the tree. The smell of cedar and peppermint filled the place where mold and mice had been only days ago. My mom and her friends baked plates of cookies.

The morning of the party, the heat was on, the tree lights lit, and one by one people started to arrive, clumping up the steps of the front porch. My sister and I played hostess while Mama drove off to get the guest of honor. "Hey, any of y'all feel like going for a ride?" Mama said, and bundled Hazel into her warm coat. "Why, where we goin'?" Hazel asked. Her face gleamed like a candle when she stepped into her "home sweet home" filled with light and friends. My mother pinned a Christmas corsage—a plastic bell with golden glitter that she had found on the dresser—to Hazel's dress. Hazel moved through her house like a queen that day. My father and my sister played their violins in the parlor, "Silent Night" and "Joy to the World," while I ladled out sweet red punch. I don't remember much more about the party, except Hazel falling asleep on the way home.

Just a few years later, we left Kentucky to move back north. My mom was glad to be going home, to have her maples instead of oaks, but saying good-bye to Hazel was hard. She saved it for last. Hazel gave her a going-away present, a rocking chair and a little box with a couple of her old-time Christmas ornaments inside. A celluloid drum and a silver plastic bird, missing its tail feathers. My mother still hangs them on her tree every year and tells the story of that party as if it were the best Christmas she ever had. We got word that Hazel had died a couple of years after we moved.

"Gone, all gone with the wind," she would have said.

There are some aches witch hazel can't assuage; for those, we need each other. My mother and Hazel Barnett, unlikely sisters, I suppose, learned well from the plants they both loved—they made a balm for loneliness together, a strengthening tea for the pain of longing.

Now, when the red leaves are all down and the geese are gone, I go looking for witch hazel. It never lets me down, always carrying the memory of that Christmas and how their friendship was medicine for each other. I cherish a witch hazel kind of day, a scrap of color, a light in the window when winter is closing all around.

A Mother's Work

I wanted to be a good mother, that's all—like Skywoman maybe. Somehow this led me into hip waders filled with brown water. The rubber boots that were intended to keep the pond at bay now contain it. And me. And one tadpole. I feel a flutter at the back of my other knee. Make that two tadpoles.

When I left Kentucky to go house hunting in upstate New York, my two small daughters gave me an explicit wish list for our new home: trees big enough for tree forts, one apiece; a stone walk lined with pansies like the one in Larkin's favorite book; a red barn; a pond to swim in; a purple bedroom. The last request gave me some comfort. Their dad had just pulled up stakes, left the country—and us. He said that he no longer wanted a life with so much responsibility, so the responsibility was all mine. I was grateful that, if nothing else, I could at least paint a bedroom purple.

All winter long I looked at house after house, none of which made sense for either my budget or my hopes. Real estate listings—"3BR, 2B, raised ranch, landscaping"—are pretty thin on vital information like trees suitable for tree houses. I confess that I was thinking more about mortgages and school districts and whether I was going to end up in a trailer park at the end of the road. But the girls' wish list surfaced in my mind when the agent drove me to an old farmhouse surrounded by immense sugar maples, two with low, spreading branches perfect for tree houses. This was a possibility. But there was the matter of sagging shutters and a porch that hadn't seen level in half a century. On the plus side, it sat on seven acres, including what was described as a trout pond, which was only a smooth expanse of ice surrounded by trees at the time. The house was empty, cold, and unloved, but as I opened doors to the musty rooms, wonder of wonders: the corner bedroom was the color of spring violets. It was a sign. This is where we would fall to earth.

We moved in that spring. Not long after, the girls and I cobbled together tree forts in the maples, one apiece. Imagine our surprise when the snow melted to reveal a flagstone walk overgrown with weeds leading to the front door. We met the neighbors, explored the hilltops with picnic lunches, planted pansies, and started to put down the roots of happiness. Being the good mother, good enough for two parents, seemed within my grasp. All that remained to complete the wish list for home was a swimmable pond.

The deed described a deep spring-fed pond, and a hundred years ago it might have been exactly that. One of my neighbors whose family has been here for generations told me that it was the favorite pond in the valley. In summer, after haying, the boys would park their wagons and hike up to the pond for a swim. "We'd throw off our clothes and jump in," he said. "The way it sits, no girls would be able to see us, buck naked as we were. And cold! That spring kept the water icy cold and it felt so good after working hay. We'd lie in the grass afterward, just to warm up." Our pond nestles in the hill up behind the house. The slopes rise around it on three sides and a copse of apple trees on the other side entirely shield it from view. At its back is a limestone cliff where rock was quarried to build my house more than two hundred years ago. It was hard to believe that anyone would dip even a toe in that pond today. My daughters certainly would not. It was so choked with green that you could not tell where weeds left off and water began.

The ducks didn't help. If anything, they were what you might politely call a major source of nutrient input. They were so cute in the feed store—just downy yellow fluff connecting outsize beaks and enormous orange feet, waddling around in a crate of wood chips. It was spring, almost Easter, and all the good reasons not to take them home

evaporated with the girls' delight. Wouldn't a good mother adopt ducklings? Isn't that what a pond is for?

We kept them in a cardboard box in the garage with a heat lamp,
closely watched so neither box nor ducklings would ignite. The girls
accepted full responsibility for their care and dutifully fed and cleaned
them. I came home from work one afternoon to see them floating in
the kitchen sink, quacking and dabbling, shaking water off their backs
while the girls just beamed. The condition of the sink should have given
me a clue of what was to come. For the next few weeks they ate and def-
ecated with equal enthusiasm. But within a month we carried the box of
six glossy white ducks up to the pond and released them.

They preened and splashed. All was well for the first few days, but
apparently, in the absence of their own good mother to protect and teach
them, they didn't have the essential survival skills for life outside the
box. Every day there was one less duck; five remained, then four, and
then finally three who had the right stuff to fend off foxes and snapping turtles and the marsh hawk who had taken to cruising the shore.
These three flourished. They looked so placid, so pastoral gliding over
the pond. But the pond itself began to get even greener than before.

They were perfect pets until winter came and their delinquent ten-
dencies emerged. Despite the little hut we made for them—a floating
A-frame lodge with a wraparound porch—despite the corn we showered around them like confetti, they were discontent. They developed a
fondness for dog food and the warmth of my back porch. I would come
out on a January morning to find the dog bowl empty and the dog cow-
ering outside while three snowy-white ducks sat in a row on the bench,
wiggling their tails in contentment.

It gets cold where I live. Really cold. Duck turds were frozen into
coiled mounds like half-finished clay pots solidly affixed to my porch
floor. It took an ice pick to chip them away. I would shoo them, close the
porch door, and lay a trail of corn kernels back up to the pond, and they
would follow in a gabbling line. But the next morning they'd be back.

Winter and a daily dose of duck splats must freeze up the part of the
brain devoted to compassion for animals, for I began to hope for their

demise. Unfortunately, I didn't have the heart to dispatch them, and who among our rural friends would welcome the dubious gift of ducks in the dead of winter? Even with plum sauce. I secretly contemplated spraying them with fox lure. Or tying slices of roast beef to their legs in hopes of interesting the coyotes that howled at the ridgetop. But instead I was a good mother; I fed them, rasped my shovel over the crust on the porch floor, and waited for spring. One balmy day they trundled back up to the pond and within a month they were gone, leaving piles of feathers like a drift of late snow on the shore.

The ducks were gone but their legacy lived on. By May the pond was a thick soup of green algae. A pair of Canada geese had settled in to take their place and raised a brood under the willows. One afternoon I walked up to see if the goose babies had sprouted pinfeathers yet, only to hear a distressed quacking. A fuzzy brown gosling out for a swim had gotten snared in the floating masses of algae. It was squawking and flapping its wings trying to get free. While I tried to think of how to rescue it, it gave a mighty kick and popped up to the surface, where it began to walk on the algal mat.

That was a moment of resolve for me. You should not be able to walk on a pond. It should be an invitation to wildlife, not a snare. The likelihood of making the pond swimmable, even for geese, seemed remote at best. But I am an ecologist, so I was confident that I could at least improve the situation. The word *ecology* is derived from the Greek *oikos*, the word for home. I could use ecology to make a good home for goslings and girls.

Like many an old farm pond, mine was the victim of eutrophication, the natural process of nutrient enrichment that comes with age. Generations of algae and lily pads and fallen leaves and autumn's apples falling into the pond built up the sediments, layering the once clean gravel at the bottom in a sheet of muck. All those nutrients fueled the growth of new plants, which fueled the growth of more new plants, in an accelerating cycle. This is the way for many ponds—the bottom gradually fills in until the pond becomes a marsh and maybe someday a meadow and then a forest. Ponds grow old, and though I will too, I like the ecological idea of aging as progressive enrichment, rather than progressive loss.

Sometimes the process of eutrophication is accelerated by human activities: nutrient-rich runoff from fertilized fields or septic tanks ends up in the water, where it supports exponential growth of algae. My pond was buffered from such influences—its source was a cold spring coming out of the hill, and a swath of trees on the uphill side formed a nitrogen-grabbing filter for runoff from the surrounding pastures. My battle was not with pollution, but with time. Making my pond swimmable would be an exercise in turning back time. That's just what I wanted, to turn back time. My daughters were growing up too fast, my time as a mother slipping away, and my promise of a swimming pond yet to be fulfilled.

Being a good mother meant fixing the pond for my kids. A highly productive food chain might be good for frogs and herons, but not for swimming. The best swimming lakes are not eutrophic, but cold, clear, and oligotrophic, or poor in nutrients.

I carried my small solo canoe up to the pond to serve as a floating platform for algae removal. I envisioned scooping up the algae with a long-handled rake, filling the canoe as if it was a garbage scow, emptying it on the shore, and then going for a nice swim. But only the swimming part worked out—and it wasn't nice. As I tried to skim the algae, I discovered that they hung like sheer green curtains through the water. If you reach far out of a light canoe and try to lift a heavy mat of algae at the end of a rake, physics dictates that swimming will occur.

My attempts at skimming were useless. I was addressing only the symptoms of scum and not the cause. I read as much as I could about pond rehabilitation and weighed my options. To undo what time and ducks had accomplished I needed to remove nutrients from the pond, not just skim the foam. When I waded in the shallow end of the pond, the muck squished between my toes, but beneath it I could feel the clean gravel that was the pond's original basin. Maybe I could dredge up the muck and cart it away in buckets. But when I brought my broadest snow shovel to scoop up the mud, by the time it reached the surface there was a brown cloud all around me and a mere handful of soil in the shovel. I stood in the water laughing out loud. Shoveling muck was like trying to catch wind in a butterfly net.

Next I used old window screens to make a sieve that we could lift up through the sediments. But the muck was far too fine and my improvised net came up empty. This was not ordinary mud. The organic matter in the sediments occurs as tiny particles, dissolved nutrients that flocculate in specks small enough to be bite-size snacks for zooplankton. Clearly, I was powerless to haul the nutrients out of the water. Fortunately, the plants were not.

A mat of algae is really nothing more than dissolved phosphorous and nitrogen made solid through the alchemy of photosynthesis. I couldn't remove nutrients by shoveling, but once they are fixed into the bodies of plants they can be forked out of the water with the application of biceps and bent back and carted away by the wheelbarrowful.

The average phosphate molecule in a farm pond has a cycling time of less than two weeks from the time it is absorbed out of the water, made into living tissue, is eaten or dies, decomposes, and is recycled back to feed yet another algal strand. My plan was to interrupt this endless recycling by capturing nutrients in plants and hauling them away before they could once again be turned into algae. I could slowly, steadily deplete the stores of nutrients circulating in the pond.

I'm a botanist by trade, and so of course I needed to know who these algae were. There are probably as many kinds of algae as there are species of tree, and I would do a disservice to their lives and to my task if I didn't know who they were. You wouldn't try to restore a forest without knowing what kind of trees you were working with, so I scooped up a jarful of green slime and took it to my microscope with the top screwed tightly to contain the smell.

I teased apart the slippery green wads into tiny wisps that would fit beneath my microscope. In this single tuft were long threads of *Cladophora*, shining like satin ribbons. Wound around them were translucent strands of *Spirogyra*, in which the chloroplasts spiral like a green staircase. The whole green field was in motion, with iridescent tumbleweeds of *Volvox* and pulsing euglenoids stretching their way among the strands. So much life in a single drop of water, water that previously looked like scum in a jar. Here were my partners in restoration.

Progress was slow with pond restoration hours squeezed between years' worth of Girl Scout meetings, bake sales, camping trips, and a more-than-full-time job. All moms have treasured ways to spend the few precious hours they have to themselves, curling up with a book or sewing, but I mostly went to the water, the birds and the wind and the quiet were what I needed. This was one place where I somehow felt as if I could make things right. At school I taught ecology, but on a Saturday afternoon when the kids were off at a friend's, I got to *do* ecology.

After the canoe debacle, I decided it was wiser to stand on the shore with a rake and stretch out as far as I could reach. The rake brought sticks draped in *Cladophora* like a comb matted with long green hair. Every stroke of the rake combed up another sheet from the bottom and added to a quickly growing mound, which I had to get out of the watershed by moving it downhill from the pond. If I left it to rot on the shore, the nutrients released in decay would return to the pond in short order. I flung the wads of algae onto a sled—my kids' little red plastic toboggan—and dragged it up the steep bank to empty it into the waiting wheelbarrow.

I really didn't want to stand in the mucky ooze, so I worked cautiously from the edges in old sneakers. I could reach out and dredge up heaps of algae, but there was so much more just beyond my reach. Sneakers evolved to Wellingtons, extending my sphere of influence just enough for me to know that it was ineffective, and thus Wellingtons came to waders. But waders give you a false sense of security, and before long I reached just a little too far and felt the icy pond rush in over their tops. Waders are darn heavy when they fill up, and I found myself anchored in the muck. A good mother does not drown. The next time I just wore shorts.

I simply gave myself up to the task. I remember the liberation of just walking right in to my waist the first time, the lightness of my T-shirt floating around me, the swirl of the water against my bare skin. I finally felt at home. The tickles at my legs were just wisps of *Spirogyra*, the nudges just curious perch. Now I could see the algael curtains stretched out before me, much more beautiful than dangling at the end of my rake. I could see the way *Cladophora* bloomed from old sticks and watch diving beetles swim among them.

I developed a new relationship with mud. Instead of trying to protect myself from it, I became oblivious to it, noticing its presence only when I would go back to the house and see strands of algae caught in my hair or the water in the shower turning decidedly brown. I came to know the feel of the gravelly bottom below the muck, the sucking mud by the cattails and the cold stillness where the bottom dropped away from the shallows. Transformation is not accomplished by tentative wading at the edge.

One spring day my rake came up draped with a mass of algae so heavy it bent the bamboo handle. I let it drip to lighten the load and then flipped it onto the shore. I was about to go for another load when I heard a wet smacking from the pile, the slap of a watery tail. A lump was wiggling in a frenzy below the surface of the heaped algae. I picked the threads apart, opening the weave to see what was struggling within. A plump brown body; a bullfrog tadpole as big as my thumb was caught there. Tadpoles can swim easily through a net that is suspended in the water, but when the net is drawn up by the rake it collapses around them like a purse seine. I picked him up, squishy and cold, between thumb and forefinger and tossed him back into the pond, where he rested, suspended for a moment in the water, and then swam off. The next rake came up in a smooth dripping sheet studded with so many tadpoles that they looked like nuts caught in a tray of peanut brittle. I bent and untangled them, every one.

This was a problem. There was so much to rake. I could dredge the algae out, slap it into piles, and be done with it. I could work so much faster if I didn't have to stop and pick tadpoles from the tangle of every moral dilemma. I told myself that my intention was not to hurt them; I was just trying to improve the habitat and they were the collateral damage. But my good intentions meant nothing to tadpoles if they struggled and died in a compost pile. I sighed, but I knew what I had to do. I was driven to this chore by a mothering urge, to make a swimmable pond.

In the process, I could hardly sacrifice another mother's children, who, after all, already have a pond to swim in.

Now I was not only a pond raker, but also a tadpole plucker. It was amazing what I found in the mesh of algae: predaceous diving beetles with sharp black mandibles; small fish; dragonfly larvae. I stuck my fingers in to free a wiggle and felt a sharp pain like a bee sting. My hand flinched back with a big crayfish attached to my fingertip. A whole food web was dangling from my rake, and those were just the critters I could see, just the tip of the iceberg, the top of the food chain. Under my microscope, I had seen the web of algae teeming with invertebrates—copepods, daphnia, whirling rotifers, and creatures so much smaller: threadlike worms, globes of green algae, protozoans with cilia beating in unison. I knew they were there, but I couldn't possibly pick them out. So I bargained with myself over the chain of responsibility and tried to convince myself that their demise served a greater good.

Raking a pond provides you with a lot of mental free space for philosophizing. As I raked and plucked, it challenged my conviction that all lives are valuable, protozoan or not. As a theoretical matter, I hold this to be true, but on a practical level it gets murky, the spiritual and the pragmatic bumping heads. With every rake I knew that I was prioritizing. Short, single-cell lives were ended because I wanted a clear pond. I'm bigger, I have a rake, so I win. That's not a worldview I readily endorse. But it didn't keep me awake at night, or halt my efforts; I simply acknowledged the choices I was making. The best I could do was to be respectful and not let the small lives go to waste. I plucked out whatever wee beasties I could and the rest went into the compost pile, to start the cycle again as soil.

At first I hauled carts of freshly raked algae, but I soon realized that trundling hundreds of pounds of water was hard work. I learned to heap the algae on the shore and watch it dribble moisture back to the pond. In the following days the algae bleached in the sun into light papery sheets, easily lifted into the wheelbarrow. Filamentous algae like *Spirogyra* and *Cladophora* have a nutrient content equivalent to that of high-quality forage grasses. I was hauling away the equivalent nutrient load of bales of good dairy hay. Load after load of algae domed up in the compost pile, on its way to making good black humus. The pond was literally feeding the garden, *Cladophora* reborn as carrots. I began to see a difference in the pond. A span of days would go by when the surface was clear, but the fuzzy green mats always returned.

I began to notice other sponges for my pond's excess nutrients in addition to the algae. All along the shore, the willows reached their feathery red roots into the shallow water to troll for nitrogen and phosphorous to pull into their root systems to become leaves and willow withes. I came along the shore with my loppers and cut the willows, stem by swaying stem. Dragging the piles of willow branches away, I was removing storehouses of nutrients they had sucked from the pond bottom. The brush pile in the field grew taller, soon to be browsed by cottontails and redistributed far and wide as rabbit droppings. Willow responds vigorously to cutting and sends up long straight shoots that can tower over my head in a single growing season. I left the thickets away from the water for rabbits and songbirds, but those right at the shore I cut and bundled for making baskets. The larger stems became the foundation for garden trellises for pole beans and morning glories. I also gathered mint and other herbs along the banks. As with the willows, the more I picked, the more it seemed to grow back. Everything I took moved the pond a step closer to clear. Every cup of mint tea struck a blow for nutrient removal.

Cleaning the pond by cutting willows really seemed to help. I cut with renewed enthusiasm, moving in a mindless rhythm with my loppers— *snick, snick, snick*—clearing whole swaths of shoreline as willow stems fell at my feet. Then something, perhaps a movement glimpsed out of the corner of my eye, perhaps a silent plea, made me stop. In the last stem left standing was a beautiful little nest, a cup woven sweetly of *Juncus* rushes and threadlike roots around a fork in the tree, a marvel of homemaking. I peered inside and there were three eggs the size of lima beans lying in a circlet of pine needles. What a treasure I had nearly destroyed in my zeal to "improve" the habitat. Nearby, the mother, a yellow warbler, flitted in the bushes, calling in alarm. I was so quick and single-minded about what I was doing that I forgot to look. I forgot to acknowledge that creating the home that I wanted for my children jeopardized the homemaking of other mothers whose intents were no different from mine.

It came to me once again that restoring a habitat, no matter how well intentioned, produces casualties. We set ourselves up as arbiters of what is good when often our standards of goodness are driven by narrow interests, by what we want. I piled the cut brush back up near the nest in some semblance of the protective cover I had destroyed and sat on a rock, concealed on the other side of the pond, to see if she would come back. What did she think as she watched me come closer and closer, laying waste to the home she had carefully chosen, threatening her family? There are powerful forces of destruction loose in the world, advancing inexorably toward her children and mine. The onslaught of progress, well-intentioned to improve human habitat, threatens the nest I've chosen for my children as surely as I threatened hers. What does a good mother do?

I continued to clear out the algae, let the silt settle, and it looked better. But I went back a week later to a foamy green mass. It's kind of like cleaning the kitchen: you get everything put away, wipe off the countertops, and before you know it there are drips of peanut butter and jelly everywhere and you have to do it all over again. Life adds up. It's eutrophic. But I could see ahead to a time when my kitchen would stay too clean. I would have an oligotrophic kitchen. Without the girls to mess it up, I would be longing for leftover cereal bowls, for a eutrophic kitchen. For signs of life.

I pull my red toboggan to the other end of the pond and start to work in the shallows. Immediately, my rake gets stalled with a heavy load of weeds that I drag slowly to the surface. This mat has a different weight and texture than the slippery sheets of *Cladophora* that I've been dredging. I lay it down on the grass for a closer look and spread the film with my fingers until it stretches into what looks like a green fishnet stocking—a fine mesh network like a drift net suspended in the water. This is *Hydrodictyon*.

I stretch it between my fingers and it glistens, almost weightless after the water has drained away. As orderly as a honeycomb, *Hydrodictyon* is a geometric surprise in the seemingly random stew of a murky pond. It hangs in the water, a colony of tiny nets all fused together.

Under the microscope, the fabric of *Hydrodictyon* is made up of tiny six-sided polygons, a mesh of linked green cells that surround the holes of the net. It multiplies quickly because of a unique means of clonal reproduction. Inside each of the net cells, daughter cells are born. They arrange themselves into hexagons, neat replicas of the mother net. In order to disperse her young, the mother cell must disintegrate, freeing the daughter cells into the water. The floating newborn hexagons fuse with others, forging new connections and weaving a new net.

I look out at the expanse of *Hydrodictyon* visible just below the surface. I imagine the liberation of new cells, the daughters spinning off on their own. What does a good mother do when mothering time is done? As I stand in the water, my eyes brim and drop salt tears into the freshwater at my feet. Fortunately, my daughters are not clones of their mother, nor must I disintegrate to set them free, but I wonder how the fabric is changed when the release of daughters tears a hole. Does it heal over quickly, or does the empty space remain? And how do the daughter cells make new connections? How is the fabric rewoven?

Hydrodictyon is a safe place, a nursery for fish and insects, a shelter from predators, a safety net for the small beings of the pond. *Hydrodictyon*—Latin for "the water net." What a curious thing. A fishnet catches fish, a bug net catches bugs. But a water net catches nothing, save what cannot be held. Mothering is like that, a net of living threads to lovingly encircle what it cannot possibly hold, what will eventually move through it. But right then my job was reversing succession, turning back time to make these waters swimmable for my daughters. So I wiped my eyes and with all due respect for the lessons of *Hydrodictyon*, I raked it up onto the shore.

When my sister came to visit, her kids, raised in the dry California hills, were smitten with water. They waded after frogs and splashed with abandon while I worked at the algae. My brother-in-law called out from the shade, "Hey, who is the biggest kid here?" I can't deny it—I've never outgrown my desire to play in the mud. But isn't play the way we get limbered up for the work of the world? My sister defended my pond-raking with the reminder that it was sacred play.

Among our Potawatomi people, women are the Keepers of Water. We carry the sacred water to ceremonies and act on its behalf. "Women have a natural bond with water, because we are both life bearers," my sister said. "We carry our babies in internal ponds and they come forth into the world on a wave of water. It is our responsibility to safeguard the water for all our relations." Being a good mother includes the caretaking of water.

On Saturday mornings, Sunday afternoons, year after year, I would go to the solitude of the pond and get to work. I tried grass carp and barley straw, and every new change provoked a new reaction. The job is never over; it simply changes from one task to the next. What I'm looking for, I suppose, is balance, and that is a moving target. Balance is not a passive resting place—it takes work, balancing the giving and the taking, the raking out and the putting in.

Skating in winter, peepers in the spring, summer sunbathing, autumn bonfires; swimmable or not, the pond became like another room in our house. I planted sweetgrass around the edge. The girls and their friends had campfires on the flat meadow of the shore, slumber parties in the tent, summer suppers on the picnic table, and long sun-washed afternoons sunbathing, rising on one elbow when the gust of a heron's wings stirred the air.

I cannot count the hours that I've spent here. Almost without notice the hours stretched out to years. My dog used to bound up the hill after me and race back and forth along the shore as I worked. As the pond grew clearer, he grew more feeble but would always go with me, to sleep in the sun and drink at the edge. We buried him nearby. The pond built my muscles, wove my baskets, mulched my garden, made my tea, and trellised my morning glories. Our lives became entwined in ways both material and spiritual. It's been a balanced exchange: I worked on the pond and the pond worked on me, and together we made a good home.

One spring Saturday, while I was raking algae, there was a rally downtown in support of the cleanup of Onondaga Lake, on whose shore our city stands. The lake is held sacred by the Onondaga Nation, the people who have fished and gathered on its shore for millennia. It was here that the great Haudenosaunee (Iroquois) Confederacy was formed.

Today, Onondaga Lake has the dubious reputation of being one of the most polluted lakes in the country. The problem at Onondaga Lake is not too much life, but too little. As I dredge up another heavy rakeful of slime, I feel also the weight of responsibility. In one short life where does responsibility lie? I spend countless hours improving the water quality of my half-acre pond. I stand here raking algae so that my kids can swim in clear water, while standing silent on the cleanup of Onondaga, where no one can swim.

Being a good mother means teaching your children to care for the world, and so I've shown the girls how to grow a garden, how to prune an apple tree. The apple tree leans out over the water and makes for a shadowy arbor. In spring a drift of pink and white blossoms send plumes of fragrance wafting down the hill and a rain of petals on the water. For years now I've watched her seasons, from frothy pink blossoms, to gently swelling ovaries as the petals fall away, to sour green marbles of adolescent fruit, to the ripe golden apples of September. That tree has been a good mother. Most years she nurtures a full crop of apples, gathering the energy of the world into herself and passing it on. She sends her young out into the world well provisioned for the journey, packaged in sweetness to share with the world.

My girls, too, have grown up strong and beautiful here, rooted like the willows and flying off like their windblown seeds. And now, after twelve years, the pond is nearly swimmable, if you don't mind the weeds that tickle your legs. My older daughter left for college long before the pond was clean. I recruited my younger daughter to help me carry buckets of pea gravel to pour ourselves a beach. Having become so intimate with muck and tadpoles, I don't mind the occasional green strand that wraps around my arm, but the beach makes a small ramp that lets me wade in and plunge into the deep clear pool at the center without raising a cloud. On a hot day it feels wonderful to submerge in the icy spring water and watch the pollywogs flee. Emerging with a shiver, I have to pluck bits of algae from my wet skin. The girls will take a quick dip to please me, but, in truth, I've not succeeded in turning back time.

It is Labor Day now, the last day of summer vacation. A day to savor the mellow sunshine. This summer is my last with a child at home. Yellow apples plop into the water from an overhanging tree. I am mesmerized by the yellow apples on the dark surface of the pond, globes of light dancing and turning. The breeze off the hill sets the water in motion. In a circular current from west to east and back again, the wind is stirring the pond, so gently you wouldn't see it but for the fruit. The apples ride the current, a procession of yellow rafts following each other along the shoreline. They move quickly from under the apple tree and follow the curve beneath the elms. As the wind carries them away, more fall from the tree so that the whole pond surface is stenciled with moving arcs of yellow, like a procession of yellow candles against a dark night. They spiral around and around in an ever widening gyre.

Paula Gunn Allen, in her book *Grandmothers of the Light*, writes of the changing roles of women as they spiral through the phases of life, like the changing face of the moon. We begin our lives, she says, walking the Way of the Daughter. This is the time for learning, for gathering experiences in the shelter of our parents. We move next to self-reliance, when the necessary task of the age is to learn who you are in the world. The path brings us next to the Way of the Mother. This, Gunn relates, is a time when "her spiritual knowledge and values are all called into service of her children." Life unfolds in a growing spiral, as children begin their own paths and mothers, rich with knowledge and experience, have a new task set before them. Allen tells us that our strengths turn now to a circle wider than our own children, to the well-being of the community. The net stretches larger and larger. The circle bends round again and grandmothers walk the Way of the Teacher, becoming models for younger women to follow. And in the fullness of age, Allen reminds us, our work is not yet done. The spiral widens farther and farther, so that the sphere of a wise woman is beyond herself, beyond her family, beyond the human community, embracing the planet, mothering the earth.

So it is my grandchildren who will swim in this pond, and others whom the years will bring. The circle of care grows larger and caregiving for my little pond spills over to caregiving for other waters. The outlet from my pond runs downhill to my good neighbor's pond. What I do here matters. Everybody lives downstream. My pond drains to the brook, to the creek, to a great and needful lake. The water net connects us all. I have shed tears into that flow when I thought that motherhood would end. But the pond has shown me that being a good mother doesn't end with creating a home where just my children can flourish. A good mother grows into a richly eutrophic old woman, knowing that her work doesn't end until she creates a home where all of life's beings can flourish. There are grandchildren to nurture, and frog children, nestlings, goslings, seedlings, and spores, and I still want to be a good mother.

The Consolation of Water Lilies

Before I knew it, and long before the pond was ready for swimming, they were gone. My daughter Linden chose to leave the little pond and put her feet in the ocean at a redwood college far from home. I went to visit her that first semester and we spent a lazy Sunday afternoon admiring the rocks of the agate beach at Patrick's Point.

Walking the shore, I spotted a smooth green pebble threaded with carnelian, just like one I'd passed by a few steps earlier. I walked back, searching the strand until I found it again. I reunited the two pebbles, letting them lie together, shining wet in the sun until the tide came back and pulled them apart, rolling their edges smoother and their bodies smaller. The whole beach was like that for me, a gallery of beautiful pebbles divided from each other and from the shore. Linden's way on the beach was different. She too was rearranging, but her method was to place gray with black basalt and pink beside a spruce green oval. Her eye was finding new pairings; mine was searching out the old.

I had known it would happen from the first time I held her—from that moment on, all her growing would be away from me. It is the fundamental unfairness of parenthood that if we do our jobs well, the deepest bond we are given will walk out the door with a wave over the shoulder. We get good training along the way. We learn to say "Have a great time, sweetie" while we are longing to pull them back to safety. And against all the evolutionary imperatives of protecting our gene pool, we give them car keys. And freedom. It's our job. And I wanted to be a good mother.

I was happy for her, of course, poised at the beginning of a new adventure, but I was sad for myself, enduring the agony of missing her. My friends who had already weathered this passage counseled me to remember the parts of having a house full of children that I wouldn't miss a bit. I would be glad to retire from the worried nights when the roads are snowy, waiting for the sound of tires in the driveway exactly one minute before curfew. The half-done chores and the mysteriously emptying refrigerator.

There were days when I'd get up in the morning and the animals had beaten me to the kitchen. The calico cat yelled from her perch: *Feed me!* The longhair stood by his bowl silently with an accusing stare. The dog threw herself against my legs with happiness and looked expectant. *Feed me!* And I did. I dropped handfuls of oatmeal and cranberries into one pot and stirred hot chocolate in another. The girls came downstairs sleepy-eyed and needing that homework paper from last night. *Feed me,* they said. And I did. I tipped the scraps into the compost bucket so when the next summer's tomato seedlings say *feed me,* I can. And when I kiss the girls good-bye at the door, the horses whicker at the fence for their bucket of grain and the chickadees call from their empty seed tray: *Feed me me me. Feed me me me.* The fern on the windowsill droops its fronds in silent request. When I put the key in the ignition of the car it starts to ping: *fill me.* Which I do. I listen to public radio all the way to school and thank goodness it's not pledge week.

I remember my babies at the breast, the *first* feeding, the long deep suck that drew up from my innermost well, which was filled and filled again, by the look that passed between us, the reciprocity of mother and child. I suppose I should welcome the freedom from all that feeding and worrying, but I'll miss it. Maybe not the laundry, but the immediacy of those looks, the presence of our reciprocal love is hard to say good-bye to.

I understood that part of my sadness at Linden's departure was because I did not know who I would be when I was no longer known as "Linden's Mother." But I had a bit of a reprieve from that crisis, as I am also justly famous for being "Larkin's Mother." But this, too, would pass.

Before my younger daughter, Larkin, left, she and I had a last camp-fire up at the pond and watched the stars come out. "Thank you," she whispered, "for all of this." The next morning she had the car all packed with dorm furnishings and school supplies. The quilt that I made for her before she was born showed through one of the big plastic tubs of essentials. When everything she needed was stuffed in back, then she helped me load mine on the roof.

After we'd unloaded and decorated the dorm room and went out to lunch as if nothing was happening, I knew it was time for my exit. My work was done and hers was beginning.

I saw girls dismiss their parents with a waggle of fingers, but Larkin walked me out to the dorm parking lot where the herds of minivans were still disgorging their cargos. Under the gaze of deliberately cheerful dads and strained-looking moms, we hugged again and shed some smiley tears that we both thought had already been used up. As I opened the car door, she started to walk away and called out loudly, "Mom, if you break down in uncontrollable sobs on the highway, please pull over!" The entire parking lot erupted in laughter and then we were all released.

I did not need Kleenex or the breakdown lane. After all, I wasn't going home. I could manage leaving her at college, but I did not want to go home to an empty house. Even the horses were gone and the old family dog had died that spring. There would be no welcoming committee.

I had planned for this with my special grief-containment system strapped on top of my car. Spending every weekend at track meets or hosting slumber parties, I rarely found time to go paddling alone. Now I was going to celebrate my freedom rather than mourn my loss. You hear about those shiny, red midlife crisis Corvettes? Well, mine was strapped on top of the car. I drove down the road to Labrador Pond and slipped my new red kayak into the water.

Just remembering the sound of the first bow wave brings back the whole of the day. Late summer afternoon, golden sun and lapis sky between the hills that fold around the pond. Red-winged blackbirds cackling in the cattails. Not a breath of wind disturbed the glassy pond. Open water sparkled ahead, but first I had to traverse the marshy edges, beds of pickerelweed and water lilies so thick they covered the water. The long petioles of the spatterdock lilies, stretching six feet from the mucky bottom to the surface, tangled around my paddle as if they wanted to keep me from moving forward. Pulling away the weeds that stuck to my hull, I could see inside their broken stalks. They were packed with spongy white cells filled with air, like a pith of Styrofoam, that botanists call *aerenchyma*. These air cells are unique to floating water plants and give the leaves buoyancy, like a built-in life jacket. This characteristic makes them very hard to paddle through but they serve a larger purpose.

Pond lily leaves get their light and air at the surface, but are attached at the bottom of the lake to a living rhizome as thick as your wrist and as long as your arm. The rhizome inhabits the anaerobic depths of the pond, but without oxygen it will perish. So the aerenchyma forms a convoluted chain of air-filled cells, a conduit between the surface and the depths so that oxygen can slowly diffuse to the buried rhizome. If I pushed the leaves aside I could see them resting below.

Mired in the weeds, I rested for a bit surrounded by water shield, fragrant water lily, rushes, wild calla, and the eccentric flowers known variously as yellow pond lily, bullhead lily, *Nuphar luteum*, spatterdock, and brandybottle. That last name, rarely heard, is perhaps most apt, as the yellow flowers sticking up from the dark water emit a sweet alcoholic scent. It made me wish I had brought a bottle of wine.

Once the showy brandybottle flowers have accomplished their goal of attracting pollinators, they bend below the surface for several weeks, suddenly reclusive while their ovaries swell. When the seeds are mature, the stalks straighten again and lift up above the water the fruit—a curiously flask-shaped pod with a brightly colored lid that looks like its namesake, a miniature brandy cask about the size of a shot glass. I've never witnessed it myself, but I'm told that the seeds pop dramatically from the pod onto the surface, earning one of their other names, spatterdock. All around me there were lilies in all stages of rising and sinking and reemerging, a waterscape of change that is hard to move through, but I bent to the task, pushing my red boat through the green.

I paddled hard and strong out to the deep water, pulling against the weight of the restraining vegetation, eventually breaking free. When I had exhausted my shoulders so they were as empty as my heart, I rested on the water, closed my eyes, and let the sadness come, adrift.

Maybe a little breeze came up, maybe a hidden current, or the earth tilting on its axis to slosh the pond, but whatever the invisible hand, my little boat began to rock gently, like a cradle on the water. Held by the hills and rocked by the water, the hand of the breeze against my cheek, I gave myself over to the comfort that came, unbidden.

I don't know how long I floated, but my little red boat drifted the length of the lake. Rustling whispers around my hull drew me from reverie and the first thing I saw upon opening my eyes were polished green leaves of water lilies and spatterdock smiling up at me again, rooted in darkness and floating in the light. I found myself surrounded by hearts on the water, luminous green hearts. The lilies seemed to pulse with light, green hearts beating with my own. There were young heart leaves below the water on their way up and old leaves on the surface, some with edges tattered by a summer of wind and waves and, no doubt, kayak paddles.

Scientists used to think that the movement of oxygen from the surface leaves of lilies to the rhizome was merely the slow process of diffusion, an inefficient drift of molecules from a region of high concentration in the air to low concentration under water. But new inquiries revealed a flow we could have known by intuition if we had remembered the teachings of plants.

The new leaves take up oxygen into the tightly packed air spaces of their young, developing tissues, whose density creates a pressure gradient. The older leaves, with looser air spaces created by the tatters and tears that open the leaf, create a low-pressure region where oxygen can be released into the atmosphere. This gradient exerts a pull on the air taken in by the young leaf. Since they are connected by air-filled capillary networks, the oxygen moves by mass flow from the young leaves to the old, passing through and oxygenating the rhizome in the process. The young and the old are linked in one long breath, an inhalation that calls for reciprocal exhalation, nourishing the common root from which they both arose. New leaf to old, old to new, mother to daughter—mutuality endures. I am consoled by the lesson of lilies.

I paddled more easily back to the shore. Loading the kayak onto the car in the fading light, I was doused with the leftover pond water draining onto my head. I smiled at the illusion of my grief-containment system: there is no such thing. We spill over into the world and the world spills over into us.

The earth, that first among good mothers, gives us the gift that we cannot provide ourselves. I hadn't realized that I had come to the lake and said *feed me,* but my empty heart was fed. I had a good mother. She gives what we need without being asked. I wonder if she gets tired, old Mother Earth. Or if she too is fed by the giving. "Thanks," I whispered, "for all of this."

It was nearly dark when I got home, but my plan had included leaving the porch light on because a dark house would have been one assault too many. I carried my life jacket into the porch and got out my house keys before I noticed a pile of presents, all beautifully wrapped in brightly colored tissue paper, as if a piñata had burst over my door. A bottle of wine with a single glass on the doorsill. There was a going-away party on the porch and Larkin had missed it. "She's one lucky girl," I thought, "showered with love."

I looked through the gifts for tags or a card, but there was nothing to show who had made the late delivery. The wrapping was just tissue paper so I hunted for a clue. I smoothed the purple paper tight on one gift to read the label underneath. It was a jar of Vicks VapoRub! A little note fell from the twisted tissue paper: "Take comfort." I recognized the handwriting immediately as my cousin's, dear enough to be my sister, who lives hours away. My fairy godmother left eighteen notes and presents, one for every year of mothering Larkin. A compass: "To find your new path." A packet of smoked salmon: "Because they always come home." Pens: "Celebrate having time to write."

We are showered every day with gifts, but they are not meant for us to keep. Their life is in their movement, the inhale and the exhale of our shared breath. Our work and our joy is to pass along the gift and to trust that what we put out into the universe will always come back.

Allegiance to Gratitude

There was a time, not so long ago, when my morning ritual was to rise before dawn and start the oatmeal and coffee before waking the girls. Then I would get them up to feed the horses before school. That done, I would pack lunches, find lost papers, and kiss pink cheeks as the school bus chugged up the hill, all before filling bowls for the cats and dog, finding something presentable to wear, and previewing my morning lecture as I drove to school. *Reflection* was not a word frequently on my mind those days.

But on Thursdays, I didn't have a morning class and could linger a little, so I would walk the pasture to the top of the hill to start the day properly, with birdsong and shoes soaked in dew and the clouds still pink with sunrise over the barn, a down payment on a debt of gratitude. One Thursday I was distracted from the robins and new leaves by a call I received from my sixth-grade daughter's teacher the night before. Apparently, my daughter had begun refusing to stand with the class for the Pledge of Allegiance. The teacher assured me she wasn't being disruptive, really, or misbehaving, but just sat quietly in her seat and wouldn't join in. After a couple of days other students began following suit, so the teacher was calling "just because I thought you'd like to know."

I remember how that ritual used to begin my day, too, from kindergarten through high school. Like the tap of the conductor's baton, it gathered our attention from the hubbub of the school bus and the jostling hallway. We would be shuffling our chairs and putting lunch boxes away in the cubbies when the loudspeaker grabbed us by the collar. We stood beside our desks facing the flag that hung on a stick at the corner of the blackboard, as ubiquitous as the smell of floor wax and school paste. Hand over heart, we recited the Pledge of Allegiance. The pledge was a puzzlement to me, as I'm sure it is to most students. I had no earthly idea what a republic even was, and was none too sure about God, either. And you didn't have to be an eight-year-old Indian to know that "liberty and justice for all" was a questionable premise.

But during school assemblies, when three hundred voices all joined together, all those voices, in measured cadence, from the gray-haired school nurse's to the kindergarteners', made me feel part of something. It was as if for a moment our minds were one. I could imagine then that if we all spoke for that elusive justice, it might be within our reach.

From where I stand today, though, the idea of asking schoolchildren to pledge loyalty to a political system seems exceedingly curious. Especially since we know full well that the practice of recitation will largely be abandoned in adulthood, when the age of reason has presumably been attained. Apparently my daughter had reached that age and I was not about to interfere. "Mom, I'm not going to stand there and lie," she explained. "And it's not exactly liberty if they force you to say it, is it?"

She knew different morning rituals, her grandfather's pouring of coffee on the ground and the one I carried out on the hill above our house, and that was enough for me. The sunrise ceremony is our Potawatomi way of sending gratitude into the world, to recognize all that we are given and to offer our choicest thanks in return. Many Native peoples across the world, despite myriad cultural differences, have this in common—we are rooted in cultures of gratitude.

Our old farm is within the ancestral homelands of the Onondaga Nation and their reserve lies a few ridges to the west of my hilltop. There, just like on my side of the ridge, school buses discharge a herd of kids who run even after the bus monitors bark "Walk!" But at Onondaga, the flag flying outside the entrance is purple and white, depicting the Hiawatha wampum belt, the symbol of the Haudenosaunee Confederacy.

With bright backpacks too big for their little shoulders, the kids stream in through doors painted the traditional Haudenosaunee purple, under the words *Nya wenhah Ska: nonh*, a greeting of health and peace. Black-haired children run circles around the atrium, through sun shafts, over clan symbols etched on the slate floor.

Here the school week begins and ends not with the Pledge of Allegiance, but with the Thanksgiving Address, a river of words as old as the people themselves, known more accurately in the Onondaga language as the Words That Come Before All Else. This ancient order of protocol sets gratitude as the highest priority. The gratitude is directed straight to the ones who share their gifts with the world.

All the classes stand together in the atrium, and one grade each week has responsibility for the oratory. Together, in a language older than English, they begin the recitation. It is said that the people were instructed to stand and offer these words whenever they gathered, no matter how many or how few, before anything else was done. In this ritual, their teachers remind them that every day, "beginning with where our feet first touch the earth, we send greetings and thanks to all members of the natural world."

Today it is the third grade's turn. There are only eleven of them and they do their best to start together, giggling a little, and nudging the ones who just stare at the floor. Their little faces are screwed up with concentration and they glance at their teacher for prompts when they stumble on the words. In their own language they say the words they've heard nearly every day of their lives.

Today we have gathered and when we look upon the faces around us we see that the cycles of life continue. We have been given the duty to live in balance and harmony with each other and all living things. So now let us bring our minds together as one as we give greetings and thanks to each other as People. Now our minds are one.*

---

* The actual wording of the Thanksgiving Address varies with the speaker. This text is the widely-publicised version of John Stokes and Kanawahientun, 1993.

There is a pause and the kids murmur their assent.

We are thankful to our Mother the Earth, for she gives us every-
thing that we need for life. She supports our feet as we walk about
upon her. It gives us joy that she still continues to care for us, just as
she has from the beginning of time. To our Mother, we send thanks-
giving, love, and respect. Now our minds are one.

The kids sit remarkably still, listening. You can tell they've been
raised in the longhouse.

The Pledge has no place here. Onondaga is sovereign territory,
surrounded on every side by the *Republicforwhichitstands,* but outside the jurisdiction of the United States. Starting the day with the
Thanksgiving Address is a statement of identity and an exercise of
sovereignty, both political and cultural. And so much more.

The Address is sometimes mistakenly viewed as a prayer, but the children's heads are not bowed. The elders at Onondaga teach otherwise, that
the Address is far more than a pledge, a prayer, or a poem alone.

Two little girls step forward with arms linked and take up the
words again:

We give thanks to all of the waters of the world for quenching our
thirst, for providing strength and nurturing life for all beings. We
know its power in many forms—waterfalls and rain, mists and
streams, rivers and oceans, snow and ice. We are grateful that the
waters are still here and meeting their responsibility to the rest of
Creation. Can we agree that water is important to our lives and
bring our minds together as one to send greetings and thanks to the
Water? Now our minds are one.

I'm told that the Thanksgiving Address is at heart an invocation
of gratitude, but it is also a material, scientific inventory of the natural world. Another name for the oration is Greetings and Thanks to
the Natural World. As it goes forward, each element of the ecosystem
is named in its turn, along with its function. It is a lesson in Native
science.

We turn our thoughts to all of the Fish life in the water. They were instructed to cleanse and purify the water. They also give them-selves to us as food. We are grateful that they continue to do their duties and we send to the Fish our greetings and our thanks. Now our minds are one.

Now we turn toward the vast fields of Plant life. As far as the eye can see, the Plants grow, working many wonders. They sustain many life forms. With our minds gathered together, we give thanks and look forward to seeing Plant life for many generations to come. Now our minds are one.

When we look about us, we see that the berries are still here, providing us with delicious foods. The leader of the berries is the strawberry, the first to ripen in the spring. Can we agree that we are grateful that the berries are with us in the world and send our thanksgiving, love, and respect to the berries? Now our minds are one.

I wonder if there are kids here who, like my daughter, rebel, who refuse to stand and say thank you to the earth. It seems hard to argue with gratitude for berries.

With one mind, we honor and thank all the Food Plants we harvest from the garden, especially the Three Sisters who feed the people with such abundance. Since the beginning of time, the grains, vege-tables, beans, and fruit have helped the people survive. Many other living things draw strength from them as well. We gather together in our minds all the plant foods and send them a greeting and thanks. Now our minds are one.

The kids take note of each addition and nod in agreement. Especially for food. A little boy in a Red Hawks lacrosse shirt steps forward to speak:

Now we turn to the Medicine Herbs of the world. From the begin-ning they were instructed to take away sickness. They are always waiting and ready to heal us. We are so happy that there are still among us those special few who remember how to use the plants for healing. With one mind, we send thanksgiving, love, and respect to the Medicines and the keepers of the Medicines. Now our minds are one.

Standing around us we see all the Trees. The Earth has many families of Trees who each have their own instructions and uses. Some provide shelter and shade, others fruit and beauty and many useful gifts. The Maple is the leader of the trees, to recognize its gift of sugar when the People need it most. Many peoples of the world recognize a Tree as a symbol of peace and strength. With one mind we greet and thank the Tree life. Now our minds are one.

The Address is, by its very nature of greetings to all who sustain us, *long*. But it can be done in abbreviated form or in long and loving detail. At the school, it is tailored to the language skills of the children speaking it.

Part of its power surely rests in the length of time it takes to send greetings and thanks to so many. The listeners reciprocate the gift of the speaker's words with their attention, and by putting their minds into the place where gathered minds meet. You could be passive and just let the words and the time flow by, but each call asks for the response: "Now our minds are one." You have to concentrate; you have to give yourself to the listening. It takes effort, especially in a time when we are accustomed to sound bites and immediate gratification.

When the long version is done at joint meetings with non-Native business or government officials, they often get a little fidgety— especially the lawyers. They want to get on with it, their eyes darting around the room, trying *so hard* not to look at their watches. My own students profess to cherish the opportunity to share this experience of the Thanksgiving Address, and yet it never fails that one or a few comment that it goes on too long. "Poor you," I sympathize. "What a pity that we have so much to be thankful for."

We gather our minds together to send our greetings and thanks to all the beautiful animal life of the world, who walk about with us.

They have many things to teach us as people. We are grateful that
they continue to share their lives with us and hope that it will always
be so. Let us put our minds together as one and send our thanks to
the Animals. Now our minds are one.

Imagine raising children in a culture in which gratitude is the first
priority. Freida Jacques works at the Onondaga Nation School. She is a
clan mother, the school-community liaison, and a generous teacher. She
explains to me that the Thanksgiving Address embodies the Onondaga
relationship with the world. Each part of Creation is thanked in turn for
fulfilling its Creator-given duty to the others. "It reminds you every
day that you have enough," she says. "More than enough. Everything
needed to sustain life is already here. When we do this, every day, it
leads us to an outlook of contentment and respect for all of Creation."

You can't listen to the Thanksgiving Address without feeling
wealthy. And, while expressing gratitude seems innocent enough, it
is a revolutionary idea. In a consumer society, contentment is a radical proposition. Recognizing abundance rather than scarcity under-
mines an economy that thrives by creating unmet desires. Gratitude
cultivates an ethic of fullness, but the economy needs emptiness. The
Thanksgiving Address reminds you that you already have everything
you need. Gratitude doesn't send you out shopping to find satisfaction;
it comes as a gift rather than a commodity, subverting the foundation
of the whole economy. That's good medicine for land and people alike.

We put our minds together as one and thank all the birds who move
and fly about over our heads. The Creator gave them the gift of
beautiful songs. Each morning they greet the day and with their
songs remind us to enjoy and appreciate life. The Eagle was chosen
to be their leader and to watch over the world. To all the Birds, from
the smallest to the largest, we send our joyful greetings and thanks.
Now our minds are one.

The oratory is more than an economic model; it's a civics lesson,
too. Freida emphasizes that hearing the Thanksgiving Address every

day lifts up models of leadership for the young people: the strawberry as leader of the berries, the eagle as leader of the birds. "It reminds them that much is expected of them eventually. It says this is what it means to be a good leader, to have vision, and to be generous, to sacrifice on behalf of the people. Like the maple, leaders are the first to offer their gifts." It reminds the whole community that leadership is rooted not in power and authority, but in service and wisdom.

We are all thankful for the powers we know as the Four Winds. We hear their voices in the moving air as they refresh us and purify the air we breathe. They help to bring the change of seasons. From the four directions they come, bringing us messages and giving us strength. With one mind we send our greetings and thanks to the Four Winds. Now our minds are one.

As Freida says, "The Thanksgiving Address is a reminder we cannot hear too often, that we human beings are not in charge of the world, but are subject to the same forces as all of the rest of life."

For me, the cumulative impact of the Pledge of Allegiance, from my time as a schoolgirl to my adulthood, was the cultivation of cynicism and a sense of the nation's hypocrisy—not the pride it was meant to instill. As I grew to understand the gifts of the earth, I couldn't understand how "love of country" could omit recognition of the actual country itself. The only promise it requires is to a flag. What of the promises to each other and to the land?

What would it be like to be raised on gratitude, to speak to the natural world as a member of the democracy of species, to raise a pledge of *inter*dependence? No declarations of political loyalty are required, just a response to a repeated question: "Can we agree to be grateful for all that is given?" In the Thanksgiving Address, I hear respect toward all our nonhuman relatives, not one political entity, but to all of life. What happens to nationalism, to political boundaries, when allegiance lies with winds and waters that know no boundaries, that cannot be bought or sold?

Now we turn to the west where our grandfathers the Thunder Beings live. With lightning and thundering voices they bring with them the water that renews life. We bring our minds together as one to send greetings and thanks to our Grandfathers, the Thunderers.

We now send greetings and thanks to our eldest brother the Sun. Each day without fail he travels the sky from east to west, bringing the light of a new day. He is the source of all the fires of life. With one mind, we send greetings and thanks to our Brother, the Sun. Now our minds are one.

The Haudenosaunee have been recognized for centuries as masters of negotiation, for the political prowess by which they've survived against all odds. The Thanksgiving Address serves the people in myriad ways, including diplomacy. Most everyone knows the tension that squeezes your jaw before a difficult conversation or a meeting that is bound to be contentious. You straighten your pile of papers more than once while the arguments you have prepared stand at attention like soldiers in your throat, ready to be deployed. But then the Words That Come Before All Else begin to flow, and you start to answer. Yes, of course we can agree that we are grateful for Mother Earth. Yes, the same sun shines on each and every one of us. Yes, we are united in our respect for the trees. By the time we greet Grandmother Moon, the harsh faces have softened a bit in the gentle light of remembrance. Piece by piece, the cadence begins to eddy around the boulder of disagreement and erode the edges of the barriers between us. Yes, we can all agree that the waters are still here. Yes, we can unite our minds in gratitude for the winds. Not surprisingly, Haudenosaunee decision-making proceeds from consensus, not by a vote of the majority. A decision is made only "when our minds are one." Those words are a brilliant political preamble to negotiation, strong medicine for soothing partisan fervor. Imagine if our government meetings began with the Thanksgiving Address. What if our leaders first found common ground before fighting over their differences?

We put our minds together and give thanks to our oldest Grandmother, the Moon, who lights the nighttime sky. She is the leader of women all over the world and she governs the movement of the ocean tides. By her changing face we measure time and it is the Moon who watches over the arrival of children here on Earth. Let us gather our thanks for Grandmother Moon together in a pile, layer upon layer of gratitude, and then joyfully fling that pile of thanks high into the night sky that she will know. With one mind, we send greetings and thanks to our Grandmother, the Moon.

We give thanks to the Stars who are spread across the sky like jewelry. We see them at night, helping the Moon to light the darkness and bringing dew to the gardens and growing things. When we travel at night, they guide us home. With our minds gathered as one, we send greetings and thanks to all the Stars. Now our minds are one.

Thanksgiving also reminds us of how the world was meant to be in its original condition. We can compare the roll call of gifts bestowed on us with their current status. Are all the pieces of the ecosystem still here and doing their duty? Is the water still supporting life? Are all those birds still healthy? When we can no longer see the stars because of light pollution, the words of Thanksgiving should awaken us to our loss and spur us to restorative action. Like the stars themselves, the words can guide us back home.

We gather our minds to greet and thank the enlightened Teachers who have come to help throughout the ages. When we forget how to live in harmony, they remind us of the way we were instructed to live as people. With one mind, we send greetings and thanks to these caring Teachers. Now our minds are one.

While there is a clear structure and progression to the oratory, it is usually not recited verbatim or exactly the same by different speakers. Some renditions are low murmurs, barely discernible. Some are nearly songs. I love to hear elder Tom Porter hold a circle of listeners in the bowl of his hand. He lights up every face and no matter how long the delivery, you wish it was longer. Tommy says, "Let us pile up our thanks like a heap of flowers on a blanket. We will each take a corner and toss it high into the sky. And so our thanks should be as rich as the gifts of the world that shower down upon us," and we stand there together, grateful in the rain of blessings.

We now turn our thoughts to the Creator, or Great Spirit, and send greetings and thanks for all the gifts of Creation. Everything we need to live a good life is here on Mother Earth. For all the love that is still around us, we gather our minds together as one and send our choicest words of greetings and thanks to the Creator. Now our minds are one.

The words are simple, but in the art of their joining, they become a statement of sovereignty, a political structure, a Bill of Responsibilities, an educational model, a family tree, and a scientific inventory of ecosystem services. It is a powerful political document, a social contract, a way of being—all in one piece. But first and foremost, it is the credo for a culture of gratitude.

Cultures of gratitude must also be cultures of reciprocity. Each person, human or no, is bound to every other in a reciprocal relationship. Just as all beings have a duty to me, I have a duty to them. If an animal gives its life to feed me, I am in turn bound to support its life. If I receive a stream's gift of pure water, then I am responsible for returning a gift in kind. An integral part of a human's education is to know those duties and how to perform them.

The Thanksgiving Address reminds us that duties and gifts are two sides of the same coin. Eagles were given the gift of far sight, so it is their duty to watch over us. Rain fulfills its duty as it falls, because it was given the gift of sustaining life. What is the duty of humans? If gifts and responsibilities are one, then asking "What is our responsibility?" is the same as asking "What is our gift?" It is said that only humans have the capacity for gratitude. This is among our gifts.

It's such a simple thing, but we all know the power of gratitude to incite a cycle of reciprocity. If my girls run out the door with lunch in hand without a "Thanks, Mama!" I confess I get to feeling a tad miserly with my time and energy. But when I get a hug of appreciation, I want to stay up late to bake cookies for tomorrow's lunch bag. We know that appreciation begets abundance. Why should it not be so for Mother Earth, who packs us a lunch every single day?

Living as a neighbor to the Haudenosaunee, I have heard the Thanksgiving Address in many forms, spoken by many different voices, and I raise my heart to it like raising my face to the rain. But I am not a Haudenosaunee citizen or scholar—just a respectful neighbor and a listener. Because I feared overstepping my boundaries in sharing what I have been told, I asked permission to write about it and how it has influenced my own thinking. Over and over, I was told that these words are a gift of the Haudenosaunee to the world. When I asked Onondaga Faithkeeper Oren Lyons about it, he gave his signature slightly bemused smile and said, "Of course you should write about it. It's supposed to be shared, otherwise how can it work? We've been waiting five hundred years for people to listen. If they'd understood the Thanksgiving then, we wouldn't be in this mess."

The Haudenosaunee have published the Address widely and it has now been translated into over forty languages and is heard all around the world. Why not here in this land? I'm trying to imagine how it would be if schools transformed their mornings to include something like the Thanksgiving Address. I mean no disrespect for the white-haired veterans in my town, who stand with hand on heart as the flag goes by, whose eyes fill with tears as they recite the Pledge in raspy voices. I love my country too, and its hopes for freedom and justice. But the boundaries of what I honor are bigger than the republic. Let us pledge reciprocity with the living world. The Thanksgiving Address describes our mutual allegiance as human delegates to the democracy of species. If what we want for our people is patriotism, then let us inspire true love of country by invoking the land herself. If we want to raise good leaders, let us remind our children of the eagle and the maple. If we want to grow good citizens, then let us teach reciprocity. If what we aspire to is justice for all, then let it be justice for all of Creation.

We have now arrived at the place where we end our words. Of all the things we have named, it is not our intention to leave anything out. If something was forgotten, we leave it to each individual to send such greetings and thanks in their own way. And now our minds are one.

Every day, with these words, the people give thanks to the land. In the silence that falls at the end of those words I listen, longing for the day when we can hear the land give thanks for the people in return.

Picking Sweetgrass

Sweetgrass is harvested in midsummer, when the leaves are

long and shiny. The blades are taken one by one and dried in

the shade to preserve the color. A gift is always left in return.

Epiphany in the Beans

It came to me while picking beans, the secret of happiness.

I was hunting among the spiraling vines that envelop my teepees of pole beans, lifting the dark-green leaves to find handfuls of pods, long and green, firm and furred with tender fuzz. I snapped them off where they hung in slender twosomes, bit into one, and tasted nothing but August, distilled into pure, crisp beaniness. This summer abundance is destined for the freezer, to emerge again in deep midwinter when the air tastes only of snow. By the time I finished searching through just one trellis, my basket was full.

To go and empty it in the kitchen, I stepped between heavy squash vines and around tomato plants fallen under the weight of their fruit. They sprawled at the feet of the sunflowers, whose heads bowed with the weight of maturing seeds. Lifting my basket over the row of potatoes, I noticed an open furrow revealing a nest of red skins where the girls left off harvesting that morning. I kicked some soil over them so the sun wouldn't green them up.

They complain about garden chores, as kids are supposed to do, but once they start they get caught up in the softness of the dirt and the smell of the day and it is hours later when they come back into the house. Seeds for this basket of beans were poked into the ground by their fingers back in May. Seeing them plant and harvest makes me feel like a good mother, teaching them how to provide for themselves.

The seeds, though, we did not provide for ourselves. When Skywoman buried her beloved daughter in the earth, the plants that are special gifts to the people sprang from her body. Tobacco grew from her head. From her hair, sweetgrass. Her heart gave us the strawberry. From her breasts grew corn, from her belly the squash, and we see in her hands the long-fingered clusters of beans.

How do I show my girls I love them on a morning in June? I pick them wild strawberries. On a February afternoon we build snowmen and then sit by the fire. In March we make maple syrup. We pick violets in May and go swimming in July. On an August night we lay out blankets and watch meteor showers. In November, that great teacher the woodpile comes into our lives. That's just the beginning. How do we show our children our love? Each in our own way by a shower of gifts and a heavy rain of lessons.

Maybe it was the smell of ripe tomatoes, or the oriole singing, or that certain slant of light on a yellow afternoon and the beans hanging thick around me. It just came to me in a wash of happiness that made me laugh out loud, startling the chickadees who were picking at the sunflowers, raining black and white hulls on the ground. I knew it with a certainty as warm and clear as the September sunshine. The land loves us back. She loves us with beans and tomatoes, with roasting ears and blackberries and birdsongs. By a shower of gifts and a heavy rain of lessons. She provides for us and teaches us to provide for ourselves. That's what good mothers do.

I looked around at the garden and could feel her delight in giving us these beautiful raspberries, squash, basil, potatoes, asparagus, lettuce, kale and beets, broccoli, peppers, brussels sprouts, carrots, dill, onions, leeks, spinach. It reminded me of my little girls' answer to "How much do I love you?" "Thiiiiiiiis much," with arms stretched wide, they replied. This is really why I made my daughters learn to garden—so they would always have a mother to love them, long after I am gone.

The epiphany in the beans. I spend a lot of time thinking about our relationships with land, how we are given so much and what we might give back. I try to work through the equations of reciprocity and responsibility, the whys and wherefores of building sustainable relationships with ecosystems. All in my head. But suddenly there was no intellectualizing, no rationalizing, just the pure sensation of baskets full of mother love. The ultimate reciprocity, loving and being loved in return.

Now, the plant scientist who sits at my desk and wears my clothes and sometimes borrows my car—she might cringe to hear me assert that a garden is a way that the land says, "I love you." Isn't it supposed to be just a matter of increasing net primary productivity of the artificially selected domesticated genotypes, manipulating environmental conditions through input of labor and materials to enhance yield? Adaptive cultural behaviors that produce a nutritious diet and increase individual fitness are selected for. What's love got to do with it? If a garden thrives, it loves you? If a garden fails, do you attribute potato blight to a withdrawal of affection? Do unripe peppers signal a rift in the relationship?

I have to explain things to her sometimes. Gardens are simultaneously a material and a spiritual undertaking. That's hard for scientists, so fully brainwashed by Cartesian dualism, to grasp. "Well, how would you know it's love and not just good soil?" she asks. "Where's the evidence? What are the key elements for detecting loving behavior?"

That's easy. No one would doubt that I love my children, and even a quantitative social psychologist would find no fault with my list of loving behaviors:

- nurturing health and well-being
- protection from harm
- encouraging individual growth and development
- desire to be together
- generous sharing of resources
- working together for a common goal
- celebration of shared values
- interdependence
- sacrifice by one for the other
- creation of beauty

If we observed these behaviors between humans, we would say, "She loves that person." You might also observe these actions between a person and a bit of carefully tended ground and say, "She loves that garden." Why then, seeing this list, would you not make the leap to say that the garden loves her back?

The exchange between plants and people has shaped the evolutionary history of both. Farms, orchards, and vineyards are stocked with species we have domesticated. Our appetite for their fruits leads us to till, prune, irrigate, fertilize, and weed on their behalf. Perhaps they have domesticated us. Wild plants have changed to stand in well-behaved rows and wild humans have changed to settle alongside the fields and care for the plants—a kind of mutual taming.

We are linked in a co-evolutionary circle. The sweeter the peach, the more frequently we disperse its seeds, nurture its young, and protect them from harm. Food plants and people act as selective forces on each other's evolution—the thriving of one in the best interest of the other. This, to me, sounds a bit like love.

I sat once in a graduate writing workshop on relationships to the land. The students all demonstrated a deep respect and affection for nature. They said that nature was the place where they experienced the greatest sense of belonging and well-being. They professed without reservation that they loved the earth. And then I asked them, "Do you think that the earth loves you back?" No one was willing to answer that. It was as if I had brought a two-headed porcupine into the classroom. Unexpected. Prickly. They backed slowly away. Here was a room full of writers, passionately wallowing in unrequited love of nature.

So I made it hypothetical and asked, "What do you suppose would happen *if* people believed this crazy notion that the earth loved them back?" The floodgates opened. They all wanted to talk at once. We were suddenly off the deep end, heading for world peace and perfect harmony.

One student summed it up: "You wouldn't harm what gives you love."

Knowing that you love the earth changes you, activates you to defend and protect and celebrate. But when you feel that the earth loves you in return, that feeling transforms the relationship from a one-way street into a sacred bond.

My daughter Linden grows one of my favorite gardens in the world. She brings up all kinds of good things to eat from her thin mountain soil, things I can only dream of, like tomatillos and chile. She makes compost and flowers, but the best part isn't the plants. It's that she phones me to chat while she weeds. We water and weed and harvest, visiting happily as we did when she was a girl despite the three thousand miles between us. Linden is immensely busy, and so I ask her why she gardens, given how much time it takes.

She does it for the food and the satisfaction of hard work yielding something so prolific, she says. And it makes her feel at home in a place, to have her hands in the earth. I ask her, "Do you love your garden?" even though I already know the answer. But then I ask, tentatively, "Do you feel that your garden loves you back?" She's quiet for a minute; she's never glib about such things. "I'm certain of it," she says. "My garden takes care of me like my own mama." I can die happy.

I once knew and loved a man who lived most of his life in the city, but when he was dragged off to the ocean or the woods he seemed to enjoy it well enough—as long as he could find an Internet connection. He had lived in a lot of places, so I asked him where he found his greatest sense of place. He didn't understand the expression. I explained that I wanted to know where he felt most nurtured and supported. What is the place that you understand best? That you know best and knows you in return?

He didn't take long to answer. "My car," he said. "In my car. It provides me with everything I need, in just the way I like it. My favorite music. Seat position fully adjustable. Automatic mirrors. Two cup holders. I'm safe. And it always takes me where I want to go." Years later, he tried to kill himself. In his car.

He never grew a relationship with the land, choosing instead the splendid isolation of technology. He was like one of those little withered seeds you find in the bottom of the seed packet, the one who never touched the earth.

I wonder if much that ails our society stems from the fact that we have allowed ourselves to be cut off from that love of, and from, the land. It is medicine for broken land and empty hearts.

Larkin used to complain mightily about weeding. But now when she comes home, she asks if she can go dig potatoes. I see her on her knees, unearthing red skins and Yukon Golds and singing to herself. Larkin is in graduate school now, studying food systems and working with urban gardeners, growing vegetables for the food pantry on land reclaimed from empty lots. At-risk youth do the planting and hoeing and harvesting. The kids are surprised that the food they harvest is free. They've had to pay for everything they've ever gotten before. They greet fresh carrots, straight from the ground, with suspicion at first, until they eat one. She is passing on the gift, and the transformation is profound.

Of course, much of what fills our mouths is taken forcibly from the earth. That form of taking does no honor to the farmer, to the plants, or to the disappearing soil. It's hard to recognize food that is mummified in plastic, bought and sold, as a gift anymore. Everybody knows you can't buy love.

In a garden, food arises from partnership. If I don't pick rocks and pull weeds, I'm not fulfilling my end of the bargain. I can do these things with my handy opposable thumb and capacity to use tools, to shovel manure. But I can no more create a tomato or embroider a trellis in beans than I can turn lead into gold. That is the plants' responsibility and their gift: animating the inanimate. Now *there* is a gift.

People often ask me what one thing I would recommend to restore relationship between land and people. My answer is almost always, "Plant a garden." It's good for the health of the earth and it's good for the health of people. A garden is a nursery for nurturing connection, the soil for cultivation of practical reverence. And its power goes far beyond the garden gate—once you develop a relationship with a little patch of earth, it becomes a seed itself.

Something essential happens in a vegetable garden. It's a place where if you can't say "I love you" out loud, you can say it in seeds. And the land will reciprocate, in beans.

The Three Sisters

I t should be them who tell this story. Corn leaves rustle with a signature sound, a papery conversation with each other and the breeze. On a hot day in July—when the corn can grow six inches in a single day—there is a squeak of internodes expanding, stretching the stem toward the light. Leaves escape their sheaths with a drawn-out creak and sometimes, when all is still, you can hear the sudden pop of ruptured pith when water-filled cells become too large and turgid for the confines of the stem. These are the sounds of being, but they are not the voice.

The beans must make a caressing sound, a tiny hiss as a soft-haired leader twines around the scabrous stem of corn. Surfaces vibrate delicately against each other, tendrils pulse as they cinch around a stem, something only a nearby flea beetle could hear. But this is not the song of beans.

I've lain among ripening pumpkins and heard creaking as the parasol leaves rock back and forth, tethered by their tendrils, wind lifting their edges and easing them down again. A microphone in the hollow of a swelling pumpkin would reveal the pop of seeds expanding and the rush of water filling succulent orange flesh. These are sounds, but not the story. Plants tell their stories not by what they say, but by what they do.

What if you were a teacher but had no voice to speak your knowledge? What if you had no language at all and yet there was something you needed to say? Wouldn't you dance it? Wouldn't you act it out? Wouldn't your every movement tell the story? In time you would become so eloquent that just to gaze upon you would reveal it all. And so it is with these silent green lives. A sculpture is just a piece of rock with topography hammered out and chiseled in, but that piece of rock can open your heart in a way that makes you different for having seen it. It brings its message without a single word. Not everyone will get it, though; the language of stone is difficult. Rock mumbles. But plants speak in a tongue that every breathing thing can understand. Plants teach in a universal language: food.

Years ago, Awiakta, a Cherokee writer, pressed a small packet into my hand. It was a corn leaf, dry and folded into a pouch, tied with a bit of string. She smiled and warned, "Don't open 'til spring." In May I untie the packet and there is the gift: three seeds. One is a golden triangle, a kernel of corn with a broadly dimpled top that narrows to a hard white tip. The glossy bean is speckled brown, curved and sleek, its inner belly marked with a white eye—the hilum. It slides like a polished stone between my thumb and forefinger, but this is no stone. And there is a pumpkin seed like an oval china dish, its edge crimped shut like a piecrust bulging with filling. I hold in my hand the genius of Indigenous agriculture, the Three Sisters. Together these plants—corn, beans, and squash—feed the people, feed the land, and feed our imaginations, telling us how we might live.

For millennia, from Mexico to Montana, women have mounded up the earth and laid these three seeds in the ground, all in the same square foot of soil. When the colonists on the Massachusetts shore first saw Indigenous gardens, they inferred that the savages did not know how to farm. To their minds, a garden meant straight rows of single species, not a three-dimensional sprawl of abundance. And yet they ate their fill and asked for more, and more again.

Once planted in the May-moist earth, the corn seed takes on water quickly, its seed coat thin and its starchy contents, the endosperm, drawing water to it. The moisture triggers enzymes under the skin that cleave the starch into sugars, fueling the growth of the corn embryo that is nestled in the point of the seed. Thus corn is the first to emerge from the ground, a slender white spike that greens within hours of finding the light. A single leaf unfurls, and then another. Corn is all alone at first, while the others are getting ready.

Drinking in soil water, the bean seed swells and bursts its speckled coat and sends a rootling down deep in the ground. Only after the root is secure does the stem bend to the shape of a hook and elbow its way above ground. Beans can take their time in finding the light because they are well provisioned: their first leaves were already packaged in the two halves of the bean seed. This pair of fleshy leaves now breaks the soil surface to join the corn, which is already six inches tall.

Pumpkins and squash take their time—they are the slow sister. It may be weeks before the first stems poke up, still caught in their seed coat until the leaves split its seams and break free. I'm told that our ancestors would put the squash seeds in a deerskin bag with a little water or urine a week before planting to try to hurry them along. But each plant has its own pace and the sequence of their germination, their birth order, is important to their relationship and to the success of the crop.

The corn is the firstborn and grows straight and stiff; it is a stem with a lofty goal. Laddering upward, leaf by long-ribbed leaf, it must grow tall quickly. Making a strong stem is its highest priority at first. It needs to be there for its younger sister, the bean. Beans put out a pair of heart-shaped leaves on just a stub of a stem, then another pair, and another, all low to the ground. The bean focuses on leaf growth while the corn concentrates on height. Just about the time that the corn is knee high, the bean shoot changes its mind, as middle children are wont to do. Instead of making leaves, it extends itself into a long vine, a slender green string with a mission. In this teenage phase, hormones set the shoot tip to wandering, inscribing a circle in the air, a process known as circumnutation. The tip can travel a meter in a day, pirouetting in a loopy circle dance until it finds what it's looking for—a corn stem or some other vertical support. Touch receptors along the vine guide it to wrap itself around the corn in a graceful upward spiral. For now, it holds back on making leaves, giving itself over to embracing the corn, keeping pace with its height growth. Had the corn not started early, the bean vine would strangle it, but if the timing is right, the corn can easily carry the bean.

Meanwhile, the squash, the late bloomer of the family, is steadily extending herself over the ground, moving away from the corn and beans, setting up broad lobed leaves like a stand of umbrellas waving at the ends of hollow petioles. The leaves and vines are distinctly bristly, giving second thoughts to nibbling caterpillars. As the leaves grow wider, they shelter the soil at the base of the corn and beans, keeping moisture in, and other plants out.

Native people speak of this gardening style as the Three Sisters. There are many stories of how they came to be, but they all share the understanding of these plants as women, sisters. Some stories tell of a long winter when the people were dropping from hunger. Three beautiful women came to their dwellings on a snowy night. One was a tall woman dressed all in yellow, with long flowing hair. The second wore green, and the third was robed in orange. The three came inside to shelter by the fire. Food was scarce but the visiting strangers were fed generously, sharing in the little that the people had left. In gratitude for their generosity, the three sisters revealed their true identities—corn, beans, and squash— and gave themselves to the people in a bundle of seeds so that they might never go hungry again.

At the height of the summer, when the days are long and bright, and the thunderers come to soak the ground, the lessons of reciprocity are written clearly in a Three Sisters garden. Together their stems inscribe what looks to me like a blueprint for the world, a map of balance and harmony. The corn stands eight feet tall; rippling green ribbons of leaf curl away from the stem in every direction to catch the sun. No leaf sits directly over the next, so that each can gather light without shading the others. The bean twines around the corn stalk, weaving itself between the leaves of corn, never interfering with their work. In the spaces where corn leaves are not, buds appear on the vining bean and expand into outstretched leaves and clusters of fragrant flowers. The bean leaves droop and are held close to the stem of the corn. Spread around the feet of the corn and beans is a carpet of big broad squash leaves that intercept the light that falls among the pillars of corn. Their layered spacing uses the light, a gift from the sun, efficiently, with no waste. The organic symmetry of forms belongs together; the placement of every leaf, the harmony of shapes speak their message. Respect one another, support one another, bring your gift to the world and receive the gifts of others, and there will be enough for all.

By late summer, the beans hang in heavy clusters of smooth green pods, ears of corn angle out from the stalk, fattening in the sunshine, and pumpkins swell at your feet. Acre for acre, a Three Sisters garden yields more food than if you grew each of the sisters alone.

You can tell they are sisters: one twines easily around the other in relaxed embrace while the sweet baby sister lolls at their feet, close, but not too close—cooperating, not competing. Seems to me I've seen this before in human families, in the interplay of sisters. After all, there are three girls in my family. The firstborn girl knows that she is clearly in charge; tall and direct, upright and efficient, she creates the template for everyone else to follow. That's the corn sister. There's not room for more than one corn woman in the same house, so the middle sister is likely to adapt in different ways. This bean girl learns to be flexible, adaptable, to find a way around the dominant structure to get the light that she needs. The sweet baby sister is free to choose a different path, as expectations have already been fulfilled. Well grounded, she has nothing to prove and finds her own way, a way that contributes to the good of the whole.

Without the corn's support, the beans would be an unruly tangle on the ground, vulnerable to bean-hungry predators. It might seem as if she is taking a free ride in this garden, benefiting from the corn's height and the squash's shade, but by the rules of reciprocity none can take more than she gives. The corn takes care of making light available; the squash reduces weeds. What about the beans? To see her gift you have to look underground.

The sisters cooperate above ground with the placement of their leaves, carefully avoiding one another's space. The same is true below ground. Corn is classified as a monocot, basically an overgrown grass, so its roots are fine and fibrous. With the soil shaken off, they look like a stringy mop head at the end of a cornstalk handle. They don't go very deep at all; instead they make a shallow network, calling first dibs on incoming rain. After they've had their drink, the water descends out of reach of the corn roots. As the water goes deeper, the deep taproots of the bean are poised there to absorb it. The squash finds its share by moving away from the others. Wherever a squash stem touches soil, it can put out a tuft of adventitious roots, collecting water far from the corn and bean roots. They share the soil by the same techniques that they share the light, leaving enough for everyone.

But there is one thing they all need that is always in short supply: nitrogen. That nitrogen should be the factor that limits growth is an ecological paradox: fully 78 percent of the atmosphere is nitrogen gas. The problem is that most plants simply can't use atmospheric nitrogen. They need mineral nitrogen, nitrate or ammonium. The nitrogen in the atmosphere might as well be food locked away in full sight of a starving person. But there are ways to transform that nitrogen, and one of the best ways is named "beans."

Beans are members of the legume family, which has the remarkable ability to take nitrogen from the atmosphere and turn it into usable nutrients. But they don't do it alone. My students often run to me with a handful of roots from a bean they've unearthed, with little white balls clinging to strands of root. "Is this a disease?" they ask. "Is something wrong with these roots?" In fact, I reply, there's something very right.

These glistening nodules house the *Rhizobium* bacteria, the nitrogen fixers. *Rhizobium* can only convert nitrogen under a special set of circumstances. Its catalytic enzymes will not work in the presence of oxygen. Since an average handful of soil is more than 50 percent air space, the *Rhizobium* needs a refuge in order to do its work. Happily, the bean obliges. When a bean root meets a microscopic rod of *Rhizobium* underground, chemical communications are exchanged and a deal is negotiated. The bean will grow an oxygen-free nodule to house the bacterium and, in return, the bacterium shares its nitrogen with the plant. Together, they create nitrogen fertilizer that enters the soil and fuels the growth of the corn and the squash, too. There are layers upon layers of reciprocity in this garden: between the bean and the bacterium, the bean and the corn, the corn and the squash, and, ultimately, with the people.

It's tempting to imagine that these three are deliberate in working together, and perhaps they are. But the beauty of the partnership is that each plant does what it does in order to increase its own growth. But as it happens, when the individuals flourish, so does the whole.

The way of the Three Sisters reminds me of one of the basic teachings of our people. The most important thing each of us can know is our unique gift and how to use it in the world. Individuality is cherished and nurtured, because, in order for the whole to flourish, each of us has to be strong in who we are and carry our gifts with conviction, so they can be shared with others. Being among the sisters provides a visible manifestation of what a community can become when its members understand and share their gifts. In reciprocity, we fill our spirits as well as our bellies.

For years, I taught General Botany in a lecture hall with slides and diagrams and stories of plants that could not fail to inflame the enthusiasm of eighteen-year-olds for the marvels of photosynthesis. How could they be anything but elated to learn how roots find their way through the soil, sitting on the edge of their seats waiting to hear more about pollen? The sea of blank looks suggested that most of them found this as interesting as, literally, watching grass grow. When I would wax eloquent about the grace with which a bean seedling pushes its way up in the spring, the first row would eagerly nod their heads and raise their hands while the rest of the class slept.

In a fit of frustration, I asked for a show of hands: "How many of you have ever grown anything?" Every hand in the front row went up, and there were a few halfhearted waves from the back from someone whose mother had an African violet that had died a withering death. Suddenly I understood their boredom. I was teaching from memory, drawing on images of plant lives that I had witnessed over the years. The green images I thought we shared as human beings were not theirs, thanks to the supplanting of gardens by supermarkets. The front-row students had seen these things as well and wanted to know how such everyday miracles were possible. But most of the class had no experience of seeds and soil, had never watched a flower transform itself into an apple. They needed a new teacher.

And so now each fall I begin my class in a garden, where they have the best teachers I know, three beautiful sisters. For a whole September afternoon they sit with the Three Sisters. They measure yield and growth and get to know the anatomy of the plants who feed them. I ask them first to just look. They observe and draw the way the three live in relationship. One of my students is an artist, and the more she looks the more excited she becomes. "Look at the composition," she says. "It's just like our art teacher described the elements of design in studio today. There is unity, balance, color. It's perfect." I look at the sketch in her notebook, and she's seeing it like a painting. Long leaves, round leaves, lobed and smooth, yellow, orange, tan on a matrix of green. "See the way it works? Corn is the vertical element, squash horizontal, and it's all tied together with these curvilinear vines, the beans. Ravishing," she claims with a flourish.

One of the girls is dressed for allure that might work in a dance club, but not on a botany field trip. She has avoided any contact with the dirt so far. To ease her into the work, I suggest that she take the relatively clean task of simply following a squash vine from one end to another and diagramming the flowers. Way out at the young tip of the vine are orange squash blossoms as ruffled and splashy as her skirt. I point out the swollen ovary of the flower after it has been pollinated. Such is the outcome of successful seduction. Mincing carefully in her heels, she follows the vine back toward its source; the older flowers have wilted and a tiny little squash has appeared where the flower's pistil had been. Closer and closer to the plant, the squashes become larger, from a penny-size nub with flower still attached, to the full ripeness of a ten-inch squash. It's like watching a pregnancy unfold. Together we pick a ripe butternut squash and slice it open so she can see the seeds in the cavity within.

"You mean a squash comes from a flower?" she says incredulously, seeing the progression along the vine. "I love this kind of squash at Thanksgiving."

"Yes," I tell her, "this is the ripened ovary of that first flower."

Her eyes widen in shock. "You mean all these years I've been eating ovaries? Blech—I'll never eat a squash again."

There is an earthy sexuality to a garden, and most of the students get drawn in to the revelation of fruit. I have them carefully open an ear of corn without disturbing the corn silk that plumes from the end. First the coarse outer husks are pulled away, then layer after layer of inner leaves, each thinner than the next until the last layer is exposed, so thin and tightly pressed to the corn that the shape of the kernels show through it. As we draw aside the last layer, the sweet milky scent of corn rises from the exposed ear, rows upon rows of round yellow kernels. We look closely and follow an individual strand of corn silk. Outside the husk it is brown and curly, but inside it is colorless and crisply succulent, as if filled with water. Each little strand of silk connects a different kernel inside the husk to the world outside.

A corncob is an ingenious sort of flower in which the silk is a greatly elongated flower pistil. One end of the silk waves in the breeze to collect pollen, while the other end attaches to the ovary. The silk is the water-filled conduit for sperm released from the pollen grains caught there. The corn sperm swim down the silken tube to the milky-white kernel—the ovary. Only when the corn kernels are so fertilized will they grow plump and yellow. A corncob is the mother of hundreds, as many children as there are kernels, each with potentially a different father. Is it any wonder she is called the Corn Mother?

Beans too grow like babies in the womb. The students are contentedly munching fresh pole beans. I ask them to first open a slender pod, to see what they're eating. Jed slits a pod with his thumbnail and opens it. There they are, bean babies, ten in a row. Each little beanlet is attached to the pod by a fragile green cord, the funiculus. Just a few millimeters long, it is the analog to the human umbilical cord. Through this cord, the mother plant nourishes her growing offspring. The students crowd around to look. Jed asks, "Does that mean a bean has a belly button?" Everybody laughs, but the answer is right there. Every bean has a little scar from the funiculus, a colored spot on its seed coat, the hilum. Every bean does have a belly button. These plant mothers feed us and leave their children behind as seeds, to feed us again and again.

In August, I like to have a Three Sisters potluck. I spread tablecloths on the tables beneath the maples and stuff bouquets of wildflowers in canning jars on every table. Then my friends start to arrive, each with a dish or a basket. The tables fill up with trays of golden cornbread, three-bean salad, round brown bean cakes, black bean chili, and summer squash casserole. My friend Lee brings a platter of small pumpkins stuffed with cheesy polenta. There's a steaming pot of Three Sisters soup, all green and yellow, with slices of summer squash floating in the broth.

As if there wasn't enough to eat already, our ritual is to go to the garden together, once everyone arrives, and pick some more. The corn ears fill a bushel basket. The kids are delegated to shuck the corn while parents fill a bowl with new green beans and the littlest kids peek under prickly leaves looking for squash blossoms. We carefully spoon a batter of cheese and cornmeal into the orange throat of each flower, close it up, and fry it until it's crisp. They disappear from the plate as fast as we can make them.

The genius of the Three Sisters lies not only in the process by which they grow, but also in the complementarity of the three species on the kitchen table. They taste good together, and the Three Sisters also form a nutritional triad that can sustain a people. Corn, in all its guises, is a superb form of starch. All summer, the corn turns sunshine into carbohydrate, so that all winter, people can have food energy. But a human cannot subsist on corn alone; it is not nutritionally complete. Just as the bean complements the corn in the garden, it collaborates in the diet as well. By virtue of their nitrogen-fixing capacity, beans are high in protein and fill in the nutritional gaps left by corn. A person can live well on a diet of beans and corn; neither alone would suffice. But neither beans nor corn have the vitamins that squash provide in their carotene-rich flesh. Together, they are once again greater than alone.

After dinner we are too full for dessert. There is a dish of Indian pudding and maple corncakes waiting for us, but we just sit and look out over the valley while the kids run around. The land below us is mostly planted to corn, the long rectangular fields butting right up against the woodlots. In the afternoon light, the rows of corn throw shadows on one another, outlining the contours of the hill. From a distance they look like lines of text on a page, long lines of green writing across the hillside. The truth of our relationship with the soil is written more clearly on the land than in any book. I read across that hill a story about people who value uniformity and the efficiency it yields, a story in which the land is shaped for the convenience of machines and the demands of a market.

In Indigenous agriculture, the practice is to modify the plants to fit the land. As a result, there are many varieties of corn domesticated by our ancestors, all adapted to grow in many different places. Modern agriculture, with its big engines and fossil fuels, took the opposite approach: modify the land to fit the plants, which are frighteningly similar clones.

Once you know corn as a sister, it's hard to unknow it. But the long ranks of corn in the conventional fields seem like a different being altogether. The relationships disappear and individuals are lost in anonymity. You can hardly recognize a beloved face lost in a uniformed crowd. These acres are beautiful in their own way, but after the companionship of a Three Sisters garden, I wonder if they're lonely.

There must be millions of corn plants out there, standing shoulder to shoulder, with no beans, no squash, and scarcely a weed in sight. These are my neighbor's fields, and I've seen the many passes with the tractor that produce such a "clean" field. Tank sprayers on the tractor have delivered applications of fertilizer; you can smell it in the spring as it drifts off the fields. A dose of ammonium nitrate substitutes for the partnership of a bean. And the tractors return with herbicides to suppress weeds in lieu of squash leaves.

There were certainly bugs and weeds back when these valleys were Three Sisters gardens, and yet they flourished without insecticides. Polycultures—fields with many species of plants—are less susceptible to pest outbreaks than monocultures. The diversity of plant forms provides habitats for a wide array of insects. Some, like corn worms and bean beetles and squash borers, are there with the intent of feeding on the crop. But the diversity of plants also creates habitat for insects who eat the crop eaters. Predatory beetles and parasitic wasps coexist with the garden and keep the crop eaters under control. More than people are fed by this garden, but there is enough to go around.

The Three Sisters offer us a new metaphor for an emerging relationship between Indigenous knowledge and Western science, both of which are rooted in the earth. I think of the corn as traditional ecological knowledge, the physical and spiritual framework that can guide the curious bean of science, which twines like a double helix. The squash creates the ethical habitat for coexistence and mutual flourishing. I envision a time when the intellectual monoculture of science will be replaced with a polyculture of complementary knowledges. And so all may be fed.

Fran brings out a bowl of whipped cream for the Indian pudding. We spoon up the soft custard, rich with molasses and cornmeal, and watch the light fade on the fields. There's a squash pie, too. By this feast, I want the Three Sisters to know that we've heard their story. Use your gift to take care of each other, work together, and all will be fed, they say.

They've all brought their gifts to this table, but they've not done it alone. They remind us that there is another partner in the symbiosis. She is sitting here at the table and across the valley in the farmhouse, too. She's the one who noticed the ways of each species and imagined how they might live together. Perhaps we should consider this a Four Sisters garden, for the planter is also an essential partner. It is she who turns up the soil, she who scares away the crows, and she who pushes seeds into the soil. We are the planters, the ones who clear the land, pull the weeds, and pick the bugs; we save the seeds over winter and plant them again next spring. We are midwives to their gifts. We cannot live without them, but it's also true that they cannot live without us. Corn, beans, and squash are fully domesticated; they rely on us to create the conditions under which they can grow. We too are part of the reciprocity. They can't meet their responsibilities unless we meet ours.

Of all the wise teachers who have come into my life, none are more eloquent than these, who wordlessly in leaf and vine embody the knowledge of relationship. Alone, a bean is just a vine, squash an oversize leaf.

Only when standing together with corn does a whole emerge which transcends the individual. The gifts of each are more fully expressed when they are nurtured together than alone. In ripe ears and swelling fruit, they counsel us that all gifts are multiplied in relationship. This is how the world keeps going.

Wisgaak Gokpenagen:
A Black Ash Basket

Doonk, *doonk, doonk.* Silence. *Doonk, doonk, doonk.*

The back of the ax meets the log to make a hollow music. It drops three times on one spot and then John's eyes shift a fraction down the log, where he strikes again. *Doonk, doonk, doonk.* As he raises the ax above his head, his hands slide apart on the upstroke, then together on the down, shoulders pulling tight under his chambray shirt, his thin braid jumping with every impact. All the way down the log he pounds triplets of crushing blows.

Straddling the end of the log, he works his fingers under a split in the cut end and gives it a tug. Slow and steady, he peels off a strip of wood the width of the ax head in a thick ribbon. He takes up the ax and pounds another few feet. *Doonk, doonk, doonk.* Again he grasps the base of the strip and peels it back along the pounded line, taking the log apart strip by strip. By the time he pounds the last few feet, he has worked off an eight-foot splint of gleaming white wood. He holds it to his nose to breathe in the goodness of new wood and passes it around for us all to see. John coils it into a neat hoop, ties it fast, and hangs it on a nearby tree branch. "Your turn," he says and hands off the ax.

My teacher this warm summer day is John Pigeon, a member of the large, renowned Pigeon family of Potawatomi basket makers. Since that first initiation to pounding a log, I'm grateful to have sat in on black ash basket classes with several generations of the extended family of

Pigeons—Steve, Kitt, Ed, Stephanie, Pearl, Angie, and more, children and grandchildren—with splints in their hands. All gifted basket makers, carriers of culture, and generous teachers. The log is a good teacher, too.

It's harder than it looks, making the ax repeat its pattern evenly down the log. Too much impact in one spot will break the fibers; too little and the strip won't fully break free, leaving a thin spot. Each of us beginners works differently, some with sharp strokes from overhead, some with dull thudding as if we were hammering nails. The sound changes with the pounder: a high ringing note like the call of wild geese, a bark like a startled coyote's, the muffled thumping of a drumming grouse.

When John was a kid the sound of log pounding was heard all through the community. Walking home from school, he could tell who was out working by the sound of their swing. Uncle Chester was a hard, fast *crack, crack, crack*. From across the hedgerow he could hear Grandma Bell's slow *thuds* separated by long pauses while she caught her breath. But now the village grows quieter and quieter as elders walk on and kids seem more interested in video games than in tromping through the swamp. So John Pigeon teaches any who will come, to pass on what he's learned from his elders and the trees.

John is both a master basket maker and a carrier of tradition. Pigeon family baskets can be found in the Smithsonian and other museums and galleries around the world. But they are also available here, at the family's booth at the annual Potawatomi Gathering of Nations. Their table is loaded with colorful baskets, no two alike. There are fancy baskets the size of a bird's nest, gathering baskets, potato baskets, corn-washing baskets. His whole family weaves, and no one at the Gathering wants to go home without a Pigeon basket. I save up each year for one.

Like the rest of the family, John is also a master teacher, committed to sharing what has been passed on by generations who came before. What was given to him, he now gives back to the people. Some basket classes I've taken start with a neat pile of materials, all assembled on a clean table. But John doesn't hold with teaching basket weaving where the splints come ready made—he teaches basket *making*, beginning with a living tree.

Black Ash *(Fraxinus nigra)* likes to have its feet wet. In floodplain forests and edges of swamps, black ash mingles with red maples, elms, and willows. It is never the most common tree—you only find it in scattered patches—so it can take a long day of tromping over boot-sucking ground to find the right tree. Scanning a wet forest, you can pick out the black ash by its bark. You pass by maples with bark of rigid gray plates, the braided corky ridges of elm, the deeply furrowed willows, and instead seek out the fine pattern of interlocked ridges and warty knobs of black ash. The knobs feel spongy under your fingertips when you give them a squeeze. There are other species of ash growing in the swamp, so it's good to check the leaves overhead as well. All ashes—green, white, blue, pumpkin, and black—have compound leaves borne opposite one another on stout, corky twigs.

And yet it's not enough to simply find black ash; it has to be the right one—a tree ready to be a basket. An ideal basket ash has a straight, clear bole with no branches in the lower trunk. Branches make knots that interrupt the straight grain of the splint. A good tree is about a handbreadth across, the crown full and vigorous, a healthy tree. A tree that has grown directly up toward the sun will be straight and fine grained, while those that have wandered a bit to find the light show twists and turns in the grain. Some basket makers will choose only trees perched on a hummock in the swamp, while others will avoid a black ash growing next to a cedar.

Trees are affected by their sapling days as much as people are by their childhoods. The history of a tree appears in its growth rings, of course. Good years yield a wide ring, poor years a thin one, and the pattern of rings is critical to the process of basket making.

Growth rings are formed by the cycle of the seasons, by the waking and resting of the fragile layer of cells that lies between the bark and the newest wood, the cambium. Peel away the bark and you feel the cambium's slippery wetness. The cells of the cambium are perpetually embryonic, always dividing to add to the girth of the tree. In the spring, when the buds detect the lengthening of the days and the sap starts to rise, the cambium grows cells made for feast days, big, wide-mouthed tubes to carry the abundant water leafward. These lines of large vessels are what you count to determine a tree's age. They grow quickly and so their walls tend to be thin. Wood scientists call this part of the annual ring springwood or early wood. When spring turns to summer, nutrients and water become scarce and the cambium produces smaller, thicker cells for leaner times. These densely packed cells are called late wood or summerwood. When the days shorten and leaves fall, the cambium settles in for a winter's rest and stops dividing altogether. But as soon as spring is imminent, the cambium once again bursts into action, making large springwood cells. The abrupt transition between the last year's small-celled late wood and the early wood of spring creates the appearance of a line, a growth ring.

John has developed a practiced eye for these things. But sometimes, just to be sure, he'll unsheathe his knife and cut out a wedge for a look at the rings. John prefers a tree in the range of thirty to forty growth rings, each ring as wide as a nickel. When he's found the right one, the harvest begins. Not with a saw, though, but rather with a conversation.

Traditional harvesters recognize the individuality of each tree as a person, a nonhuman forest person. Trees are not taken, but requested. Respectfully, the cutter explains his purpose and the tree is asked permission for harvest. Sometimes the answer is no. It might be a cue in the surroundings—a vireo nest in the branches, or the bark's adamant resistance to the questioning knife—that suggests a tree is not willing, or it might be the ineffable knowing that turns him away. If consent is granted, a prayer is made and tobacco is left as a reciprocating gift. The tree is felled with great care so as not to damage it or others in the fall. Sometimes a cutter will make a bed of spruce boughs to cushion the landing of the tree. When they finish, John and his son hoist the log to their shoulders and begin the long walk home.

John and his extended family make a lot of baskets. His mother prefers to pound her own log, although he and the boys will often do it when her arthritis is bothering her. They'll weave all year round, but there are certain seasons for the best harvest. It's a good idea to pound a log soon after harvest, while it is still moist, although John says you can bury a log in a trench covered with damp earth to keep it fresh. His favorite times are spring—when "the sap is rising and the energy of the earth is flowing into the tree"—and fall, "when the energy is flowing back to the ground."

Today, John scales away the spongy bark, which would deflect the power of the ax, and gets to work. When he pulls the edge of the first strip, you can see what's happening: Beating the log crushes the thin-walled cells of the early wood, breaking them down and separating them from the late wood. The log fractures at the dividing line between springwood and summer, so the strip that peels off is the wood between annual rings.

Depending on the individual history of the tree and its pattern of rings, a strip might come off carrying the wood of five years or sometimes just one. Every tree is different, but as the basket makers pound and peel, he is always moving back through time. The tree's life is coming off in his hands, layer by layer. As the hoops of splint grow more numerous, the log itself grows smaller and within hours is a skinny pole. "See," John shows us, "we've stripped all the way back to the time it was a sapling." He gestures to the big pile of splint we've accumulated. "Don't ever forget that. It's the whole life of that tree you've got piled up there."

The long strips of wood vary in thickness, so the next step is splitting the strip into its component layers, further separating the annual rings. Thick splints are needed for a big laundry hamper or a trapper's pack basket. The finest fancy baskets use only a ribbon of less than one year's wood. From the back of his new white pickup, John pulls out his splitters: two pieces of wood joined with a clamp to make what looks like a giant clothespin. He sits on the edge of his chair and holds the splitter between his knees so its open legs are on the ground and the peaked end rises from his lap. He threads a full eight-foot length of splint up through the clamp and fastens it there with an inch or so protruding. He flicks open his knife and wedges the blade into the cut end of the strip, wiggling it along the growth ring to open a cut. His brown hands grasp either side of the cut and he pulls them apart in a smooth motion, yielding strips as smooth and even as two long blades of grass.

"That's all there is to it," he says, but there's laughter in his eyes as they meet mine. I thread the splint, try to balance the splitter steady between my thighs, and then make the cut that will start the split. I discover quickly that you need to grip the splitter hard between your legs—something I can barely manage. "Yup," John laughs, "this is an old Indian invention—the thigh master!" By the time I'm through, my splint looks like a chipmunk has been gnawing on the end. John is a patient teacher, but he won't do it for me. He just smiles, smartly severs my frayed end, and says, "Try it again." Eventually I get two sides that I can pull, but they're uneven and my pulling yields only a twelve-inch splinter, thin on one side, thick on the other. John circles among us, offering encouragement. He has learned everyone's name and picked up something of what each one of us needs. Some he joshes about their weak biceps, others he pats warmly on the shoulder. With the frustrated he sits gently alongside and says, "Don't try so hard. Be easier on yourself." For others, he just pulls the strip and gives it to them. He's as good a judge of people as he is of trees.

"This tree's a good teacher," he says. "That's what we've always been taught. The work of being a human is finding balance, and making splints will not let you forget it."

When you get the hang of it, the splint pulls apart evenly, the inner faces of the splint unexpectedly beautiful: glossy and warm, they catch the light like a ribbon of cream satin. The outer surface is uneven and roughened with splintered ends that leave long "hairs."

"You need a very sharp knife now," he says. "I have to use the whetstone every day. And it's awfully easy to cut yourself." John hands each of us a "leg," cut from worn blue jeans, and shows us how to lay the double thickness of denim over our left thighs. "Deerskin is really the best thing to use," he says, "if you've got some lying around. But blue jeans work fine. Just be careful." He sits with us individually to demonstrate, for the difference between success and bloodshed is a small degree in the angle of the knife and the pressure of the hand. He lays the strip across his thigh, rough side up, and sets the knife edge against it. With his other hand, he draws the strip out from beneath the knife in a continuous motion like a skate blade skimming over ice. The shavings gather on the knife as the strip pulls by. The result is a polished surface. This too he makes look easy. I've seen Kitt Pigeon pull satiny strips as if she were pulling ribbon from a spool, but my knife snags and I end up cutting gouges instead of planing it smooth. The angle of my knife is too sharp and I cut right through, rendering a long pretty strip into a scrap.

"You're about up to a loaf of bread," John says, shaking his head when I ruin yet another piece. "That's what my mother would say when we spoiled splints." Basket making was and is the livelihood of the Pigeon family. In their grandfather's time the lake, woods, and gardens gave them most of their food and other provisions, but at times they also needed store goods, and baskets were the cash crop that bought bread, canned peaches, and school shoes. Spoiled splints were like food thrown away. Depending on the size and design, a black ash basket can sell for good money. "People get a little mad when they see the prices," John says. "People think it's 'just' basket weaving, but 80 percent of the work comes long before you weave. With finding the tree, pounding and pulling, and all, you barely make minimum wage."

With splints finally prepared, we're poised for weaving—what we had mistakenly thought was the real work of a basket. But John stops the class, his gentle voice gaining a hard edge. "You've missed the most important thing," he says. "Look around you." We look—at the forest, at the camp, at each other. "At the *ground!*" he says. In a circle around each novice is a litter of scraps. "Stop and think what you're holding. That ash tree was growing out there in that swamp for thirty years, putting out leaves, dropping them, putting out more. It got eaten by deer, hit by a freeze, but it kept working year in and year out, laying down those rings of wood. A splint fallen on the ground is a whole year of that tree's life and you're about to step on it, bend it, grind it into the dirt? That tree honored you with its life. There's no shame in messing up a splint; you're just learning. But whatever you do, you owe that tree respect and should never waste it." And so he guides us as we sort through the debris we've made. Short strips go into a pile for small baskets and decoration. The miscellaneous bits and shavings get tossed into a box to be dried and used for tinder. John keeps to the tradition of the Honorable Harvest: take only what you need and use everything you take.

His words echo what I've often heard from my folks. They grew up during the Depression, with the imperative not to waste, and there were certainly no scraps on the floor then. But "use it up, wear it out, make it do, or do without" is an ethic both economical and ecological. The waste of splints both dishonors the tree and diminishes the household budget.

Just about everything we use is the result of another's life, but that simple reality is rarely acknowledged in our society. The ash curls we make are almost paper thin. They say that the "waste stream" in this country is dominated by paper. Just as much as an ash splint, a sheet of paper is a tree's life, along with the water and energy and toxic by-products that went into making it. And yet we use it as if it were nothing. The short path from mailbox to waste bin tells the story. But what would happen, I wonder, to the mountain of junk mail if we could see in it the trees it once had been? If John was there to remind us of the worthiness of their lives?

In some parts of the range, basket makers began to observe a decline in the numbers of black ash. They worried that overharvesting might be to blame, a decline caused by too much attention for the baskets in the marketplace and too little for their sources in the woods. My graduate student Tom Touchet and I decided to investigate. We began by ana-lyzing the population structure of black ashes around us in New York State, to understand where in the trees' life cycle the difficulty might lie. In every swamp we visited, we counted all the black ash we could find and wrapped a tape around them to get their size. Tom cored a few in every site to check their ages. In stand after stand, Tom found that there were old trees and seedlings, but hardly any trees in between. There was a big hole in the demographic census. He found plenty of seeds, plenty of young seedlings, but most of the next age class—the saplings, the future of the forest—were dead or missing.

There were only two places where he found an abundance of adoles-cent trees. One was in gaps in the forest canopy, where disease or a wind-storm had brought down a few old trees, letting light through. Curiously enough, he found that where Dutch elm disease had killed off elms, black ash was replacing them in a balance between loss of one species and gain of another. To make the transition from seedling to tree, the young black ash needed an opening. If they remained in full shade they would die.

The other place where saplings were thriving was near communities of basket makers. Where the tradition of black ash basketry was alive and well, so were the trees. We hypothesized that the apparent decline in ash trees might be due not to overharvesting but to *under*harvesting. When communities echoed with *Doonk, doonk, doonk,* there were plenty of basket makers in the woods, creating gaps where the light would reach the seedlings and the young trees could shoot to the canopy and become adults. In places where the basket makers disappeared, or were few, the forest didn't get opened up enough for black ash to flourish.

Black ash and basket makers are partners in a symbiosis between harvesters and harvested: ash relies on people as the people rely on ash. Their fates are linked.

The Pigeons' teaching of this linkage is part of a growing movement to revive traditional basketry, tied to the revitalization of Indigenous lands, language, culture, and philosophies. All over Turtle Island, Native peoples are leading a resurgence in traditional knowledge and lifeways that nearly disappeared under the pressures of newcomers. But just as the revival of ash basketry is gaining strength, it is being threatened by yet another invading species.

John sends us off for a break, a cool drink, and a stretch for tired fingers. "You need a clear mind for the next part," he says. As we mill about, shaking out the cramps in our necks and hands, John gives us each a U.S. Department of Agriculture pamphlet with a photo of a shiny green beetle on the cover. "If you care about ash trees," he says, "you'd better pay attention. They're under attack."

The emerald ash borer, introduced from China, lays its eggs in tree trunks. After the larvae hatch, they chew up the cambium until they pupate, when the beetle bores its way out of the tree and flies off to find a new nursery. But wherever it lands, it is inevitably fatal for the infested trees. Unfortunately for the people of the Great Lakes region and New

England, the beetle's favorite host is ash. Today there is a quarantine on moving logs and firewood in an effort to contain their spread, but the insect is moving faster than scientists predicted.

"So, be on the lookout," John says. "We have to protect our trees, that's our job." When he and his family are harvesting logs in the fall, they take special care to gather up fallen seeds and spread them around as they move through the wetlands. "It's like anything else," he reminds us. "You can't take something without giving back. This tree takes care of us, so we have to take care of it."

Already, vast areas of ash in Michigan have died; beloved basket grounds are now boneyards of barkless trees. There is a rupture in the chain of relationship that stretches back through time immemorial. The swamp where the Pigeons have gathered and cared for black ash for generations is now infested. Angie Pigeon writes, "Our trees are all gone. I don't know if there will be any more baskets." To most people, an invasive species represents losses in a landscape, the empty spaces to be filled by something else. To those who carry the responsibility of an ancient relationship, the empty niche means empty hands and a hole in the collective heart.

Now, when so many trees have fallen and the tradition passed on by generations is at risk, the Pigeons work to protect both trees and the tradition. They are partnering with forest scientists to resist the insect and to adapt to its aftermath. There are reweavers among us.

John and his family are not alone in their efforts to protect the black ash. At Akwesasne, a Mohawk reserve that straddles the border between New York State and Canada, black ash has yet more guardians. Over the past three decades, Les Benedict, Richard David, and Mike Bridgen have led an effort to bring traditional ecological knowledge as well as scientific tools to bear in the protection of black ash. They have grown thousands of black ash seedlings to give away to Indigenous communities throughout the region. Les even convinced the New York State Tree Nursery to grow them for planting in places ranging from school yards to Superfund sites. Thousands had already been planted in resurgent forests, in resurgent communities, just as the ash borer appeared on our shores.

As the threat wings its way closer to their homelands every fall, Les and his colleagues gather the willing to collect the best seeds they can find, storing seed to keep faith with the future, to replant the forest after the wave of invasion has passed. Every species needs its Les Benedict, its Pigeon family, its allies and protectors. Many of our traditional teachings recognize that certain species are our helpers and guides. The Original Instructions remind us that we must return the favor. It is an honor to be the guardian of another species—an honor within each person's reach that we too often forget. A Black Ash basket is a gift that reminds us of the gifts of other beings, gifts we can gratefully return through advocacy and care. ·

John calls us back to the circle for the next step: assembling the bottom of the basket. We're doing a traditional round bottom, so the first two strips are laid out at right angles in a symmetrical cross. Easy. "Now take a look at what you've done," John says. "You've started with the four directions in front of you. It's the heart of your basket. Everything else is built around that." Our people honor the four sacred directions and the powers resident there. Where the two basket strips meet, at the intersection of those four directions, is right where we stand as humans, trying to find balance among them. "See there," John says, "everything we do in life is sacred. The four directions are what we build on. That's why we start like that."

Once the eight spokes of the framework are twined into place with the thinnest possible strips, each basket begins to grow. We look to John for the next set of instructions, but there are none. He says, "You're on your own now. The design of the basket is up to you. No one can tell you what to create." We have thick and thin splints to work with, and John shakes out a bag full of brightly dyed splints in every color. The tangled pile looks like the singing ribbons on the men's ribbon shirts in the evening powwows. "Just think of the tree and all its hard work before you start," he says. "It gave its life for this basket, so you know your responsibility. Make something beautiful in return."

Responsibility to the tree makes everyone pause before beginning. Sometimes I have that same sense when I face a blank sheet of paper. For me, writing is an act of reciprocity with the world; it is what I can give back in return for everything that has been given to me. And now there's another layer of responsibility, writing on a thin sheet of tree and hoping the words are worth it. Such a thought could make a person set down her pen.

The first two rows of the basket are the hardest. On the first go-round, the splint seems to have a will of its own and wants to wander from the over-under rhythm around the circle. It resists the pattern and looks all loose and wobbly. This is when John steps in to help, offering encouragement and a steady hand to anchor the escaping splints. The second row is almost as frustrating; the spacing is all wrong and you have to clamp the weaver in place to get it to stay. Even then, it comes loose and slaps you in the face with its wet end. John just laughs. It is a mess of unruly pieces, nothing like a whole. But then there's the third row—my favorite. At this point, the tension of over is balanced by the tension of under, and the opposing forces start to come into balance. The give and take—reciprocity—begins to take hold and the parts begin to become a whole. The weaving becomes easy as splints fall snugly into place. Order and stability emerge out of chaos.

In weaving well-being for land and people, we need to pay attention to the lessons of the three rows. Ecological well-being and the laws of nature are always the first row. Without them, there is no basket of plenty. Only if that first circle is in place can we weave the second. The second reveals material welfare, the subsistence of human needs. Economy built upon ecology. But with only two rows in place, the basket is still in jeopardy of pulling apart. It's only when the third row comes that the first two can hold together. Here is where ecology, economics, and spirit are woven together. By using materials as if they were a gift, and returning that gift through worthy use, we find balance. I think that third row goes by many names: Respect. Reciprocity. All Our Relations. I think of it as the spirit row. Whatever the name, the three rows represent recognition that our lives depend on one another, human needs being only one row in the basket that must hold us all. In relationship, the separate splints become a whole basket, sturdy and resilient enough to carry us into the future.

While we're working, a gaggle of little kids comes by to watch. John is pulled in many directions to help us all, but he stops and gives his full attention to the boys. They're too little to join in, but they want to be there, so he takes up a handful of the short strips from our debris. His hands, now deliberate and slow, bend and twist the strips until a few minutes later a little toy horse sits in the palm of his hand. He gives the boys some scraps, the model, and a few words in Potawatomi, but doesn't tell them how to make a horse. They're used to this kind of teaching and don't ask questions. They look and look some more and then set to work to figure it out. Before long, a herd of horses is galloping over the table and little boys are watching baskets grow.

Toward the end of the afternoon, in the lengthening shadows, the work table begins to fill with completed baskets. John helps us add the decorative curls that are traditional on small baskets. The black ash ribbons are so flexible that you can embroider the surface of the basket with loops and twists that show off the glossy sheen of the ash. We've made low round trays, tall thin vases, plump apple baskets in textures and colors of every kind. "Here's the last step," he says, handing out Sharpie markers. "You've got to sign your basket. Take pride in what you did. That basket didn't make itself. Claim it, mistakes and all." He makes us line up for a photograph, all holding our baskets. "This is a special occasion," he says, beaming like a proud father. "Look what you've learned today. I want you to see what the baskets have shown you. Every one of them is beautiful. Every one of them is different and yet every one of them began in the same tree. They are all made of the same stuff and yet each is itself. That's the way it is with our people, too, all made of the same thing and each their own kind of beautiful."

That night I see the powwow circle with new eyes. I notice that the cedar arbor sheltering the drums is supported by poles set in the four directions. The drum, the heartbeat, calls us out to dance. There is one beat, but each dancer has a distinctive step: dipping grass dancers, crouching buffalo dancers, the twirl of fancy shawl dancers, high-stepping jingle-dress girls, the dignified pace of the women's traditional dancers. Each man, each woman, each child, all dressed in their dreamed-of colors, ribbons flying, fringes swaying, all beautiful, all dancing to the heartbeat. Around the circle we go all night, together weaving a basket.

Today, my house is full of baskets and my favorites are Pigeons. In them I can hear John's voice, can hear the *doonk, doonk, doonk,* and smell the swamp. They remind me of the years of a tree's life that I hold in my hands. What would it be like, I wondered, to live with that heightened sensitivity to the lives given for ours? To consider the tree in the Kleenex, the algae in the toothpaste, the oaks in the floor, the grapes in the wine; to follow back the thread of life in everything and pay it respect? Once you start, it's hard to stop, and you begin to feel yourself awash in gifts.

I open the cupboard, a likely place for gifts. I think, "I greet you, jar of jam. You glass who once was sand upon the beach, washed back and forth and bathed in foam and seagull cries, but who are formed into a glass until you once again return to the sea. And you, berries, plump in your June-ness, now in my February pantry. And you, sugar, so far from your Caribbean home—thanks for making the trip."

In that awareness, looking over the objects on my desk—the basket, the candle, the paper—I delight in following their origins back to the ground. I twirl a pencil—a magic wand lathed from incense cedar—between my fingers. The willow bark in the aspirin. Even the metal of my lamp asks me to consider its roots in the strata of the earth. But I notice that my eyes and my thoughts pass quickly over the plastic on my desk. I hardly give the computer a second glance. I can muster no reflective moment for plastic. It is so far removed from the natural world. I wonder if that's a place where the disconnection began, the loss of respect, when we could no longer easily see the life within the object.

And yet I mean no disrespect for the diatoms and marine invertebrates who two hundred million years ago lived well and fell to the bottom of an ancient sea, where under great pressure of a shifting earth they became oil that was pumped from the ground to a refinery where it was broken down and then polymerized to make the case of my laptop or the cap of the aspirin bottle—but being mindful in the vast network of hyperindustrialized goods really gives me a headache. We weren't made for that sort of constant awareness. We've got work to do.

But every once in a while, with a basket in hand, or a peach or a pencil, there is that moment when the mind and spirit open to all the connections, to all the lives and our responsibility to use them well. And just in that moment, I can hear John Pigeon say, "Slow down—it's thirty years of a tree's life you've got in your hands there. Don't you owe it a few minutes to think about what you'll do with it?"

Mishkos Kenomagwen: The
Teachings of Grass

I. INTRODUCTION

You can smell it before you see it, a sweetgrass meadow on a summer day. The scent flickers on the breeze, you sniff like a dog on a scent, and then it's gone, replaced by the boggy tang of wet ground. And then it's back, the sweet vanilla fragrance, beckoning.

II. LITERATURE REVIEW

Lena is not fooled easily, though. She wanders into the meadow with the certainty of her years, parting grasses with her slender form. A tiny, gray-haired elder, she is up to her waist in grass. She casts her gaze over all the other species and then makes a beeline to a patch that to the uninitiated looks like all the rest. She runs a ribbon of grass through the thumb and forefinger of her wrinkled brown hand. "See how glossy it is? It can hide from you among the others, but it wants to be found. That's why it shines like this." But she passes this patch by, letting it slide through her fingers. She obeys the teachings of her ancestors to never take the first plant that you see.

I follow behind her as her hands trail lovingly over the boneset and the goldenrod. She spies a gleam in the sward and her step quickens. "Ah, *Bozho*," she says. Hello. From the pocket of her old nylon jacket she takes her pouch, deerskin with a beaded red edge, and shakes a little tobacco into the palm of her hand. Eyes closed, murmuring, she raises a hand to the four directions and then scatters the tobacco to the ground. "You know this," she says, her eyebrows a question mark. "To always leave a gift for the plants, to ask if we might take them? It would be rude not to ask first." Only then does she stoop and pinch off a grass stem at its base, careful not to disturb the roots. She parts the nearby clumps, finding another and another until she has gathered a thick sheaf of shining stems. A winding path marks her progress where the meadow canopy was opened by the trail of her passage.

She passes right by many dense patches, leaving them to sway in the breeze. "It's our way," she says, "to take only what we need. I've always been told that you never take more than half." Sometimes she doesn't take any at all, but just comes here to check on the meadow, to see how the plants are doing. "Our teachings," she says, "are very strong. They wouldn't get handed on if they weren't useful. The most important thing to remember is what my grandmother always said: 'If we use a plant respectfully it will stay with us and flourish. If we ignore it, it will go away. If you don't give it respect it will leave us.'" The plants themselves have shown us this—*mishkos kenomagwen*. As we leave the meadow for the path back through the woods, she twists a handful of timothy into a loose knot upon itself, beside the trail. "This tells other pickers that I've been here," she says, "so that they know not to take any more. This place always gives good sweetgrass since we tend to it right. But other places it's getting hard to find. I'm thinking that they might not be picking right. Some people, they're in a hurry and they pull up the whole plant. Even the roots come up. That's not the way I was taught."

I've been with pickers who did that, yanking up a handful that left a little bare spot in the turf and a fuzz of broken roots on the uprooted stems. They too made offerings of tobacco and took only half, and they assured me that their method of picking was the correct one. They were defensive about the charges that their harvesting was depleting sweetgrass. I asked Lena about it and she just shrugged.

III. HYPOTHESIS

In many places, sweetgrass is disappearing from its historic locales, so the basket makers had a request for the botanists: to see if the different ways of harvesting might be the cause of sweetgrass's leaving.

I want to help, but I'm a little wary. Sweetgrass is not an experimental unit for me; it's a gift. There is a barrier of language and meaning between science and traditional knowledge, different ways of knowing, different ways of communicating. I'm not sure I want to force the teachings of grass into the tight uniform of scientific thinking and technical writing that is required of the academy: Introduction, Literature Review, Hypothesis, Methods, Results, Discussion, Conclusions, Acknowledgments, References Cited. But I've been asked on behalf of sweetgrass, and I know my responsibility.

To be heard, you must speak the language of the one you want to listen. So, back at school, I proposed the idea as a thesis project to my graduate student Laurie. Not content with purely academic questions, she had been looking for a research project that would, as she said, "mean something to someone" instead of just sitting on the shelf.

IV. METHODS

Laurie was eager to begin, but she hadn't met Sweetgrass before. "It's the grass that will teach you," I advised, "so you have to get to know it." I took her out to our restored sweetgrass meadows and it was love at first sniff. It didn't take her long to recognize Sweetgrass after that. It was as if the plant wanted her to find it.

Together we designed experiments to compare the effects of the two harvesting methods the basket makers had explained. Laurie's education so far was full of the scientific method, but I wanted her to live out a slightly different style of research. To me, an experiment is a kind of conversation with plants: I have a question for them, but since we don't speak the same language, I can't ask them directly and they won't answer verbally. But plants can be eloquent in their physical responses and behaviors. Plants answer questions by the way they live, by their responses to change; you just need to learn how to ask. I smile when I hear my colleagues say "I discovered X." That's kind of like Columbus claiming to have discovered America. It was here all along, it's just that he didn't know it. Experiments are not about discovery but about listening and translating the knowledge of other beings.

My colleagues might scoff at the notion of basket makers as scientists, but when Lena and her daughters take 50 percent of the sweetgrass, observe the result, evaluate their findings, and then create management guidelines from them, that sounds a lot like experimental science to me. Generations of data collection and validation through time builds up to well-tested theories.

At my university, as at many others, graduate students must present their thesis ideas to a faculty committee. Laurie did a wonderful job of outlining the proposed experiment, ably describing multiple study sites, the many replicates, and intensive sampling techniques. But when she was through speaking there was an uneasy silence in the conference room. One professor shuffled through the proposal pages and pushed them aside dismissively. "I don't see anything new here for science," he said. "There's not even a theoretical framework."

A theory, to scientists, means something rather different from its popular use, which suggests something speculative or untested. A scientific theory is a cohesive body of knowledge, an explanation that is consistent among a range of cases and can allow you to predict what might happen in unknown situations. Like this one. Our research was most definitely grounded in theory—Lena's, primarily—in the traditional ecological knowledge of Indigenous peoples: If we use a plant respectfully, it will flourish. If we ignore it, it will go away. This is a theory generated from millennia of observations of plant response to harvest, subject to peer review by generations of practitioners, from basket makers to herbalists. Despite the weight of this truth, the committee could only struggle not to roll their eyes.

The dean looked over the glasses that had slid down his nose, fixing Laurie with a pointed stare and directing a sidelong glance toward me. "*Anyone* knows that harvesting a plant will damage the population. You're wasting your time. And I'm afraid I don't find this whole traditional knowledge thing very convincing." Like the former schoolteacher she was, Laurie was unfailingly calm and gracious as she explained further, but her eyes were steely.

Later, though, they were filled with tears. Mine, too. In the early years, no matter how carefully you prepared, this was nearly a rite of passage for women scientists—the condescension, the verbal smackdown from academic authorities, especially if you had the audacity to ground your work in the observations of old women who had probably not finished high school, and talked to plants to boot.

Getting scientists to consider the validity of Indigenous knowledge is like swimming upstream in cold, cold water. They've been so conditioned to be skeptical of even the hardest of hard data that bending their minds toward theories that are verified without the expected graphs or equations is tough. Couple that with the unblinking assumption that science has cornered the market on truth and there's not much room for discussion.

Undeterred, we carried on. The basket makers had given us the prerequisites of the scientific method: observation, pattern, and a testable hypothesis. That sounded like science to me. So we began by setting up experimental plots in the meadows to ask the plants the question "Do these two different harvest methods contribute to decline?" And then we tried to detect their answer. We chose dense sweetgrass stands where the population had been restored rather than compromising native stands where pickers were active.

With incredible patience, Laurie did a census of the sweetgrass population in every plot to obtain precise measures of population density prior to harvest. She even marked individual stems of grass with colored plastic ties to keep track of them. When all had been tallied, she then began the harvest.

The plots were subject to one of the two harvest methods the basket makers had described. Laurie took half of the stems in each plot, pinching them off one by one carefully at the base in some plots and yanking up a tuft and leaving a small ragged gap in the sod in others. Experiments must have controls, of course, so she left an equal number of plots alone and did not harvest them at all. Pink flagging festooned the meadows to mark her study areas.

One day in the field we sat in the sun and talked about whether the method really duplicated the traditional harvest. "I know that it doesn't," she said, "because I'm not replicating the relationship. I don't speak to the plants or make an offering." She had wrestled with this but settled on excluding it: "I honor that traditional relationship, but I couldn't ever do it as part of an experiment. It wouldn't be right on any level—to add a variable that I don't understand and that science can't even attempt to measure. And besides, I'm not qualified to speak to sweetgrass." Later, she admitted that it was hard to stay neutral in her research and avoid affection for the plants; after so many days among them, learning and listening, neutrality proved impossible. Eventually she was just careful to show them all her mindful respect, making her care a constant as well, so that she would not sway the results one way or the other. The sweetgrass she harvested was counted, weighed, and given away to basket makers.

Every few months, Laurie counted and marked all the grass in her plots: dead shoots, living ones, and brand-new shoots just pushing up from the ground. She charted the birth, the death, and the reproduction of all her grass stems. When the next July rolled around she harvested once more, just as women were doing in the native stands. For two years she harvested and measured the response of the grass along with a team of student interns. It was a little tough at first to recruit student helpers given that their task would be watching grass grow.

V. RESULTS

Laurie observed carefully and filled her notebook with measurements, charting the vigor of each plot. She worried a little when the control plots were looking a little sickly. She was relying on these controls, the unharvested patches, to be the reference point for comparing the effects of harvesting in the other plots. We hoped they would perk up when spring came.

By the second year, Laurie was expecting her first child. The grass grew and grew, as did her belly. Bending and stooping became a little more difficult, to say nothing of lying in the grass to read plant tags.

But she was faithful to her plants, sitting in the dirt among them, counting and marking. She said the quiet of fieldwork, the calm of sitting in a flower-strewn meadow with the smell of sweetgrass all around, was a good beginning for a baby. I think she was right.

As the summer wore on, it became a race to finish the research before the baby was born. Just weeks away from delivery, it became a team effort. When Laurie was done with a plot, she would call out for her field crew to help hoist her to her feet. This too was a rite of passage for women field biologists.

As her baby grew, Laurie came to believe with increasing conviction in the knowledge of her basket-making mentors, recognizing, as Western science often does not, the quality of observations from the women who had long had close relationships with plants and their habitats. They shared many of their teachings with her, and they knit many baby hats.

Baby Celia was born in the early fall, and a braid of sweetgrass was hung over her crib. While Celia slept nearby, Laurie put her data on the computer and began to make the comparisons between the harvesting methods. From the twist ties on every stem, Laurie could chart the births and deaths in the sample plots. Some plots were full of new young shoots that signaled a thriving population, and some were not.

Her statistical analyses were all sound and thorough, but she hardly needed graphs to tell the story. From across the field you could see the difference: some plots gleamed shiny golden green and some were dull and brown. The committee's criticism hovered in her mind: "Anyone knows that harvesting a plant will damage the population."

The surprise was that the failing plots were not the harvested ones, as predicted, but the unharvested controls. The sweetgrass that had not been picked or disturbed in any way was choked with dead stems while the harvested plots were thriving. Even though half of all stems had been harvested each year, they quickly grew back, completely replacing everything that had been gathered, in fact producing more shoots than were present before harvest. Picking sweetgrass seemed to actually stimulate growth. In the first year's harvest, the plants that grew the very best were the ones that had been yanked up in a handful. But, whether it was pinched singly or pulled in a clump, the end result was nearly the same: it didn't seem to matter how the grass was harvested, only that it was.

Laurie's graduate committee had dismissed this possibility from the outset. They had been taught that harvesting causes decline. And yet the grasses themselves unequivocally argued the opposite point. After the grilling Laurie received over her research proposal, you might imagine she was dreading the thesis defense. But she had one thing skeptical scientists value most: data. While Celia slept in her proud father's arms, Laurie presented her graphs and tables to demonstrate that sweetgrass flourishes when it's harvested and declines when it is not. The doubting dean was silent. The basket makers smiled.

VI. DISCUSSION

We are all the product of our worldviews—even scientists who claim pure objectivity. Their predictions for sweetgrass were consistent with their Western science worldview, which sets human beings outside of "nature" and judges their interactions with other species as largely negative. They had been schooled that the best way to protect a dwindling species was to leave it alone and keep people away. But the grassy meadows tell us that for sweetgrass, human beings are part of the system, a vital part. Laurie's findings might have been surprising to academic ecologists but were consistent with the theory voiced by our ancestors. "If we use a plant respectfully it will stay with us and flourish. If we ignore it, it will go away."

"Your experiment seems to demonstrate a significant effect," said the dean. "But how do you explain it? Are you implying that the grass that was unharvested had its feelings hurt by being ignored? What is the mechanism responsible for this?"

Laurie admitted that the scientific literature held no explanations for the relationship between basket makers and sweetgrass since such questions were not generally deemed worthy of scientific attention. She turned to studies of how grasses respond to other factors, such as fire or grazing. She discovered that the stimulated growth she had observed was well known to range scientists. After all, grasses are beautifully adapted to disturbance—it's why we plant lawns. When we mow them they multiply. Grasses carry their growing points just beneath the soil surface so that when their leaves are lost to a mower, a grazing animal, or a fire, they quickly recover.

She explained how harvesting thinned the population, allowing the remaining shoots to respond to the extra space and light by reproducing quickly. Even the pulling method was beneficial. The underground stem that connects the shoots is dotted with buds. When it's gently tugged, the stem breaks and all those buds produce thrifty young shoots to fill the gap.

Many grasses undergo a physiological change known as compensatory growth in which the plant compensates for loss of foliage by quickly growing more. It seems counterintuitive, but when a herd of buffalo grazes down a sward of fresh grass, it actually grows faster in response. This helps the plant recover, but also invites the buffalo back for dinner later in the season. It's even been discovered that there is an enzyme in the saliva of grazing buffalo that actually stimulates grass growth. To say nothing of the fertilizer produced by a passing herd. Grass gives to buffalo and buffalo give to grass.

The system is well balanced, but only if the herd uses the grass respectfully. Free-range buffalo graze and move on, not returning to the same place for many months. Thus they obey the rule of not taking more than half, of not overgrazing. Why shouldn't it also be true for people and sweetgrass? We are no more than the buffalo and no less, governed by the same natural laws.

With a long, long history of cultural use, sweetgrass has apparently become dependent on humans to create the "disturbance" that stimulates its compensatory growth. Humans participate in a symbiosis in which sweetgrass provides its fragrant blades to the people and people, by harvesting, create the conditions for sweetgrass to flourish.

It's intriguing to wonder whether the regional decline in sweetgrass might be due not to overharvesting but rather to underharvesting. Laurie and I pored over the map of historical locations for sweetgrass created by a former student, Daniela Shebitz. There were blue dots where sweetgrass used to be found but has since disappeared. Red dots marked the few places where sweetgrass was reported historically and where it is still thriving. These red dots are not randomly scattered. They are clustered around Native communities, particularly those known for their sweetgrass basketry. Sweetgrass thrives where it is used and disappears elsewhere.

Science and traditional knowledge may ask different questions and speak different languages, but they may converge when both truly listen to the plants. To relate the story the ancestors told us to the academics in the room, however, we needed to use scientific explanations expressed in the language of mechanism and objectification: "If we remove 50 percent of the plant biomass, the stems are released from resource competition. The stimulus of compensatory growth causes an increase in population density and plant vigor. In the absence of disturbance, resource depletion and competition result in a loss of vigor and increased mortality."

The scientists gave Laurie a warm round of applause. She had spoken their language and made a convincing case for the stimulatory effect of harvesters, indeed for the reciprocity between harvesters and sweetgrass. One even retracted his initial criticism that this research would "add nothing new to science." The basket makers who sat at the table simply nodded their heads in agreement. Wasn't this just as the elders have said?

The question was, how do we show respect? Sweetgrass told us the answer as we experimented: sustainable harvesting can be the way we treat a plant with respect, by respectfully receiving its gift.

Perhaps it is no coincidence that it is Sweetgrass that reveals this story. *Wiingaashk* was the first to be planted by Skywoman on the back of Turtle Island. The grass gives its fragrant self to us and we receive it with gratitude. In return, through the very act of accepting the gift, the pickers open some space, let the light come in, and with a gentle tug bestir the dormant buds that make new grass. Reciprocity is a matter of keeping the gift in motion through self-perpetuating cycles of giving and receiving.

Our elders taught that the relationship between plants and humans must be one of balance. People can take too much and exceed the capacity of the plants to share again. That's the voice of hard experience that resonates in the teachings of "never take more than half." And yet, they also teach that we can take too little. If we allow traditions to die, relationships to fade, the land will suffer. These laws are the product of hard experience, of past mistakes. And not all plants are the same; each has its own way of regenerating. Some, unlike sweetgrass, are easily harmed by harvest. Lena would say that the key is to know them well enough to respect the difference.

VII. CONCLUSIONS

With their tobacco and their thanks, our people say to the Sweetgrass, "I need you." By its renewal after picking, the grass says to the people, "I need you, too."

Mishkos kenomagwen. Isn't this the lesson of grass? Through reciprocity the gift is replenished. All of our flourishing is mutual.

VIII. ACKNOWLEDGMENTS

In a field of tall grass, with only the wind for company, there is a language that transcends the differences between scientific and traditional understandings, the data or the prayer. The wind moves through and carries the grass song. It sounds to me like *mishhhhkos,* over and over again on ripples of moving grass. After all it has taught us, I want to say thank you.

IX. REFERENCES CITED

Wiingaashk, Buffalo, Lena, the Ancestors.

Maple Nation: A Citizenship Guide

There's just one gas station in my community. It's right there at the stoplight, also the only one. You get the picture. I'm sure that it has an official name, but we just call it the Pompey Mall. Coffee, milk, ice, dog food, you can get most anything essential to life at the mall. Duct tape to hold things together and WD-40 to get them apart. There are tins of last year's maple syrup, which I pass up, since I'm on my way to the sugar house where new syrup awaits. The clientele runs largely to pickup trucks and now and then a Prius. There aren't any snowmobiles revving at the pumps today, because the snow is just about gone.

Since it's the only place to fuel up, the lines are often long and today people stand outside in the spring sunshine, leaning against the cars, waiting their turn. Conversation, like the shelves inside, tends toward essentials—the price of gas, how the sap is running, who's got their taxes done. Sugaring season and tax season overlap around here.

"Between the price of gas and the tax man, I'm just about bled dry," Kerm gripes as he replaces the nozzle and wipes his hands on greasy Carhartts. "Now they want to raise taxes for a windmill down to the school? All on account of global warming. Not on my dime." One of our town officials is ahead of me in line. She's an ample woman, a former social studies teacher at the school, and does not hesitate to wag a finger in the banter. She probably had Kerm in class. "You don't like it? Don't complain if you're not there. Show up to a damn meeting."

There's still snow under the trees, a bright blanket beneath the gray trunks and the blush of reddening maple buds. Last night, a tiny sliver of moon hung in the deep-blue dark of early spring. That new moon ushers in our Anishinaabe new year—the *Ziҙibaskwet Giiҙis,* Maple Sugar Moon. It is when the earth starts to wake up from her well-deserved rest and renews her gifts to the people. To celebrate, I'm going sugaring.

I received my census form today; it's on the seat beside me as I drive out through the hills toward the sugarbush. If you took a biologically inclusive census of the people in this town, the maples would outnumber humans a hundred to one. In our Anishinaabe way, we count trees as people, "the standing people." Even though the government only counts humans in our township, there's no denying that we live in the nation of maples.

There's a beautiful map of bioregions drawn by an organization dedicated to restoring ancient food traditions. State boundaries disappear and are replaced by ecological regions, defined by the leading denizens of the region, the iconic beings who shape the landscape, influence our daily lives, and feed us—both materially and spiritually. The map shows the Salmon Nation of the Pacific Northwest and the Pinyon Nation of the Southwest, among others. We in the Northeast are in the embrace of the Maple Nation.

I'm thinking about what it would mean to declare citizenship in Maple Nation. Kerm would probably answer with two terse words of resentment: pay taxes. And he's right, being a citizen does mean sharing in the support of your community.

Here it is, almost tax day, when my fellow humans are getting ready to make their contribution to the well-being of the community, but the maples have been giving all year long. Their contribution of limb wood kept my old neighbor Mr. Keller's house warm all winter when he couldn't pay the oil bill. The volunteer fire department and the ambulance squad as well rely on maple contributions to their monthly pancake breakfast, to raise funds for a new engine. The trees make a real dent in the energy bill for the school with their shade, and, thanks to big canopies of maples, nobody I know ever pays a bill for air-conditioning. They donate shade to the Memorial Day parade every year without even being asked. If it weren't for the maples' ability to break the wind, the highway department would have to plow snowdrifts off the road twice as often.

Both of my parents have been active in their town government for years, so I've seen firsthand how stewardship of a community happens. "Good communities don't make themselves," my dad said. "We've got a lot to be grateful for, and we all have to do our part to keep it going." He just retired as town supervisor. My mom is on the zoning board. From them I learned that town government is invisible to most citizens, which is perhaps as it should be—necessary services are delivered so smoothly that folks just take them for granted. The roads get plowed, the water is kept clean, the parks are kept up, and the new senior citizens center finally got built, all without much fanfare. Most people are indifferent, unless their self-interest is at stake. Then there are the chronic complainers, always on the phone to contest the tax levy, and also on the phone to object to cutbacks when the same tax levies fail.

Fortunately, there are those in every organization, few but invaluable, who know their responsibilities and seem to thrive on meeting them. They get things done. These are the ones we all rely upon, the people who take care of the rest of us, quiet leaders.

My Onondaga Nation neighbors call the maple the leader of the trees. Trees constitute the environmental quality committee—running air and water purification service 24-7. They're on every task force, from the historical society picnic to the highway department, school board, and library. When it comes to civic beautification, they alone create the crimson fall with little recognition.

We haven't even mentioned how they create habitat for songbirds, and wildlife cover, golden leaves to shuffle through, tree forts and branches for swings. Centuries of their falling leaves have built this soil, now farmed for strawberries, apples, sweet corn, and hay. How much of the oxygen in our valley comes from our maples? How much carbon is taken from the atmosphere and stored away? These processes are what ecological scientists term ecosystem services, the structures and functions of the natural world that make life possible. We can assign an economic value to maple timber, or gallons of syrup, but ecosystem services are far more precious. And yet these services go unaccounted for in the human economy. As with the services of local government, we don't think about them unless they are missing. There is no official tax system to pay for these services, as we pay for snowplowing and schoolbooks. We get them for free, donated continually by maples. They do their share for us. The question is: How well do we do by them?

By the time I get to the sugar house, the guys already have the pan at full boil. A forceful plume of steam billows from the open vents, signaling to folks down the road and across the valley that they're boiling today. While I'm there, a steady stream of people drop by for conversation and a gallon of new syrup. As they step into the shed, they all stop right at the door; their glasses fog up and the sweet aroma of boiling sap stops them in their tracks. I like to walk in and out over and over again, just for the rush of fragrance.

The sugar house itself is a rough wood building with a character-istic vented cupola running its length to allow the steam to escape. It whooshes up to join the downy clouds in a soft spring sky.

The fresh sap goes in at one end of the open evaporator and moves along channels under its own increasing gravity as the water is boiled away. The boil at the beginning is wild and frothy with big random bubbles and more sedate at the end as it thickens, moving from clear at the start to deep caramel at the end. You've got to take the syrup off at just the right time and density. Let it go too far and the whole affair could crystallize into a delicious brick.

It's hard work, and the two guys watching and testing have been here since early this morning. I brought along a pie so they can grab forkfuls every now and then, between tasks. As we all watch the boil, I ask them my question: What does it mean to be a good citizen of Maple Nation?

Larry is the stoker. Every ten minutes he pulls on elbow-length gloves and dons a face shield before opening the door to the fire. The heat is intense as he adds another armload of three-foot lengths of firewood one by one. "You've gotta keep it boiling heavy," he says. "We do it the old-fashioned way. Some folks have gone to fuel oil or gas burners, but I hope we always stick with wood. It feels right."

The woodpile is easily as big as the sugar house itself, stacked ten feet high with cord upon cord of dry split ash and birch and, of course, good hard maple. The forestry students cut and gather a fair bit of the wood from dead trees along all of our trails. "See, it works out good. To keep the sugar bush productive we thin out the competition so our sap trees can grow a nice full canopy. The trees we thin out usually end up right here, as firewood. Nothing gets wasted. That's a kind of being a good citizen, isn't it? You take care of the trees and they'll take care of you." I don't imagine there are many colleges that run their own sugarbushes, and I'm grateful that ours does.

Bart sits by the bottling tank and chimes in: "We should save the oil for where we've got to have it. Wood can do this job better—and besides, it's carbon neutral. The carbon we release from burning wood for syrup came from the trees that took it in, in the first place. It will go right back to them, with no net increase." He goes on to explain that these forests are part of the college's plan to be totally carbon neutral: "We actually get a tax credit by keeping our forests intact, so they can absorb carbon dioxide."

I suppose that one of the features of being a member of a nation is shared currency. In Maple Nation, the currency is carbon. It is traded, exchanged, bartered among community members from atmosphere to tree to beetle to woodpecker to fungus to log to firewood to atmosphere and back to tree. No waste, shared wealth, balance, and reciprocity. What better model for a sustainable economy do we need?

What does it mean to be a citizen of Maple Nation? I put this question to Mark, who handles the finishing with a big paddle and the hydrometer to test the sugar concentration. "That's a good question," he says as he pours a few drops of cream onto the boiling syrup to quell the foam. He doesn't answer, but opens the spigot at the bottom of the finishing pan, filling a bucket with new syrup. Later, when it has cooled a bit, he pours out a little cup for each of us, golden and warm, and raises his in a toast. "I guess this is what you do," he says. "You make syrup. You enjoy it. You take what you're given and you treat it right."

Drinking maple syrup gives you quite a sugar rush. This too is what it means to be a citizen of Maple Nation, having maple in your bloodstream, maple in your bones. We are what we eat, and with every golden spoonful maple carbon becomes human carbon. Our traditional thinking had it right: maples are people, people are maples.

Our Anishinaabe word for maple is *anenemik*, the man tree. "My wife makes maple cake," says Mark, "and we always give out candy maple leaves at Christmas." Larry's favorite is to just pour it on vanilla ice cream. My ninety-six-year-old grandma likes to take a pure spoonful once in a while, when she's feeling low. She calls it vitamin M. Next month, the college will hold a pancake breakfast here, where staff and faculty and families gather to celebrate sticky-fingered membership in Maple Nation, our bond to each other and to this land. Citizens also celebrate together.

The pan is running low, so I go with Larry down the road to the sugar bush, where a tank is slowly filling with fresh sap, drip by drip. We walk around the woods for a while, ducking under the network of tubes that gurgle like a brook, carrying the sap inside to the collecting tank. It's not the same plinking music of old-time sap buckets, but it enables two people to do the work of twenty.

The woods are the same as countless springs before this one; the citizens of Maple Nation are starting to wake up. Snowfleas pepper the wells of deer tracks. Mosses drip with snowmelt at the base of trees, and geese race by, their V in disarray with their eagerness to be home.

As we drive back with a brimming tank, he says, "Of course sugaring is a gamble every year. It's not like you can control the sap flow. Some years are good and some aren't. You take what you get and be grateful for it. It all depends on the temperature, and that's out of our hands." But that's not entirely true anymore. Our addiction to fossil fuel and current energy policies accelerate carbon dioxide inputs every year, unequivocally causing a global rise in temperatures. Spring comes nearly a week earlier than it did just twenty years ago.

I hate to leave, but I have to get back to my desk. On the drive home, I continue to think about citizenship. When my kids were in school they had to memorize the Bill of Rights, but I would venture to guess that maple seedlings would be schooled instead in a Bill of Responsibilities.

When I get home, I look up the citizenship oaths for various human nations. They have many elements in common. Some require allegiance to a leader. Most are a pledge of loyalty, an expression of shared beliefs and an oath to obey the laws of the land. The United States rarely permits dual citizenship—you have to choose. On what basis do we select where to invest our allegiance? If I were forced, I would choose Maple Nation. If citizenship is a matter of shared beliefs, then I believe in the democracy of species. If citizenship means an oath of loyalty to a leader, then I choose the leader of the trees. If good citizens agree to uphold the laws of the nation, then I choose natural law, the law of reciprocity, of regeneration, of mutual flourishing.

The oath of citizenship for the United States stipulates that citizens will defend the nation against all enemies and take up arms if they are called to do so. If that same oath held in Maple Nation, the trumpet call would be echoing through these wooded hills. Maples of the United States face a grave enemy. The most highly regarded models predict that the climate of New England will become hostile to sugar maples within fifty years. Rising temperatures will reduce seedling success and regeneration will thereby start to fail. It already is failing. Insects will follow, and the oaks will get the upper hand. Imagine New England without maples. Unthinkable. A brown fall instead of hills afire. Sugar houses boarded up. No more fragrant clouds of steam. Would we even recognize our homes? Is that a heartbreak we can bear?

It's a running threat on the left and the right: "If things don't change, I'm moving to Canada." It looks like the maples will have to do just that. Like the displaced farmers of Bangladesh fleeing rising sea levels, maples will become climate refugees. To survive they must migrate northward to find homes at the boreal fringe. Our energy policy is forcing them to leave. They will be exiled from their homelands for the price of cheap gas.

We do not pay at the pump for the cost of climate change, for the loss of ecosystem services provided by maples and others. Cheap gas now or maples for the next generation? Call me crazy, but I'd welcome the tax that would resolve that question.

Individuals far wiser than I have said that we get the government we deserve. That may be true. But the maples, our most generous of benefactors and most responsible of citizens, do not deserve our government. They deserve you and me speaking up on their behalf. To quote our town council woman, "Show up at the damn meeting." Political action, civic engagement—these are powerful acts of reciprocity with the land. The Maple Nation Bill of Responsibilities asks us to stand up for the standing people, to lead with the wisdom of Maples.

The Honorable Harvest

The crows see me coming across the field, a woman with a basket, and argue my provenance loudly among themselves. The soil is hard under my feet, bare except for a scattering of plow-scraped rocks and a few of last year's corn stalks, their remnant prop roots squatting like bleached-out spider legs. Years of herbicides and continuous corn have left the field sterile. Even in rain-soaked April not a blade of green shows its face. By August it will once again be a monoculture of corn plants in straight rows of indentured servitude, but for now it's my cross-country route to the woods.

My entourage of crows leaves me at the stone wall, a loose windrow of glacial cobbles raked from the field to mark its boundary. On the other side the ground is soft underfoot and deep in centuries of leaf mold, the forest floor flocked with tiny pink spring beauties and clumps of yellow violets. The humus stirs with trout lilies and trillium poised to rise through the winter-brown mat of leaves. A wood thrush hangs a silvery trill on the still-bare branches of the maples. The dense patches of leeks are among the first to appear in the spring, their green so vivid that they signal like a neon sign: PICK ME!

I resist the urge to answer their call immediately and instead address the plants the way I've been taught: introducing myself in case they've forgotten, even though we've been meeting like this for years. I explain why I've come and ask their permission to harvest, inquiring politely if they would be willing to share.

Eating leeks is a spring tonic that blurs the line between food and medicine. It wakens the body from its winter lassitude and quickens the blood. But I have another need, too, that only greens from this particular woods can satisfy. Both of my daughters will be home for the weekend from the far places where they live. I ask these leeks to renew the bonds between this ground and my children, so that they will always carry the substance of home in the mineral of their bones.

Some of the leaves are already expanded—stretching toward the sun—while others are still rolled into a spear, thrusting up through the duff. I dig my trowel in around the edge of the clump, but they're deeply rooted and tightly packed, resisting my efforts. It's just a small trowel and it hurts my winter-softened hand, but at last I pry out a clump and shake away the dark earth.

I expected a cluster of fat white bulbs, but in their place I find ragged papery sheathes where the bulbs should be. Withered and flaccid, they look as if all the juice has already been sucked out of them. Which it has. If you ask permission, you have to listen to the answer. I tuck them back in the soil and go home. Along the stone wall, the elderberries have broken bud and their embryonic leaves reach out like gloved purple hands.

On a day like this, when the fiddleheads are unfurling and the air is petal soft, I am awash in longing. I know that "thou shalt not covet thy neighbor's chloroplasts" is good advice and yet I must confess to full-blown chlorophyll envy. Sometimes I wish I could photosynthesize so that just by being, just by shimmering at the meadow's edge or floating lazily on a pond, I could be doing the work of the world while standing silent in the sun. The shadowy hemlocks and the waving grasses are spinning out sugar molecules and passing them on to hungry mouths and mandibles all the while listening to the warblers and watching the light dance on the water.

It would be so satisfying to provide for the well-being of others—like being a mother again, like being needed. Shade, medicine, berries, roots; there would be no end to it. As a plant I could make the campfire, hold the nest, heal the wound, fill the brimming pot.

But this generosity is beyond my realm, as I am a mere heterotroph, a feeder on the carbon transmuted by others. In order to live, I must consume. That's the way the world works, the exchange of a life for a life, the endless cycling between my body and the body of the world. Forced to choose, I must admit I actually like my heterotroph role. Besides, if I could photosynthesize, I couldn't eat leeks.

So instead I live vicariously through the photosynthesis of others. I am not the vibrant leaves on the forest floor—I am the woman with the basket, and how I fill it is a question that matters. If we are fully awake, a moral question arises as we extinguish the other lives around us on behalf of our own. Whether we are digging wild leeks or going to the mall, how do we consume in a way that does justice to the lives that we take?

In our oldest stories, we are reminded that this was a question of profound concern for our ancestors. When we rely deeply on other lives, there is urgency to protect them. Our ancestors, who had so few material possessions, devoted a great deal of attention to this question, while we who are drowning in possessions scarcely give it a thought. The cultural landscape may have changed, but the conundrum has not—the need to resolve the inescapable tension between honoring life around us and taking it in order to live is part of being human.

A few weeks later I take up my basket and again cross the field, still bare while the earth on the other side of the wall is drifted in snowy white trillium blossoms like a late-season snowfall. I must look like a ballet dancer tiptoeing and spinning between clumps of delicate Dutchman's-breeches, mysterious blue shoots of cohosh, patches of bloodroot, and the green shoots of jack-in-the-pulpit and mayapple surging up through the leaves. I greet them one by one and feel as if they're glad to see me, too.

We are told to take only that which is given, and when I was here last the leeks had nothing to give. Bulbs hold energy saved up for the next generation like money in the bank. Last fall the bulbs were sleek and fat, but, in the first days of spring, that savings account gets depleted as the roots send their stored energy into the emerging leaves to fuel their journey from soil to sunshine. In their first few days, the leaves are consumers, taking from the root, shriveling it up and giving nothing back. But as they unfurl they become a powerful solar array that will recharge the energy of the roots, playing out the reciprocity between consuming and producing in a few short weeks.

The leeks today are twice the size they were on my first visit and the scent of onions is strong where a deer has bruised the leaves. I pass by the first clump and kneel by the second. Once again, I quietly ask permission.

Asking permission shows respect for the personhood of the plant, but it is also an assessment of the well-being of the population. Thus I must use both sides of my brain to listen to the answer. The analytic left reads the empirical signs to judge whether the population is large and healthy enough to sustain a harvest, whether it has enough to share. The intuitive right hemisphere is reading something else, a sense of generosity, an open-handed radiance that says *take me,* or sometimes a tight-lipped recalcitrance that makes me put my trowel away. I can't explain it, but it is a kind of knowing that is for me just as compelling as a no-trespassing sign. This time, when I push my trowel deep I come up with a thick cluster of gleaming white bulbs, plump, slippery, and aromatic. I hear *yes,* so I make a gift from the soft old tobacco pouch in my pocket and begin to dig.

Leeks are clonal plants that multiply by division, spreading the patch wider and wider. As a result, they tend to become crowded in the center of a patch, so I try to harvest there. In this way my taking can help the growth of the remaining plants by thinning them out. From camas bulbs to sweet-grass, blueberries to basket willow, our ancestors found ways to harvest that bring long-term benefit to plants and people.

While a sharp shovel would make digging more efficient, the truth is that it makes the work too fast. If I could get all the leeks I needed in five minutes, I'd lose that time on my knees watching the ginger poke up and listening to the oriole that has just returned home. This is truly a choice for "slow food." Besides, that simple shift in technology would also make it easy to slice through neighboring plants and take too much. Woods throughout the country are losing their leeks to harvesters who love them to extinction. The difficulty of digging is an important constraint. Not everything should be convenient.

The traditional ecological knowledge of Indigenous harvesters is rich in prescriptions for sustainability. They are found in Native science and philosophy, in lifeways and practices, but most of all in stories, the ones that are told to help restore balance, to locate ourselves once again in the circle.

Anishinaabe elder Basil Johnston tells of the time our teacher Nanabozho was fishing in the lake for supper, as he often did, with hook and line. Heron came striding along through the reeds on his long, bent legs, his beak like a spear. Heron is a good fisherman and a sharing friend, so he told Nanabozho about a new way to fish that would make his life much easier. Heron cautioned him to be careful not to take too many fish, but Nanabozho was already thinking of a feast. He went out early the next day and soon had a whole basketful of fish, so heavy he could barely carry it and far more than he could eat. So he cleaned all those fish and set them out to dry on the racks outside his lodge. The next day, with his belly still full, he went back to the lake and again did what Heron had showed him. "Aah," he thought as he carried home the fish, "I will have plenty to eat this winter."

Day after day he stuffed himself and, as the lake grew empty, his drying racks grew full, sending out a delicious smell into the forest where Fox was licking his lips. Again he went to the lake, so proud of himself. But that day his nets came up empty and Heron looked down on him as he flew over the lake with a critical eye. When Nanabozho got home to his lodge, he learned a key rule—never take more than you need. The racks of fish were toppled in the dirt and every bite was gone.

Cautionary stories of the consequences of taking too much are ubiquitous in Native cultures, but it's hard to recall a single one in English. Perhaps this helps to explain why we seem to be caught in a trap of over-consumption, which is as destructive to ourselves as to those we consume.

Collectively, the Indigenous canon of principles and practices that govern the exchange of life for life is known as the Honorable Harvest. They are rules of sorts that govern our taking, shape our relationships with the natural world, and rein in our tendency to consume—that the world might be as rich for the seventh generation as it is for our own.

The details are highly specific to different cultures and ecosystems, but the fundamental principles are nearly universal among peoples who live close to the land.

I am a student of this way of thinking, not a scholar. As a human being who cannot photosynthesize, I must struggle to participate in the Honorable Harvest. So I lean in close to watch and listen to those who are far wiser than I am. What I share here, in the same way they were shared with me, are seeds gleaned from the fields of their collective wisdom, the barest surface, the moss on the mountain of their knowledge. I feel grateful for their teachings and responsible for passing them on as best I can.

My friend is the town clerk in a small Adirondack village. In the summer and fall there is a line outside her door for fishing and hunting licenses. With every laminated card, she hands out the harvesting regulations, pocket-size booklets on thin newsprint, printed in black and white except for glossy inserts with photos of the actual prey, just in case people don't know what they're shooting at. It happens: every year there is a story about triumphal deer hunters being stopped on the highway with a Jersey calf tied to their bumper.

A friend of mine once worked at a hunting check station during partridge season. A guy drove up in a big white Oldsmobile and proudly opened his trunk for inspection of his take. The birds were all neatly laid out on a canvas sheet, lined up beak to back with plumage scarcely ruffled, a whole brace of yellow-shafted flickers.

Traditional peoples who feed their families from the land have harvest guidelines too: detailed protocols designed to maintain the health and vigor of wildlife species. Like the state regulations, they too are based on sophisticated ecological knowledge and long-term monitoring of populations. They share the common goal of protecting what hunting managers call "the resource," both for its own sake and to safeguard the sustainable supply for future generations.

Early colonists on Turtle Island were stunned by the plenitude they found here, attributing the richness to the bounty of nature.

Settlers in the Great Lakes wrote in their journals about the extraordinary abundance of wild rice harvested by Native peoples; in just a few days, they could fill their canoes with enough rice to last all year. But the settlers were puzzled by the fact that, as one of them wrote, "the savages stopped gathering long before all the rice was harvested." She observed that "the rice harvest starts with a ceremony of thanksgiving and prayers for good weather for the next four days. They will harvest dawn till dusk for the prescribed four days and then stop, often leaving much rice to stand unreaped. This rice, they say, is not for them but for the Thunders. Nothing will compel them to continue, therefore much goes to waste." The settlers took this as certain evidence of laziness and lack of industry on the part of the heathens. They did not understand how Indigenous land-care practices might contribute to the wealth they encountered.

I once met an engineering student visiting from Europe who told me excitedly about going ricing in Minnesota with his friend's Ojibwe family. He was eager to experience a bit of Native American culture. They were on the lake by dawn and all day long they poled through the rice beds, knocking the ripe seed into the canoe. "It didn't take long to collect quite a bit," he reported, "but it's not very efficient. At least half of the rice just falls in the water and they didn't seem to care. It's wasted." As a gesture of thanks to his hosts, a traditional ricing family, he offered to design a grain capture system that could be attached to the gunwales of their canoes. He sketched it out for them, showing how his technique could get 85 percent more rice. His hosts listened respectfully, then said, "Yes, we could get more that way. But it's got to seed itself for next year. And what we leave behind is not wasted. You know, we're not the only ones who like rice. Do you think the ducks would stop here if we took it all?" Our teachings tell us to never take more than half.

When my basket holds enough leeks for dinner, I head home. Walking back through the flowers, I see a whole patch of snakeroot spreading its glistening leaves, which reminds me of a story told by an herbalist

I know. She taught me one of the cardinal rules of gathering plants: "Never take the first plant you find, as it might be the last—and you want that first one to speak well of you to the others of her kind." That's not too hard to do when you come upon a whole stream bank of coltsfoot, when there's a third and a fourth right behind the first, but it's harder when the plants are few and the desire is great.

"Once I dreamed of a snakeroot and that I should bring it with me on a journey the next day. There was a need but I didn't know what it was. But it was still too early to harvest. The leaves wouldn't be up for another week or so. There was a chance it might be up early somewhere—maybe in a sunny spot, so I went to look in the usual place I pick those medicines," the herbalist recalled for me. The blood-root was out and the spring beauties, too. She greeted them as she walked past, but saw none of the plant she sought. She stepped more slowly, opening her awareness, making her whole self into a halo of peripheral vision. Nestled at the base of a maple, on the southeast side, the snakeroot made itself visible, a glossy mass of dark-green leaves. She knelt, smiling, and spoke quietly. She thought of her upcoming journey, the empty bag in her pocket, and then slowly rose to her feet. Though her knees were stiff with age, she walked away, refraining from taking the first one.

She wandered through the woods, admiring the trillium just poking their heads up. And the leeks. But there was no more snakeroot. "I just figured I'd have to do without. I was halfway home when I found I'd lost my little shovel, the one I always use for digging medicine. So I had to go back. Well, I found it all right—it's got a red handle so it's easy to find. And you know, it had fallen from my pocket right in a patch of root. So I talked to that plant, addressed it just like you would a person whose help you needed, and it gave me a bit of itself. When I got where I was going, sure enough, there was a woman there who needed that snake-root medicine and I could pass on the gift. That plant reminded me that if we harvest with respect, the plants will help us."

The guidelines for the Honorable Harvest are not written down, or even consistently spoken of as a whole—they are reinforced in small acts of daily life. But if you were to list them, they might look something like this:

> *Know the ways of the ones who take care of you, so that you may*
>   *take care of them.*
> *Introduce yourself. Be accountable as the one who comes asking for life.*
> *Ask permission before taking. Abide by the answer.*
> *Never take the first. Never take the last.*
> *Take only what you need.*
> *Take only that which is given.*
> *Never take more than half. Leave some for others.*
> *Harvest in a way that minimizes harm.*
> *Use it respectfully. Never waste what you have taken.*
> *Share.*
> *Give thanks for what you have been given.*
> *Give a gift, in reciprocity for what you have taken.*
> *Sustain the ones who sustain you and the earth will last forever.*

The state guidelines on hunting and gathering are based exclusively in the biophysical realm, while the rules of the Honorable Harvest are based on accountability to both the physical and the metaphysical worlds. The taking of another life to support your own is far more significant when you recognize the beings who are harvested as persons, nonhuman persons vested with awareness, intelligence, spirit—and who have families waiting for them at home. Killing a *who* demands something different than killing an *it*. When you regard those non-human persons as kinfolk, another set of harvesting regulations extends beyond bag limits and legal seasons.

The state regulations are, by and large, lists of illegal practices: "It is unlawful to keep a rainbow trout whose length from snout to posterior fin does not exceed twelve inches." The consequences for breaking the law are clearly stipulated and involve a financial transaction after a visit with your friendly conservation officer.

Unlike the state laws, the Honorable Harvest is not an enforced legal policy, but it is an agreement nonetheless, among people and most especially between consumers and providers. The providers have the upper hand. The deer, the sturgeon, the berries, and the leeks say, "If you follow these rules, we will continue to give our lives so that you may live."

Imagination is one of our most powerful tools. What we imagine, we can become. I like to imagine what it would be like if the Honorable Harvest were the law of the land today, as it was in our past. Imagine if a developer, eying open land for a shopping mall, had to ask the goldenrod, the meadowlarks, and the monarch butterflies for permission to take their homeland. What if he had to abide by the answer? Why not?

I like to imagine a laminated card, like the one my friend the town clerk hands out with the hunting and fishing licenses, embossed with the rules of the Honorable Harvest. Everyone would be subject to the same laws, since they are, after all, the dictates of the *real* government: the democracy of species, the laws of Mother Nature.

When I ask my elders about the ways our people lived in order to keep the world whole and healthy, I hear the mandate to take only what you need. But we human people, descendants of Nanabozho, struggle, as he did, with self-restraint. The dictum to take only what you need leaves a lot of room for interpretation when our needs get so tangled with our wants.

This gray area yields then to a rule more primal than need, an old teaching nearly forgotten now in the din of industry and technology. Deeply rooted in cultures of gratitude, this ancient rule is not just to take only what you need, but to take only that which is given.

At the level of human interactions, we already do this. It's what we teach our kids. If you're visiting your sweet grandma and she offers you homemade cookies on her favorite china plate, you know what to do. You accept them with many "thank yous" and cherish the relationship reinforced by cinnamon and sugar. You gratefully take what has been given. But you wouldn't dream of breaking into her pantry and just taking all the cookies without invitation, grabbing her china plate for good measure. That would be at a minimum a breach of good manners, a betrayal of the loving relationship. What's more, your grandma would be heartbroken, and not inclined to bake more cookies for you any time soon.

As a culture, though, we seem unable to extend these good manners to the natural world. The dishonorable harvest has become a way of life—we take what doesn't belong to us and destroy it beyond repair: Onondaga Lake, the Alberta tar sands, the rainforests of Malaysia, the list is endless. They are gifts from our sweet Grandmother Earth, which we take without asking. How do we find the Honorable Harvest again?

If we're picking berries or gathering nuts, taking only what is given makes a lot of sense. They offer themselves and by taking them we fulfill our reciprocal responsibility. After all, the plants have made these fruits with the express purpose of our taking them, to disperse and plant. By our use of their gifts, both species prosper and life is magnified. But what about when something is taken without a clear avenue for mutual benefit, when someone is going to lose?

How can we distinguish between that which is given by the earth and that which is not? When does taking become outright theft? I think my elders would counsel that there is no one path, that each of us must find our own way. In my wandering with this question, I've found dead ends and clear openings. Discerning all that it might mean is like bushwhacking through dense undergrowth. Sometimes I get faint glimpses of a deer trail.

It is hunting season and we are sitting on the porch of the cookhouse at Onondaga on a hazy October day. The leaves are smoky gold and fluttering down while we listen to the men tell stories. Jake, with a red bandanna around his hair, gets everybody laughing with a story about Junior's never-fail turkey call. With his feet on the railing and black braid hanging over the back of his chair, Kent tells about following a blood trail over new-fallen snow, bear tracking, and the one that got away. For the most part they're young men with reputations to build, along with one elder.

In a Seventh Generation ball cap and a thin gray ponytail, Oren gets his turn at a story and leads us along with him, through thickets and down ravines to get to his favorite hunting spot. Smiling in recollection, he says, "I must have seen ten deer that day, but I only took one shot." He tips his chair back and looks at the hill, remembering. The young men listen, looking intently at the porch floor. "The first one came crunching through the dry leaves, but was shielded by the brush as it wove down the hill. It never saw me sitting there. Then a young buck came moving upwind toward me and then stepped behind a boulder. I could have tracked it and followed it across the crick, but I knew it wasn't the one." Deer by deer, he recounts the day's encounters for which he never even raised his rifle: the doe by the water, the three-pointer concealed behind a basswood with only its rump showing. "I only take one bullet with me," he says.

The young men in T-shirts lean forward on the bench across from him. "And then, without explanation, there's one who walks right into the clearing and looks you in the eye. He knows full well that you're there and what you're doing. He turns his flank right toward you for a clear shot. I know he's the one, and so does he. There's a kind of nod exchanged. That's why I only carry one shot. I wait for the one. He gave himself to me. That's what I was taught: take only what is given, and then treat it with respect." Oren reminds his listeners, "That's why we thank the deer as the leader of the animals, for its generosity in feeding the people. Acknowledging the lives that support ours and living in a way that demonstrates our gratitude is a force that keeps the world in motion."

The Honorable Harvest does not ask us to photosynthesize. It does not say *don't take*, but offers inspiration and a model for what we *should* take. It's not so much a list of "do not's" as a list of "do's." *Do* eat food that is honorably harvested, and celebrate every mouthful. *Do* use technologies that minimize harm; *do* take what is given. This philosophy guides not only our taking of food, but also any taking of the gifts of Mother Earth—air, water, and the literal body of the earth: the rocks and soil and fossil fuels.

Taking coal buried deep in the earth, for which we must inflict irreparable damage, violates every precept of the code. By no stretch of the imagination is coal "given" to us. We have to wound the land and water to gouge it from Mother Earth. What if a coal company planning mountaintop removal in the ancient folds of the Appalachians were compelled by law to take only that which is given? Don't you long to hand them the laminated card and announce that the rules have changed?

It doesn't mean that we can't consume the energy we need, but it does mean that we honorably take only what is given. The wind blows every day, every day the sun shines, every day the waves roll against the shore, and the earth is warm below us. We can understand these renewable sources of energy as given to us, since they are the sources that have powered life on the planet for as long as there has been a planet. We need not destroy the earth to make use of them. Solar, wind, geothermal, and tidal energy—the so-called "clean energy" harvests—when they are wisely used seem to me to be consistent with the ancient rules of the Honorable Harvest.

And the code might ask of any harvest, including energy, that our purpose be worthy of the harvest. Oren's deer made moccasins and fed three families. What will we use our energy for?

I once gave a lecture titled "Cultures of Gratitude" at a small private college where tuition ran upwards of $40,000 a year. For the allocated fifty-five minutes, I talked about the Thanksgiving Address of the Haudenosaunee, the potlatch tradition of the Pacific Northwest, and the gift economies of Polynesia. Then I told a traditional story of the years when the corn harvests were so plentiful that the caches were full. The fields had been so generous with the villagers that the people scarcely needed to work. So they didn't. Hoes leaned against a tree, idle. The people became so lazy that they let the time for corn ceremonies go by without a single song of gratitude. They began to use the corn in ways the Three Sisters had not intended when they gave the people corn as a sacred gift of food. They burned it for fuel when they couldn't be bothered to cut firewood. The dogs dragged it off from the untidy heaps the people made instead of storing the harvest in secure granaries. No one stopped the kids when they kicked ears around the village in their games.

Saddened by the lack of respect, the Corn Spirit decided to leave, to go where she would be appreciated. At first the people didn't even notice. But the next year, the cornfields were nothing but weeds. The caches were nearly empty and the grain that had been left untended was moldy and mouse-chewed. There was nothing to eat. The people sat about in despair, growing thinner and thinner. When they abandoned gratitude, the gifts abandoned them.

One small child walked out from the village and wandered for hungry days until he found the Corn Spirit in a sunlit clearing in the woods. He begged her to return to his people. She smiled kindly at him and instructed him to teach his people the gratitude and respect that they had forgotten. Only then would she return. He did as she asked and after a hard winter without corn, to remind them of the cost, she returned to them in the spring.*

Several students in my audience yawned. They could not imagine such a thing. The aisles of the grocery store were always well stocked. At a reception afterward the students filled their Styrofoam plates with the usual fare. We exchanged questions and comments while we balanced plastic cups of punch. The students grazed on cheese and crackers, a profusion of cut vegetables, and buckets of dip. There was enough food to feast a small village. The leftovers were swept into trash bins placed conveniently next to the tables.

A beautiful young girl, dark hair tied up in a headscarf, was hanging back from the discussion, waiting her turn. When nearly everyone had left she approached me, gesturing with an apologetic smile at the wasted remains of the reception. "I don't want you to think no one understands what you were saying," she said. "I do. You sound like my grandmother, back in my village in Turkey. I will tell her she must have a sister here in the United States. The Honorable Harvest is her way, too. In her house, we learned that everything we put in our mouths, everything that allows us to live, is the gift of another life. I remember lying with her at night as she made us thank the rafters of her house and the wool blankets we slept in. My grandma wouldn't let us forget that these are all gifts, which is why you take care of everything, to show respect for that life. In

---

* This story is known from the southwest to the northeast. One version is told by Joseph Bruchac, in Caduto and Bruchac's *Keepers of Life*.

my grandmother's house we were taught to kiss the rice. If a single grain fell to the ground, we learned to pick it up and kiss it, to show we meant no disrespect in wasting it." The student told me that, when she came to the United States, the greatest culture shock she experienced was not language or food or technology, but waste.

"I've never told anyone before," she said, "but the cafeteria made me sick, because of the way people treated their food. What people throw away here after one lunch would supply my village for days. I could not speak to anyone of this; no one else would understand to kiss the grain of rice." I thanked her for her story and she said, "Please, take it as a gift, and give it to someone else."

I've heard it said that sometimes, in return for the gifts of the earth, gratitude is enough. It is our uniquely human gift to express thanks, because we have the awareness and the collective memory to remember that the world could well be otherwise, less generous than it is. But I think we are called to go beyond cultures of gratitude, to once again become cultures of reciprocity.

I met Carol Crowe, an Algonquin ecologist, at a meeting on Indigenous models of sustainability. She told the story of requesting funding from her tribal council to attend the conference. They asked her, "What is this all about, this notion of sustainability? What are they talking about?" She gave them a summary of the standard definitions of sustainable development, including "the management of natural resources and social institutions in such a manner as to ensure the attainment and continued satisfaction of human needs for present and future generations." They were quiet for a while, considering. Finally one elder said, "This sustainable development sounds to me like they just want to be able to keep on taking like they always have. It's always about taking. You go there and tell them that in our way, our first thoughts are not 'What can we take?' but 'What can we give to Mother Earth?' That's how it's supposed to be."

The Honorable Harvest asks us to give back, in reciprocity, for what we have been given. Reciprocity helps resolve the moral tension of taking a life by giving in return something of value that sustains the ones who sustain us. One of our responsibilities as human people is to find ways to enter into reciprocity with the more-than-human world. We can do it through gratitude, through ceremony, through land stewardship, science, art, and in everyday acts of practical reverence.

I have to confess that I'd shuttered my mind before I even met him. There was nothing a fur trapper could say that I wanted to hear. Berries, nuts, leeks, and, arguably, that deer who looks you in the eye, are all part of the matrix of the Honorable Harvest, but laying snares for snowy ermine and soft-footed lynx in order to adorn wealthy women is hard to justify. But I would certainly be respectful and listen.

Lionel grew up in the north woods, hunting, fishing, guiding, making a living off the land in a remote log cabin, carrying on the tradition of the *coureurs des bois*. He learned trapping from his Indian grandfather who was renowned for his skills on the trapline. To catch a mink, you have to be able to think like a mink. His grandpa was a successful trapper because of his deep respect for the knowledge of the animals, where they traveled, how they hunted, where they would den up in bad weather. He could see the world through ermine eyes and so provided for his family.

"I loved living in the bush," Lionel says, "and I loved the animals." Fishing and hunting gave the family their food; the trees gave them heat; and after their needs for warm hats and mittens were provided for, the furs they sold every year gave them cash for kerosene, coffee, beans, and school clothes. It was assumed that he would follow in the trade, but as a young man he refused. He wanted nothing more of trapping in the years when leg-hold traps became the norm. It was a cruel technology. He'd seen the animals who gnawed off their feet to free themselves. "Animals do have to die for us to live, but they don't have to suffer," he says.

To stay in the bush he tried logging. He was practiced in the old methods for sledding out timber in the winter along an ice road, felling while the snow blanket protected the earth. But the old, low-impact practices had given way to big machines that ripped up the forest and wrecked the land his animals needed. The dark forest turned to ragged stumps, the clear streams to muddy trenches. He tried to work in the cab of the D9 Cat, and a feller-buncher, a machine designed to take it all. But he couldn't do it.

Then Lionel went to work in the mines at Sudbury, Ontario, left the woods to work underground, digging nickel ore from the earth to be fed into the maw of furnaces. Sulfur dioxide and heavy metals poured from the stacks, making a toxic acid rain that killed every living thing for miles, a gigantic burn mark on the land. Without vegetation, the soil all washed away, leaving a moonscape so bare that NASA used it to test lunar vehicles. The metal smelters at Sudbury held the earth in a leg-hold trap, and the forest was dying a slow and painful death. Too late, after the damage was done, Sudbury became the poster child for clean-air legislation.

There is no shame in working the mines to feed your family—an exchange of hard labor in return for food and shelter—but you want your labor to count for something more. Driving home each night through the moonscape his labor created, he felt blood on his hands, and so he quit.

Today Lionel spends his winter days on snowshoes on his trapline and winter nights preparing furs. Unlike the harsh chemicals of the factory, brain tanning yields the softest, most durable hide. He says with wonder in his voice and a soft moose hide on his lap, "There is just enough in each animal's brain to tan its own hide." His own brain and his heart led him back home to the woods.

Lionel is of the Métis Nation; he calls himself "a blue-eyed Indian," raised in the deep woods of northern Quebec, as his melodious accent suggests. His conversation is so delightfully sauced with "*Oui, oui, madame*" that I imagine he will kiss my hand at any moment. His own hands are telling: woodsman's hands broad and strong enough to set a trap or a logging chain but sensitive enough to stroke a pelt to gauge its thickness. By the time we spoke, leg-hold traps had been banned in Canada and only body-hold traps that ensure a sudden death were permitted. He demonstrates one: it takes two strong arms to open and set, and its powerful snap would break a neck in an instant.

Trappers spend more time on the land than anyone else these days, and they maintain detailed records of their harvest. Lionel keeps a thickly penciled notebook in his vest pocket; he takes it out and waves it, saying, "Wanna see my new BlackBerry? I just download my data to my bush computer, runs on propane, don't you know."

His traplines yield beaver, lynx, coyote, fisher, mink, and ermine. He runs his hand over the pelts, explaining about the density of the winter undercoat and the long guard hairs, how you can judge the health of an animal by its fur. He pauses when he comes to martens, whose pelage is legendary in its silky-soft luxury—the American sable. It is beautifully colored and feather light.

Martens are part of Lionel's life here—they're his neighbors and he is thankful that they have rebounded from near extirpation. Trappers like him are on the front line of monitoring wildlife populations and well-being. They have a responsibility to take care of the species they rely upon, and every visit to the trapline produces data that govern the trapper's response. "If we catch only male martens, we will keep the traps open," he says. When there is an excess of unpaired males, they are wandering and easy to trap. Too many young males can leave less food for the others. "But as soon as we get a female, we stop trapping. That means we've skimmed off the excess and we don't touch the rest. That way the population doesn't get too crowded, none will go hungry, but their population will continue to grow."

In late winter, when the snow is still heavy but the days are lengthening, Lionel drags down the ladder from the rafters in his garage. He straps on his snowshoes and stomps out into the bush with the ladder on his shoulder and hammer, nails, and scrap wood in his pack basket. He scouts out just the right spots: big old trees with cavities are best, as long as the size and shape of the hole dictates that only a single species can use it. He climbs to where the ladder, anchored in the snow, leans against a high branch and he constructs a platform. He makes it home before dark and rises the next day to do it again. It's hard work lugging a ladder through the woods. When he's done with the platforms, he pulls a white plastic pail from the freezer and sets it by the woodstove to thaw.

All summer long Lionel serves as a fishing guide on the remote lakes and rivers of his birth. He jokes that he works for only himself now and he calls his company See More and Do Less. Not a bad business plan. When he and his "sports" clean their catch he scrapes the guts into big white pails and keeps them in his freezer. He overheard his clients whispering, "Must be he eats fish-gut stew in the winter."

The next day he's off again, pulling the bucket on a sled, miles down the trapline. At every platform tree, he scrambles up the ladder, with somewhat less grace than a weasel, one-handed. (You don't want to slop fish guts all over yourself.) He shovels out a big smelly scoop onto each platform and then hikes off to the next.

Like many predators, martens are slow reproducers, which makes them vulnerable to decline, especially when they're exploited. Gestation is about nine months, and they don't give birth until they're three years old. They'll have from one to four young and raise only as many as the food supply allows. "I put out the gut piles in the last weeks before the little mothers give birth," Lionel says. "If you put them where nothing else can get them, those mothers will have some extra-good meals. That will help them to nurse their babies so more will survive, especially if we get a late snow or something." The tenderness in his voice makes me think of a neighbor delivering a warm casserole to a shut-in. It's not how I've thought of trappers. "Well," he says, blushing a little, "dose little martens take care of me and I take care of dem."

The teachings tell us that a harvest is made honorable by what you give in return for what you take. There is no escaping the fact that Lionel's care will result in more martens on his trapline. There is no escaping the fact that they will also be killed. Feeding mama martens is not altruism; it is deep respect for the way the world works, for the connections between us, of life flowing into life. The more he gives, the more he can take, and he goes the extra mile to give more than he takes.

I'm moved by Lionel's affection and respect for these animals, for the care that flows from his intimate knowledge of their needs. He lives the tension of loving his prey and resolves it for himself by practicing the tenets of the Honorable Harvest. But there is also no escaping the fact that the marten pelts are likely to become a luxury coat for a very wealthy person, perhaps the owner of the Sudbury mine.

These animals will die by his hand, but first they will live well, in part by his hand. His lifestyle, which I had condemned without understanding, protects the forest, protects the lakes and rivers, not just for him and the furbearers, but for all the forest beings. A harvest is made honorable when it sustains the giver as well as the taker. And today Lionel is also a gifted teacher, invited to schools far and wide to share his traditional knowledge of wildlife and conservation. He is giving back what was given to him.

It's hard for the guy wearing the sable in the corner office of Sudbury to imagine Lionel's world, to even conceive of a way of living that would require him to consider taking only what he needs, to give back in reciprocity for what he takes, to nurture the world that nurtures him, to carry meals to a nursing mother in a wild treetop den. But unless we want more wastelands, he needs to learn.

These may seem like charming anachronisms, rules for hunting and gathering whose relevance vanished along with the buffalo. But remember that the buffalo are not extinct and in fact are making a resurgence under the care of those who remember. The canon of the Honorable Harvest is poised to make its comeback, too, as people remember that what's good for the land is also good for the people.

We need acts of restoration, not only for polluted waters and degraded lands, but also for our relationship to the world. We need to restore honor to the way we live, so that when we walk through the world we don't have to avert our eyes with shame, so that we can hold our heads up high and receive the respectful acknowledgment of the rest of the earth's beings.

I feel lucky to have wild leeks, dandelion greens, marsh marigolds, and hickory nuts—if I get there before the squirrels do. But these are decorations on a diet that comes mostly from my garden and from the grocery store, like everyone else, especially now that more people live in urban centers than the countryside.

Cities are like the mitochondria in our animal cells—they are consumers, fed by the autotrophs, the photosynthesis of a distant green landscape. We could lament that urban dwellers have little means of exercising direct reciprocity with the land. Yet while city folks may be separated from the sources of what they consume, they can exercise reciprocity through how they spend their money. While the digging of the leeks and the digging of the coal may be too far removed to see, we consumers have a potent tool of reciprocity right in our pockets. We can use our dollars as the indirect currency of reciprocity.

Perhaps we can think of the Honorable Harvest as a mirror by which we judge our purchases. What do we see in the mirror? A purchase worthy of the lives consumed? Dollars become a surrogate, a proxy for the harvester with hands in the earth, and they can be used in support of the Honorable Harvest—or not.

It's easy to make this argument, and I believe that the principles of the Honorable Harvest have great resonance in an era when overconsumption threatens every dimension of our well-being. But it can be too easy to shift the burden of responsibility to the coal company or the land developers. What about me, the one who buys what they sell, who is complicit in the dishonorable harvest?

I live in the country, where I grow a big garden, get eggs from my neighbor's farm, buy apples from the next valley over, pick berries and greens from my few rewilding acres. A lot of what I own is secondhand, or third. The desk that I'm writing on was once a fine dining table that someone set out on the curb. But while I heat with wood, compost and recycle, and do myriad other responsible things, if I did an honest inventory of my household, most of it would probably not make the grade of the Honorable Harvest.

I want to do the experiment, to see if one can subsist in this market economy and still practice the rules of the Honorable Harvest. So I take my shopping list and go forth.

Actually, our local grocery store makes it pretty easy to be mindful of the choices and the mantra of mutual benefit for land and people. They've partnered with farmers for local organic goods at a price normal people can afford. They're big on "green" and recycled products, too, so I can hold my toilet paper purchase up to the mirror of the Honorable Harvest without flinching. When I walk the aisles with open eyes, the source of the food is mostly evident, although Cheetos and Ding Dongs remain an ecological mystery. For the most part, I can use dollars as the currency of good ecological choices, alongside my questionable but persistent need for chocolate.

I don't have much patience with food proselytizers who refuse all but organic, free-range, fair-trade gerbil milk. We each do what we can; the Honorable Harvest is as much about the relationships as about the materials. A friend of mine says she buys just one green item a week—that's all she can do, so she does it. "I want to vote with my dollar," she says. I can make choices because I have the disposable income to choose "green" over less-expensive goods, and I hope that will drive the market in the right direction. In the food deserts of the South Side there is no such choice, and the dishonor in that inequity runs far deeper than the food supply.

I am stopped in my tracks in the produce section. There on a Styrofoam tray, sheathed in plastic and tagged at the princely sum of $15.50 per pound, are Wild Leeks. The plastic presses down on them: they look trapped and suffocated. Alarm bells go off in my head, alarms of commoditization of what should be regarded as a gift and all the dangers that follow from that kind of thinking. Selling leeks makes them into mere objects and cheapens them, even at $15.50 per pound. Wild things should not be for sale.

Next stop is the mall, a place I try to avoid at all costs, but today I will go into the belly of the beast in service to my experiment. I sit in the car for a few minutes trying to rouse the same attunement and outlook with which I go to the woods, receptive, observant, and grateful, but I'll be gathering a new stock of paper and pens instead of wild leeks.

There is a stone wall to cross here, too, the three-story edifice of the mall, bordered by another lifeless field of parking lot, with crows perched on the stanchions. As I cross the wall, the floor is hard beneath my feet and heels click on the faux-marble tile. I pause to take in the sounds. Inside, there are neither crows nor wood thrushes, but rather a soundtrack of strangely sanitized oldies set to strings, hovering above the drone of the ventilation system. The light is dim fluorescent with spotlights to dapple the floor, the better to highlight the splashes of color which identify the shops, their logos as readily identifiable as patches of bloodroot across the forest. Like in the spring woods, the air is a patchwork of scents that I walk among: coffee here, cinnamon buns there, a shop of scented candles, and beneath it all the pervasive tang of fast-food Chinese from the food court.

At the end of the wing, I spy the habitat of my quarry. I navigate easily, as I've been coming here for years for my traditional harvest of writing supplies. At the store entrance is a stack of bright red plastic shopping bins with metal handles. I pick one up and again become the woman with the basket. In the paper aisle I am confronted with a great diversity of species of paper—wide ruled and narrow, copier paper, stationery, spiral bound, loose-leaf—arrayed in clonal patches by brand and purpose. I see just what I want, my favorite legal pads, as yellow as a downy violet.

I stand before them trying to conjure the gathering mentality, to bring all the rules of the Honorable Harvest to bear, but I can't do it without the bite of mockery. I try to sense the trees in that stack of paper and address my thoughts to them, but the taking of their lives is so far removed from this shelf that there is just a distant echo. I think about the harvesting method: were they clear-cut? I think about the stink of the paper mill, the effluent, the dioxin. Fortunately, there is a stack labeled "Recycled," so I choose those, paying a little more for the privilege. I pause and consider whether the yellow dyed may be worse than the white bleached. I have my suspicions, but I choose the yellow as I always do. It looks so nice with green or purple ink, like a garden.

I wander next to the pen aisle, or as they call it, "writing instruments." The choices here are even more numerous and I have no idea at all where they came from, except some petrochemical synthesis.

How can I bring honor to this purchase, use my dollars as the currency of honor when the lives behind the product are invisible? I stand there so long that an "associate" comes to ask if I'm looking for anything in particular. I guess I look like a shoplifter planning a heist of "writing instruments" with my little red basket. I'd like to ask him, "Where did these things come from? What are they made of and which one was made with a technology that inflicts minimal damage on the earth? Can I buy pens with the same mentality with which a person digs wild leeks?" But I suspect he would call security on the little earpiece attached to his jaunty store cap, so I just choose my favorite, for the feel of the nib against the paper and the purple and green ink. At the checkout I engage in reciprocity, tendering my credit card in return for writing supplies. Both the clerk and I say thank you, but not to the trees.

I'm trying hard to make this work, but what I feel in the woods, the pulsing animacy, is simply not here. I realize why the tenets of reciprocity don't work here, why this glittering labyrinth seems to make a mockery of the Honorable Harvest. It's so obvious, but I didn't see it, so intent was I on searching for the lives behind the products. I couldn't find them because the lives aren't here. Everything for sale here is dead.

I get a cup of coffee and sit on a bench to watch the scene unfold, gathering evidence as best I can, notebook open in my lap. Sullen teenagers wanting to buy their selfhood and sad-looking old men sitting alone at the food court. Even the plants are plastic. I've never been shopping like this before, with such intentional awareness of what goes on here. I suppose I've blocked it out in my usual hurry to get in, make my purchase, and get out. But now I scan the landscape with all senses heightened. Open to the T-shirts, the plastic earrings, and the iPods. Open to shoes that hurt, delusions that hurt, and mountains of needless stuff that hurts the chances that my grandchildren will have a good green earth to care for. It hurts me even to bring the ideas of the Honorable Harvest here; I feel protective of them. I want to cup them like a small warm animal in my hands and shelter them from the onslaught of their antithesis. But I know they are stronger than this.

It's not the Honorable Harvest that is the aberration, though—it is this marketplace. As leeks cannot survive in a cutover forest, the Honorable Harvest cannot survive in this habitat. We have constructed an artifice, a Potemkin village of an ecosystem where we perpetrate the illusion that the things we consume have just fallen off the back of Santa's sleigh, not been ripped from the earth. The illusion enables us to imagine that the only choices we have are between brands.

Back home I wash away the last bits of black soil and trim the long white roots. One big handful of leeks we set aside, unwashed. The girls chop the slender bulbs and the leaves, and they all go into my favorite cast iron skillet with way more butter than a person should probably have. The aroma of sautéed leeks fills the kitchen. Just breathing it in is good medicine. The sharp pungency dissipates quickly and the fragrance that lingers is deep and savory, with a hint of leaf mold and rainwater. Potato leek soup, wild leek risotto, or just a bowl of leeks are nourishment for body and soul. When my daughters leave on Sunday, I'm happy to know that something of their childhood woods will travel with them.

After dinner, I take the basket of unwashed leeks to the tiny patch of forest above my pond to plant them. The harvesting process now unfolds in reverse. I ask permission to bring them here, to open the earth for their arrival. I search out the rich moist hollows and tuck them into the soil, emptying my basket instead of filling it. These woods are second or third growth and sadly lost their leeks long ago. It turns out that when forests around here grow back after agricultural clearing, the trees come back readily but the understory plants do not.

From a distance the new postagricultural woods look healthy; the trees came back thick and strong. But inside something is missing. The April showers do not bring May flowers. No trillium, no mayapple, no bloodroot. Even after a century of regrowth, the postfarming forests are impoverished, while the untilled forests just across the wall are an explosion of blossoms. The medicines are missing, for reasons ecologists do not yet understand. It might be microhabitat, it might be dispersal, but it is clear that the original habitat for these old medicines was obliterated in a cascade of unintended consequences as the land was turned to corn. The land is no longer hospitable for the medicines and we don't know why.

The Skywoman woods across the valley have never been plowed, so they still have their full glory, but most other woods are missing their forest floor. Leek-laden woods have become a rarity. Left to time and chance alone, my cutover woods would probably never recover their leeks or their trillium. The way I see it, it's up to me to carry them over the wall. Over the years, this replanting on my hillside has yielded small patches of vibrant green in April and nurtures the hope that the leeks can return to their homelands and that when I'm an old lady I'll have a celebratory spring supper close at hand. They give to me, I give to them. Reciprocity is an investment in abundance for both the eater and the eaten.

We need the Honorable Harvest today. But like the leeks and the marten, it is an endangered species that arose in another landscape, another time, from a legacy of traditional knowledge. That ethic of reciprocity was cleared away along with the forests, the beauty of justice traded away for more stuff. We've created a cultural and economic landscape that is hospitable to the growth of neither leeks nor honor. If the earth is nothing more than inanimate matter, if lives are nothing more than commodities, then the way of the Honorable Harvest, too, is dead. But when you stand in the stirring spring woods, you know otherwise.

It is an animate earth that we hear calling to us to feed the martens and kiss the rice. Wild leeks and wild ideas are in jeopardy. We have to transplant them both and nurture their return to the lands of their birth. We have to carry them across the wall, restoring the Honorable Harvest, bringing back the medicine.

Braiding Sweetgrass

Sweetgrass, as the hair of Mother Earth, is traditionally braided to show loving care for her well-being. Braids, plaited of three strands, are given away as signs of kindness and gratitude.

In the Footsteps of Nanabozho:
Becoming Indigenous to Place

F og shrouds the land. There is just this rock in the half-darkness and the surf, rising and falling with a thunderous roar, reminding me how tenuous my perch is on this tiny island. I almost feel her feet on these cold, wet rocks instead of my own; Skywoman on a speck of land, alone in a cold dark sea, before she made our home. When she fell from Skyworld, Turtle Island was her Plymouth Rock, her Ellis Island. The Mother of the People was first an immigrant.

I'm new here too, on this shore at the western edge of the continent, new to how land appears and disappears in this place with the tides and with the fog. No one knows my name here, and I don't know theirs. Without this exchange of the barest recognition, I feel like I could disappear in the fog along with everything else.

It is said that the Creator gathered together the four sacred elements and breathed life into them to give form to Original Man before setting him upon Turtle Island. The last of all beings to be created, First Man was given the name Nanabozho. The Creator called out the name to the four directions so that the others would know who was coming. Nanabozho, part man, part *manido*—a powerful spirit-being—is the personification of life forces, the Anishinaabe culture hero, and our great teacher of how to be human. In Nanabozho's form as Original Man and in our own, we humans are the newest arrivals on earth, the youngsters, just learning to find our way.

I can imagine how it might have been for him in the beginning, before anyone knew him and he did not know them. I too was a stranger at first in this dark dripping forest perched at the edge of the sea, but I sought out an elder, my Sitka Spruce grandmother with a lap wide enough for many grandchildren. I introduced myself, told her my name and why I had come. I offered her tobacco from my pouch and asked if I might visit in her community for a time. She asked me to sit down, and there was a place right between her roots. Her canopy towers above the forest and her swaying foliage is constantly murmuring to her neighbors. I know she'll eventually pass the word and my name on the wind.

Nanabozho did not know his parentage or his origins—only that he was set down into a fully peopled world of plants and animals, winds, and water. He was an immigrant too. Before he arrived, the world was all here, in balance and harmony, each one fulfilling their purpose in the Creation. He understood, as some did not, that this was not the "New World," but one that was ancient before he came.

The ground where I sit with Sitka Grandmother is deep with needles, soft with centuries of humus; the trees are so old that my lifetime compared to theirs is just a birdsong long. I suspect that Nanabozho walked like I do, in awe, looking up into the trees so often I stumble.

The Creator gave Nanabozho some tasks in his role as Original Man, his Original Instructions.* Anishinaabe elder Eddie Benton-Banai beautifully retells the story of Nanabozho's first work: to walk through the world that Skywoman had danced into life. His instructions were to walk in such a way "that each step is a greeting to Mother Earth," but he wasn't quite sure yet what that meant. Fortunately, although his were the First Man's prints upon the earth, there were many paths to follow, made by all those whose home this already was.

The time when the Original Instructions were given we might call "a long time ago." For in the popular way of thinking, history draws a time "line," as if time marched in lockstep in only one direction. Some people say that time is a river into which we can step but once, as it flows in a

---

* This traditional teaching has been published in Eddie Benton-Banais's *The Mishomis Book*.

straight path to the sea. But Nanabozho's people know time as a circle. Time is not a river running inexorably to the sea, but the sea itself—its tides that appear and disappear, the fog that rises to become rain in a different river. All things that were will come again.

In the way of linear time, you might hear Nanabozho's stories as mythic lore of history, a recounting of the long-ago past and how things came to be. But in circular time, these stories are both history and prophecy, stories for a time yet to come. If time is a turning circle, there is a place where history and prophecy converge—the footprints of First Man lie on the path behind us and on the path ahead.

With all the power and all the failings of a human being, Nanabozho did his best with the Original Instructions and tried to become native to his new home. His legacy is that we are still trying. But the instructions have gotten tattered along the way and many have been forgotten.

After all these generations since Columbus, some of the wisest of Native elders still puzzle over the people who came to our shores. They look at the toll on the land and say, "The problem with these new people is that they don't have both feet on the shore. One is still on the boat. They don't seem to know whether they're staying or not." This same observation is heard from some contemporary scholars who see in the social pathologies and relentlessly materialist culture the fruit of homelessness, a rootless past. America has been called the home of second chances. For the sake of the peoples and the land, the urgent work of the Second Man may be to set aside the ways of the colonist and become Indigenous to place. But can Americans, as a nation of immigrants, learn to live here as if we were staying? With both feet on the shore?

What happens when we truly become native to a place, when we finally make a home? Where are the stories that lead the way? If time does in fact eddy back on itself, maybe the journey of the First Man will provide footsteps to guide the journey of the Second.

Nanabozho's journey first took him toward the rising sun, to the place where the day begins. As he walked, he worried how he would eat, especially as he was already hungry. How would he find his way? He considered the Original Instructions and understood that all the knowledge he needed in order to live was present in the land. His role was not to control or change the world as a human, but to learn from the world how to be human.

Wabunong—the East—is the direction of knowledge. We send gratitude to the East for the chance to learn every day, to start anew. In the East, Nanabozho received the lesson that Mother Earth is our wisest teacher. He came to know *sema*, the sacred tobacco, and how to use it to carry his thoughts to the Creator.

As he continued exploring the land, Nanabozho was given a new responsibility: to learn the names of all the beings. He watched them carefully to see how they lived and spoke with them to learn what gifts they carried in order to discern their true names. Right away he began to feel more at home and was not lonely anymore when he could call the others by name and they called out to him when he passed, *"Bozho!"*—still our greeting to one another today.

Today, far from my neighbors in Maple Nation, I see some species I recognize and many I do not, so I walk as Original Man may have done, seeing them for the first time. I try to turn off my science mind and name them with a Nanabozho mind. I've noticed that once some folks attach a scientific label to a being, they stop exploring who it is. But with newly created names I keep looking even closer, to see if I've gotten it right. And so today it is not *Picea sitchensis* but *strong arms covered in moss. Branch like a wing* instead of *Thuja plicata*.

Most people don't know the names of these relatives; in fact, they hardly even see them. Names are the way we humans build relationship, not only with each other but with the living world. I'm trying to imagine what it would be like going through life not knowing the names of the plants and animals around you. Given who I am and what I do, I can't know what that's like, but I think it would be a little scary and disorienting—like being lost in a foreign city where you can't read the street signs. Philosophers call this state of isolation and disconnection "species loneliness"—a deep, unnamed sadness stemming from estrangement from the rest of Creation, from the loss of relationship. As our human dominance of the world has grown, we have become more isolated, more lonely when we can no longer call out to our neighbors. It's no wonder that naming was the first job the Creator gave Nanabozho.

He walked the land, handing out names to all he met, an Anishinaabe Linnaeus. I like to think of the two of them walking together. Linnaeus the Swedish botanist and zoologist, in his loden jacket and woolen trousers, with felt hat cocked back on his forehead and a vasculum under his arm, and Nanabozho naked but for his breechcloth and a single feather, with a buckskin bag under his arm. They stroll along discussing the names for things. They're both so enthusiastic, pointing out the beautiful leaf shapes, the incomparable flowers. Linnaeus explains his *Systema Naturae*, a scheme designed to show the ways in which all things are related. Nanabozho nods enthusiastically, "Yes, that is also our way: we say, 'We are all related.'" He explains that there was a time when all beings spoke the same language and could understand one another, so all of Creation knew each other's names. Linnaeus looks wistful about that. "I ended up having to translate everything into Latin," he says of binomial nomenclature. "We lost any other common language long ago." Linnaeus lends Nanabozho his magnifying glass so he can see the tiny floral parts. Nanabozho gives Linnaeus a song so he can see their spirits. And neither of them are lonely.

After his eastern sojourn, Nanabozho's footsteps took him next to the South, *zhawanong*, the land of birth and growth. From the South comes the green that covers the world in spring, carried on the warm winds. There, cedar, *kizhig*, the sacred plant of the South, shared her teachings with him. Her branches are medicine that purify and protect life within her embrace. He carried *kizhig* with him to remind him that to be Indigenous is to protect life on earth.

Following the Original Instructions, Benton-Banai recounts that Nanabozho also had the task to learn how to live from his elder brothers and sisters. When he needed food, he noticed what the animals were eating and copied them. Heron taught him to gather wild rice. One night by the creek, he saw a little ring-tailed animal carefully washing his food with delicate hands. He thought, "Ahh, I am supposed to put only clean food in my body."

Nanabozho was counseled by many plants too, who shared gifts, and learned to treat them always with the greatest respect. After all, plants were here first on the earth and have had a long time to figure things out. Together, all the beings, both plants and animals, taught him what he needed to know. The Creator had told him it would be this way.

His elder brothers and sisters also inspired Nanabozho to make new things in order to survive. Beaver showed him how to make an ax; Whale gave him the shape for his canoe. He'd been instructed that if he could combine the lessons from nature with the strength of his own good mind, he could discover new things that would be useful for the people to come. In his mind, Grandmother Spider's web became a fish-net. He followed the winter lessons of squirrels to create maple sugar. The lessons Nanabozho learned are the mythic roots of Native science, medicine, architecture, agriculture, and ecological knowledge.

But true to the circle of time, science and technology are starting to catch up with Native science by adopting the Nanabozho approach— looking to nature for models of design, by the architects of biomimicry. By honoring the knowledge in the land, and caring for its keepers, we start to become Indigenous to place.

To each of the four directions Nanabozho wandered on long, strong legs. Singing loudly as he went, he didn't hear the bird's chirps of caution and was duly surprised when Grizzly challenged him. After that, when he came near the territories of others, he did not just blunder in as if the whole world belonged to him. He learned to sit quietly at the edge of the woods and wait to be invited. Then, Benton-Banai recounts, Nanabozho would rise and speak these words to the citizens of that place: "I wish not to mar the beauty of the earth or to disturb my brother's purpose. I ask that I be allowed to pass."

He saw flowers blooming through the snow, Ravens who spoke to Wolves, and insects who lit the prairie nights. His gratitude for their abilities grew and he came to understand that to carry a gift is also to carry a responsibility. The Creator gave Wood Thrush the gift of a beautiful song, with the duty to sing the forest good-night. Late at night he was grateful that the stars were sparkling to guide his way. Breathing under water, flying to the ends of the earth and back, digging earthen dens, making medicines. Every being with a gift, every being with a responsibility. He considered his own empty hands. He had to rely on the world to take care of him.

From my high bluff on the coast I look east and the hills before me are a ragged range of clear-cut forests. To the south I see an estuary dammed and diked so that salmon may no longer pass. On the western horizon, a bottom-dragging trawler scrapes up the ocean floor. And far away to the north, the earth is torn open for oil.

Had the new people learned what Original Man was taught at a council of animals—never damage Creation, and never interfere with the sacred purpose of another being—the eagle would look down on a different world. The salmon would be crowding up the rivers, and passenger pigeons would darken the sky. Wolves, cranes, *Nehalem*, cougars, *Lenape*, old-growth forests would still be here, each fulfilling their sacred purpose. I would be speaking Potawatomi. We would see what Nanabozho saw. It does not bear too much imagining, for in that direction lies heartbreak.

Against the backdrop of that history, an invitation to settler society to become Indigenous to place feels like a free ticket to a house-breaking party. It could be read as an open invitation to take what little is left. Can settlers be trusted to follow Nanabozho, to walk so that "each step is a greeting to Mother Earth"? Grief and fear still sit in the shadows, behind the glimmer of hope. Together they try to hold my heart closed.

But I need to remember that the grief is the settlers' as well. They too will never walk in a tallgrass prairie where sunflowers dance with goldfinches. Their children have also lost the chance to sing at the Maple Dance. They can't drink the water either.

In his journey to the North, Nanabozho found the medicine teachers. They gave him *Wiingaashk* to teach him the ways of compassion, kindness, and healing, even for those who have made bad mistakes, for who has not? To become Indigenous is to grow the circle of healing to include all of Creation. Sweetgrass, in a long braid, offers protection to a traveler, and Nanabozho put some in his bag. A path scented with sweetgrass leads to a landscape of forgiveness and healing for all who need it. She doesn't give her gift only to some.

When Nanabozho came to the West, he found many things that frightened him. The earth shook beneath his feet. He saw great fires consume the land. Sage, *mshkodewashk,* the sacred plant of the west, was there to help him, to wash away fear. Benton-Banai reminds us that Firekeeper himself came to Nanabozho. "This is the same fire that warms your lodge," he said. "All powers have two sides, the power to create and the power to destroy. We must recognize them both, but invest our gifts on the side of creation."

Nanabozho learned that in the duality of all things, he had a twin brother who was as committed to making imbalance as Nanabozho was dedicated to balance. That twin had learned the interplay of creation and destruction and rocked it like a boat on a choppy sea to keep people out of balance. He found that the arrogance of power could be used to unleash unlimited growth—an unrestrained, cancerous sort of creation that would lead to destruction. Nanabozho vowed to walk with humility in order to try to balance his twin's arrogance. That too is the task of those who would walk in his footsteps.

I go to sit with my Sitka Spruce grandmother to think. I am not from here, just a stranger who comes with gratitude and respect and questions of how it is we come to belong to a place. And yet she makes me welcome, just as we are told the big trees of the west kindly looked after Nanabozho.

Even as I sit in her still shadow, my thoughts are all tangled. Like my elders before me, I want to envision a way that an immigrant society could become Indigenous to place, but I'm stumbling on the words. Immigrants cannot by definition be Indigenous. *Indigenous* is a birthright word. No amount of time or caring changes history or substitutes for soul-deep fusion with the land. Following Nanabozho's footsteps doesn't guarantee transformation of Second Man to First. But if people do not feel "Indigenous," can they nevertheless enter into the deep reciprocity that renews the world? Is this something that can be learned? Where are the teachers? I'm remembering the words of elder Henry Lickers. "You know, they came here thinking they'd get rich by working on the land. So they dug their mines and cut down the trees. But the land is the one with the power—while they were working on the land, the land was working on them. Teaching them."

I sit a long time and eventually the sound of the wind in Grandmother Sitka's branches washes words away and I lose myself in just listening—to the crisp voice of laurels, the chatter of alders, the whispers of lichens. I have to be reminded—just like Nanabozho—that the plants are our oldest teachers.

I get up from my needle-soft nook between Grandmother's roots and walk back to the trail, where I am stopped in my tracks. Bedazzled by my new neighbors—giant firs, sword fern, and salal—I had passed by an old friend without recognition. I'm embarrassed to not have greeted him before. From the east coast to the edge of the west, he had walked here. Our people have a name for this round-leafed plant: White Man's Footstep.

Just a low circle of leaves, pressed close to the ground with no stem to speak of, it arrived with the first settlers and followed them everywhere they went. It trotted along paths through the woods, along wagon roads and railroads, like a faithful dog so as to be near them. Linnaeus called it *Plantago major*, the common plantain. Its Latin epithet *Plantago* refers to the sole of a foot.

At first the Native people were distrustful of a plant that came with so much trouble trailing behind. But Nanabozho's people knew that all things have a purpose and that we must not interfere with its fulfillment. When it became clear that White Man's Footstep would be staying on Turtle Island, they began to learn about its gifts. In spring it makes a good pot of greens, before summer heat turns the leaves tough. The people became glad for its constant presence when they learned that the leaves, when they are rolled or chewed to a poultice, make a fine first aid for cuts, burns, and especially insect bites. Every part of the plant is useful. Those tiny seeds are good medicine for digestion. The leaves can halt bleeding right away and heal wounds without infection.

This wise and generous plant, faithfully following the people, became an honored member of the plant community. It's a foreigner, an immigrant, but after five hundred years of living as a good neighbor, people forget that kind of thing.

Our immigrant plant teachers offer a lot of different models for how *not* to make themselves welcome on a new continent. Garlic mustard poisons the soil so that native species will die. Tamarisk uses up all the water. Foreign invaders like loosestrife, kudzu, and cheat grass have the colonizing habit of taking over others' homes and growing without regard to limits. But Plantain is not like that. Its strategy was to be useful, to fit into small places, to coexist with others around the dooryard, to heal wounds. Plantain is so prevalent, so well integrated, that we think of it as native. It has earned the name bestowed by botanists for plants that have become our own. Plantain is not Indigenous but "naturalized." This is the same term we use for the foreign-born when they become citizens in our country. They pledge to uphold the laws of the state. They might well uphold Nanabozho's Original Instructions, too.

Maybe the task assigned to Second Man is to unlearn the model of kudzu and follow the teachings of White Man's Footstep, to strive to become naturalized to place, to throw off the mind-set of the immigrant. Being naturalized to place means to live as if this is the land that feeds you, as if these are the streams from which you drink, that build your body and fill your spirit. To become naturalized is to know that your ancestors lie in this ground. Here you will give your gifts and meet your responsibilities. To become naturalized is to live as if your children's future matters, to take care of the land as if our lives and the lives of all our relatives depend on it. Because they do.

As time circles around on itself again, maybe White Man's Footstep *is* following in Nanabozho's. Perhaps Plantain will line the homeward path. We could follow. White Man's Footstep, generous and healing, grows with its leaves so close to the ground that each step is a greeting to Mother Earth.

The Sound of Silverbells

I'd never wanted to live in the South, but when my husband's job took us there I duly learned the flora and tried to cultivate affection for the drab oaks when I longed for fiery maples. Even if I did not feel fully at home, the least I could do was help my students develop a sense of botanical belonging.

In pursuit of this humble goal, I had taken my premed students to a local nature reserve where the forest marched up the slope in bands of color signifying ribbons of different species from the floodplain to the ridge. I asked them to invent a hypothesis or two to explain why the striking pattern existed.

"It's all part of God's plan," said one student. "You know, the grand design?" After ten years of immersion in the primacy of materialist science as the explanation for the function of the world, I had to swallow hard. Where I'm from, an answer like that would have drawn laughter or at least rolled eyes, but in this group it simply yielded nods of assent, or at the least tolerance. "That's an important perspective," I said carefully, "but scientists have a different explanation for the distribution of vegetation over the landscape, maples in one place, and spruce in another."

This was a dance I was trying to get used to, teaching in the Bible Belt. I stumbled over two very left feet. "Have you ever wondered how the world got to be put together so beautifully? Why certain plants grow here and not there?" Judging by their polite blankness, this was not a burning question for them. Their total disinterest in ecology pained me. To me ecological insight was the music of the spheres, but to them it was just one more requirement in their premed education. A biological story that wasn't about humans was of little interest. I didn't understand how one could be a biologist without being able to see the land, to know natural history and the elegant flow of natural forces. The earth is so richly endowed that the least we can do in return is to pay attention. And so, with a little evangelical fervor of my own, I set my sights on the conversion of their scientific souls.

All eyes were on me, waiting for failure, so I paid attention to every little detail, just to prove them wrong. Vans idled in the circle in front of the administration building while I checked my list one more time: maps prepared, campsites reserved, eighteen pairs of binoculars, six field microscopes, three days of food, first aid kits, and reams of handouts of graphs and scientific names. The dean argued that it was too expensive to take students into the field. I argued that it was too costly not to. Whether the passengers were willing or not, our little convoy of college vans was headed down the highway through the sheared-off mountaintops of coal country where the streams run red with acid. Shouldn't students devoted to a profession in health see this firsthand?

The hours on a dark highway gave me plenty of time to consider the wisdom of trying the dean's patience in my very first job. The college was already struggling with finances, and I was just a part-time instructor teaching a few classes while I finished my dissertation. I'd left my baby girls at home with their dad in order to introduce other people's children to something they cared little about. This exclusive little college had built its reputation in the South on the successful admission of its students to medical school. Accordingly, the sons and daughters of the bluegrass aristocracy were sent here for their first step toward lives of privilege.

In keeping with this medical mission, the dean ritually donned a white coat every morning as a priest dons his vestments. His desk calendar called only for administrative meetings, budget reviews, and alumni functions, but the lab coat was a fixture. Though I never saw him in an actual lab, it was no wonder that he harbored doubts about a flannel-shirt scientist like me.

The biologist Paul Ehrlich called ecology "the subversive science" for its power to cause us to reconsider the place of humans in the natural world. So far, these students had devoted several years to the study of a single species: themselves. I had a whole three days to be subversive, to distract them from *Homo sapiens* for a glimpse of the six million other species with whom we share the planet. The dean voiced his concerns about funding a "mere camping trip," but I argued that the Great Smoky Mountains were a major reservoir of biodiversity and promised that it would be a legitimate scientific expedition. I was tempted to add that we'd wear lab coats for good measure. He sighed and signed the requisition.

The composer Aaron Copland got it right. An Appalachian spring is music for dancing. The woods dance with the colors of wildflowers, nodding sprays of white dogwood and the pink froth of redbuds, rushing streams and the embroidered solemnity of dark mountains. But we were here to work. I got out of my tent the first morning with clipboard in hand and lessons in mind.

The range spread out above us in our valley campsite. The Smokies in early spring are a patchwork of diffuse colors, like a map with individual nations colored: pale green for the newly-leafed poplars, gray blocks of the still-dormant oaks, and dusty rose for the maples breaking bud. Here and there, hot pink tracts of redbud and swaths of white reveal where the dogwoods bloom and lines of dark green hemlock trace the watercourses like a cartographer's pen. Back in the classroom, hands white with chalk dust, I had diagrammed the gradients of temperature, soils, and growing season. Before us, the mountainside spread the pastel map of our field trip, the abstract translated into flowers.

Moving up the mountainside was the ecological equivalent of walking to Canada. The warm valley floor could give us a Georgia summer, while the five-thousand-foot summits are akin to Toronto. "Bring your warm jackets," I told them. An increase of one thousand feet is equivalent to moving a hundred miles northward and therefore many steps back into spring. The dogwoods on the lower slopes were in full bloom, creamy-white sprays against the emerging leaves. Moving upslope they reversed like a time-lapse camera running backward from open blossoms to tightly bound buds not yet awakened by heat. Midway up the slope, where the growing season is too short, the dogwoods disappear altogether, their place taken by another tree more tolerant of the late-season frosts, silverbells.

For three days we wandered over this ecological map, traversing elevational zones from deep cove forests of tulip poplar and cucumber magnolia to the summits. The lush coves were a garden of wildflowers, glossy patches of wild ginger and nine species of trillium. The students dutifully wrote down whatever I told them, creating a mirror image of my internal checklist of things to see without much apparent interest. They asked for the spelling of scientific names so often that I felt like I was in a woodland spelling bee. The dean would be proud.

For three days I checked the species and ecosystems off the list to justify the trip. We mapped vegetation, soils, and temperature with the fervor of Alexander von Humboldt. At night we drew graphs around the campfire. Oak-hickory at midelevation, coarse gravelly soil— check. Reduced stature and increased wind speed at high elevation— check. Phenological patterns with elevational change—check. Endemic salamanders, niche diversification—check. I so wanted them to see the world beyond the boundaries of their own skins. I was conscientious not to waste a single teaching opportunity and filled the quiet woods with facts and figures. My jaw ached at the end of the day when I crawled into my sleeping bag.

This was hard work. When I hike, I like to do it quietly, just looking, just being there. Here I was constantly talking, pointing things out, generating discussion questions in my head. Being the teacher.

I only lost it once. The road became steeper as we approached the top of the range. The vans labored around sharp switchbacks and were buffeted by strong winds. No more soft maples and pink froth of redbud. At this elevation the snows had only recently melted away from beneath the firs. Looking out over the land, we could see how narrow this band of boreal forest was, a thin strip of Canadian habitat way down here in North Carolina, hundreds of miles north from the nearest spruce-fir woods, just a remnant from the day when ice covered the north. Today these high mountaintops offer a refuge that feels like home to spruce and fir, islands in a sea of southern hardwoods, perched high enough to duplicate the Canadian climate.

These islands of northern woods felt like home to me too, and in the fresh cold air I slipped the leash of my lectures. We prowled among the trees, breathing in the scent of balsam. The soft mattress of needles, wintergreen, trailing arbutus, bunchberry—all my familiars from home carpeted the forest floor. They made me realize suddenly how displaced I felt to be teaching in someone else's home forest, when I was so far from my own.

I lay down on a carpet of moss and held class from a spider's perspective. High on these summits live the world's last populations of the endangered spruce-fir moss spider. I didn't expect premed students to give a damn, but I had to speak up for the spiders. They have persisted here since the glaciers picked up and left, living their tiny lives spinning webs among mossy rocks. Global warming is the major threat to this habitat and these animals. As the climate warms, this island of boreal forest will melt away and with it the last of many lives, never to return. Already insects and disease from warmer elevations are claiming them. When you live on the summit, there's no place else to go when the hot air rises. They will balloon away on strands of spider silk, but there will be no refuge.

I ran my hand over a mossy rock, thinking of the unraveling of ecosystems and the hand that pulls the loosened thread. "We have no right to take their homes from them," I thought. Maybe I spoke out loud or had a zealot's look in my eye, because one student suddenly asked, "Is this like your religion or something?"

Ever since a student had challenged my teaching of evolution, I'd learned to tread lightly on these matters. I felt all of their eyes upon me, good Christians, every one. So I hemmed and hawed about loving the woods, started to explain about Indigenous environmental philosophies and kinship with the other members of Creation, but they looked at me so quizzically that I stopped and then hastened off to point out a nearby clump of sporulating ferns. At that time in my life, in that setting, I felt that I couldn't explain the ecology of spirit, a sense that went so far from Christianity and science alike that I was sure they wouldn't understand. And besides, we were there for Science. I should have just answered yes.

After many miles and many lectures, at last it was Sunday afternoon. Job done, mountains climbed, data collected. My premed students were dirty and tired, their notebooks filled with more than a hundred and fifty nonhuman species and the mechanisms behind their distributions. I'd have a good report for the dean.

We hiked back to the vans in the late golden light, through a stand filled with the pendant blooms of mountain silverbell that seemed to glow from within like pearly lanterns. The students were awfully quiet, tired, I imagined. With mission accomplished, I was happy just to watch the slant of hazy light over the mountains for which the park is justly famous. A Hermit Thrush sang out from the shadows and a little breeze brought a shower of white petals around us as we walked in that amazing place. I was suddenly so sad. In that moment, I knew that I had failed. I had failed to teach the kind of science that I had longed for as a young student seeking the secret of Asters and Goldenrod, a science deeper than data.

I had given them so much information, all the patterns and processes laid on so thick as to obscure the most important truth. I missed my chance, leading them down every path save the one that matters most. How will people ever care for the fate of moss spiders if we don't teach students to recognize and respond to the world as gift? I'd told them all about how it works and nothing of what it meant. We may as well have stayed home and read about the Smokies. In effect, against all my prejudices, I'd worn a white lab coat into the wilderness. Betrayal is a heavy load and I plodded along, suddenly weary.

I turned to see the students coming down the trail behind me, a petal-strewn path in gauzy light. One person, I don't know who, began to sing, ever so quietly, those familiar first notes. The ones that open your throat, irresistibly calling you to sing. *Amazing grace, how sweet the sound.* One by one they joined in, singing in the long shadows and a drift of white petals settling on our shoulders. *That saved a wretch like me. I once was lost but now I'm found.*

I was humbled. Their singing said everything that my well-intentioned lectures did not. On and on they went, adding harmonies as they walked. They understood harmony in a way that I did not. I heard in their raised voices the same outpouring of love and gratitude for the Creation that Skywoman first sang on the back of Turtle Island. In their caress of that old hymn I came to know that it wasn't naming the source of wonder that mattered, it was wonder itself. Despite my manic efforts and my checklist of scientific names, I knew now that they hadn't missed it all. *Was blind, but now I see.* And they did. And so did I. If I forget every genus and species I ever knew, I'll never forget that moment. The worst teacher in the world or the best teacher in the world—neither can be heard over the voices of Silverbells and Hermit Thrushes. The rush of waterfalls and the silence of mosses have the last word.

As an enthusiastic young PhD, colonized by the arrogance of science, I had been fooling myself that I was the only teacher. The land is the real teacher. All we need as students is mindfulness. Paying attention is a form of reciprocity with the living world, receiving the gifts with open eyes and open heart. My job was just to lead them into the presence and ready them to hear. On that smoky afternoon, the mountains taught the students and the students taught the teacher.

As I drove home that night, the students slept or studied by dimming flashlight. That Sunday afternoon changed forever my way of teaching. A teacher comes, they say, when you are ready. And if you ignore its presence, it will speak to you more loudly. But you have to be quiet to hear.

Sitting in a Circle

B rad arrives at our wilderness field station for ethnobotany class in loafers and a polo shirt. I watch him wander the shoreline, looking in vain for a cell phone signal, looking like he really needs to talk to somebody. "Nature's great and all," he says as I show him around, but the remoteness makes him uneasy. "There's nothing here but trees."

Most of our students come to the Cranberry Lake Biological Station with effervescent enthusiasm, but there are always a few who arrive with only resignation to endure five weeks away from the wired world—a graduation requirement. Over the years, the demeanor of the students has become a pretty good mirror for the changing relationships to nature. They used to arrive motivated by childhoods filled with camping or fishing or messing about in the woods. Today, while their passion for wilderness has not diminished, they now report that their inspiration comes from Animal Planet or the National Geographic channel. More and more often, the reality of nature outside the living room takes them by surprise.

I try to reassure Brad that the woods are just about the safest place in the world. I confess that I experience the same unease when I go to the city, a slight panic of not knowing how to take care of myself, where there's nothing but people. But I know it is a tough transition: We are seven miles across the lake with no road access, not a scrap of pavement, and completely surrounded by wilderness for a day's walk in any direction. It's easily an hour to medical help and three to a Walmart. "I mean, what if you need something?" he says. I guess he's going to find out.

After just a few days of being here, the students start to metamor-phose into field biologists. Their confidence with the equipment and the insider jargon gives them a new swagger. They constantly practice learning Latin names and count coup by using them. At the evening volleyball games it's perfectly excusable in biostation culture to miss the ball if your opponents call out *"Megaceryle alcyon!"* when a kingfisher rattles along the shore. These are good things to know, to begin to dis-criminate the living world into individuals, to discern the threads in the weave of the woods, to attune to the body of the land.

But I also see that when we put scientific instruments in their hands they trust their own senses less. And when they put more energy into memorizing Latin names, they spend less time looking at the beings themselves. The students come already knowing a lot about ecosystems and can identify an impressive list of plants. But when I ask how these plants take care of them, they cannot say.

So, at the start of my ethnobotany class, we brainstorm a list of human needs, with the goal of discovering which of them the Adirondack plants might be able to meet. It's a familiar list: food, shelter, heat, clothing. I'm glad that oxygen and water make it into the top ten. Some of the students have studied Maslow's hierarchy of human needs and take it beyond sur-vival into the "higher" levels of art, companionship, and spirituality. This of course elicits some dubious comedy about people whose needs for interpersonal connection are met by carrots. Putting that observa-tion aside, we begin with shelter—by building our classroom.

They've chosen the site, marked the geometry on the ground, har-vested saplings and set them deep in the soil, so we have a twelve-foot circle of neatly spaced maple poles. It's hot and sweaty work, at first done mostly as individuals. But when the circle is complete and the first pair of saplings are joined in an arch, the need for a team becomes clear: the tallest to grab the treetops, the heaviest to hold them down, the small-est to scramble up and lash them in place. The creation of one arch calls for the next and they are led by the emerging shape of the wigwam. Its inherent symmetry makes any mistakes obvious and the students tie and untie until they get it right. The woods are full of their bright voices.

When the last pair of saplings is tied, quiet falls as they see what they have made. It looks like an upside-down bird's nest, a basket of thick saplings domed like a turtle's back. You want to be inside.

All fifteen of us can find a comfortable seat around the perimeter. Even without a covering, it feels cozy. Few of us live in round houses anymore, where there are no walls or corners. Indigenous architecture tends to the small and round, though, following the model of nests and dens and burrows and redds and eggs and wombs—as if there were some universal pattern for home. With our backs leaning against the saplings, we consider this convergence of design. A sphere has the highest ratio of volume to surface area, minimizing the materials needed for living space. Its form sheds water and distributes the weight of a snow load. It is efficient to heat and resistant to wind. Beyond material considerations, there is cultural meaning to living within the teachings of a circle. I tell them that the doorway always faces east and they quickly assess its utility, given the prevailing westerly winds. The utility of greeting the dawn is not yet part of their thinking, but the sun will show them.

This bare frame of a wigwam is not done teaching. It needs walls of cattail mats and a birch bark roof tied with spruce root. There's still work to be done.

I see Brad before class and he's still looking glum. I try to cheer him up and tell him, "We're going shopping across the lake today!" There *is* a tiny shop in the town across the lake, the Emporium Marine, the kind of general store you find off the beaten track that always seems to have the very thing you need, next to the shoelaces, cat food, coffee filters, a can of Hungry-Man stew, and a bottle of Pepto-Bismol. But that's not where we're going. The cattail marsh has *something* in common with the Emporium, but I suppose a comparison to Walmart is more appropriate, as they both sprawl over acres of land. Today we will shop at the marsh.

At one time marshes had a bad reputation for slimy beasts, disease, stink, and all manner of unpleasantness until people realized how valuable they are. Our students now sing the praises of wetland biodiversity and their ecosystem functions, but that still doesn't mean they want to walk in them, and they eye me skeptically when I explain that gathering cattails is most efficiently accomplished *in* the water. I reassure them that there are no poisonous water snakes this far north, no quicksand, and that the snapping turtles generally hunker down when they hear us coming. I do not say the word *leeches* aloud.

Eventually they all follow me and manage to exit their canoes without capsizing. We wade like herons through the marsh, minus the grace and poise, the students tentative among the floating islets of shrubs and grasses, feeling for solidity before committing their weight to the next step. If their young lives have not already shown them, they will learn today that solidity is an illusion. The lake bottom here lies under several feet of suspended muck, as solid as chocolate pudding.

Chris is the most fearless, and—bless him—he leads the way. Grinning like a five-year-old, he stands nonchalantly in the channel, waist deep, elbow resting against a sedge hummock as if it were an armchair. He's never done this before but encourages the others anyway, offering advice to those teetering on a log: "Just get it over with so you can relax and have fun." Natalie takes the plunge as she shouts, "Become one with your inner muskrat!" Claudia steps back to avoid the muddy splash. She's scared. Like an elegant doorman, Chris gallantly offers her a hand into the muck. Then a long trail of bubbles rises up behind him and breaks the surface in a loud burble. He blushes under his mud-streaked face and shifts his feet as everyone eyes him. Another long trill of foul-smelling bubbles erupts behind him. The class cracks up and soon everybody is smooshing through the water. Swamp walking releases a stream of fart jokes as inevitably as methane "swamp gas" is released by our footsteps. The water is about thigh deep in most places, but every now and then there is a shriek—and then laughter—when someone discovers the chest-deep holes. I hope it's not Brad.

To pull cattails, you reach under water to the base of the plant and tug. If the sediments are loose enough or if you're strong enough, you can pull up the whole plant, rhizome and all. The problem is that you can't tell whether the shoot will snap or not until you tug with all your might and it suddenly breaks free, leaving you sitting in the water with muck dripping from your ears.

The rhizomes, essentially underground stems, are a real prize. Brown and fibrous on the outside, they are white and starchy on the inside, almost like a potato, and they taste pretty good roasted in the fire. Soak cut rhizomes in clean water and you'll soon have a bowl of pasty white starch that can become flour or porridge. Some of the hairy rhizomes have a stiff white shoot emerging from their end, a more than vaguely phallic organ of horizontal propagation. This is the growing point that will spread the cattails through the marsh. Invoking the hierarchy of human needs, some of the guys have a little fun with them when they think I'm not looking.

The cattail plant—*Typha latifolia*—is like a giant grass: no distinct stem, but rather a rolled bundle of leaves that sheathe around each other in concentric layers. No one leaf could withstand wind and wave action, but the collective is strong and the extensive underwater network of rhizomes anchors them in place. Harvested in June, they're three feet high. Wait until August and you have leaves eight feet long, each about an inch wide and strengthened by the parallel veins running from base to softly waving leaf tip. These circular veins are themselves encircled by sturdy fibers, all working to support the plant. In turn, the plant supports the people. Cattail leaves, split and twisted, are one of the easiest sources of plant cordage, our string and twine. Back at camp, we'll make twine for the wigwam and thread fine enough for weaving.

Before long, the canoes are brimming with bundles of leaves and look like a flotilla of rafts on a tropical river. We tow them to shore, where we begin to sort and clean them by taking each plant apart, leaf by leaf, from the outside in. As she strips off the leaves, Natalie drops hers quickly to the ground. "Ooh, it's all slimy," she says, and starts to wipe her hands on her muddy pants, as if that will help. When you pull the leaf bases apart, gobs of cattail gel stretch like clear watery mucus between the leaves. At first it seems gross, but then you notice how good your hands feel. I've often heard herbalists say that "the cure grows near to the cause," and, accordingly, though gathering cattails is guaranteed to get you sunburned and itchy, the antidote to discomfort is in the plants themselves. Clear and cool and clean, the gel is refreshing and antimicrobial, the swamp's answer to aloe vera gel. The cattails make the gel as a defense against microbes and to keep the leaf bases moist when water levels drop. These same properties that protect the plant protect us too. It feels so soothing on sunburn that soon the students are smearing themselves with slime.

Cattails have evolved other features that are perfectly adapted for a life spent standing in the marsh. The bases of the leaves are under water, but they still need oxygen for respiration. So, like scuba divers with air tanks, they equip themselves with spongy, air-filled tissue, nature's Bubble Wrap. These white cells, called aerenchyma, are big enough to be seen with the naked eye and make a buoyant, cushiony layer at the base of each leaf. The leaves are also coated with a waxy layer, a waterproof barrier like a raincoat. But this raincoat works in reverse, keeping water-soluble nutrients inside, so that they don't leach away into the water.

This is all good for the plant, of course—and it's good for people. The cattails have made a superb material for shelter in leaves that are long, water repellent, and packed with closed-cell foam for insulation. In the old times, fine mats of cattail leaves were sewn or twined to sheathe a summer wigwam. In dry weather, the leaves shrink apart from one another and let the breeze waft between them for ventilation. When the rains come, they swell and close the gap, making the mat waterproof. Cattails also make fine sleeping mats. The wax keeps away moisture from the ground and the aerenchyma provide cushioning and insulation. A couple of cattail mats—soft, dry, and smelling like fresh hay— under your sleeping bag make for a cozy night.

Squeezing the soft leaves between her fingers, Natalie says, "It's almost as if the plants made these things for us." The parallels between the adaptations evolved by the plants and the needs of the people are indeed striking. In some Native languages the term for plants translates to "those who take care of us." Through natural selection the cattails developed sophisticated adaptations that increase their survival in the marsh. The people were attentive students and borrowed solutions from the plants, which increased *their* likelihood of survival. The plants adapt, the people adopt.

As we keep peeling away leaves they get thinner and thinner, like the husks of corn as you get near the cob. At the center the leaves nearly merge with the stem, a soft column of white pith as thick as your pinkie and as crisp as a summer squash. I snap the pith into bite-size pieces and pass it around. Only after I eat mine do the students venture a nibble, looking at each other sideways. Moments later they're hungrily stripping stalks for themselves like pandas in a bamboo patch. Sometimes called Cossacks' asparagus, the raw pith tastes like a cucumber. It can be sautéed, boiled, or simply eaten fresh on the lakeshore by hungry college students after their bag lunches are just a memory.

Back across the marsh, you can easily see where we've been harvesting. It looks like big muskrats have been at work. The students wade into a heated conversation about their own impact.

Our shopping canoes are already filled with leaves for clothing, mats, twine, and shelter. We have buckets of rhizomes for carbohydrate energy, stalks of pith for vegetables—what more could people need? The students compare our haul to their list of human needs. They note that while the cattails are impressive in their versatility, there are some gaps: protein, fire, light, music. Natalie wants pancakes added to the list. "Toilet paper!" offers Claudia. Brad has an iPod on his list of essentials.

We wander the aisles of the supermarket of the swamp to search out additional products. The students start pretending they're at an actual Walmart, Lance offering to be the greeter at the door of Walmarsh so he doesn't have to wade back in. "Pancakes, ma'am? Aisle five. Flashlights? Aisle three. Sorry—we don't carry iPods."

Cattail flowers hardly look like flowers at all. The stalk is about five feet tall and ends in a plump green cylinder, neatly tucked at the waist into two halves, males above and females below. Wind pollinated, the froth of male flowers bursts open to release a cloud of sulfur-yellow pollen into the air. The pancake crew scans the marsh for these beacons. They gently slip a small paper bag over the stalk, crumple it tightly closed, and then shake. At the bottom of the bag there is about a table-spoon of bright yellow powder and perhaps an equivalent volume of bugs. Pollen (and bugs) are almost pure protein, a high-quality food to complement the starchy rhizomes back in the canoe. Once the bugs are picked out, it can be added to biscuits and pancakes, adding nutritional value and a beautiful golden color. Not all of the pollen ends up in the bag and the students emerge decorated with tie-dye splashes of yellow.

The female half of the stalk looks like a skinny green hot dog on a stick, a nubbly sponge of tightly packed ovaries waiting for pollen. We'll boil them in a little salt water and then drench them in butter. Holding both ends of the stalk like an ear of corn, you just nibble off the immature flowers as if the stalk were a skewer. The taste and texture are remarkably like an artichoke's. Cattail kebabs for dinner.

I hear shouting and see clouds of fluff drifting on the air, so I know that the students have reached Walmarsh aisle three. Each tiny flower matures to a seed attached to a plume of fluff, making up the familiar cattail, a handsome brown sausage at the end of the stalk. At this time of year, wind and winter have picked away at them until they are just wads like cotton batting. The students tear it from the stalk and stuff it into sacks, destined for pillows or bedding. Our foremothers must have been grateful for a thick marsh. One of the names for cattail in the Potawatomi language is *bewiieskwinuk*, meaning "we wrap the baby in it." Soft, warm, absorbent—it was both insulation and diaper.

Elliot calls back to us: "I found the flashlights!" The stalks with matted fuzz traditionally were dipped in fat and lit to make a serviceable torch. The stalk itself is remarkably straight and smooth, almost like a lathed dowel. Our people gathered these for many uses, including arrow shafts and drills for creating handmade friction fire. A puff of cattail fluff was usually kept in a fire-making bundle as tinder. The students gather it all and bring their bargains back to the canoes. Natalie still wades nearby; she calls out that she's going to "Marsh-alls" next. Chris is not back yet.

On wings of fluff, the seeds blow far and wide to establish new colonies. Cattails grow in nearly all types of wetlands, wherever there is adequate sun, plentiful nutrients, and soggy ground. Midway between land

and water, freshwater marshes are among the most highly productive ecosystems on earth, rivaling the tropical rainforest. People valued the supermarket of the swamp for the cattails, but also as a rich source of fish and game. Fish spawn in the shallows; frogs and salamanders abound. Waterfowl nest here in the safety of the dense sward, and migratory birds seek out cattail marshes for sanctuary on their journeys.

Not surprisingly, hunger for this productive land precipitated a 90 percent loss of the wetlands—as well as the Native people who depended upon them. Cattails are also soil builders. All those leaves and rhizomes return to the sediments when the cattails die back. What hasn't been eaten lies beneath the water, only partially decomposing in the anaerobic waters, building up peat. It is rich in nutrients and has the water-holding capacity of a sponge, making it ideal for truck crops. Decried as "wastelands," marsh draining for agriculture was carried out on a huge scale. So-called "muck farms" plow under the black soil of drained marshes, and a landscape that once supported some of the world's highest biodiversity now supports a single crop. In some places the old wetlands are just paved over for parking. A true waste of land.

Just as we're tying down the load in our canoes, Chris comes walking along the shore with a secret smirk and something behind his back. "Here you go, Brad. I found your iPods." He has two dry milkweed pods, which he fits over his eyes and holds in place with a squint: eye pods.

By the end of the mucky, sunburned, laughing, and leech-free day, we have boats piled high with material for rope, bedding, insulation, light, food, heat, shelter, rain gear, shoes, tools, and medicine. As we're paddling home, I wonder if Brad is still worried that we might "need something."

A few days later, fingers roughened by harvesting and weaving mats, we gather in the wigwam with slits of sun coming through our walls of cattail mats, sitting on cattail cushions. The top of the dome is still open to the sky. Surrounded by our woven classroom, it feels like being an apple in a basket, everyone nestled together. The roof is the last step, and rain is in the forecast. We already have a pile of birch bark sheets waiting to become our ceiling, so we head out to gather the last materials.

I used to teach just the way I was taught, but now I let someone else do all the work for me. If plants are our oldest teachers, why not let them teach?

After the long hike from camp, our shovels clanking against rocks and the relentless torment of deerflies on sweaty skin, the shade feels like a dip into cool water. Still swatting, we drop our packs by the trail to rest for a moment in the mossy hush. The air is redolent with DEET and impatience. Maybe the students already sense the line of welts that the blackflies will leave, where that gap of unprotected skin opens between shirt and pants when you're down on all fours, grubbing for roots. They'll lose some blood but still I envy them the experience to come, the beginner's mind.

The forest floor here is all spruce needles, rusty brown, deep and soft, with the occasional pale drift of maple or black cherry leaves. Ferns, mosses, and trailing partridgeberry glow in the few sun flecks that penetrate the dense canopy. We're here to harvest *watap*, the roots of white spruce, *Picea glauca*—a cultural keystone for Indigenous peoples throughout the Great Lakes, strong enough to stitch together birch bark canoes and wigwams, flexible enough for beautiful baskets. The roots of other spruces are serviceable, but it's worth hunting for the glaucous foliage and pungent feline odor of white spruce.

We thread our way among the spruces, snapping off dead branches that threaten to poke out an eye as we search for just the right spot. I want them to learn how to read the forest floor, to develop the X-ray vision that helps you see the roots beneath the surface, but it's hard to break down intuition into a formula. Choose a place between two spruces to maximize your chances, as level as possible, and avoid a spot with rocks. A well-decayed log nearby is welcome and a mossy layer is a good sign.

In gathering roots, just plunging in will get you nothing but a hole. We have to unlearn hurrying. This is all about slowness. "First we give. Then we take." Whether it's cattails or birch or roots, the students have gotten used to this preharvest ritual, invoking the Honorable Harvest. Some close their eyes and join me and some realize it's a good time to fumble through their backpacks for a missing pencil. I murmur to the

Spruces who I am and why I've come. Using bits of Potawatomi and bits of English, I ask their kind permission for digging. I ask if they'll share with these dear young people what only they can give, their physical bodies and their teachings. I'm asking for something more than roots and leave a little tobacco in return.

The students gather round, leaning on their shovels. I brush away the layer of old leaves, flaky and fragrant like aged pipe tobacco. I take out my knife and make the first incision through the duff—not deep enough to sever veins or muscle, just a superficial slice through the forest skin—slide my fingers beneath the cut edge, and pull back. The top layer peels away and I set it aside for safekeeping, to replace when we're done. A centipede runs blindly in the unaccustomed light. A beetle dives for cover. Laying open the soil is like a careful dissection and there is the same astonishment among the students at the orderly beauty of the organs, the harmony of how they rest against one another, form to function. These are the viscera of the forest.

Against the black humus, colors stand out like neon lights on a dark wet street. Juicy school bus orange, goldthread roots crisscross the ground. A web of creamy roots, each as thick as a pencil, connects all the sarsaparillas. Chris says right away, "It looks like a map." With roads of different colors and sizes, it really does. There are interstates of heavy red roots whose origins I do not know. We tug on one and few feet away a blueberry bush jounces in reply. White tubers of Canada mayflower are connected by translucent threads like county roads between villages. A mycelial fan of pale yellow spreads out from a clump of dark organic matter, like the small dead-end streets of a cul-de-sac. A great dense metropolis of fibrous brown roots emanates from a young hemlock. They all have their hands in it now, tracing the lines, trying to match the root colors to the aboveground plants, reading the map of the world.

The students think they've seen soil before. They've dug in their gardens, planted a tree, held a handful of freshly turned earth—warm, crumbly, and ready for a seed. But that handful of tilled soil is a poor cousin to the soil of the forest, as a pound of hamburger is to the whole blooming pasture of cows and bees and clover, meadowlarks, woodchucks, and all that binds them together. Backyard soil is like ground meat: it may be nutritious but it has been homogenized beyond recognition of its origins. Humans make agricultural soils by tilling; forest soils simply make themselves through a web of reciprocal processes that few have the chance to witness.

Carefully lift away the sod of herb roots and the soil beneath is as black as morning java before the cream—humus, moist and dense, black flour as silky as the finest coffee grounds. There is nothing "dirty" about soil. This soft black humus is so sweet and clean you could eat it by the spoonful. We have to excavate a bit of this gorgeous soil to find the tree roots and sort out which is which. The maples, birches, and cherries are too brittle—we only want spruce. The spruce roots, you can tell by feel; they're taut and springy. You can pluck one like a guitar string and it twangs against the ground, resilient and strong. Those are the ones we're looking for.

Slip your fingers around it. Tug and it starts to pull up from the ground, leading you off to the north, so you clear a little channel in that direction to free it. But then its path is intersected by another coming in from the east, straight and sure, as if it knows where it's going. So you excavate there, too. Dig some more and then there are three. Before long, it looks like a bear has been clawing up the ground. I go back to the first, cut an end free, and then duck it under the others, over, under, over, under. I'm separating a single wire in the scaffold that holds up the forest, but I find that it can't be freed without unraveling the others. A dozen roots are exposed, and somehow you need to choose one and follow it without breaking it, so that you have one great, long continuous strand. It's not easy.

I send the students off gathering, to read the land and see where it says *roots*. They go crashing off through the woods, their laughter flashing bright in the dim coolness. For a time they continue to call to each other, loudly cursing the flies biting under the edge of their untucked shirts.

They disperse so as not to concentrate the harvest in any one spot. The root mat is easily as big as the canopy above. Harvesting a few roots won't cause real harm, but we're careful to repair the damage we do. I remind them to fill in the furrows we've made, set the goldthread and the mosses back in place, and empty their water bottles over their wilting leaves when the harvest is done.

I stay at my patch, working my roots and listening to the chatter slowly subside. I hear an occasional grunt of frustration nearby. A splutter when soil flies up in someone's face. I know what their hands are doing and sense where their minds are as well. Digging spruce roots takes you someplace else. The map in the ground asks you over and over, Which root to take? Which is the scenic route, which is the dead end? The fine root you'd chosen and so carefully excavated suddenly dives deep under a rock where you can't follow. Do you abandon that path and choose another? The roots may spread out like a map, but a map only helps if you know where you want to go. Some roots branch. Some break. I look at the students' faces, poised midway between childhood and adulthood. I think the tangle of choices speaks clearly to them. Which route to take? Isn't that always the question?

Before long all the chatter ceases and a mossy hush befalls us. There is just the *ssshhhh* of wind in the spruce, and a calling winter wren. Time goes by. Way longer than the fifty-minute classes they're used to. Still, no one speaks. I'm waiting for it, hoping. There is a certain energy in the air, a hum. And then I hear it, someone singing, low and contented. I feel the smile spread across my face and breathe a sigh of relief. It happens every time.

In the Apache language, the root word for land is the same as the word for mind. Gathering roots holds up a mirror between the map in the earth and the map of our minds. This is what happens, I think, in the silence and the singing and with hands in the earth. At a certain angle of that mirror, the routes converge and we find our way back home.

Recent research has shown that the smell of humus exerts a physiological effect on humans. Breathing in the scent of Mother Earth stimulates the release of the hormone oxytocin, the same chemical that promotes bonding between mother and child, between lovers. Held in loving arms, no wonder we sing in response.

I remember the first time I dug roots. I came looking for raw materials, for something I could transform into a basket, but it was me who was transformed. The crisscross patterns, the interweaving of colors—the basket was already in the ground, stronger and more beautiful than any I could make. Spruce and blueberries, deerflies and winter wren, the whole forest held in a wild native basket the size of a hill. Big enough to hold me too.

We rendezvous back at the trail and show off our coils of root, the guys bragging about whose is biggest. Elliot stretches his out on the ground and lies next to it—more than eight feet from toes to outstretched fingertips. "It went right through a rotten log," he says, "so I went, too." "Yeah, mine too," adds Claudia. "I think it was following the nutrients." Most of their coils are shortish pieces, but the stories are longer: a sleeping toad mistaken for a rock, a lens of buried charcoal from a long-ago fire, a root that suddenly broke and showered Natalie in soil. "I loved it. I didn't want to stop," she says. "It's like the roots were just waiting there for us."

My students are always different after root gathering. There is something tender in them, and open, as if they are emerging from the embrace of arms they did not know were there. Through them I get to remember what it is to open to the world as gift, to be flooded with the knowledge that the earth will take care of you, everything you need right there.

We also show off our root-gathering hands: black to the elbow, black under every nail, black in every crevice like a ritual glove of henna, our nails like tea-stained china. "See?" says Claudia, pinkies raised for tea with the queen, "I got the special spruce root manicure."

On the way back to camp, we stop at the stream to clean the roots. Sitting on rocks, we soak them awhile, along with our bare feet. I show them how to peel the roots with a little vise made of a split sapling. The rough bark and fleshy cortex strip away like a dirty sock from a slender white leg. Beneath, the root is clean and creamy. It spools around your hand like thread, but will dry as hard as wood. It smells clean and sprucy.

After unweaving the roots from the ground, we sit by the brook and weave our first baskets. With beginner's hands they turn out lopsided but they hold us nonetheless. Imperfect they may be, but I believe they are a beginning of a reweaving of the bond between people and the land.

The wigwam roof goes on easily as the students sit on each other's shoulders to reach the top and tie the bark in place with roots. Pulling cattails and bending saplings, they remember why we need each other. In the tedium of weaving mats and with the absence of iPods, storytellers emerge to relieve the boredom and songs arise to keep the fingers flying as if they remembered this, too.

In our time together, we've built our classroom, feasted on cattail kebabs, roasted rhizomes, and eaten pollen pancakes. Our bug bites were soothed by cattail gel. And there are cordage and baskets to finish, so in the roundness of the wigwam, we sit together, twining and talking.

I tell them how Darryl Thompson, a Mohawk elder and scholar, once sat with us as we made cattail baskets. "It makes me so happy," he said, "to see young people getting to know this plant. She gives us all that we need to live." Cattails are a sacred plant and appear in the Mohawk Creation stories. As it turns out, the Mohawk word for cattail has much in common with the Potawatomi word. Their word also refers to cattails in the cradleboard, but with a twist so lovely that tears spring to my eyes. In Potawatomi, the word means "we wrap the baby in it"; in Mohawk, it means that the cattail wraps humans in her gifts, as if *we* were *her* babies. In that one word we are carried in the cradleboard of Mother Earth.

How can we ever reciprocate such a wealth of care? Knowing that she carries us, could we shoulder a burden for her? I'm mulling over how to ask this when Claudia edges in with a comment that mirrors my thoughts: "I don't mean this to sound disrespectful or anything. I think it's great to ask the plants if we can take them, and give them tobacco, but is that enough? We're taking an awful lot of stuff. We were pretending like we were shopping for cattails, right? But we just took all this stuff without paying for it. When you really think about it, we just shoplifted at the swamp." And she's right. If cattails are the Walmart of the marsh, then the security alarms at the exits would be blaring at our canoes full of stolen merchandise. In a sense, unless we find a way to enter into reciprocity, we are walking away with goods for which we have not paid.

I remind them that the gift of tobacco is not a material one, but a spiritual gift, a means of conveying our highest regard. I've asked some elders about this over the years and heard a range of answers. One man said that gratitude is our only responsibility. He cautioned against the arrogance of thinking we have the capacity to give back to Mother Earth anything approaching what she gives us. I honor the *edbesendowen*, the humility inherent in that perspective. And yet it seems to me we humans have gifts in addition to gratitude that we might offer in return. The philosophy of reciprocity is beautiful in the abstract, but the practical is harder.

Having your hands busy tends to free up your mind, and the students play with the idea as we twine cattail fiber between our fingers. I ask them what we can possibly offer cattail or birch or spruce. Lance snorts at the idea: "They're just plants. It's cool that we can use them, but it's not like we owe them anything. They're just there." The others groan and then look at me, waiting for a reaction. Chris is planning to go to law school, so he takes over the conversation like a natural. He says, "If cattails are 'free' then they're a gift and all we owe is gratitude. You don't pay for a gift, you just graciously accept." But Natalie objects: "Just because it's a gift, does that make you any less beholden? You should always give something back." Whether it's a gift or a commodity, you still have incurred an unpaid debt. One moral, the other legal. So, were we to act ethically, don't we have to somehow compensate the plants for what we received?

I love listening to them consider such a question. I don't believe that average Walmart shoppers stop to consider their debt to the land that has produced their purchases. The students ramble and laugh as we work and weave, but come up with a long list of suggestions. Brad proposes a permit system in which we do pay for what we take, a fee to the state that goes to support wetland protection. A couple of kids take the route of generating appreciation for wetlands, proposing school workshops on the values of cattails. They also suggest defensive strategies:

to reciprocate with protection against the things that threaten cattails, to organize pulls of invasive species like phragmites or purple loosestrife. To go to a town planning board meeting and speak up for wetland preservation. To vote. Natalie promises to get a rain barrel at her apartment, to reduce water pollution. Lance swears that he'll boycott fertilizing the lawn next time his parents give him that chore, to stop runoff. To join Ducks Unlimited or the Nature Conservancy. Claudia vows to weave coasters of cattail and give them to everyone for Christmas, so they'll remember to love wetlands whenever they use them. I thought they would have no answer, but I was humbled by their creativity. The gifts they might return to cattails are as diverse as those the cattails gave them. This is our work, to discover what we can give. Isn't this the purpose of education, to learn the nature of your own gifts and how to use them for good in the world?

As I listen to them, I hear another whisper from the swaying stand of cattails, from spruce boughs in the wind, a reminder that caring is not abstract. The circle of ecological compassion we feel is enlarged by direct experience of the living world, and shrunken by its lack. Had we not waded waist deep in the swamp, had we not followed muskrat trails and rubbed ourselves with soothing slime, had we never made a spruce root basket or eaten cattail pancakes, would they even be debating what gifts they could offer in return? In learning reciprocity, the hands can lead the heart.

On the last night of the course, we decide to sleep in our wigwam, hauling our sleeping bags down the trail at dusk and laughing around the fire until late. Claudia says, "I'm sad to leave here tomorrow. I'm going to miss feeling so connected to the land when I'm not sleeping on cattails." It takes real effort to remember that it's not just in a wigwam that the earth gives us everything we need. The exchange of recognition, gratitude, and reciprocity for these gifts is just as important in a Brooklyn flat as under a birch bark roof.

When the students start to leave the fire circle with their flashlights in twos and threes to whisper, I sense a conspiracy. Before I know it they are lined up with makeshift song sheets like a choir in the firelight. "We have a little something for you," they say and start a marvelous anthem of their own creation, filled with crazy rhymes of spruce roots and hiking boots, human needs and marshy reeds, cattail torches on our porches. The song crescendos to a rousing chorus of "no matter where I roam, when I'm with plants I'll be at home." I couldn't imagine a more perfect gift.

With all of us packed into the wigwam like down caterpillars, the slow slide to sleep is punctuated by laughs and last scraps of conversation. Remembering the improbable rhyme of "ecotones and baked rhizomes," I start to giggle too, sending a ripple across the sleeping bags like a wave across a pond. As we eventually drift off, I feel us all held beneath the dome of our bark roof, an echo of the starry dome above. The quiet settles in until all I can hear is their breathing and the whisper of the cattail walls. I feel like a good mother.

When the sun pours in the eastern door, Natalie wakes first, tiptoes over the others, and steps outside. Through the slits in the cattails I watch as she raises her arms and speaks her thanks to the new day.

Burning Cascade Head

"The dance of renewal, the dance that made the world, was always danced here at the edge of things, on the brink, on the foggy coast."   —URSULA K. LE GUIN

Far out beyond the surf they felt it. Beyond the reach of any canoe, half a sea away, something stirred inside them, an ancient clock of bone and blood that said, "It's time." Silver-scaled body its own sort of compass needle spinning in the sea, the floating arrow turned toward home. From all directions they came, the sea a funnel of fish, narrowing their path as they gathered closer and closer, until their silver bodies lit up the water, redd-mates sent to sea, prodigal salmon coming home.

The coastline here is scalloped with countless coves, clothed in fog banks, and cut with rainforest rivers, an easy place to lose your way, where landmarks can vanish in the fog. The spruce are heavy on the shore, their black cloaks hiding signs of home. The elders speak of lost canoes that strayed in the wind and landed on a sand spit not their own. When the boats are too long gone, their families go down to the beach to light a blaze among the driftwood, a beacon to sing them home to safety. When the canoes finally approach, laden with food from the sea, the hunters are honored in dances and songs, their dangerous journey repaid by faces alight with gratitude.

And so it is too that the people make ready for the arrival of their brothers who bring food in the canoe of their bodies. The people watch and wait. The women sew one more row of dentalia shells upon their finest garments for the dance. They pile alder wood for the welcome feast and sharpen huckleberry skewers. While they mend nets, they practice the old songs. But still their brothers do not come. The people go down to the shore, looking out to sea for a sign. Perhaps they have forgotten. Perhaps they wander, lost at sea, uncertain of their welcome with those they left behind.

The rains are late, the water low, the forest trails turned dusty and dry and covered in a steady rain of yellow spruce needles. The prairies up on the headland are crisp and brown, without even fog to moisten them.

Far out, beyond the pounding surf, beyond the reach of canoes, in the inky darkness that swallows light, they move as one body, a school, turning neither east nor west until they know.

So he walks the path at nightfall with a bundle in his hand. Into a nest of cedar bark and twisted grass he lays the coal and feeds it with his breath. It dances and then subsides. Smoke pools darkly as the grasses melt to black and then erupt into flame, climbing one stem and then another. All around the meadow, others do the same, setting in the grass a crackling ring of fire that quickens and gathers, white smoke curling upward in the fading light, breathing into itself, panting across the slope until its convective gasp sets the night alight. A beacon to bring their brothers home.

They are burning the headland. Flames race on the wind until they are stopped by the wet green wall of the forest. Fourteen hundred feet above the surf it blazes, a tower of fire: yellow, orange, and red, a massive flare. The burning prairie billows smoke, roiling white with undersides of salmon pink in the darkness. They mean for it to say, "Come, come, flesh of my flesh. My brothers. Come back to the river where your lives began. We have made a welcome feast in your honor."

Out at sea, beyond where the canoes can go, there is a pinprick of light on a pitch-black coast, a match in the darkness, flickering, beckoning below the white plume that drifts down the coast to mingle with the fog. A spark in the vastness. The time has come. As one body they turn to the east, toward the shore and the river of home. When they can smell the water of their natal stream, they pause in their journey and rest on the slackening tide. Above them all, on the headland, the sparkling tower of fire reflects on the water, kissing the reddened wave tops and glinting off silver scales.

By sunrise the headland is gray and white, as if dusted by an early snow. A cold drift of ash falls on the forest below and the wind carries the tang of burnt grass. But no one notices, for they are all standing along the river singing a welcome, a song of praise as the food swims up the river, fin to fin. The nets stay on the shore; the spears still hang in the houses. The hook-jawed leaders are allowed to pass, to guide the others and to carry the message to their upriver relatives that the people are grateful and full of respect.

The fish course by the camp in great throngs, unmolested as they make their way upstream. Only after four days of fish have moved safely by is the First Salmon taken by the most honored fisher and prepared with ritual care. It is carried to the feast in great ceremony on a cedar plank in a bed of ferns. And then they feast on the sacred foods—salmon, venison, roots, and berries—in sequence for their places in the watershed. They celebrate the water that connects them all in a ritual passing of the cup. They dance in long lines, singing thanks for all that is given. The salmon bones are placed back in the river, their heads facing upstream so that their spirits might follow the others. They are destined to die as we are all destined to die, but first they have bound themselves to life in an ancient agreement to pass it on, to pass it on. In so doing, the world itself is renewed.

Only then the nets are set out, the weirs are put in place, and the harvest begins. Everyone has a task. An elder counsels the young one with a spear, "Take only what you need and let the rest go by and the fish will last forever." When the drying racks are full with winter food, they simply stop fishing.

And so, at the time of dry grasses, the fall Chinook arrived in legendary numbers. The story is told that when Salmon first arrived he was greeted on the shore by Skunk Cabbage, who had been keeping the people from starvation all those years. "Thank you, brother, for taking care of my people," said Salmon, and he gave Skunk Cabbage gifts—an elk hide blanket and a war club—and then set him in the soft, moist ground so he could rest.

The diversity of salmon in the river—Chinook, Chum, Pink and Coho—ensured that the people would not go hungry, likewise the forests. Swimming many miles inland, they brought a much-needed resource for the trees: nitrogen. The spent carcasses of spawned-out salmon, dragged into the woods by bears and eagles and people, fertilized the trees as well as Skunk Cabbage. Using stable isotope analysis, scientists traced the source of nitrogen in the wood of ancient forests all the way back to the ocean. Salmon fed everyone.

When spring returns, the headland becomes a beacon again, shining with the intense green light of new grass. The burnt and blackened soil heats up quickly and urges the shoots upward, fueled by the fertilizing ash, giving the elk and their calves a lush pasture in the midst of dark forests of Sitka spruce. As the season unfolds, the prairie is awash with wildflowers. The healers make the long climb to gather the medicines they need, which grow only here on the mountain they call "the place where the wind always blows."

The headland juts out from the shore and the sea curls around its base in white curls. It is a place for the long view. To the north, the rocky coast. To the east, ridge after ancient ridge of moss-draped rainforest. To the west, the unbroken sea. And to the south, the estuary. An enormous sand spit arcs across the mouth of the bay, enclosing it and forcing the river through a narrow path. All the forces that shape the meeting of land and sea are written there, in sand and water.

Overhead, Eagles, bringers of vision, soar on the thermals that rise off the head. This was sacred ground, reserved for seekers of a vision who would sacrifice by fasting alone for days in this place where the grasses give themselves to fire. They would sacrifice for the Salmon, for the People, to hear the Creator's voice, to dream.

Only fragments of the story of the head remain with us. The people who know it were lost before their knowledge could be captured and the death was too thorough to have left many tellers behind. But the prairie kept the story of the ritual fires long after there were people here to speak of it.

A tsunami of disease swept the Oregon coast in the 1830s, the germs traveling faster than covered wagons could. Smallpox and measles came to the Native peoples, diseases for which they had no more resistance than did grass before a fire. By the time the squatters arrived around 1850, most of the villages were ghost towns. Settlers' diaries record their surprise at finding a densely forested place with a pasture all ready for their livestock, and they eagerly set their cows out to fatten on the native grasses. In the way of all cows, these no doubt followed the paths that already lay on the land, pressing them even more decisively into the soil. Their presence did some of the work of the lost fires by preventing encroachment by forest and fertilizing the grasses.

As more people arrived to take the remaining lands of the Nechesne, they wanted even more pasture for their Holsteins. Flat land is a hard thing to come by in these parts, so they cast a covetous eye on the salt marshes of the estuary.

Situated at the meeting point between ecosystems, with a mix of river, ocean, forest, soil, sand, and sunlight at this edge of all edges, estuaries can have the highest biodiversity and productivity of any wetland. They are a breeding ground for invertebrates of all sorts. The dense sponge of vegetation and sediment is riddled with channels of all sizes, matching the sizes of salmon that are coming and going through its network. The estuary is a nursery for salmon, from tiny fry just days out of the redd to fattening smolt adjusting to salt water. Herons, ducks, eagles, and shellfish could make a living there, but not cows—that sea of grasses was too wet. So they built dikes to keep the water out, engineering they called "reclaiming land from the sea," turning wetlands into pasture.

The diking changed the river from a capillary system to a single straightened flow to hurry the river to the sea. It might have been good for cows, but it was disastrous for young salmon who were now unceremoniously flushed to the sea.

The transition to salt water is a major assault on the body chemistry of a salmon born in freshwater. One fish biologist likens it to the rigors of a chemotherapy transfusion. The fish need a gradual transition zone, a halfway house of sorts. The brackish water of estuaries, the wetland buffer between river and ocean, plays a critical role in salmon survival.

Drawn by the prospect of fortunes to be made from canneries, salmon fishing exploded. But there was no more honoring of the returning fish, no guarantee of safe passage upstream for the early arrivers. Adding insult to injury, construction of upstream dams created rivers of no return, and degradation by cattle grazing and industrial forestry reduced spawning to nil. The commodity mind-set drove fish that had fed the people for thousands of years close to extinction. To preserve the revenue stream, they built salmon hatcheries, turning out industrial fish. They thought they could make salmon without rivers.

From the sea the wild salmon watched for the blaze on the headland and saw nothing for years. But they have a covenant with the People and a promise to Skunk Cabbage to care for them, and so they came, but fewer and fewer every time. The ones that made it though came home to an empty house, dark and lonely. There were no songs or fern-decked tables. No light on the shore to say welcome back.

According to the laws of thermodynamics, everything has to go someplace. Where did the relationship of loving respect and mutual caregiving between people and fish go?

The path rises abruptly from the river in steps cut into the steep slope. My legs burn as they push up over roots of massive Sitka spruces. Moss, fern, and conifer repeat a pattern of feathery forms, a tessellation of green fronds block-printed on the walls of the forest, which draw close.

The branches brush my shoulder and compress my view to the path and my feet. Walking this trail turns me inward, under the small dome of my own head, my busy mind clicking away over an interior landscape of lists and remembrances. I hear only the tread of my own feet, the swish of my rain pants, and my heartbeat until I arrive at a stream crossing where the water sings as it falls over the sheer drop, throwing up a fine mist. It opens my eyes to the forest: a winter wren chatters at me from the sword ferns; an orange-bellied newt crosses my path.

The spruce shade eventually gives way to dappled light as the trail ascends to enter a skirt of white-stemmed alder below the summit. I want to walk a little quicker, knowing what is ahead, but the transition is so seductive that I force myself to step slowly and savor the anticipation, taste the change in the air and the lift in the breeze. The very last alder leans away from the thread of the trail, as if to set me free.

Black against the golden grass and many inches deep into prairie earth, the trail follows the natural contours as if centuries of footfalls have preceded my own. It's just me, the grass, and the sky, and two bald eagles riding the thermals. Cresting the ridge releases me into an explosion of light and space and wind. My head catches fire at the sight. I cannot tell you more of that high and holy place. Words blow away. Even thought dissipates like wisps of cloud sailing up the headland. There is only being.

Before I knew this story, before the fire lit my dreams, I would have hiked here like everyone else, snapping photos at scenic viewpoints. I would have admired the great sickle curve of the yellow sand spit enclosing the bay and the lace-edge waves riding up the beach. I would crane around the knoll to see how the river cuts a sinuous silver line through the salt marsh far below, on its way from the dark line of the Coast Range. Like the others, I would edge toward the bluff and thrill to the vertiginous drop to the surf pounding the base of the headland a thousand feet below. Listen to the seals barking in the echo chamber of the cove. Watch the wind ripple the grass like a cougar pelt. And the sky going on and on. And the sea.

Before I knew the story, I would have written some field notes, consulted my field guide about rare plants, and unpacked my lunch. I would not have talked on my cell phone, though, as the guy at the next overlook is doing.

Instead I just stand there, tears running down my cheeks in nameless emotion that tastes of joy and of grief. Joy for the being of the shimmering world and grief for what we have lost. The grasses remember the nights they were consumed by fire, lighting the way back with a conflagration of love between species. Who today even knows what that means? I drop to my knees in the grass and I can hear the sadness, as if the land itself was crying for its people: *Come home. Come home.*

There are often other walkers here. I suppose that's what it means when they put down the camera and stand on the headland, straining to hear above the wind with that wistful look, the gaze out to sea. They look like they're trying to remember what it would be like to love the world.

It is an odd dichotomy we have set for ourselves, between loving people and loving land. We know that loving a person has agency and power—we know it can change everything. Yet we act as if loving the land is an internal affair that has no energy outside the confines of our head and heart. On the high prairie at Cascade Head another truth is revealed, the active force of love for land is made visible. Here the ritual burning of the headland cemented the people's connection to salmon, to each other, and to the spirit world, but it also created biodiversity. The ceremonial fires converted forests to fingers of seaside prairie, islands of open habitat in a matrix of fog-dark trees. Burning created the headland meadows that are home to fire-dependent species that occur nowhere else on earth.

Likewise, the First Salmon Ceremony, in all its beauty, reverberates through all the domes of the world. The feasts of love and gratitude were not just internal emotional expressions but actually aided the upstream passage of the fish by releasing them from predation for a critical time. Laying salmon bones back in the streams returned nutrients to the system. These are ceremonies of practical reverence.

The burning beacon is a beautiful poem, but it is a poem written physically, deeply on the land.

People loved the salmon the way fire loves grass
and the blaze loves the darkness of the sea.

Today we only write it on postcards ("Terrific view from Cascade Head—wish you were here") and grocery lists ("Pick up salmon, 1½ pounds").

Ceremony focuses attention so that attention becomes intention. If you stand together and profess a thing before your community, it holds you accountable.

Ceremonies transcend the boundaries of the individual and resonate beyond the human realm. These acts of reverence are powerfully pragmatic. These are ceremonies that magnify life.

In many Indigenous communities, the hems of our ceremonial robes have been unraveled by time and history, but the fabric remains strong. In the dominant society, though, ceremony seems to have withered away. I suppose there are many reasons for that: the frenetic pace of life, dissolution of community, the sense that ceremony is an artifact of organized religion forced upon participants rather than a celebration joyfully chosen.

The ceremonies that persist—birthdays, weddings, funerals—focus only on ourselves, marking rites of personal transition. Perhaps the most universal is high school graduation. I love graduation in my small town, with the whole community dressed up and filling the auditorium on a June evening, whether you have a kid graduating or not. There's a sense of community in the shared emotions. Pride for the young people walking across the stage. Relief for some. A good dose of nostalgia and remembrance. We celebrate those beautiful young people who have enriched our lives; we honor their hard work and accomplishment against all odds. We tell them that they are our hope for the future. We encourage them to go off into the world and pray that they will come back home. We applaud for them. They applaud for us. Everyone cries a little. And then the parties begin.

And, at least in our little town, we know it's not an empty ritual. The ceremony has power. Our collective good wishes really do fuel the confidence and strength of young people about to leave home. The ceremony reminds them of where they come from and their responsibilities to the community that has supported them. We hope it inspires them. And the checks tucked into the graduation cards really do help them make their way in the world. These ceremonies too magnify life.

We know how to carry out this rite for each other and we do it well. But imagine standing by the river, flooded with those same feelings as the Salmon march into the auditorium of their estuary. Rise in their honor, thank them for all the ways they have enriched our lives, sing to honor their hard work and accomplishments against all odds, tell them they are our hope for the future, encourage them to go off into the world to grow, and pray that they will come home. Then the feasting begins. Can we extend our bonds of celebration and support from our own species to the others who need us?

Many Indigenous traditions still recognize the place of ceremony and often focus their celebrations on other species and events in the cycle of the seasons. In a colonist society the ceremonies that endure are not about land; they're about family and culture, values that are transportable from the old country. Ceremonies for the land no doubt existed there, but it seems they did not survive emigration in any substantial way. I think there is wisdom in regenerating them here, as a means to form bonds with this land.

To have agency in the world, ceremonies should be reciprocal cocreations, organic in nature, in which the community creates ceremony and the ceremony creates communities. They should not be cultural appropriations from Native peoples. But generating new ceremony in today's world is hard to do. There are towns I know that hold apple festivals and Moose Mania, but despite the wonderful food, they tend toward the commercial. Educational events like wildflower weekends and Christmas bird counts are all steps in the right direction, but they lack an active, reciprocal relationship with the more-than-human world.

I want to stand by the river in my finest dress. I want to sing, strong and hard, and stomp my feet with a hundred others so that the waters hum with our happiness. I want to dance for the renewal of the world.

On the banks of the Salmon River estuary today, people are again waiting by the stream, watching. Their faces are alight with anticipation and sometimes furrowed with concern. Instead of their finest clothes, they wear tall rubber boots and canvas vests. Some wade in with nets, while others tend buckets. From time to time they whoop and yell with delight at what they find. It's a First Salmon Ceremony of a different kind.

Beginning in 1976, the U.S. Forest Service and a host of partner organizations led by Oregon State University initiated a restoration project for the estuary. Their plan was to remove the dikes and dams and tidegates and once again let the tidal waters go where they were meant to go, to fulfill their purpose. Hoping that the land remembered how to be an estuary, the teams worked to dismantle the human structures, one by one.

The plan was guided by many cumulative lifetimes of ecological research, endless hours in the lab, scorching sunburns in the field, and shivering winter days of collecting data in the rain, as well as gorgeous summer days when new species miraculously returned. This is what we field biologists live for: the chance to be outside in the vital presence of other species, who are generally way more interesting than we are. We get to sit at their feet and listen. Potawatomi stories remember that all the plants and animals, including humans, used to speak the same language. We could share with one another what our lives were like. But that gift is gone and we are the poorer for it.

Because we can't speak the same language, our work as scientists is to piece the story together as best we can. We can't ask the salmon directly what they need, so we ask them with experiments and listen carefully to their answers. We stay up half the night at the microscope looking at the annual rings in fish ear bones in order to know how the fish react to water temperature. So we can fix it. We run experiments on the effects of salinity on the growth of invasive grasses. So we can fix it. We measure and record and analyze in ways that might seem lifeless but to us are the conduits to understanding the inscrutable lives of species not our own. Doing science with awe and humility is a powerful act of reciprocity with the more-than-human world.

I've never met an ecologist who came to the field for the love of data or for the wonder of a p-value. These are just ways we have of crossing the species boundary, of slipping off our human skin and wearing fins or feathers or foliage, trying to know others as fully as we can. Science can be a way of forming intimacy and respect with other species that is rivaled only by the observations of traditional knowledge holders. It can be a path to kinship.

These too are my people. Heart-driven scientists whose notebooks, smudged with salt marsh mud and filled with columns of numbers, are love letters to salmon. In their own way, they are lighting a beacon for salmon, to call them back home.

When the dikes and dams were removed, the land did remember how to be a salt marsh. Water remembered how it was supposed to distribute itself through tiny drainage channels in the sediment. Insects remembered where they were supposed to lay their eggs. Today the natural curvaceous flow of the river has been restored. From the headland, the river looks like an etching of a gnarled old shore pine, on a background of waving sedges. Sandbars and deep pools swirl patterns of gold and blue. And in this reborn water world, young salmon rest in every curve. The only straight lines are the old boundaries of the dikes, a reminder of how the flow was interrupted and how it was renewed.

The First Salmon Ceremonies were not conducted for the people. They were for the Salmon themselves, and for all the glittering realms of Creation, for the renewal of the world. People understood that when lives are given on their behalf they have received something precious. Ceremonies are a way to give something precious in return.

When the season turns and the grasses dry on the headland, preparations begin; they repair the nets and get their gear together. They come every year at this time. They gather together all the traditional foods, as there will be many mouths to feed on the crew. The data recorders are all calibrated and ready. With waders and boats, the biologists are on the river to dip nets into the restored channels of the estuary, to take its pulse. They come now every day to check, go down to the shore and gaze out to sea. And still the salmon do not come. So the waiting scientists roll out their sleeping bags and turn off the lab equipment. All but one. A single microscope light is left on.

Out beyond the surf they gather, tasting the waters of home. They see it against the dark of the headland. Someone has left a light on, blazing a tiny beacon into the night, calling the salmon back home.

Putting Down Roots

A summer day on the banks of the Mohawk River: *Én:ska, tékeni, áhsen*. Bend and pull, bend and pull. *Kaié:ri, wísk, iá:ia'k, tsiá:ta*, she calls to her granddaughter, standing waist deep in the grass. Her bundle grows thicker with every stoop of her back. She straightens up, rubs the small of her back, and tilts her head up to the blue summer sky, her black braid swinging in the arch of her back. Bank swallows twitter over the river. The breeze off the water sets the grasses waving and carries the fragrance of sweetgrass that rises from her footsteps.

A spring morning four hundred years later:

Én:ska, tékeni, áhsen. One, two, three; bend and dig, bend and dig. My bundle grows smaller with every stoop of my back. I drive my trowel into the soft ground and rock it back and forth. It scrapes against a buried stone and I dig my fingers in to unearth it, cast the stone aside to make an apple-sized hole big enough for the roots. From the tangled bundle wrapped in burlap, my fingers separate out a single clump of sweetgrass. I set it in the hole, scoop soil around it, speak words of welcome, and tamp it down. I straighten up and rub the small of my aching back. The sunshine pours down around us, warming the grass and releasing its scent. Red stake flags flutter in the breeze, marking the outlines of our plots.

Kaié:ri, wísk, iá:ia'k, tsiá:ta. From time beyond memory, Mohawk people inhabited this river valley that now bears their name. Back then the river was full of fish and its spring floods brought silt to fertilize their cornfields. Sweetgrass, called *wenserakon ohonte* in Mohawk, flourished on the banks. That language has not been heard here for centuries. Replaced by waves of immigrants, the Mohawk people were pushed from this generous valley in upstate New York to the very margins of the country. The once dominant culture of the great Haudenosaunee (Iroquois) Confederacy was reduced to a patchwork of small reservations. The language that first gave voice to ideas like democracy, women's equality, and the Great Law of Peace became an endangered species.

Mohawk language and culture didn't disappear on their own. Forced assimilation, the government policy to deal with the so-called Indian problem, shipped Mohawk children to the barracks at Carlisle, Pennsylvania, where the school's avowed mission was "Kill the Indian to Save the Man." Braids were cut off and Native languages forbidden. Girls were trained to cook and clean and wear white gloves on Sunday. The scent of sweetgrass was replaced by the soap smells of the barracks laundry. Boys learned sports and skills useful to a settled village life: carpentry, farming, and how to handle money in their pockets. The government's goal of breaking the link between land, language, and Native people was nearly a success. But the Mohawk call themselves the *Kanienkeha*—People of the Flint—and flint does not melt easily into the great American melting pot.

Over the top of the waving grasses I can see two other heads bent to the soil. The shiny black curls tied back with a red bandanna belong to Daniela. She pushes herself up from her knees and I watch her tally the number of plants in her plot . . . 47, 48, 49. Without looking up she makes notes on her clipboard, slings her bundle over her shoulder, and moves on. Daniela is a graduate student and for months we have been planning for this day. This work has become her thesis project and she's anxious about getting it right. On graduate school forms it says that I'm her professor, but I've been telling her all along that it is the plant who will be her greatest teacher.

On the other side of the field, Theresa looks up, swinging her braid over her shoulder. She's rolled the sleeves of her T-shirt, which reads IROQUOIS NATIONALS LACROSSE, and her forearms are streaked with dirt. Theresa is a Mohawk basket maker and is an integral part of our research team. She's taken the day off from work to kneel in the dirt with us and she grins from ear to ear. Sensing our flagging energy, she starts a counting chant to lift our spirits. *"Kaié:ri, wísk, iá:ia'k, tsiá:ta,"* she calls out, and together we count out the rows of plants. In rows of seven, for seven generations, we are putting roots in the ground welcoming the sweetgrass back home.

Despite Carlisle, despite exile, despite a siege four hundred years long, there is something, some heart of living stone, that will not surrender. I don't know just what sustained the people, but I believe it was carried in words. Pockets of the language survived among those who stayed rooted to place. Among those remaining, the Thanksgiving Address was spoken to greet the day: "Let us put our minds together as one and send greetings and thanks to our Mother Earth, who sustains our lives with her many gifts." Grateful reciprocity with the world, as solid as a stone, sustained them when all else was stripped away.

In the 1700s, the Mohawks had to flee their homelands in the Mohawk Valley and settled at Akwesasne, straddling the border with Canada. Theresa comes from a long line of Akwesasne basket makers.

The marvel of a basket is in its transformation, its journey from wholeness as a living plant to fragmented strands and back to wholeness again as a basket. A basket knows the dual powers of destruction and creation that shape the world. Strands once separated are rewoven into a new whole. The journey of a basket is also the journey of a people.

With their roots in riverside wetlands, both black ash and sweetgrass are neighbors on the land. They are reunited as neighbors in the Mohawk baskets. Braids of sweetgrass are woven among the splints of ash. Theresa remembers many childhood hours spent making braids from individual leaves of sweetgrass, twining them tight and even to reveal their glossy shine. Also woven into the baskets are the laughter and the stories of the gathered women, where English and Mohawk blend together in the same sentence. Sweetgrass coils around the basket rim and threads the lids, so that even an empty basket contains the smell of the land, weaving the link between people and place, language and identity. Basket making also brings economic security. A woman who knows how to weave will not go hungry. Making sweetgrass baskets has become almost synonymous with being Mohawk.

Traditional Mohawks speak the words of thanksgiving to the land, but these days the lands along the St. Lawrence River have little to be grateful for. When parts of the reserve were flooded by power dams, heavy industry moved in to take advantage of the cheap electricity and easy shipping routes. Alcoa, General Motors, and Domtar don't view the world through the prism of the Thanksgiving Address, and Akwesasne became one of the most contaminated communities in the country. The families of fishermen can no longer eat what they catch. Mother's milk at Akwesasne carries a heavy burden of PCBs and dioxin. Industrial pollution made following traditional lifeways unsafe, threatening the bond between people and the land. Industrial toxins were poised to finish what was started at Carlisle.

Sakokwenionkwas, also known as Tom Porter, is a member of the Bear Clan. The Bear is known for protecting the people and as the keeper of medicine knowledge. Just so, twenty years ago, Tom and a handful of others set out with healing in mind. As a boy, he had heard his grandmother repeat the old prophecy that someday a small band of Mohawks would return to inhabit their old home along the Mohawk River. In 1993, that someday arrived when Tom and friends left Akwesasne for ancestral lands in the Mohawk Valley. Their vision was to create a new community on old lands, far from PCBs and power dams.

They settled on four hundred acres of woods and farms at Kanatsiohareke. It's a place name from the time when this valley was dense with longhouses. In researching the land's history, they found that Kanatsiohareke was the site of an ancient Bear Clan village. Today the old memories are weaving among new stories. A barn and houses nestle at the foot of a bluff in a bend of the river. Silty floodplain loams run right down to the banks. The hills, once laid waste by lumbermen, have regrown with straight stands of pine and oak. A powerful artesian well pours from a cleft in the bluff with a strength that endures even the deepest drought and fills a clear mossy pool. In the still water, you can see your own face. The land speaks the language of renewal.

When Tom and others arrived, the buildings were in a sad state of disrepair. Over the years, scores of volunteers have banded together to repair roofs and replace windows. The big kitchen once again smells of corn soup and strawberry drink on feast days. An arbor for dancing was built among the old apple trees, making a place where people can gather to relearn and celebrate Haudenosaunee culture. The goal was "Carlisle in reverse": Kanatsiohareke would return to the people what was taken from them—their language, their culture, their spirituality, their identity. The children of the lost generation could come home.

After rebuilding, the next step was to teach the language, Tom's anti-Carlisle motto being "Heal the Indian, Save the Language." Kids at Carlisle and other mission schools all over the country had their knuckles rapped—and much worse—for speaking their native language. Boarding school survivors did not teach their children the language of their birth, in order to spare them hardship. And so the language dwindled right along with the land. Only a few fluent speakers remained, most over the age of seventy. The language was teetering on extinction, like an endangered species with no habitat to rear its young.

When a language dies, so much more than words are lost. Language is the dwelling place of ideas that do not exist anywhere else. It is a prism through which to see the world. Tom says that even words as basic as numbers are imbued with layers of meaning. The numbers we use to count plants in the sweetgrass meadow also recall the Creation Story. *Én:ska*—one. This word invokes the fall of Skywoman from the world above. All alone, *én:ska*, she fell toward the earth. But she was not alone, for in her womb a second life was growing. *Tékeni*—there were two. Skywoman gave birth to a daughter, who bore twin sons and so then there were three—*áhsen*. Every time the Haudenosaunee count to three in their own language, they reaffirm their bond to Creation.

Plants are also integral to reweaving the connection between land and people. A place becomes a home when it sustains you, when it feeds you in body as well as spirit. To recreate a home, the plants must also return. When I heard of the homecoming at Kanatsiohareke, visions of sweetgrass rose in my mind. I began looking for a way to bring them back to their old home.

One morning in March I stopped by Tom's place to talk about planting sweetgrass in the spring. I was full of plans for an experimental restoration, but I'd forgotten myself. No work could be done before guests were fed, and we sat down to a big breakfast of pancakes and thick maple syrup. Tom stood at the stove in a red flannel shirt, a powerfully built man, his pitch hair streaked with gray, but his face is scarcely wrinkled despite his more than seventy years. Words flow from him as water flows from the spring at the foot of the bluff—stories, dreams, and jokes that warm the kitchen like the scent of maple syrup. He refilled my plate with a smile and a story, ancient teachings braided into his conversation as naturally as comments on the weather. Strands of spirit and matter are woven together like black ash and sweetgrass.

"What's a Potawatomi doing way out here?" he asks. "Aren't you a long way from home?"

I need only one word: *Carlisle*.

We lingered over coffee and our talk turned to his dreams for Kanatsiohareke. On this land he sees a working farm where people learn again how to grow traditional foods, a place for the traditional ceremonies to honor the cycle of the seasons, where "the words that come before all else" are spoken. He spoke for a long time about the Thanksgiving Address as the core of Mohawk relationship to land. I remembered a question that had long been on my mind.

At the end of the words that come before all else, when thanks have been given to all the beings of the land, I asked, "has the land ever been known to say thank you in reply?" Tom was quiet for a second, piled more pancakes on my plate, and set the syrup jug in front of me. That's as good an answer as I know.

From a drawer in the table Tom took out a bag of fringed buckskin and laid a piece of soft deerskin on the table. He poured onto it a rattling pile of smooth peach seeds, one side painted black, the other white. He drew us into the gambling game, guessing how many pits in each throw will be white and how many black. His pile of winnings mounded up while ours dwindled. While we shook the pits and threw them down he told me about the time this game was played for very high stakes.

The twin grandsons of Skywoman had long struggled over the making and unmaking of the world. Now their struggle came down to this one game. If all the pits came up black, then all the life that had been created would be destroyed. If all the pits were white, then the beautiful earth would remain. They played and played without resolution and finally they came to the final roll. If all came up black, it would be done. The twin who made sweetness in the world sent his thoughts out to all the living beings he had made and asked them to help, to stand on the side of life. Tom told us how in the final roll, as the peach stones hung for a moment in the air, all the members of Creation joined their voices together and gave a mighty shout for life. And turned the last pit white. The choice is always there.

Tom's daughter came to join the game. She held a red velvet bag in her hands and poured its contents onto the deerskin. Diamonds. The sharp facets threw rainbows of color. She beamed at us as we oohed and aahed. Tom explained that these are Herkimer diamonds, beautiful quartz crystals as clear as water and harder than flint. Buried in the earth, they are washed along by the river and turn up from time to time, a blessing from the land.

We put on our jackets and walked out over the fields. Tom paused at the paddock to offer apples to the big Belgians. All was quiet, the river slipping along the banks. With the right eyes you can almost un-see Route 5, the railroad tracks, and I-90 across the river. You can almost see fields of Iroquois white corn and riverside meadows where women are picking sweetgrass. Bend and pull, bend and pull. But the fields where we walk are neither sweetgrass nor corn.

When Skywoman first scattered the plants, sweetgrass flourished along this river, but today it is gone. Just as the Mohawk language was replaced by English and Italian and Polish, the sweetgrass was crowded out by immigrants. Losing a plant can threaten a culture in much the same way as losing a language. Without sweetgrass, the grandmothers don't bring the granddaughters to the meadows in July. Then what becomes of their stories? Without sweetgrass, what happens to the baskets? To the ceremony that uses these baskets?

The history of the plants is inextricably tied up with the history of the people, with the forces of destruction and creation. At graduation ceremonies at Carlisle, the young men were required to take an oath: "I am no longer an Indian man. I will lay down the bow and arrow forever and put my hand to the plow." Plows and cows brought tremendous changes to the vegetation. Just as Mohawk identity is tied to the plants the people use, so it was for the European immigrants who sought to make a home here. They brought along their familiar plants, and the associated weeds followed the plow to supplant the natives. Plants mirror changes in culture and ownership of land. Today this field is choked by a vigorous sward of foreign plants that the first sweetgrass pickers would not recognize: quackgrass, timothy, clover, daisies. A wave of invasive purple loosestrife threatens from along the slough. To restore sweetgrass here we'll need to loosen the hold of the colonists, opening a way for the return of the natives.

Tom asked me what it would take to bring sweetgrass back, to create a meadow where basket makers can once again find materials. Scientists have not devoted much effort to the study of sweetgrass, but basket makers know that it can be found in a wide array of conditions, from wetlands to dry railroad tracks. It thrives in full sun and especially favors moist, open soil. Tom bent and picked up a handful of the floodplain soil and let it sift through his fingers. Except for the dense turf of exotic species, this seems like a good place for sweetgrass. Tom glanced at the old Farmall tractor in the lane, covered with a blue tarp. "Where can we get some seeds?"

It's a strange thing about sweetgrass seed. The plant sends up flowering stalks in early June, but the seeds it makes are rarely viable. If you sow a hundred seeds, you might get one plant if you're lucky. Sweetgrass has its own way of multiplying. Every shiny green shoot that pokes up above ground also produces a long, slender white rhizome, winding its way through the soil. All along its length are buds, which will sprout up and emerge into the sunshine. Sweetgrass can send its rhizomes many feet out from the parent. In this way, the plant could travel freely all along the riversides. This was a good plan when the land was whole.

But those tender white rhizomes cannot make their way across a highway or a parking lot. When a patch of sweetgrass was lost to the plow it could not be replenished by seed from outside. Daniela has revisited many places where historical records show sweetgrass once lived, more than half of which no longer carry its fragrance. The major cause of decline seems to be development, native populations eliminated by wetland draining, converting wild places to agriculture and pavement. As nonnative species come in, they may also crowd out the sweetgrass— plants repeating the history of their people.

In nursery beds back at the university, I've been growing up a stock of sweetgrass, waiting for this day. I had searched far and wide for a grower who could sell us plants to begin the nursery and finally located an operation in California that had some. This seemed odd, since *Hierochloe odorata* does not occur naturally in California. When I asked about where their planting stock came from, I got a surprising answer: Akwesasne. It was a sign. I bought it all.

Under irrigation and fertilizer, the beds have grown thick. But cultivation is miles removed from restoration. The science of restoration ecology depends upon myriad other factors—soil, insects, pathogens, herbivores, competition. Plants are seemingly equipped with their own sense about where they will live, defying the predictions of science, for there is yet another dimension to sweetgrass' requirements. The most vigorous stands are the ones tended by basket makers. Reciprocity is a key to success. When the sweetgrass is cared for and treated with respect, it will flourish, but if the relationship fails, so does the plant.

What we contemplate here is more than ecological restoration; it is the restoration of relationship between plants and people. Scientists have made a dent in understanding how to put ecosystems back together, but our experiments focus on soil pH and hydrology—matter, to the exclusion of spirit. We might look to the Thanksgiving Address for guidance on weaving the two. We are dreaming of a time when the land might give thanks for the people.

We walked back up to the house, imagining basket classes in years to come. Maybe Theresa would be the teacher, leading her granddaughter into the field that she herself has helped to plant. Kanatsiohareke runs a gift shop to raise funds for the work of the community. The shop is filled with books and beautiful artwork, beaded moccasins, antler carvings, and, of course, baskets. Tom unlocked the door and we stepped inside. The still air smelled of sweetgrass hanging from the rafters. What words can capture that smell? The fragrance of your mother's newly washed hair as she holds you close, the melancholy smell of summer slipping into fall, the smell of memory that makes you close your eyes for a moment, and then a moment longer.

When I was young, I had no one to tell me that, like the Mohawks, Potawatomi people revere sweetgrass as one of the four sacred plants. No one to say that it was the first plant to grow on Mother Earth and so we braid it, as if it were our mother's hair, to show our loving care for her. The runners of the story could not find their way through a fragmented cultural landscape to me. The story was stolen at Carlisle.

Tom walks over to the bookshelf and chooses a thick red volume to lay on the counter. *The Indian Industrial School, Carlisle Pennsylvania.* 1879–1918. In the back of the book is a list of names, pages and pages of them: Charlotte Bigtree (Mohawk), Stephen Silver Heels (Oneida), Thomas Medicine Horse (Sioux). Tom points to show me his uncle's name. "That's why we're doing this," he says, "undoing Carlisle."

My grandfather is in this book too, I know. I run my finger down the long columns of names and stop at Asa Wall (Potawatomi). A pecan-picking Oklahoma boy just nine years old sent on the train across the prairies to Carlisle. His brother's name comes next, Uncle Oliver, who ran away back home. But Asa did not. He was one of the lost generation, one who never could go home again. He tried, but after Carlisle he didn't fit anywhere, so he joined the army. Instead of returning to a life among his family in Indian Territory he settled in upstate New York, not far from this riverbank, and raised his children in the immigrant world. At a time when cars were novel he became a superb mechanic. He was always fixing broken cars, always mending, seeking to make things whole. I think that same need, the need to make things whole, propels my work in ecological restoration. I imagine his knife-nose profile leaning over the hood of a car, his brown hands wiped on a greasy rag. During the Depression people flocked to his garage. Payment, if there was any, was often in eggs or turnips from the garden. But there were some things he couldn't make whole.

He didn't talk much about those days, but I wonder if he thought of the pecan grove in Shawnee where his family lived without him, the lost boy. The aunties would send boxes for us grandchildren: moccasins, a pipe, a buckskin doll. They were boxed away in the attic until our nana would lovingly take them out to show us, to whisper, "Remember who you are."

I suppose he achieved what he had been taught to want, a better life for his children and grandchildren, the American life he was taught to honor. My mind thanks him for his sacrifice, but my heart grieves for the one who could have told me stories of sweetgrass. All my life I have felt that loss. What was stolen at Carlisle has been a knot of sorrow I've carried like a stone buried in my heart. I am not alone. That grief lives on in all the families of those whose names appear on the pages of that big red book. The broken link between land and people, between the past and the present, aches like a badly broken bone still unknit.

The city of Carlisle, Pennsylvania, is proud of its history and wears its age well. To celebrate its tricentennial, people looked hard and honestly at the scope of its history. The city began as the Carlisle Barracks, a mustering ground for soldiers of the Revolutionary War. Back when Federal Indian Affairs was still a branch of the War Department, the same buildings became the Carlisle Indian School, the fire beneath the great melting pot. Today the spartan barracks that once held rows of iron cots for Lakota, Nez Perce, Potawatomi, and Mohawk children are genteel officer's quarters, with blooming dogwoods at the doorstep.

In honor of the anniversary, the descendants of all those lost children were invited back to Carlisle for what were called "ceremonies of remembrance and reconciliation." Three generations of my family traveled together to be there. With hundreds of other children and grandchildren, we converged on Carlisle. This was the first time most laid eyes on a place only hinted of in family stories, or not spoken of at all.

The town was decked out in star-spangled bunting draped from every window; a banner on the main street announced the upcoming tricentennial parade. It was lovely, a postcard-perfect town of narrow brick streets and buildings of rosy brick restored to colonial charm. Wrought iron fences and brass plaques with dates celebrate its antiquity. How surreal it seems that Carlisle has earned a reputation in America for fervent preservation of its heritage, while in Indian Country the name is a chilling emblem of a heritage killer. I walked silently among the barracks. Forgiveness was hard to find.

We gathered at the cemetery, a small-fenced rectangle beside the parade ground, with four rows of stones. Not all of the kids who came to Carlisle left. There lay the dust that was born a child in Oklahoma, in Arizona, at Akwesasne. Drums sounded in the rain-washed air. The scent of burning sage and sweetgrass wrapped the small crowd in prayer. Sweetgrass is a healing medicine, a smudge that invokes kindness and compassion, coming as it does from our first Mother. The sacred words of healing rose up around us.

Stolen children. Lost bonds. The burden of loss hangs in the air and mingles with the scent of the sweetgrass, reminding us that there was a time when all the peach stones threatened to turn black side up. One could choose to assuage the grief of that loss by anger and the forces of self-destruction. But all things come in twos, white peach stones and black, destruction and creation. If the people give a mighty shout for life, the peach stone game can have a different ending. For grief can also be comforted by creation, by rebuilding the homeland that was taken. The fragments, like ash splints, can be rewoven into a new whole. And so we are here along the river, kneeling in the earth with the smell of sweetgrass on our hands.

Here on my knees in the dirt, I find my own ceremony of reconciliation. Bend and dig, bend and dig. By now my hands are earth colored as I settle the last of the plants, whisper words of welcome, and tamp them down. I look over at Theresa. She is intent, finishing up her last bundle of transplants. Daniela is making her final notes.

The light is growing golden at the end of the day over our newly planted field of spindly sweetgrass. If I look at it just right, I can almost see the women walking a few years ahead. Bend and pull, bend and pull, their bundles growing thicker. Feeling blessed for this day by the river, I murmur to myself the words of thanksgiving.

The many paths from Carlisle—Tom's, Theresa's, and mine— converge here. In putting roots in the ground, we can join the mighty shout that turned the peach pit from black to white. I can take the buried stone from my heart and plant it here, restoring land, restoring culture, restoring myself.

My trowel digs deep into the soil and strikes against a rock. I scrape away the earth and pry it up to make room for the roots. I almost cast it aside, but it is strangely light in my hand. I pause for a closer look. It is nearly the size of an egg. With muddy thumb I rub away the dirt and a glassy surface is revealed, then another and another. Even beneath the dirt it gleams as clear as water. One face is rough and cloudy, abraded by time and history, but the rest is brilliant. There is light shining through. It is a prism and the fading light refracts, throwing rainbows from within the buried stone.

I dip it in the river to wash it clean and call Daniela and Theresa to come see. We are all struck with wonder as I cradle it in my hand. I wonder if it's right to keep it, but I'm torn by thoughts of laying it back in its home. Having found it, I find I cannot let it go. We pack up our tools and head up to the house to say our good-byes for the day. I open my hand to show the stone to Tom, to ask the question. "This is the way the world works," he says, "in reciprocity." We gave sweetgrass and the land gave a diamond. A smile lights his face and he closes my fingers over the stone. "This is for you," he says.

Umbilicaria: The Belly Button
of the World

Glacial erratics stud the Adirondack landscape, granite boulders dropped in place when the glaciers got tired of rolling them and melted their way back home to the north. The granite in these parts is anorthosite, among the oldest rocks on earth and resistant to weathering. Most of the boulders have been rounded by their journey, but some still stand tall and sharp-edged, like this one, which is as big as a dump truck. I run my fingers over its surface. Veined with quartz, its top is a knife edge and its sides too steep to climb.

This elder has sat silently in these lakeshore woods for ten thousand years as forests have come and gone, lake levels ebbed and flowed. And after all that time, it is still a microcosm of the postglacial era when the world was a cold desert of rubble and scraped earth. Alternately baking in the summer sun and snow-blasted in the long winter, without soil in a world still treeless, the glacial till provided a forbidding home for pioneers.

Undaunted, lichens volunteered to put down roots and homestead stone—metaphorically, of course, since they have no roots. This is an asset when there is no soil. Lichens have no roots, no leaves, no flowers. They are life at its most basic. From a dusting of propagules that lodged in tiny pits and fissures just a pinprick deep, they settled the bare granite. This microtopography gave protection from the wind and offered concavities where water might rest after a rain in a microscopic puddle. It wasn't much, but it was enough.

In the span of centuries the rock became glazed with a gray-green crust of lichen almost indistinguishable from the rock itself, a bare coating of life. The steep faces and exposure to the winds off the lake have prevented any accumulation of soil, its surface a last relic of the Ice Age.

I come here sometimes just to be in the presence of such ancient beings. The sides of the boulder are festooned with *Umbilicaria americana* in raggedy ruffles of brown and green, the most magnificent of northeastern lichens. Unlike those of its tiny crustose forebearers, the *Umbilicaria*'s thallus—its body—can span an outstretched hand. The largest one recorded was measured at just over two feet. Tiny ones cluster like baby chicks around a mother hen. So charismatic a being has accumulated many names; it is most frequently known as the rock tripe and sometimes as the oakleaf lichen.

Rain cannot linger on the vertical faces, so most of the time this boulder is dry and the lichens shrink and get crisp, making the rock look scabby. Without leaves or stem, *Umbilicaria* is simply a thallus, roughly circular in shape, like a tattered scrap of brown suede. Its upper surface when dry is a mousy shade of taupe. The thallus edges curl up in a chaotic sort of ruffle, exposing the black underside, which is crisp and grainy like a charred potato chip. It is anchored tightly to the rock at its center by a short stalk, like a very short-handled umbrella. The stalk, or umbilicus, cements the thallus to the rock from underneath.

The forest the lichens inhabit is a richly textured plantscape, but they are not plants. They blur the definition of what it means to be an individual, as a lichen is not one being, but two: a fungus and an alga. These partners are as different as could be and yet are joined in a symbiosis so close that their union becomes a wholly new organism.

I once heard a Navajo herbalist explain how she understands certain kinds of plants to be "married," due to their enduring partnership and unquestioning reliance on one another. Lichens are a couple in which the whole is more than the sum of its parts. My parents will celebrate their sixtieth wedding anniversary this year and seem to have just that kind of symbiosis, a marriage in which the balance of giving and taking is dynamic, the roles of giver and receiver shifting from moment to moment. They are committed to an "us" that emerges from the shared strengths and weaknesses of the partners, an "us" that extends beyond the boundaries of coupledom and into their family and community. Some lichens are like that too; their shared lives benefit the whole ecosystem.

All lichens, from the tiny crusts to the stately *Umbilicaria*, are a mutualistic symbiosis, a partnership in which both members benefit from their association. In many Native American wedding traditions, the bride and the groom present each other with baskets of gifts, traditionally representing what each promises to bring to the marriage. Often, the woman's basket contains plants from the garden or meadows to show her agreement to provide food for her husband. The man's basket may contain meat, or animal hides, a promise to provide for the family by hunting. Plant food and animal food, autotroph and heterotroph—the alga and the fungus also bring their particular gifts to their union as a lichen.

The algal partner is a collection of single cells, gleaming like emeralds and bearing the gift of photosynthesis, the precious alchemy of turning light and air to sugar. The alga is an autotroph, or one that makes its own food and will be the cook of the family, the producer. The alga can make all the sugar it needs for energy, but it's not very good at finding the minerals it needs. It can only photosynthesize when it's moist, but it has no ability to protect itself from drying.

The fungus partner is the heterotroph, or "other feeder," since it can't make its own food but must subsist on the carbon harvested by others. The fungus is brilliant at the art of dissolving things and liberating their minerals for its use, but it can't make sugar. The fungal wedding basket would be filled with specialized compounds like acids and enzymes that digest complex materials into their simpler components. The body of the fungus, a network of delicate threads, goes out hunting for minerals and then absorbs those molecules through its huge surface area. Symbiosis enables the alga and the fungus to engage in a reciprocal exchange of sugar and minerals. The resulting organism behaves as if it were a single entity, with a single name. In a traditional human marriage, the partners may change their names to indicate that they are a unit. Likewise, a lichen is not named a fungus or an alga. We name it as if it were one new being, an interspecies family, as it were: rock tripe, *Umbilicaria americana*.

In *Umbilicaria*, the algal partner is almost always a genus that would be called *Trebouxia* if it lived alone or was not "lichenized." The fungal partner is always a type of ascomycete but not always the same species. Depending on how you look at it, the fungi are quite loyal. They always choose *Trebouxia* as their algal partner. The alga, however, is a bit more promiscuous, willing to hook up with a wider array of fungi. I guess we've all seen marriages like that, too.

In their shared architecture, the algal cells are embedded like green beads in fabric woven of fungal hyphae. If you sliced a cross section of the thallus it would be like a cake with four layers. The upper surface, the cortex, feels like the top of a mushroom, smooth and leathery. It is tightly woven of fungal filaments, or hyphae, to hold in moisture. The dusky brown coloration acts like a natural sunscreen that shields the algal layer, which lies just below, from intense sunlight.

Below the shelter of the fungal roof, the algae form a distinct medulla layer where the hyphae wrap themselves around the algal cells, like an arm draped over a shoulder or a loving embrace. Some fungal threads actually penetrate the green cells, as if they were long slender fingers reaching into a piggy bank. These fungal pickpockets help themselves to the sugars made by the alga and distribute them throughout the lichen. It has been estimated that the fungi take as much as half of the sugars the alga produces, maybe more. I've seen marriages like that, too, one partner siphoning off way more than he or she gives. Rather than thinking of lichens as a happy marriage, some researchers view them more as reciprocal parasitism. Lichens have been described as "fungi who discovered agriculture" by capturing photosynthetic beings within their fences of hyphae.

Below the medulla, the next layer is a loose tangle of fungal hyphae designed to hold water and thus keep the algae productive for longer. The bottommost layer is coal black and prickly with rhizines, microscopic hairlike extensions that help attach the lichen to the rock.

The fungal/algal symbiosis so blurs the distinction between individual and community that it has attracted a great deal of research attention. Some pairs are so specialized that they cannot live apart from one another. Nearly twenty thousand species of fungus are known to occur only as obligate members of a lichen symbiosis. Others have the capacity to live freely yet choose to join an alga to become a lichen.

Scientists are interested in how the marriage of alga and fungus occurs and so they've tried to identify the factors that induce two species to live as one. But when researchers put the two together in the laboratory and provide them with ideal conditions for both alga and fungus, they gave each other the cold shoulder and proceeded to live separate lives, in the same culture dish, like the most platonic of roommates. The scientists were puzzled and began to tinker with the habitat, altering one factor and then another, but still no lichen. It was only when they severely curtailed the resources, when they created harsh and stressful conditions, that the two would turn toward each other and begin to cooperate. Only with severe need did the hyphae curl around the alga; only when the alga was stressed did it welcome the advances.

When times are easy and there's plenty to go around, individual species can go it alone. But when conditions are harsh and life is tenuous, it takes a team sworn to reciprocity to keep life going forward. In a world of scarcity, interconnection and mutual aid become critical for survival. So say the lichens.

Lichens are opportunistic, making efficient use of resources when they're available and otherwise happily doing without. Most of the time when you encounter *Umbilicaria* it is as crisp and dry as a dead leaf, but it's far from deceased. It is only waiting, empowered with a remarkable physiology to endure drought. Like the mosses with whom it shares the rocks, lichens are poikilohydric: they can photosynthesize and grow only when they are wet, but they are not able to regulate their own water balance—their moisture content mirrors the moisture in the environment. If the rock is dry, so are they. A rain shower changes everything.

The very first drops splatter hard against the rigid surface of rock tripe, which instantly changes color. The mud-brown thallus becomes sprinkled with clay-gray polka dots, the tracks of raindrops, which deepen over the next minute to sage green, like a magic picture developing before your eyes. And then, as the green spreads, the thallus begins to move as if animated by muscle, stretching and flexing as the water expands its tissue. In a matter of minutes it is transformed from a dry scab to tender green skin, as smooth as the inside of your arm.

With the lichen restored, you can see how it got its other name. Where the umbilicus anchors the thallus to the rock, the soft skin is dimpled, with little wrinkles radiating about its center. It looks to all the world like a belly button. Some are such perfect little navels that you want to kiss them, like a little baby tummy. Some are kind of saggy and wrinkled, like the old woman whose belly carried those babies.

Since the navel lichen grows on vertical surfaces, the top will dry out faster than the bottom, where moisture collects. When the thallus starts to dry and its edges curl up, a shallow water-holding trough forms along its lower edge. As the lichen gets older, it becomes asymmetrical, the bottom half as much as 30 percent longer than the upper, a legacy of lingering moisture that permitted it to keep photosynthesizing and growing after the top half was dry and still. The trough can also collect debris, the lichen equivalent of belly-button lint.

I lean in close and find lots of baby thalli, little brown discs about the size of a pencil eraser, scattered over the rock. This is a healthy population. These juveniles arose either from broken fragments of the parent or, because of their perfect symmetry, more likely from specialized propagules called soredia—a little package of both fungus and alga designed for joint dispersal, so they'll never be without their partners.

Even the tiny thalli are dimpled with navels. How fitting that this ancient being, one of the first forms of life on the planet, should be connected to the earth by an umbilicus. The marriage of alga and fungus, *Umbilicaria* is the child of earth, life nourished by stone.

And people are nourished by *Umbilicaria*, as the name rock tripe suggests. Rock tripe is generally categorized as a starvation food, but it's not so bad. My students and I make a pot every summer. Each thallus may take decades to grow, so our harvest is minimal, just enough to taste. First we soak the thallus overnight in freshwater to remove the grit it has accumulated. The soaking water is poured off to leach away the powerful acids the lichen uses to eat away at the rock. Then we set it to boil for half an hour. It yields a lichen broth that is quite palatable and rich enough in protein to gel like consommé when it is chilled, tasting vaguely of rock and mushroom. The thallus itself we cut into strips that are like a chewy pasta, making a quite serviceable lichen noodle soup.

Umbilicaria is often the victim of its own success. Accumulation is its undoing. Slowly, slowly the lichens build up a thin layer of debris around them, perhaps their own exfoliations, or dust, or falling needles—the flotsam of the forest. The dusting of organic matter holds the moisture that the bare rock could not hold and gradually an accretion of soil creates a habitat for mosses and ferns. Through the laws of ecological succession, the lichens have done their work of laying the foundation for others, and now the others have come.

I know a whole escarpment covered with rock tripe. Water trickles down fissures in the cliff face and the trees have closed in, making a shady paradise for mosses. The lichens colonized in an earlier day, before the forest was thick and moist. Today they look like an encampment of floppy canvas tents on the rock, some now tattered, with sagging rooflines. When I scan the oldest tripe with my hand lens I see they are crusted over with algae and other crustose lichens like microscopic barnacles. Some have slippery green streaks where blue-green algae have made themselves at home. These epiphytes can impede the photosynthesis of the lichen by blocking out the sun. A deep pillow of *Hypnum* moss catches my eye, vivid against the dull lichens. I move along the ledge to admire its plush contours. Sticking out from its base like a ruffle around a pillow are the edges of an *Umbilicaria* thallus, nearly engulfed by the moss. Its time has come to an end.

The lichen, in a single body, unites the two great pathways of life: the so-called grazing food chain based on the building up of beings, and the detrital food chain based on taking them apart. Producers and decomposers, the light and the darkness, the givers and receivers wrapped in each other's arms, the warp and the weft of the same blanket so closely woven that it's impossible to discern the giving from the taking. Some of earth's oldest beings, lichens are born from reciprocity. Our elders share the teachings that these rocks, the glacial erratics, are the oldest of grand-fathers, the carriers of prophecy, and our teachers. Sometimes I go to sit among them, the proverbial navel gazer at the belly button of the world.

These ancients carry teachings in the ways that they live. They remind us of the enduring power that arises from mutualism, from the sharing of the gifts carried by each species. Balanced reciprocity has enabled them to flourish under the most stressful of conditions. Their success is measured not by consumption and growth, but by graceful longevity and simplicity, by persistence while the world changed around them. It is changing now.

While lichens can sustain humans, people have not returned the favor of caring for lichens. *Umbilicaria*, like many lichens, is highly sensitive to air pollution. When you find *Umbilicaria*, you know you're breathing the purest air. Atmospheric contaminants like sulfur dioxide and ozone will kill it outright. Pay attention when it departs.

Indeed, whole species and entire ecosystems are vanishing before our eyes in the vanguard of accelerating climate chaos. At the same time, other habitats are on the rise. Melting glaciers are exposing land where it has not been seen for millennia. At the edge of the ice, newly scraped land is emerging, a jumble of rocky till, harsh and cold. *Umbilicaria* is known to be among the first to colonize postglacial forelands today, just as it did when the earth was raw and bare, ten thousand years ago—another era of great climate change. Our Indigenous herbalists say to pay attention when plants come to you; they're bringing you something you need to learn.

For millennia, these lichens have held the responsibility of building up life and in an eyeblink of earth's history we have set about undermin-ing their work to usher in a time of great environmental stress, a barren-ness of our own making. I suspect that lichens will endure. We could, too, if we listen to their teachings. If not, I imagine *Umbilicaria* will cover the rocky ruins of our time long after our delusions of separateness have relegated us to the fossil record, a ruffled green skin adorning the crum-bling halls of power.

Rock tripe, oak leaf lichen, navel lichen. I'm told that *Umbilicaria* is known in Asia by another name: the ear of the stone. In this almost silent place I imagine them listening. To the wind, to a hermit thrush, to thunder. To our wildly growing hunger. Ear of stone, will you hear our anguish when we understand what we have done? The harsh post-glacial world in which you began may well become our own unless we listen to the wisdom carried in the mutualistic marriage of your bodies. Redemption lives in knowing that you might also hear our hymns of joy when we too marry ourselves to the earth.

Old-Growth Children

We're chatting like vireos as we hike with long, easy strides through rolling stands of Doug Fir. Then, at some invisible boundary, the temperature drops in a cool breath and we descend into a basin. The conversation halts.

Fluted trunks rise from a lawn of deep moss-green, their canopies lost in the hanging mist that suffuses the forest with hazy silver twilight. Strewn with huge logs and clumps of ferns, the forest floor is a featherbed of needles dappled with sun flecks. Light streams through holes over the heads of young trees while their grandmothers loom in shadows, great buttressed trunks eight feet in diameter. You want to be quiet in instinctive deference to the cathedral hush and because nothing you could possibly say would add a thing.

But it wasn't always quiet here. Girls were here, laughing and chatting while their grandmas sat nearby with singing sticks, supervising. A long scar runs up the tree across the way, a dull gray arrow of missing bark tapering off among the first branches, thirty feet up. The one who took this strip would have backed away, up the hill behind her, with the bark ribbon grasped in her hands, pulling until it tore loose.

In those days the ancient rainforests spread from Northern California to southeastern Alaska in a band between the mountains and the sea. Here is where the fog drips. Here is where the moisture-laden air from the Pacific rises against the mountains to produce upward of one hundred inches of rain a year, watering an ecosystem rivaled nowhere else on earth. The biggest trees in the world. Trees that were born before Columbus sailed.

And trees are just the beginning. The numbers of species of mammals, birds, amphibians, wildflowers, ferns, mosses, lichens, fungi, and insects are staggering. It's hard to write without running out of superlatives, for these were among the greatest forests on earth, forests peopled with centuries of past lives, enormous logs and snags that foster more life after their death than before. The canopy is a multilayered sculpture of vertical complexity from the lowest moss on the forest floor to the wisps of lichen hanging high in the treetops, raggedy and uneven from the gaps produced by centuries of windthrow, disease, and storms. This seeming chaos belies the tight web of interconnections between them all, stitched with filaments of fungi, silk of spiders, and silver threads of water. *Alone* is a word without meaning in this forest.

Native peoples of the coastal Pacific Northwest made rich livelihoods here for millennia, living with one foot in the forest and one on the shore, gathering the abundance of both. This is the rainy land of salmon, of wintergreen conifers, huckleberries, and sword fern. This is the land of the tree of ample hips and full baskets, the one known in the Salish languages as Maker of Rich Women, as Mother Cedar. No matter what the people needed, the cedar was ready to give, from cradleboard to coffin, holding the people.

In this wet climate, where everything is on its way back to decay, rot-resistant cedar is the ideal material. The wood is easily worked and buoyant. The huge, straight trunks practically offer themselves for seagoing craft that could carry twenty paddlers. And everything that was carried in those canoes was also the gift of cedar: paddles, fishing floats, nets, ropes, arrows, and harpoons. The paddlers even wore hats and capes of cedar, warm and soft against the wind and rain.

Along the creeks and bottomlands, the women sang their way down well-worn trails to find just the right tree for each purpose. Whatever they needed they asked for respectfully, and for whatever they received they offered prayers and gifts in return. Notching a wedge in the bark of a middle-aged tree, the women could peel off a ribbon a hands-width wide and twenty-five feet long. Harvesting bark from just a fraction of the tree's circumference, they ensured that the damage would heal over without ill effect. The dried strips were then beaten to separate the many layers, yielding inner bark with a satiny softness and a glossy sheen. A long process of shredding bark with a deer bone yielded a pile of fluffy cedar "wool." Newborn babies were delivered into a nest of this fleece. The "wool" could also be woven into warm, durable clothing and blankets. A family sat on woven mats of outer bark, slept on cedar beds, and ate from cedar dishes.

Every part of the tree was used. The ropy branches were split for tools, baskets, and fish traps. Dug and cleaned, cedars' long roots were peeled and split into a fine, strong fiber that is woven into the famous conical hats and ceremonial headgear that signify the identity of the one beneath the brim. During the famously cold and rainy winters, with a perpetual twilight of fog, who lit the house? Who warmed the house? From bow drill to tinder to fire, it was Mother Cedar.

When sickness came, the people turned again to her. Every part is medicine for the body, from the flat sprays of foliage to the flexible branches to the roots, and throughout there is powerful spiritual medicine as well. Traditional teachings recount that the power of cedars is so great and so fluid that it can flow into a worthy person who leans back into the embrace of her trunk. When death came, so came the cedar coffin. The first and last embrace of a human being was in the arms of Mother Cedar.

Just as old-growth forests are richly complex, so too were the old-growth cultures that arose at their feet. Some people equate sustainability with a diminished standard of living, but the aboriginal people of the coastal old-growth forests were among the wealthiest in the world. Wise use and care for a huge variety of marine and forest resources, allowed them to avoid overexploiting any one of them while extraordinary art, science, and architecture flowered in their midst. Rather than to greed, prosperity here gave rise to the great potlatch tradition in which material goods were ritually given away, a direct reflection of the generosity of the land to the people. Wealth meant having enough to give away, social status elevated by generosity. The cedars taught how to share wealth, and the people learned.

Scientists know Mother Cedar as *Thuja plicata*, the western red cedar. One of the venerable giants of the ancient forests, they reach heights of two hundred feet. They are not the tallest, but their enormous buttressed waistlines can be fifty feet in circumference, rivaling the girth of the redwoods. The bole tapers from the fluted base, sheathed in bark the color of driftwood. Her branches are graceful and drooping with tips that swoop upward like a bird in flight, each branch like a frond of green feathers.

Looking closely, you can see the tiny overlapping leaves that shingle each twig. The species epithet *plicata* refers to their folded, braided appearance. The tight weave and golden-green sheen make the leaves look like tiny braids of sweetgrass, as if the tree itself was woven of kindness.

Cedar unstintingly provided for the people, who responded with gratitude and reciprocity. Today, when cedar is mistaken for a commodity from the lumberyard, the idea of gift is almost lost. What can we who recognize the debt possibly give back?

The blackberries clawed at Franz Dolp's sleeves as he forced himself through the bramble. Salmonberry grabbing an ankle threatened to pull him down the nearly vertical hill, but you can't fall far before the thicket, eight feet tall, will trap you like Br'er Rabbit in the briar patch. You lose any sense of direction in the tangle; the only way is up, toward the ridgetop. Clearing trail is the first step. Nothing else is possible without access, so he pressed on, machete swinging.

Tall and lean in field pants and the tall rubber work boots that are endemic in this muddy, thorny terrain, he wore a black baseball cap pulled low. With artist's hands in worn work gloves, he was a man who knew how to sweat. That night he wrote in his journal: "This is work I should have started in my twenties, not my mid-fifties."

All afternoon he lopped and slashed a way toward the ridge, hacking blindly through the brush, his rhythm broken only by the clang of the blade off an obstacle hidden in the brambles: a huge old log, shoulder high, cedar by the looks of it. They were only milling Douglas fir in those early days, so they left the other trees to rot. Only thing is, cedar doesn't rot: it can last for a hundred years on the forest floor, maybe more. This one was a remnant of the missing forest, left over from the first cut more than a century ago. It was too big to cut through and a long way around, so Franz just created another bend in the trail.

Today, now that the old cedars are nearly gone, people want them. They scrounge old clear-cuts for the logs that were left behind. Shake-bolting, they call it, turning old logs into high-priced cedar shakes. The grain is so straight the shakes split right off.

It's amazing to think that, within the lifetime of those old trees on the ground, they have gone from being revered to being rejected to nearly being eliminated, and then somebody looked up and noticed they were gone and wanted them again.

"My tool of preference was a Cutter Mattock, commonly known in this area as a Maddox," Franz wrote. With this sharp edge, he could chop roots and grade trail, defeating, if briefly, the march of the vine maples.

It took several more days of wrangling impenetrable brush to break through to the ridgetop, where a view of Mary's Peak was the reward. "I remember the exhilaration as we reached a certain point and savored our accomplishment. Also the days when with the slopes and the weather contributing mightily to the feeling that everything had gotten out of hand and we just fell down laughing."

Franz's journals record his impressions of the view from the ridge, across a crazy-quilt landscape, the panorama broken up into forestry management units: polygons of dead brown and mottled patches of gray and green next to "dense plantations of young Doug Fir like sections of manicured lawn" in squares and wedges, all broken up like shards of shattered glass on the mountain. Only at the top of Mary's Peak, within the boundaries of a preserve, is there a continuous span of forest, rough textured and multihued from a distance, the signature of the old-growth forest, the forest that used to be.

"My work grew out of a deeply experienced sense of loss," he wrote, "the loss of what should be here."

When the Coast Range was first opened to logging in the 1880s, the trees were so big—three hundred feet tall and fifty feet around—that the bosses didn't know what to do with them. Eventually two poor sods were told to man the "misery whip," a thin, two-man crosscut saw that they pulled for weeks to fell the behemoths. These were the trees that built the cities of the west, which grew and then demanded even more. They said in those days, "You could never cut all the old growth."

About the time the chain saws last growled on these slopes, Franz was planting apple trees and thinking of cider, with his wife and kids on a farm hours away. A father, a young professor of economics, he was investing in home economics, his dream of an Oregon homestead, embedded in the forest, like the one he grew up on, and where he would stay forever.

Unknown to him, while he was raising cows and kids, the blackberries got started in the full sun above what would become his new land on Shotpouch Creek. They were doing their work of covering the stump farm and rusting remnants of logging chains, wheels, and rails. The salmonberries mingled their thorns with the rolls of barbed wire while moss reupholstered the old couch in the gully.

While his marriage was eroding and running downhill on the home farm, so was the soil at Shotpouch. The alders came to try to hold it in place, and then the maples. This was a land whose native language was conifer but now spoke only the slang of leggy hardwoods. Its dream of itself as groves of cedar and fir was gone, lost under the unrelenting chaos of brush. Straight and slow has little chance against fast and thorny. When he drove away from the farm intended for "till death do us part," the woman waving good-bye said, "I hope that your next dream turns out better than your last."

In his journal he wrote that he "made the mistake of visiting the farm after it was sold. The new owners had cut it all. I sat among the stumps and the swirling red dust and I cried. When I moved to Shotpouch after leaving the farm, I realized that making a new home required more than building a cabin or planting an apple tree. It required some healing for me and for the land."

And so it was that a wounded man moved to live on wounded land at Shotpouch Creek.

This patch of land was in the heart of the Oregon Coast Range, the same mountains where his grandfather had made a hardscrabble homestead. Old family photos show a rough cabin and grim faces, surrounded by nothing but stumps.

He wrote, "These forty acres were to be my retreat, my escape to the wild. But this was no pristine wilderness." The place he chose was near a spot on the map called Burnt Woods. Scalped Woods would have been more apt. The land was razed by a series of clear-cuts, first the venerable old forest and then its children. No sooner had the firs grown back than the loggers came for them again.

After land is clear-cut, everything changes. Sunshine is suddenly abundant. The soil has been broken open by logging equipment, raising its temperature and exposing mineral soil beneath the humus blanket. The clock of ecological succession has been reset, the alarm buzzing loudly.

Forest ecosystems have tools for dealing with massive disturbance, evolved from a history of blowdown, landslide, and fire. The early successional plant species arrive immediately and get to work on damage control. These plants—known as opportunistic, or pioneer, species—have adaptations that allow them to thrive after disturbance. Because resources like light and space are plentiful, they grow quickly. A patch of bare ground around here can disappear in a few weeks. Their goal is to grow and reproduce as fast as possible, so they don't bother themselves with making trunks but rather madly invest in leaves, leaves, and more leaves borne on the flimsiest of stems.

The key to success is to get more of everything than your neighbor, and to get it faster. That life strategy works when resources seem to be infinite. But pioneer species, not unlike pioneer humans, require cleared land, hard work, individual initiative, and numerous children. In other words, the window of *opportunity* for opportunistic species is short. Once trees arrive on the scene, the pioneers' days are numbered, so they use their photosynthetic wealth to make babies that will be carried by birds to the next clear-cut. As a result, many are berry makers: salmonberry, elderberry, huckleberry, blackberry.

The pioneers produce a community based on the principles of unlimited growth, sprawl, and high energy consumption, sucking up resources as fast as they can, wresting land from others through competition, and then moving on. When resources begin to run short, as they always will, cooperation and strategies that promote stability—strategies perfected by rainforest ecosystems—will be favored by evolution. The breadth and depth of these reciprocal symbioses are especially well developed in old-growth forests, which are designed for the long haul.

Industrial forestry, resource extraction, and other aspects of human sprawl are like salmonberry thickets—swallowing up land, reducing biodiversity, and simplifying ecosystems at the demand of societies always bent on having more. In five hundred years we exterminated old-growth cultures and old-growth ecosystems, replacing them with opportunistic culture. Pioneer human communities, just like pioneer plant communities, have an important role in regeneration, but they are not sustainable in the long run. When they reach the edge of easy energy, balance and renewal are the only way forward, wherein there is a reciprocal cycle between early and late successional systems, each opening the door for the other.

The old-growth forest is as stunning in its elegance of function as in its beauty. Under conditions of scarcity, there can be no frenzy of uncontrolled growth or waste of resources. The "green architecture" of the forest structure itself is a model of efficiency, with layers of foliage in a multilayered canopy that optimizes capture of solar energy. If we are looking for models of self-sustaining communities, we need look no further than an old-growth forest. Or the old-growth cultures they raised in symbiosis with them.

Franz's journals recall that when he compared the fragment of old growth he could see in the distance with the raw land at Shotpouch—where the only remnant of the ancient forest was an old cedar log—he knew he had found his purpose. Displaced from his own vision of how the world should be, he vowed that he would heal this place and return it to what it was meant to be. "My goal," he wrote, "is to plant an old-growth forest."

But his ambitions ranged beyond physical restoration. As Franz wrote, "It is important to engage in restoration with development of a personal relationship with the land and its living things." In working with the land, he wrote of the loving relationship that grew between them: "It was as if I discovered a lost part of myself."

After the garden and the fruit trees, his next goal was building a house that would honor the self-sufficiency and simplicity that he sought. His ideal had been to build the cabin from the red cedar—beautiful, fragrant, rot-resistant, and symbolic—left behind by the loggers on the slopes above. But the repeated logging had simply taken too much. So, regrettably, he had to purchase the cedar timber for the cabin, "with the promise that I would plant and grow more cedar trees than would ever be cut for my use."

Lightweight and highly water-repellent, sweet-smelling cedar was also the architectural choice for Indigenous rainforest peoples. Cedar houses, constructed of both logs and planks, were emblematic of the region. The wood split so readily that, in skilled hands, dimensional boards could be made without a saw. Sometimes trees were felled for lumber, but planks were more often split from naturally fallen logs. Remarkably, Mother Cedar also yielded planks from her living flanks. When a line of wedges of stone or antler were pounded into a standing tree, long boards would pop from the trunk along the straight grain. The wood itself is dead supportive tissue, so the harvest of a few boards from a big tree does not risk killing the whole organism—a practice that redefines our notions of sustainable forestry: lumber produced without killing a tree.

Now, however, industrial forestry dictates how the landscape is shaped and used. To own the land at Shotpouch, which is designated as timberlands, Franz was required to register an approved forest management plan for his new property. He wryly wrote his dismay that his land was classified "not as forestland, but timberland," as if the sawmill was the only possible destiny for a tree. Franz had an old-growth mind in a Doug Fir world.

The Oregon Department of Forestry and the College of Forestry at Oregon State University offered Franz technical assistance, prescribing herbicides to quell the brush and replanting with genetically improved Douglas fir. If you can ensure plenty of light by eliminating understory competition, Douglas fir makes timber faster than anything else around. But Franz didn't want timber. He wanted a forest.

"My love of this country motivated me to purchase land at Shotpouch," he wrote. "I wanted to do right here, even if I had little idea of what 'right' meant. To love a place is not enough. We must find ways to heal it." If he used the herbicides, the only tree that could tolerate the chemical rain was Douglas Fir, and he wanted all the species to be present. He vowed to clear the brush by hand.

Replanting an industrial forest is backbreaking labor. Crews of tree planters come in, progressing sideways on steep slopes with bulging sacks of seedlings. Walk six feet, dibble in a seedling, tamp it down. Walk six feet, repeat. One species. One pattern. But at that time there was no prescription for how to plant a natural forest, so Franz turned to the only teacher he had, the forest itself.

Observing the locations of species in the few existing old-growth plots, he tried to replicate their patterns on his own land. Douglas fir went on sunny open slopes, hemlock on the shady aspects, and cedar on the dimly lit, wet ground. Rather than getting rid of the young stands of alder and big-leaf maple as the authorities recommended, he let them stay to do their work of rebuilding soil and planted the shade-tolerant species beneath their canopy. Every tree was marked and mapped and tended. He hand-cleared the brush that threatened to swallow them up, until back surgery eventually forced him to hire a good crew.

Over time, Franz became a very good ecologist, reading his way through both the printed library and the more subtle library of texts offered by the forest itself. His goal was to match his vision for an ancient forest with the possibilities that the land provided.

His journals make it clear that there were times when he doubted the wisdom of his endeavors. He recognized that no matter what he did, the land would eventually turn back to some sort of forest whether he slogged up hills with a sack of seedlings or not. Human time is not the same as forest time. But time alone is no guarantee of the old-growth forest he imagined. When the surrounding landscape is a mosaic of clear-cut and Douglas fir lawns, it is not necessarily possible for a natural forest to reassemble itself. Where would the seeds come from? Would the land be in a condition to welcome them?

This last question is especially critical for the regeneration of "Maker of Rich Women." Despite its huge stature, cedar has tiny seeds, flakes wafted on the wind from delicate cones not more than half an inch long. Four hundred thousand cedar seeds add up to a single pound. It's a good thing that the adults have a whole millennium to reseed themselves. In the profusion of growth in these forests, such a speck of life has almost no chance at all to establish a new tree.

While adult trees are tolerant of the various stresses that an always changing world throws their way, the young are quite vulnerable. Red cedar grows more slowly than the other species who quickly overtop it and steal the sun—especially after a fire or logging, it is almost entirely outcompeted by species better adapted to the dry, open conditions. If red cedars do survive, despite being the most shade tolerant of all the western species, they do not flourish but rather bide their time, waiting for a windthrow or a death to punch a hole in the shade. Given the opportunity, they climb that transient shaft of sunlight, step by step, making their way to the canopy. But most never do. Forest ecologists estimate that the window of opportunity for cedars to get started occurs perhaps only twice in a century. So at Shotpouch, natural recolonization was out. In order to have cedars in the restored forest, Franz had to plant them.

Given all cedar's traits—slow growth, poor competitive ability, susceptibility to browsing, wildly improbable seedling establishment—one would expect it to be a rare species. But it's not. One explanation is that while cedars can't compete well on uplands, they thrive with wet feet in alluvial soils, swamps, and water edges that other species can't stand. Their favorite habitat provides them with a refuge from competition. Accordingly, Franz carefully selected creekside areas and planted them thickly with cedar.

The unique chemistry of cedar endows it with both life-saving and tree-saving medicinal properties. Rich with many highly antimicrobial compounds, it is especially resistant to fungi. Northwest forests, like any ecosystem, are susceptible to outbreaks of disease, the most significant of which is laminated root rot caused by the native fungus *Phellinus weirii*. While this fungus can be fatal for Douglas firs, hemlock, and other trees, the red cedars are blessedly immune. When root rot strikes the others, the cedars are poised to fill in the empty gaps, freed of competition. The Tree of Life survives in patches of death.

After years of working alone to keep the cedar thriving, Franz found someone who shared his notion of a good time: planting trees and chopping salmonberry. Franz's first date with Dawn was on the ridgetop at Shotpouch. Over the following eleven years, they planted more than thirteen thousand trees and created a network of trails with names that reflect intimacy with their forty acres.

Forest Service lands are often named something like Management Unit 361. At Shotpouch, more evocative place names are penned on the hand-drawn trail map of the property: Glass Canyon, Viney Glen, Cow Hip Dip. Even individual trees, remnants of the original forest, are named: Angry Maple, Spider Tree, Broken Top. One word appears on the map more than any other: Cedar Springs, Cedar Rest, Sacred Cedar, Cedar Family.

Cedar Family is especially evocative of how cedar often lives in family-like groves. Perhaps in compensation for its difficulty in sprouting from seed, cedar is a champion at vegetative reproduction. Almost any part of the tree that rests on wet ground can take root, in a process known as layering. The low swooping foliage may send roots into moist beds of moss. The flexible branches themselves can initiate new trees—even after they're cut from the tree. Native peoples probably tended the cedar groves by propagating them in this way. Even a young cedar that has tipped over or been flattened by hungry elk will reorient its branches and start over. The aboriginal names for the tree, Long Life Maker and Tree of Life, are appropriately bestowed.

One of the most touching place names on Franz's map is a spot he called Old Growth Children. To plant trees is an act of faith. Thirteen thousand acts of faith live on this land.

Franz studied and planted, studied and planted, making a lot of mistakes and learning as he went. Franz wrote, "I was a temporary steward of this land. I was its caretaker. More accurately I was its caregiver. The devil was in the details and the devil presented details at every turn." He observed the reaction of the old-growth children to their habitats and then tried to remedy whatever ailed them. "Reforestation took on the flavor of tending a garden. This was a forestry of intimacy. When I am on the land, it is very hard to keep from messing around. Planting one more tree, cutting a limb. Transplanting what has already been planted to a more favorable spot. I call it 'anticipatory redistributive naturalization.' Dawn calls it tinkering."

Cedar's generosity extends not only to people, but to many other forest dwellers as well. Its tender, low-hanging foliage is among deer and elk's favorite food. You'd think that seedlings hidden under the canopies of everything else would be camouflaged, but they are so palatable that the herbivores hunt them out as if they were hidden chocolate bars. And because they grow so slowly, they remain vulnerable at deer height for a long time.

"The unknowns pervading my work were as pervasive as shade in the forest," Franz wrote. His plan to grow cedars on the stream banks was a good one, except that's where the beavers also live. Who knew that they eat cedar for dessert? His cedar nurseries were gnawed to oblivion. So he planted them again, this time with a fence. The wildlife just snickered. Thinking like a forest, he then planted a thicket of willow, beavers' favorite meal, along the creek, hoping to distract them from his cedars.

"I definitely should have met with a council of mice, boomers, bobcats, porcupines, beaver, and deer before I started this experiment," he wrote.

Many of these cedars today are gangly teens, all limbs and floppy leader, not yet grown into themselves. Nibbled by deer and elk, they become even more awkward. Under the tangle of vine maple they struggle toward light, reaching an arm here, a branch there. But their time is coming.

After completing the final plantings, Franz wrote, "I may heal the land. Yet I have little doubt of the direction that the real benefits flow. An element of reciprocity is the rule here. What I give, I receive in return. Here on the slopes of Shotpouch Valley, I have been engaged less in a personal forestry of restoration than in a forestry of personal restoration. In restoring the land, I restore myself."

Maker of Rich Women, there is truth in her name. She made Franz rich, too, with the wealth of seeing his vision alive in the world, of giving a gift to the future that only grows more beautiful with time.

Of Shotpouch he wrote, "This was an exercise in personal forestry. But it was also an exercise in the creation of personal art. I could have been painting a landscape or composing a cycle of songs. The exercise in finding the right distribution of trees feels like revising a poem. Given my lack of technical expertise, I could not reconcile myself to the title of 'forester,' but I could live with the idea that I am a writer who works in the forest. And with the forest. A writer who practices the art of forestry and writes in trees. The practice of forestry may be changing, but I am unaware of any instances where proficiency in the arts is sought as a professional qualification by timber companies or schools of forestry. Perhaps that is what we need. Artists as foresters."

In his years on this plot, he watched the watershed start to heal from a long history of damage. His journal describes a time-travel visit to Shotpouch one hundred and fifty years in the future, when "the venerable cedars have captured the landscape where an alder thicket once stood." But he knew that, in the present, his forty acres were just a seedling, and a vulnerable one at that. Meeting his goal would require many more careful hands—and hearts and minds too. Through his art on the land and on the page, he had to help shift people toward the worldview of old-growth cultures, a renewal of relationship to land.

Old-growth cultures, like old-growth forests, have not been exterminated. The land holds their memory and the possibility of regeneration. They are not only a matter of ethnicity or history, but of relationships born out of reciprocity between land and people. Franz showed that you can plant an old-growth forest, but he also envisioned the propagation of an old-growth culture, a vision of the world, whole and healed.

To further this vision, Franz co-created the Spring Creek Project, whose "challenge is to bring together the practical wisdom of the environmental sciences, the clarity of philosophical analysis and the creative, expressive power of the written word, to find new ways to understand and reimagine our relation to the natural world." His notion of foresters as artists and poets as ecologists takes root in the forest and in the cozy cedar cabin at Shotpouch. It has become a place of inspiration and solitude for writers, writers who could be the restoration ecologists of relationship. Writers who could be like birds in a thicket of salmonberry, carrying seeds to a wounded land, making it ready for renewal of old-growth culture.

The cabin is a gathering spot for fertile collaborations among artists, scientists, and philosophers, whose works are then expressed in a dazzling array of cultural events. His inspiration has become a nurse log for the inspiration of others. Ten years, thirteen thousand trees, and countless inspired scientists and artists later, he wrote, "I had confidence now that when it came time for me to rest, I could step aside and let others pass upon a path to a very special place. To a forest of giant fir, cedar, and hemlock, to the ancient forest that was." He was right, and many have followed the path he blazed from weedy brambles to old-growth children. Franz Dolp passed away in 2004 in a collision with a paper mill truck on his way to Shotpouch Creek.

Outside the door of his cabin, the circle of young cedars look like women in green shawls, beaded with raindrops catching the light, graceful dancers in feathery fringe that sways with their steps. They spread their branches wide, opening the circle, inviting us to be part of the dance of regeneration. Clumsy at first, from generations of sitting on the sidelines, we stumble until we find the rhythm. We know these steps from deep memory, handed down from Skywoman, reclaiming our responsibility as cocreators. Here in a homemade forest, poets, writers, scientists, foresters, shovels, seeds, elk, and alder join in the circle with Mother Cedar, dancing the old-growth children into being. We're all invited. Pick up a shovel and join the dance.

Witness to the Rain

This Oregon rain, at the start of winter, falls steadily in sheets of gray, unimpeded, making a gentle hiss. You'd think that rain falls equally over the land, but it doesn't. The rhythm and the tempo change markedly from place to place. In a tangle of salal and Oregon grape, the rain strikes *ratatatat* on the hard, shiny leaves, the snare drum of sclerophylls. Rhododendron leaves, broad and flat, receive the rain with a smack that makes the leaves bounce and rebound, dancing in the downpour. Beneath a massive hemlock, the drops are fewer and the craggy trunk knows rain as dribbles down its furrows. On bare soil the rain splats on the clay while fir needles swallow it up with an audible gulp.

In contrast, the fall of rain on moss is nearly silent. I kneel among them, sinking into their softness to watch and to listen. The drops are so quick that my eye is always chasing, but not catching, their arrival. At last, by narrowing my gaze to just a single frond, I can see it. The impact bows the shoot downward, but the drop itself vanishes. It is soundless. There is no drip or splash, but I can see the front of water move, darkening the stem as it is drunk in, silently dissipating among the tiny shingled leaves.

Most other places I know, water is a discrete entity. It is hemmed in by well-defined boundaries: lakeshores, stream banks, the great rocky coastline. You can stand at its edge and say "this is water" and "this is land." Those fish and those tadpoles are of the water realm; these trees, these mosses, and these four-leggeds are creatures of the land. But here in these misty forests those edges seem to blur, with rain so fine and con-stant as to be indistinguishable from air and cedars wrapped with cloud so dense that only their outlines emerge. Water doesn't seem to make a clear distinction between gaseous phase and liquid. The air merely touches a leaf or a tendril of my hair and suddenly a drop appears.

Even the river, Lookout Creek, doesn't respect clear boundaries. It tumbles and slides down its main channel, where a dipper rides between pools. But Fred Swanson, a hydrologist here at the Andrews Experimental Forest, has told me stories of another stream, an invisible shadow of Lookout Creek, the hyporheic flow. This is the water that moves under the stream, in cobble beds and old sandbars. It edges up the toe slope to the forest, a wide unseen river that flows beneath the eddies and the splash. A deep invisible river, known to roots and rocks, the water and the land intimate beyond our knowing. It is hyporheic flow that I'm listening for.

Wandering along the banks of Lookout Creek, I lean up against an old cedar with my back nestled in its curves and try to imagine the currents below. But all I sense is water dripping down my neck. Every branch is weighed down with mossy curtains of *Isothecium* and droplets hang from the tangled ends, just as they hang from my hair. When I bend my head over, I can see them both. But the droplets on *Isothecium* are far bigger than the drops on my bangs. In fact, the drops of moss water seem larger than any I know and they hang, swelling and pregnant with gravity, far longer than the drops on me, or on twigs or bark. They dangle and rotate, reflecting the entire forest and a woman in a bright-yellow slicker.

I'm not sure I can trust what I'm seeing. I wish I had a set of calipers, so that I could measure the drops of moss water and see if they really are bigger. Surely all drops are created equal? I don't know, so I take refuge in the play of the scientist spinning out hypotheses. Perhaps the high humidity around moss makes the drops last longer? Maybe in residence among mosses, raindrops absorb some property that increases their surface tension, making them stronger against the pull of gravity? Perhaps it is just an illusion, like how the full moon looks so much bigger at the horizon. Does the diminutive scale of the moss leaves make the drops appear larger? Maybe they want to show off their sparkle just a little longer?

After hours in the penetrating rain, I am suddenly damp and chilled and the path back to the cabin is a temptation. I could so easily retreat to tea and dry clothes, but I cannot pull myself away. However alluring the thought of warmth, there is no substitute for standing in the rain to waken every sense—senses that are muted within four walls, where my attention would be on me instead of all that is more than me. Inside looking out, I could not bear the loneliness of being dry in a wet world. Here in the rainforest, I don't want to just be a bystander to rain, passive and protected; I want to be part of the downpour, to be soaked, along with the dark humus that squishes underfoot. I wish that I could stand like a shaggy cedar with rain seeping into my bark, that water could dissolve the barrier between us. I want to feel what the cedars feel and know what they know.

But I am not a cedar and I am cold. Surely there are places where the warm-blooded among us take refuge. There must be niches here and there where the rain does not reach. I try to think like a squirrel and find them. I poke my head into an undercut bank by the stream, but its back wall runs with rivulets. No shelter there, nor in the hollow of a treefall where I hoped the upturned roots would slow the rain. A spiderweb hangs between two dangling roots. Even this is filled, a silken hammock cradling a spoonful of water. My hopes rise where the vine maples are bent low to form a moss-draped dome. I push aside the *Isothecium* curtain and stoop to enter the tiny dark room, roofed with layers of moss. It's quiet and windless, just big enough for one. The light comes through the moss-woven roof like pinprick stars, but so do the drips.

As I walk back to the trail, a giant log blocks the way. It has fallen from the toe slope out into the river, where its branches drag in the rising current. Its top rests on the opposite shore. Going under looks easier than going over, so I drop to my hands and knees. And here I find my dry place. The ground mosses are brown and dry, the soil soft and powdery. The log makes a roof overhead more than a meter wide in the wedge-shaped space where the slope falls away to the stream. I can stretch out my legs, the slope angle perfectly accommodating the length of my back. I let my head rest in a dry nest of *Hylocomium* moss and sigh in contentment. My breath forms a cloud above me, up where brown tufts of moss still cling to the furrowed bark, embroidered with spiderwebs and wisps of lichen that haven't seen the sun since this tree became a log.

This log, inches above my face, weighs many tons. All that keeps it from seeking its natural angle of repose on my chest is a hinge of fractured wood at the stump and cracked branches propped on the other side of the stream. It could loose those bonds at any moment. But given the fast tempo of raindrops and the slow tempo of treefalls, I feel safe in the moment. The pace of my resting and the pace of its falling run on different clocks.

Time as objective reality has never made much sense to me. It's what happens that matters. How can minutes and years, devices of our own creation, mean the same thing to gnats and to cedars? Two hundred years is young for the trees whose tops this morning are hung with mist. It's an eyeblink of time for the river and nothing at all for the rocks. The rocks and the river and these very same trees are likely to be here in another two hundred years, if we take good care. As for me, and that chipmunk, and the cloud of gnats milling in a shaft of sunlight—we will have moved on.

If there is meaning in the past and in the imagined future, it is captured in the moment. When you have all the time in the world, you can spend it, not on going somewhere, but on being where you are. So I stretch out, close my eyes, and listen to the rain.

The cushiony moss keeps me warm and dry, and I roll over on my elbow to look out on the wet world. The drops fall heavily on a patch of *Mnium insigne,* right at eye level. This moss stands upright, nearly two inches tall. The leaves are broad and rounded, like a fig tree in miniature. One leaf among the many draws my eye because of its long tapered tip, so unlike the rounded edges of the others. The threadlike tip of the leaf is moving, animated in a most unplantlike fashion. The thread seems firmly anchored to the apex of the moss leaf, an extension of its pellucid green. But the tip is circling, waving in the air as if it is searching for something. Its motion reminds me of the way inchworms will rise up on their hind sucker feet and wave their long bodies about until they encounter the adjacent twig, to which they then attach their forelegs, release the back, and arch across the gulf of empty space.

But this is no many-legged caterpillar; it is a shiny green filament, a moss thread, lit from within like a fiber-optic element. As I watch, the wandering thread touches upon a leaf just millimeters away. It seems to tap several times at the new leaf and then, as if reassured, stretches itself out across the gap. It holds like a taut green cable, more than doubling its initial length. For just a moment, the two mosses are bridged by the shining green thread and then green light flows like a river across the bridge and vanishes, lost in the greenness of the moss. Is that not grace—to see an animal made of green light and water, a mere thread of a being who like me has gone walking in the rain?

Down by the river, I stand and listen. The sound of individual raindrops is lost in the foaming white rush and smooth glide over rock. If you didn't know better, you might not recognize raindrops and rivers as kin, so different are the particular and the collective. I lean over a still pool, reach in my hand, and let the drops fall from my fingers, just to be sure.

Between the forest and the stream lies a gravel bar, a jumble of rocks swept down from high mountains in a river-changing flood last decade. Willows and alders, brambles and moss have taken hold there, but this too shall pass, says the river.

Alder leaves lie fallen on the gravel, their drying edges upturned to form leafy cups. Rainwater has pooled in several, and it is stained red brown like tea from the tannins leached from the leaf. Strands of lichen lie scattered among them where the wind has torn them free. Suddenly I see the experiment I need to test my hypothesis; the materials are neatly laid out before me. I find two strands of lichen, equal in size and length, and blot them on my flannel shirt inside my raincoat. One strand I place in the leaf cup of red alder tea, the other I soak in a pool of pure rainwater. Slowly I lift them both up, side by side, and watch the droplets form at the ends of the strands. Sure enough, they are different. The plain water forms small, rapid drops that seem in a hurry to let go. But the droplets steeped in alder water grow large and heavy, and then hang for a long moment before gravity pulls them away. I feel the grin spreading over my face with the *aha!* moment. There *are* different kinds of drops, depending on the relationship between the water and the plant. If tannin-rich alder water increases the size of the drops, might not water seeping through a long curtain of moss also pick up tannins, making the big strong drops I thought I was seeing? One thing I've learned in the woods is that there is no such thing as random. Everything is steeped in meaning, colored by relationships, one thing with another.

Where new gravel meets old shore, a still pool has formed beneath the overhanging trees. Cut off from the main channel, it fills from the rise of hyporheic flow, the water rising from below to fill the shallow basin where summer's daisies look surprised to be submerged two feet deep now that the rains have come. In summer this pool was a flowery swale, now a sunken meadow that tells of the river's transition from low, braided channel to the full banks of winter. It is a different river in August than in October. You'd have to stand here a long time to know them both. And even longer to know the river that was here before the coming of the gravel bar, and the river that will be after it leaves.

Perhaps we cannot know the river. But what about the drops? I stand for a long time by the still backwater pool and listen. It is a mirror for the falling rain and is textured all over by the fine and steady fall. I strain to hear only rain whisper among the many sounds, and find that I can. It arrives with a high sprickley sound, a *shurrr* so light that it only blurs the glassy surface but does not disrupt the reflection. The pool is overhung with branches of vine maple reaching from the shore, a low spray of hemlock, and, from the gravel bar, alder stems inclining over the edge. Water falls from these trees into the pool, each to its own rhythm. The hemlock makes a rapid pulse. Water collects on every needle but travels to the branch tips before falling, running to the drip line, where it releases in a steady *pit, pit, pit, pit, pit,* drawing a dotted line in the water below.

Maple stems shed their water much differently. The drips from maple are big and heavy. I watch them form and then plummet to the surface of the pool. They hit with such force that the drop makes a deep and hollow sound. *Bloink.* The rebound causes the water to jump from the surface, so it looks as if it were erupting from below. There are sporadic *bloinks* beneath the maples. Why is this drop so different from the hemlock drips? I step in close to watch the way that water moves on maple. The drops don't form just anywhere along the stem. They arise mostly where past years' bud scars have formed a tiny ridge. The rainwater sheets over the smooth green bark and gets dammed up behind the wall of the bud scar. It swells and gathers until it tops the little dam and spills over, tumbling in a massive drop to the water below. *Bloink.*

Sshhhh from rain, *pitpitpit* from hemlock, *bloink* from maple, and lastly *popp* of falling alder water. Alder drops make a slow music. It takes time for fine rain to traverse the scabrous rough surface of an alder leaf. The drops aren't as big as maple drops, not enough to splash, but the *popp* ripples the surface and sends out concentric rings. I close my eyes and listen to the voices of the rain.

The reflecting surface of the pool is textured with their signatures, each one different in pace and resonance. Every drip it seems is changed by its relationship with life, whether it encounters moss or maple or fir bark or my hair. And we think of it as simply rain, as if it were one thing, as if we understood it. I think that moss knows rain better than we do, and so do maples. Maybe there is no such thing as rain; there are only raindrops, each with its own story.

Listening to rain, time disappears. If time is measured by the period between events, alder drip time is different from maple drip. This forest is textured with different kinds of time, as the surface of the pool is dimpled with different kinds of rain. Fir needles fall with the high-frequency hiss of rain, branches fall with the *bloink* of big drops, and trees fall with a rare but thunderous thud. Rare, unless you measure time like a river. And we think of it as simply time, as if it were one thing, as if we understood it. Maybe there is no such thing as time; there are only moments, each with its own story.

I can see my face reflected in a dangling drop. The fish-eye lens gives me a giant forehead and tiny ears. I suppose that's the way we humans are, thinking too much and listening too little. Paying attention acknowledges that we have something to learn from intelligences other than our own. Listening, standing witness, creates an openness to the world in which the boundaries between us can dissolve in a raindrop. The drop swells on the tip of a cedar and I catch it on my tongue like a blessing.

Burning Sweetgrass

A sweetgrass braid is burned to create a ceremonial smudge

that washes the recipient in kindness and compassion to heal

the body and the spirit.

Windigo Footprints

I n the winter brilliance, the only sounds are the rub of my jacket against itself, the soft *ploompf* of my snowshoes, the rifle-shot crack of trees bursting their hearts in the freezing temperatures, and the beating of my own heart, pumping hot blood to fingers still tingling in double mittens. In the break between squalls, the sky is painfully blue. The snowfields sparkle below like shattered glass.

This last storm has sculpted the drifts like surf on a frozen sea. Earlier, my tracks were filled with pink and yellow shadows; now they deepen to blue in the fading light. I walk alongside fox tracks, vole tunnels, and a bright-red spatter in the snow framed by the imprint of hawk wings.

Everybody's hungry.

When the wind picks up again I can smell more snow coming and within minutes the squall line roars over the treetops, carrying flakes like a gray curtain blowing straight at me. I turn to get to shelter before full dark, retracing my steps, which have already begun to fill. When I look more closely I can see that inside each of my tracks is another print that is not my tread. I scan the growing darkness for a figure, but the snow is too heavy to see. The trees thrash beneath racing clouds. A howl rises behind me. Maybe it's just the wind.

It is on nights like this that the Windigo is afoot. You can hear its unearthly shrieks as it hunts through the blizzard.

The Windigo is the legendary monster of our Anishinaabe people, the villain of a tale told on freezing nights in the north woods. You can feel it lurking behind you, a being in the shape of an outsized man, ten feet tall, with frost-white hair hanging from its shaking body. With arms like tree trunks, feet as big as snowshoes, it travels easily through the blizzards of the hungry time, stalking us. The hideous stench of its carrion breath poisons the clean scent of snow as it pants behind us. Yellow fangs hang from its mouth that is raw where it has chewed off its lips from hunger. Most telling of all, its heart is made of ice.

Windigo stories were told around the fire to scare children into safe behavior lest this Ojibwe boogeyman make a meal of them. Or worse. This monster is no bear or howling wolf, no natural beast. Windigos are not born, they are made. The Windigo is a human being who has become a cannibal monster. Its bite will transform victims into cannibals too.

When I come in from the rising blizzard and peel off my ice-coated clothes, there is a fire in the woodstove and a simmering pot of stew. It wasn't always that way for our people, when the storms would bury the lodges and the food was gone. They named this time—when the snow is too deep and the deer are gone and the caches are empty—the Hunger Moon. It is the time when an elder leaves to hunt and never returns. When sucking a bone is not enough, the infants follow. After too many days, desperation is the only soup.

Starvation in winter was a reality for our people, particularly in the era of the Little Ice Age when winters were especially hard and long. Some scholars suggest that Windigo mythology also spread quickly in the time of the fur trade, when overexploitation of game brought famine to the villages. The ever-present fear of winter famine is embodied in the icy hunger and gaping maw of the Windigo.

As the monster shrieked on the wind, the Windigo stories reinforced the taboo against cannibalism, when the madness of hunger and isolation rustled at the edge of winter lodges. Succumbing to such a repulsive urge doomed the gnawer of bones to wander as a Windigo for the rest of time. It is said that the Windigo will never enter the spirit world but will suffer the eternal pain of need, its essence a hunger that will never be sated. The more a Windigo eats, the more ravenous it becomes. It shrieks with its craving, its mind a torture of unmet want. Consumed by consumption, it lays waste to humankind.

But the Windigo is more than just a mythic monster intended to frighten children. Creation stories offer a glimpse into the worldview of a people, of how they understand themselves, their place in the world, and the ideals to which they aspire. Likewise, the collective fears and deepest values of a people are also seen in the visage of the monsters they create. Born of our fears and our failings, Windigo is the name for that within us which cares more for its own survival than for anything else.

In terms of systems science, the Windigo is a case study of a positive feedback loop, in which a change in one entity promotes a similar change in another, connected part of the system. In this case, an increase in Windigo hunger causes an increase in Windigo eating, and that increased eating promotes only more rampant hunger in an eventual frenzy of uncontrolled consumption. In the natural as well as the built environment, positive feedback leads inexorably to change—sometimes to growth, sometimes to destruction. When growth is unbalanced, however, you can't always tell the difference.

Stable, balanced systems are typified by negative feedback loops, in which a change in one component incites an opposite change in another, so they balance each other out. When hunger causes increased eating, eating causes decreased hunger; satiety is possible. Negative feedback is a form of reciprocity, a coupling of forces that create balance and sustainability.

Windigo stories sought to encourage negative feedback loops in the minds of listeners. Traditional upbringing was designed to strengthen self-discipline, to build resistance against the insidious germ of taking too much. The old teachings recognized that Windigo nature is in each of us, so the monster was created in stories, that we might learn why we should recoil from the greedy part of ourselves. This is why Anishinaabe elders like Stewart King remind us to always acknowledge the two faces—the light and the dark side of life—in order to understand ourselves. See the dark, recognize its power, but do not feed it.

The beast has been called an evil spirit that devours mankind. The very word, *Windigo*, according to Ojibwe scholar Basil Johnston, can be derived from roots meaning "fat excess" or "thinking only of oneself." Writer Steve Pitt states that "a Windigo was a human whose selfishness has overpowered their self-control to the point that satisfaction is no longer possible."

No matter what they call it, Johnston and many other scholars point to the current epidemic of self-destructive practices—addiction to alcohol, drugs, gambling, technology, and more—as a sign that Windigo is alive and well. In Ojibwe ethics, Pitt says, "any overindulgent habit is self-destructive, and self-destruction is Windigo." And just as Windigo's bite is infectious, we all know too well that self-destruction drags along many more victims—in our human families as well as in the more-than-human world.

The native habitat of the Windigo is the north woods, but the range has expanded in the last few centuries. As Johnston suggests, multinational corporations have spawned a new breed of Windigo that insatiably devours the earth's resources "not for need but for greed." The footprints are all around us, once you know what to look for.

Our plane had to land for repairs on a short paved strip in the jungle at the heart of the Ecuadorian Amazon oil fields, a few miles from the Colombian border. We flew in over unbroken rainforest, following the river shining like a blue satin ribbon below. But the water abruptly turned black when we flew over the raw gashes of red soil marking the paths of pipelines.

Our hotel was on a dirt street where dead dogs and prostitutes shared the corners under a perpetually orange sky lit by the flaring stacks. When we got the room key, the concierge told us to push a dresser against the door and not leave our rooms during the night. In the lobby was a cage of scarlet macaws, staring dully at the street, where half-naked children were begging and AK47s hung from the shoulders of boys no older than twelve, standing guard outside the houses of the narcotraffickers. We passed the night without incident.

The next morning we flew out as the sun rose over the steaming jungle. Below us was the snarling town ringed with rainbow-colored lagoons of petrochemical waste, too many to count. The footprints of the Windigo.

They're everywhere you look. They stomp in the industrial sludge of Onondaga Lake. And over a savagely clear-cut slope in the Oregon Coast Range where the earth is slumping into the river. You can see them where coal mines rip off mountaintops in West Virginia and in oil-slick footprints on the beaches of the Gulf of Mexico. A square mile of industrial soybeans. A diamond mine in Rwanda. A closet stuffed with clothes. Windigo footprints all, they are the tracks of insatiable consumption. So many have been bitten. You can see them walking the malls, eying your farm for a housing development, running for Congress.

We are all complicit. We've allowed the "market" to define what we value so that the redefined common good seems to depend on profligate lifestyles that enrich the sellers while impoverishing the soul and the earth.

Cautionary Windigo tales arose in a commons-based society where sharing was essential to survival and greed made any individual a danger to the whole. In the old times, individuals who endangered the community by taking too much for themselves were first counseled, then ostracized, and if the greed continued, they were eventually banished. The Windigo myth may have arisen from the remembrance of the banished, doomed to wander hungry and alone, wreaking vengeance on the ones who spurned them. It is a terrible punishment to be banished from the web of reciprocity, with no one to share with you and no one for you to care for.

I remember walking a street in Manhattan, where the warm light of a lavish home spilled out over the sidewalk on a man picking through the garbage for his dinner. Maybe we've all been banished to lonely corners by our obsession with private property. We've accepted banishment even from ourselves when we spend our beautiful, utterly singular lives on making more money, to buy more things that feed but never satisfy. It is the Windigo way that tricks us into believing that belongings will fill our hunger, when it is belonging that we crave.

On a grander scale, too, we seem to be living in an era of Windigo economics of fabricated demand and compulsive overconsumption. What Native peoples once sought to rein in, we are now asked to unleash in a systematic policy of sanctioned greed.

The fear for me is far greater than just acknowledging the Windigo within. The fear for me is that the world has been turned inside out, the dark side made to seem light. Indulgent self-interest that our people once held to be monstrous is now celebrated as success. We are asked to admire what our people viewed as unforgivable. The consumption-driven mindset masquerades as "quality of life" but eats us from within. It is as if we've been invited to a feast, but the table is laid with food that nourishes only emptiness, the black hole of the stomach that never fills. We have unleashed a monster.

Ecological economists argue for reforms that would ground economics in ecological principles and the constraints of thermodynamics. They urge the embrace of the radical notion that we must sustain natural capital and ecosystem services if we are to maintain quality of life. But governments still cling to the neoclassical fallacy that human consumption has no consequences. We continue to embrace economic systems that prescribe infinite growth on a finite planet, as if somehow the universe had repealed the laws of thermodynamics on our behalf. Perpetual growth is simply not compatible with natural law, and yet a leading economist like Lawrence Summers, of Harvard, the World Bank, and the U.S. National Economic Council, issues such statements as, "There are no limits to the carrying capacity of the earth that are likely to bind at any time in the foreseeable future. The idea that we should put limits on growth because of some natural limit is a profound error." Our leaders willfully ignore the wisdom and the models of every other species on the planet—except of course those that have gone extinct. Windigo thinking.

The Sacred and the Superfund

Above the spring behind my house a drop forms at the end of a mossy branch, hangs in a momentary sparkle, and then lets go. Other drips and drops join in the procession, just a few of the hundreds of rivulets from the hills. Gathering speed, they splish over rocky ledges with growing urgency to be on their way, down Nine Mile Creek until they find Onondaga Lake. I cup my hands to the spring and drink. Knowing what I know, I worry about the journey these drops will soon take, wanting to hold them here forever. But there is no stopping water.

The watershed of my home in upstate New York lies within the ancestral homelands of the Onondaga people, the central fire of the Iroquois, or Haudenosaunee, Confederacy. Traditional Onondaga understand a world in which all beings were given a gift, a gift that simultaneously engenders a responsibility to the world. Water's gift is its role as life sustainer, and its duties are manifold: making plants grow, creating homes for fish and mayflies, and, for me today, offering a cool drink.

The particular sweetness of this water comes from the surrounding hills, great shoulders of inordinately pure, fine-grained limestone. These old seafloors are almost pure calcium carbonate with scarcely a trace of other elements to discolor their pearly gray. Other springs in these hills are less sweet, emerging from limestone shelves that hide salt-filled caverns, crystal palaces lined with cubes of halite. The Onondaga used these salt springs to season their corn soup and venison and preserve the baskets of fish the waters offered up. Life was good and water rushed off to do its work, faithful to its responsibility every day. But people are not always as mindful as water—we can forget. And so the Haudenosaunee were given the Thanksgiving Address to remind themselves to greet and thank all of the members of the natural world whenever they gathered. To the waters they say:

> We give thanks to all the Waters of the world. We are grateful that the waters are still here and doing their duty of sustaining life on Mother Earth. Water is life, quenching our thirst and providing us with strength, making the plants grow and sustaining us all. Let us gather our minds together and with one mind, we send greetings and thanks to the Waters.

These words reflect the sacred purpose of the people. For just as water was given certain responsibilities for sustaining the world, so were the people. Chief among their duties was to give thanks for the gifts of the earth and to care for them.

Stories are told of long-ago times when the Haudenosaunee people *did* forget to live in gratitude. They became greedy and jealous and began fighting among themselves. Conflict brought only more conflict, until war between the nations became continuous. Soon grief was known in every longhouse and yet the violence went on. All were suffering.

During that sorry time a son was born to a Huron woman far to the west. This handsome youth grew to manhood knowing that he had a special purpose. One day he explained to his family that he must leave home to carry a message to people in the east, a message from the Creator. He built a great canoe carved of white stone and journeyed far until at last he pulled his boat ashore in the midst of the warring Haudenosaunee. Here he spoke his message of peace and became known as the Peacemaker. Few heeded him at first, but those who listened were transformed.

His life in danger, weighed down with sorrow, the Peacemaker and his allies, among them the real Hiawatha, spoke peace in times of terrible trouble. For years they traveled between villages and one by one the chiefs of the warring nations came to accept the message of peace, all but one.

Tadodaho, an Onondaga leader, refused the way of peace for his people. He was so filled with hate that his hair writhed with snakes and his body was crippled by vitriol. Tadodaho sent death and sorrow to the carriers of the message, but the peace was more powerful than he and eventually the Onondaga too accepted the message of peace. Tadodaho's twisted body was restored to health and together the messengers of peace combed the snakes from his hair. He too was transformed.

The Peacemaker gathered together the leaders of all five Haudenosaunee nations and joined them with one mind. The Great Tree of Peace, an enormous white pine, has five long green needles joined in one bundle, representing the unity of the Five Nations. With one hand the Peacemaker lifted the great tree from the soil and the assembled chiefs stepped forward to cast their weapons of war into the hole. On this very shore, the nations agreed to "bury the hatchet" and live by the Great Law of Peace, which sets out right relations among peoples and with the natural world. Four white roots spread out to the four directions, inviting all peace-loving nations to shelter under the tree's branches.

So was born the great Haudenosaunee Confederacy, the oldest living democracy on the planet. It was here, at Onondaga Lake, where this Great Law was born. For its pivotal role, the Onondaga Nation became the central fire of the Confederacy and from that time forward, the name Tadodaho has been carried by the spiritual leader of the Confederacy. As a final measure, the Peacemaker placed the far-seeing eagle atop the Great Tree to warn the people of approaching danger. For the many centuries that followed, the eagle did its work and the Haudenosaunee people lived in peace and prosperity. But then another danger—a different kind of violence—came to their home-lands. The great bird must have called and called, but its voice was lost in the maelstrom winds of change. Today, the ground where the Peacemaker walked is a Superfund site.

In fact, nine Superfund sites line the shore of Onondaga Lake, around which the present-day city of Syracuse, New York, has grown. Thanks to more than a century of industrial development, the lake known as one of North America's most sacred sites is now known as one of the most polluted lakes in the United States.

Drawn by abundant resources and the coming of the Erie Canal, the captains of industry brought their innovations to Onondaga territory. Early journals record that smokestacks made the air "a choking miasma." The manufacturers were happy to have Onondaga Lake so close at hand, to use as a dumping ground. Millions of tons of industrial waste were slurried onto the lake bottom. The growing city followed suit, adding sewage to the suffering of the waters. It is as if the newcomers to Onondaga Lake had declared war, not on each other, but with the land.

Today, the land where the Peacemaker walked and the Tree of Peace stood isn't land at all, but beds of industrial waste sixty feet deep. It sticks to shoes like thick white school paste used in kindergartens to glue cutout birds onto construction-paper trees. There aren't too many birds here, and the Tree of Peace is buried. The original people could no longer find even the familiar curve of the shore. The old contours were filled in, creating a new shoreline of more than a mile of waste beds.

It has been said that the waste beds made new land, but that is a lie. The waste beds are actually old land, chemically rearranged. This greasy sludge used to be limestone and freshwater and rich soil. The new terrain is old land that has been pulverized, extracted, and poured out the end of a pipe. It is known as Solvay waste, after the Solvay Process Company that left it behind.

The Solvay Process was a chemical breakthrough that allowed for the production of soda ash, an essential component of other industrial processes such as glass manufacturing and making detergents, pulp, and paper. Native limestone was melted in coke-fired furnaces and then reacted with salt to produce soda ash. This industry fueled the growth of the whole region, and chemical processing expanded to include organic chemicals, dyes, and chlorine gas. Train lines ran steadily past the factories, shipping out tons of products. Pipes ran in the other direction, pouring out tons of waste.

The hills of waste are the topographic inverse of the open pit mines—the largest open pit mines in New York State, still unreclaimed—

where the limestone rocks were quarried, the earth gouged out in one place to bury the ground in another. If time could run backward, like a film in reverse, we would see this mess reassemble itself into lush green hills and moss-covered ledges of limestone. The streams would run back up the hills to the springs and the salt would stay glittering in underground rooms.

I can too easily imagine what it must have been like, those first ejections from the pipe falling in chalky white splats like the droppings of an enormous mechanical bird. Splurting and pulsing at first, with air in the mile-long intestine that stretched back to the gut of the factory. But it would soon settle into a steady flow, burying the reeds and rushes. Did the frogs and mink get away in time to avoid being entombed? What about the turtles? Too slow—they wouldn't be able to escape being embedded at the bottom of the pile in a perversion of the story of the world's creation, when the earth was carried on Turtle's back.

First they filled in the lakeshore itself, sending tons of sludge into the waters in a plume that turned blue water to white paste. Then they moved the end of the pipe to the surrounding wetlands, right up to the edges of the stream. The water of Nine Mile Creek must have wanted to head back uphill, to defy gravity and find again the mossy pools beneath the springs. But it kept to its work and found its way, seeping through the waste beds and out to the lake.

Rain bound for waste beds is in trouble too. At first, the waste particles are so fine that they trap the water in white clay. Then gravity eventually pulls the drops through sixty feet of sludge and out the bottom of the pile to join a drainage ditch instead of a stream. As it passes through the chalky depths, the rain cannot help doing what it has been called to do: dissolving minerals, carrying ions intended to nurture plants and fish. By the time it reaches the bottom of the heap, the water has picked up enough chemicals to be as salty as soup and as corrosive as lye. Its beautiful name, water, is lost. It is now called leachate. Leachate seeps from the waste beds with a pH of 11. Like drain cleaner, it will burn your skin. Normal drinking water has a pH value of 7. Today, engineers collect the leachate and mix it with hydrochloric acid in order to neutralize the pH. It is then released to Nine Mile Creek and out into Onondaga Lake.

The water has been tricked. It started on its way full of innocence, full of its own purpose. Through no fault of its own it has been corrupted and, instead of being a bearer of life, it must now deliver poison. And yet it cannot stop itself from flowing. It must do what it must do, with the gifts bestowed upon it by the Creator. It is only people who have a choice.

Today, you can drive a motorboat on the lake the Peacemaker paddled. From across the water, the western shore stands out in sharp relief. Bright white bluffs gleam in the summer sun like the White Cliffs of Dover. But when you approach by water, you'll see that the cliffs are not rock at all, but sheer walls of Solvay waste. While your boat bobs on the waves, you can see erosion gullies in the wall, the weather conspiring to mix the waste into the lake: summer sun dries out the pasty surface until it blows, and subzero winter temperatures fracture it off in plates that fall to the water. A beach beckons around the point but there are no swimmers, no docks. This bright white expanse is a flat plain of waste that slumped into the water when a retaining wall collapsed many years ago. A white pavement of settled waste extends far out from shore, barely under water. The smooth shelf is punctuated by cobble-sized rocks, ghostly beneath the water, unlike any rock you know. These are oncolites, accretions of calcium carbonate, that pepper the lake bottom. Oncolites—tumorous rocks.

Pilings stick up through the flat like a backbone, remnants of the old retaining wall. Here and there, rusted pipes that carried the sludge stick out at odd angles. Where the sludge piles meet the flats of Solvay, there are small, trickling seeps that are eerily reminiscent of springs, but the liquid that emerges seems slightly thicker than water. There are plates of summer ice along the little rivulets that drain toward the lake, crystal sheets made of salt, beneath which the water bubbles like a melting stream at the end of winter. The waste beds continue to leach tons of salt into the lake every year. Before the Allied Chemical Company, successor to Solvay Process, ceased operation, the salinity of Onondaga Lake was ten times the salinity of the headwaters of Nine Mile Creek.

The salt, the oncolites, and the waste impede the growth of rooted aquatic plants. Lakes rely on their submerged plants to generate oxygen by photosynthesis. Without plants, the depths of Onondaga Lake are oxygen-poor, and without swaying beds of vegetation, fish, frogs, insects, herons—the whole food chain—are left without habitat. While rooted water plants have a hard time, floating algae flourish in Onondaga Lake. For decades high quantities of nitrogen and phosphorous from municipal sewage fertilized the lake and fueled their growth. Algae blooms cover the surface of the water, then die and sink to the bottom. Their decay depletes what little oxygen is in the water and the lake begins to smell of the dead fish that wash up on shore on hot summer days.

The fish that survive, you may not eat. Fishing was banned in 1970 due to high concentrations of mercury. It is estimated that one hundred and sixty-five thousand pounds of mercury were discharged into Onondaga Lake between 1946 and 1970. Allied Chemical used the mercury cell process to produce industrial chlorine from the native salt brines. The mercury waste, which we know to be extremely toxic, was handled freely on its way to disposal in the lake. Local people recall that a kid could make good pocket money on "reclaimed" mercury. One old-timer told me that you could go out to the waste beds with a kitchen spoon and pick up the small glistening spheres of mercury that lay on the ground. A kid could fill an old canning jar with mercury and sell it back to the company for the price of a movie ticket. Inputs of mercury were sharply curtailed in the 1970s, but the mercury remains trapped in the sediments where, when methylated, it can circulate through the aquatic food chain. It is estimated that seven million cubic yards of lake sediments are today contaminated with mercury.

A sampling core drilled into the lake bottom cuts through sludge, trapped layers of discharged gas, oil, and sticky black ooze. Analysis of these cores reveals significant concentrations of cadmium, barium, chromium, cobalt, lead, benzene, chlorobenzene, assorted xylenes, pesticides, and PCBs. Not many insects and not many fish.

Onondaga Lake in the 1880s was famed for its whitefish, served freshly caught on steaming platters alongside potatoes boiled in salty brine. Fine restaurants did a booming business along the lakeshore, where tourists came for the scenery, the amusement parks, and picnic grounds where families spread their blankets on a Sunday afternoon. A trolley delivered passengers to the grand hotels that lined its shore. One famed resort, White Beach, featured a long wooden slide lit with strings of glittering gaslights. Holidaymakers would sit in wheeled carts and whoosh down the ramp to splash into the lake below. The resort promised an "exhilarating dousing for ladies, gentlemen, and children of all ages." But swimming was banned in 1940. Beautiful Onondaga Lake. People spoke of it with pride. Now they barely speak of it at all, as if it were a family member whose demise was so shameful that the name never comes up.

You would think that such toxic waters would be nearly transparent with the absence of life, but some areas are often nearly opaque with a dark cloud of silt. The turbidity comes from a muddy plume that enters the lake from another tributary, Onondaga Creek. It flows in from the south, from the high ridge above the Tully Valley, from hillsides of forests, farms, and sweet-smelling apple orchards.

Muddy water is usually attributed to runoff from farmland, but in this case the mud comes from below. High in the watershed are the Tully mudboils, which erupt into the creek like mud volcanoes, sending tons of soft sediment downstream. There is some debate as to whether the mudboils are of natural geologic origin. The Onondaga elders remember when, not so long ago, Onondaga Creek ran so clear through their Nation that they could spearfish by lantern light. They know that there was no mud in the creek until salt mining began upstream.

When the salt wells near the factories ran out, Allied Chemical used solution mining to access the underground salt deposits up near the headwaters. The company pumped water into the subterranean deposits, dissolved them away, and then pumped the brine miles down the valley to the Solvay plant. The brine line was run through the remaining territory of the Onondaga Nation, where breaks in the line ruined the well water. Eventually the dissolved salt domes collapsed underground, creating holes through which groundwater pushed with high pressure. The resulting gushers created the mudboils that flow downstream and fill the lake with sediment. The creek that was once a fishery for Atlantic salmon, a swimming hole for kids, and a focal point of community life now runs as brown as chocolate milk. Allied Chemical and its successors deny any role in the formation of the mudboils. They claim it was an act of God. What kind of God would that be?

The wounds to these waters are as numerous as the snakes in the Tadodaho's hair, and they must be named before they can be combed out. The ancestral Onondaga territory stretches from the Pennsylvania border north to Canada. It was a mosaic of rich woodlands, expansive cornfields, clear lakes and rivers that sustained the Native people for centuries. The original territory also encompasses the site of present-day Syracuse and the sacred shores of Onondaga Lake. Onondaga rights to these lands were guaranteed by treaties between the two sovereign nations, Onondaga Nation and the United States government. But water is more faithful to its responsibilities than the United States would ever be.

When George Washington directed federal troops to exterminate the Onondaga during the Revolutionary War, a nation that had numbered in the tens of thousands was reduced to a few hundred people in a matter of one year. Afterward, every single treaty was broken. Illegal takings of land by the state of New York diminished the aboriginal Onondaga territories to a reservation of only forty-three hundred acres. The Onondaga Nation territory today is not much bigger than the Solvay waste beds. Assaults on Onondaga culture continued. Parents tried to hide their children from Indian agents, but they were taken and sent to boarding schools like Carlisle Indian School. The language that framed the Great Law of Peace was forbidden. Missionaries were dispatched to the matrilineal communities—in which men and women were equals—to show them the error of their ways. Longhouse ceremonies of thanksgiving, ceremonies meant to keep the world in balance, were banned by law.

The people have endured the pain of being bystanders to the degradation of their lands, but they never surrendered their caregiving responsibilities. They have continued the ceremonies that honor the land and their connection to it. The Onondaga people still live by the precepts of the

Great Law and still believe that, in return for the gifts of Mother Earth, human people have responsibility for caring for the nonhuman people, for stewardship of the land. Without title to their ancestral lands, however, their hands were tied to protect it. So they watched, powerless, as strangers buried the Peacemaker's footsteps. The plants, animals, and waters they were bound to protect dwindled away, though the covenant with the land was never broken. Like the springs above the lake, the people just kept doing what they were called to do, no matter what fate met them downstream. The people went on giving thanks to the land, although so much of the land had little reason to be thankful for the people.

Generations of grief, generations of loss, but also strength—the people did not surrender. They had spirit on their side. They had their traditional teachings. And they also had the law. Onondaga is a rarity in the United States, a Native nation that has never surrendered its traditional government, never given up its identity nor compromised its status as a sovereign nation. Federal laws were ignored by their own authors, but the Onondaga people still live by the precepts of the Great Law.

Out of grief and its strength has come a rising power, a resurgence that became public on March 11, 2005, when the Onondaga Nation filed a complaint in federal court with the goal of reclaiming title to their lost homelands, that they might once again exercise their care-giving responsibilities. While elders passed on and babies became elders, the people held to the dream of regaining their traditional lands, but they had no legal voice by which to do so. The halls of justice were closed to them for decades. As the judicial climate gradually changed to permit tribes to bring federal suit, other Haudenosaunee nations filed claims to recover their lands. The substance of these claims was upheld by the Supreme Court, which ruled that Haudenosaunee lands were illegally taken, and the people greatly wronged. Indian lands were unlawfully "purchased" in contravention of the United States Constitution. New York State has been ordered to forge a settlement, though remedies and reparations have proven difficult to find.

Some nations have negotiated land claims for cash payoffs or land gains and casino deals in an effort to find relief from poverty and ensure their cultural survival on the remnants of their territories. Others have sought to reclaim their original lands via outright purchase from willing sellers, land swaps with New York State, or the threat of lawsuits against individual landowners.

The Onondaga Nation took a different approach. Their claim was made under United States law, but its moral power lay in the directives of the Great Law: to act on behalf of peace, the natural world, and future generations. They did not call their suit a land claim, because they know that land is not property, but a gift, the sustainer of life. Tadodaho Sidney Hill has said that the Onondaga Nation will never seek to evict people from their homes. The Onondaga people know the pain of displacement too well to inflict it on their neighbors. Instead the suit was termed a land rights action. The motion began with a statement unprecedented in Indian Law:

> The Onondaga people wish to bring about a healing between themselves and all others who live in this region that has been the homeland of the Onondaga Nation since the dawn of time. The Nation and its people have a unique spiritual, cultural, and historic relationship with the land, which is embodied in Gayanashagowa, the Great Law of Peace. This relationship goes far beyond federal and state legal concerns of ownership, possession, or other legal rights. The people are one with the land and consider themselves stewards of it. It is the duty of the Nation's leaders to work for a healing of this land, to protect it, and to pass it on to future generations. The Onondaga Nation brings this action on behalf of its people in the hope that it may hasten the process of reconciliation and bring lasting justice, peace, and respect among all who inhabit this area.

The Onondaga land rights action sought legal recognition of title to their home, not to remove their neighbors and not for development of casinos, which they view as destructive to community life. Their intention was to gain the legal standing necessary to move restoration of the land forward. Only with title can they ensure that mines are reclaimed and that Onondaga Lake is cleaned up. Tadodaho Sidney Hill says, "We had to stand by and watch what happens to Mother Earth, but nobody listens to what we think. The land rights action will give us a voice."

The list of named defendants was headed by the state of New York, who illegally took the lands, but the suit also listed corporations that have been responsible for degradation: a quarry, a mine, an air-polluting power plant, and the more sweetly named successor to Allied Chemical, Honeywell Incorporated.

Even without the suit, Honeywell is finally being held accountable for the lake cleanup, but there is great debate about the best approach to dealing with the contaminated sediments so that natural healing can go forward: dredge, cap, or leave it alone? State, local, and federal environmental agencies are all offering solutions with a range of price tags. The scientific issues surrounding competing lake restoration proposals are complex, and each scenario offers environmental and economic trade-offs.

After decades of foot dragging, the corporation has predictably offered its own cleanup plan, which involves minimum cost and minimum benefits. Honeywell has negotiated a plan to dredge and clean the most contaminated sediments and bury them in a sealed landfill in the waste beds. That may be a good beginning, but the bulk of the contaminants lie diffused in the sediments spread over the entire lake bottom. From here they enter the food chain. The Honeywell plan is to leave those sediments in place and cover them with a four-inch layer of sand that would partially isolate them from the ecosystem. Even if isolation were technically feasible, the proposal is to cap less than half of the lake bottom, leaving the rest to circulate as usual.

Onondaga Chief Irving Powless characterized the solution as a Band-Aid on the lake bottom. Band-Aids are fine for small hurts, but "you don't prescribe a Band-Aid for cancer." The Onondaga Nation called for a thorough cleanup of the sacred lake. Without legal title, however, the powers that be will not give the nation an equal place at the negotiating table.

The hope was that history would turn itself to prophecy, as the Onondaga Nation combed the snakes from the hair of Allied Chemical. While others quarreled over cleanup costs, the Onondaga took a stance that reversed the usual equation in which economics takes priority over well-being. The Onondaga Nation land rights action stipulated a full cleanup as part of restitution; no halfway measures would be accepted. non-Native people of the watershed joined with them as allies in their call for healing, in an extraordinary partnership, the Neighbors of the Onondaga Nation.

In the midst of legal wrangling, technical debates, and environmental models, it is important to not lose sight of the sacred nature of the task: to make this most profaned lake worthy of the work of water again. The spirit of the Peacemaker still walks along these shores. The legal action concerned not only rights *to* the land but also rights *of* the land, the right to be whole and healthy.

Clan Mother Audrey Shenandoah made the goal clear. It is not casinos and not money and not revenge. "In this action," she said, "we seek justice. Justice for the waters. Justice for the four-leggeds and the wingeds, whose habitats have been taken. We seek justice, not just for ourselves, but justice for the whole of Creation."

In the spring of 2010, the federal court handed down its ruling on the Onondaga Nation's suit. The case was dismissed.

In the face of blind injustice, how do we continue? How do we live our responsibility for healing?

The first time I heard of the place, it was long past saving. But no one even knew. They kept it hidden. Until one day the sign appeared, eerily, out of nowhere.

HELP

Green block letters big enough for a football field, just off the highway. But even then, no one paid attention.

Fifteen years later, I moved back to Syracuse, where I had been a student and watched those letters fade to brown and die away along that busy stretch of road. And yet the memory of that message hadn't faded for me—I needed to see the place again for myself.

It was a fine October afternoon and I had no classes. I wasn't sure exactly how to find the place, but I'd heard rumors. The lake was so blue you could almost forget what it was. I drove past the backside of the fairgrounds, long closed for the season and desolate. But off a dirt road at the perimeter I found the security gates wide open and swinging in the wind, and I went in, mine the only vehicle in a back lot designed for thousands of fairgoers.

It's not like there were maps for what lay behind the fences, but there was a lane of sorts heading off in the general direction of the lake, so off I went, being sure to lock my car in this lonely place. I'd just be a while, back in plenty of time to pick up my girls after school.

The lane was just a rutted track through a thicket of phragmites, the reedy stems so densely packed as to make a wall on either side. I had heard that every summer the manure from the state fair barns was dumped out here. The mucked-out stalls of blue ribbon dairy cows and midway elephants all ended up on the waste beds. The city later followed suit, dumping tankers of sewage sludge. The resulting paddy was completely overgrown, plumed seed heads towering over my head by several feet. My view of the lake and my sense of direction were lost in the craze of stems, all rubbing and sawing against each other, rocking in the wind with a hypnotic sway. The lane forked off to the left and then to the right and became a walled labyrinth without landmarks of any kind. I felt like a rat in a *Phragmites* maze. I took the fork that seemed to go lakeward and began to wish I'd brought my compass.

There are fifteen hundred acres of wasteland along this shore. Even the sound of the highway, usually a good direction finder, was lost in the swishing sound of the reeds. A niggling suspicion that this was not a good place to be alone crept up the back of my neck, but I talked myself out of being afraid. There was absolutely no one here to worry about. Who would be crazy enough to come to this godforsaken place? Who but another biologist, whom I'd be happy to meet. Either that or an ax murderer disposing of a body in the reeds. It would never be found.

I followed the track as it twisted and turned until I caught a glimpse of the top of a cottonwood. I could hear its leaves in the distance, an unmistakable sound. It was a welcome landmark. Another bend in the lane brought the tree into full view, a big cottonwood with thick spreading branches that hung over the road. From the lowest branch hung a human body. Next to it an empty noose swayed in the wind.

I screamed and ran, taking any path I could find, panicked and walled in by reeds. With pounding heart I ran blindly on and on, and then met the dead end of every horror movie. Here in a tableau of terror stood an executioner with a black hood, muscled arms, and, of course, a dripping ax. A woman's body was draped over the chopping block, her blond curls spilling from her severed head. I did not move. And neither did they. At all.

A space had been cut from the thicket to form a reed-walled room like a museum diorama with life-sized figures posed at the point of murder. Relief poured off me in a cold sweat. No dead bodies. But the palpable presence of some twisted imagination was only a marginal improvement over actual corpses. To make matters worse, I was now entirely lost in the maze, wanting only to be somewhere else, most especially picking up my kids from the school bus. Thinking of them, I gathered my wits and moved as quietly as possible, wanting to avoid detection by the satanic cultists I envisioned.

On my search for a way out, I encountered additional rooms hacked into the reeds: a mocked-up prison cell with an electric chair, a hospital room with a straitjacketed patient and an ominous nurse, and, finally, an open grave with a long-nailed occupant crawling from it. After another long pass through the eerie reeds, the lane emerged into the parking lot. The light stanchions now cast long shadows and my car was visible way down at the other end. I patted for my keys in my pocket. Still there. I could probably make it. I couldn't see if the gate was open or closed. I turned for one last look behind me. Off to the side, a nicely lettered sign was pounded into the ground:

Solvay Lions Club
Haunted Hayrides
October 24–31
8 pm–midnight

I laughed myself silly. But then I had to cry.

The Solvay waste beds: how very fitting a venue for our fears. What we ought to be afraid of isn't in the haunts, but under them. Land buried under sixty feet of industrial waste, trickling toxins into the sacred waters of the Onondaga and the home of half a million people—death may be slower than the fall of the ax, but it is just as gruesome. The executioner's face is hidden, but its names are known: Solvay Process, Allied Chemical and Dye, Allied Chemical, Allied Signal, and now Honeywell.

More frightening to me than the act of execution is the mind-set that allowed it to happen, that thought it was okay to fill a lake with toxic stew. Whatever the companies are called, individual people were sitting behind those desks, fathers who took their sons fishing, who made the decision to fill the lake with sludge. Human beings made this happen, not a faceless corporation. There were no threats, no extenuating circumstances to force their hands, just business as usual. And the people of the city allowed it to happen. Interviews with Solvay workers tell the typical story: "I was just doing my job. I had a family to feed and I wasn't going to worry about what happened out there on the waste beds."

Philosopher Joanna Macy writes of the oblivion we manufacture for ourselves to keep us from looking environmental problems straight in the eye. She quotes R. J. Clifton, a psychologist studying human response to catastrophe: "Suppression of our natural responses to disaster is part of the disease of our time. The refusal to acknowledge these responses causes a dangerous splitting. It divorces our mental calculations from our intuitive, emotional, and biological embeddedness in the matrix of life. That split allows us passively to acquiesce in the preparations for our own demise."

Waste beds: a new name for an entirely new ecosystem. *Waste:* we use the word as a noun to mean "a leftover residue," "refuse or rubbish," or "a material such as feces which is produced by a living body, but not used." More contemporary uses are "an unwanted product of manufacturing," "an industrial material rejected or thrown away." Wasteland is, therefore, land that has been thrown away. As a verb, *to waste* means "to render the valuable useless," "to diminish, to dissipate, and to squander." I wonder how the public perception of the Solvay waste beds would change if, instead of hiding them, we put up a sign along the highway welcoming people to the lakeshore defined as "squandered land covered in industrial feces."

Ruined land was accepted as the collateral damage of progress. But, back in the 1970s, Professor Norm Richards of the College of Environmental Science and Forestry in Syracuse decided to conduct one of the first studies of the dysfunctional ecology of the waste beds. Frustrated by local officials' lack of concern, "Stormin' Norman" took matters into his own hands. Following the same lane I walked years later, he snuck into the fenced-off lakeshore and unloaded his guerrilla garden equipment, wheeling his backyard lawn seeder out to the long sloping beds that faced the highway. He pushed the load of grass seed and fertilizer back and forth with measured steps. North twenty paces, east ten paces, north again. A few weeks later the word *HELP* appeared, written in grass letters forty feet long on the barren slopes. The scale of the wastelands left room for a longer treatise in fertilized script, but that single word was the right one. The land had been kidnapped. Bound and gagged, it could not speak for itself.

The waste beds are not unique. The cause and the chemistry vary from my homeland to yours, but each of us can name these wounded places. We hold them in our minds and our hearts. The question is, what do we do in response?

We could take the path of fear and despair. We could document every scary scene of ecological destruction and never run out of material for a Haunted Hayride of environmental disasters, constructing a shocking nightmare tableaux of environmental tragedies, in rooms carved from a monoculture of invasive plants, on the shore of the most chemically contaminated lake in the United States. There could be scenes of oiled pelicans. How about chain saw murders on clear-cut slopes washing into rivers? Corpses of extinct Amazon primates. Prairies paved over for parking lots. Polar bears stranded on melting ice floes.

What could such a vision create other than woe and tears? Joanna Macy writes that until we can grieve for our planet we cannot love it—grieving is a sign of spiritual health. But it is not enough to weep for our lost landscapes; we have to put our hands in the earth to make ourselves whole again. Even a wounded world is feeding us. Even a wounded world holds us, giving us moments of wonder and joy. I choose joy over despair. Not because I have my head in the sand, but because joy is what the earth gives me daily and I must return the gift.

We are deluged by information regarding our destruction of the world and hear almost nothing about how to nurture it. It is no surprise then that environmentalism becomes synonymous with dire predictions and powerless feelings. Our natural inclination to do right by the world is stifled, breeding despair when it should be inspiring action. The participatory role of people in the well-being of the land has been lost, our reciprocal relations reduced to a KEEP OUT sign.

When my students learn about the latest environmental threat, they are quick to spread the word. They say, "If people only knew that snow leopards are going extinct," "If people only knew that rivers are dying." If people only knew . . . then they would, what? Stop? I honor their faith in people, but so far the *if-then* formula isn't working. People *do* know the consequences of our collective damage, they *do* know the wages of an extractive economy, but they don't stop. They get very sad, they get very quiet. So quiet that protection of the environment that enables them to eat and breathe and imagine a future for their children doesn't even make it onto a list of their top ten concerns. The Haunted Hayride of toxic waste dumps, the melting glaciers, the litany of doomsday projections—they move anyone who is still listening only to despair.

Despair is paralysis. It robs us of agency. It blinds us to our own power and the power of the earth. Environmental despair is a poison every bit as destructive as the methylated mercury in the bottom of Onondaga Lake. But how can we submit to despair while the land is saying "Help"? Restoration is a powerful antidote to despair. Restoration offers concrete means by which humans can once again enter into positive, creative relationship with the more-than-human world, meeting responsibilities that are simultaneously material and spiritual. It's not enough to grieve. It's not enough to just stop doing bad things.

We have enjoyed the feast generously laid out for us by Mother Earth, but now the plates are empty and the dining room is a mess. It's time we started doing the dishes in Mother Earth's kitchen. Doing dishes has gotten a bad rap, but everyone who migrates to the kitchen after a meal knows that that's where the laughter happens, the good conversations, the friendships. Doing dishes, like doing restoration, forms relationships.

How we approach restoration of land depends, of course, on what we believe that "land" means. If land is just real estate, then restoration looks very different than if land is the source of a subsistence economy and a spiritual home. Restoring land for production of natural resources is not the same as renewal of land as cultural identity. We have to think about what land means.

This question and more are played out on the Solvay waste beds. In a sense, the "new" land of the waste beds represents a blank slate on which a whole range of ideas have been written in response to the urgent message of HELP. They are scattered over the waste beds, in scenes every bit as evocative as the tableaux of the Haunted Hayride. A tour of the Onondaga Lake shore captures the scope of what land might mean and what restoration might look like.

Our first stop would have to be the blank slate itself, greasy, white industrial sludge poured over what once was a grassy green lakeshore. In some places, it is as bare as the day it was spewed, a chalky desert. Our diorama should include a figure of a laborer placing the outfall pipe, but behind him would be the man in the suit. The signpost at stop #1 should say: LAND AS CAPITAL. If land is only a means to make money, then these fellows are doing it right.

Norm Richards's HELP appeal started something back in the 1970s. If nutrients and seed were all it took to green the waste beds, the city had a ready answer. Slopping sewage sludge onto the terraces of the waste beds provided both nutrients for plant growth and a disposal solution for the output of the water treatment plant. The result was the nightmare swards of Phragmites, a dense monoculture of invasive reeds, ten feet high, that excludes all other forms of life. Stop #2 on our tour. The sign reads: LAND AS PROPERTY. If land is just private property, a mine of "resources," then you can do whatever you want with it and move on.

Scarcely thirty years ago, covering up your mess passed for responsibility—a kind of land-as-litter-box approach. Policy dictated only that land ruined by mining or industry had to be covered by vegetation. With this AstroTurf strategy, a mining company that destroyed a forest of two hundred species could satisfy its legal responsibilities by planting the tailings to alfalfa under a mist of irrigation and fertilizer. Once federal inspectors checked and signed off, the company could put up a MISSION ACCOMPLISHED banner, turn off the sprinklers, and walk away. The vegetation disappeared almost as quickly as the corporate executives.

Happily, scientists like Norm Richards and a host of others had a better idea. When I was at the University of Wisconsin in the early 1980s, on summer evenings I would walk with a young Bill Jordan through the trails of the arboretum, where a collection of natural ecosystems had been put in place on abandoned farmland, homage to Aldo Leopold's advice that "the first step to intelligent tinkering is to save all the pieces." At a time when the toll taken by places like the Solvay waste beds was finally being understood, Bill envisioned a whole science of restoration ecology, in which ecologists would turn their skills and philosophy to healing land, not by imposing an industrial blanket of vegetation, but by recreating natural landscapes. He didn't submit to despair. He didn't let his idea sit on the shelf. He was the catalyst for and a cofounder of the Society for Ecological Restoration.

As a result of efforts like his, new laws and policy demanded evolution in the concept of restoration: restored sites would have to not only look like nature, but have functional integrity as well. The National Research Council defined ecological restoration thus:

> The return of an ecosystem to a close approximation of its condition prior to disturbance. In restoration, ecological damage to the resource is repaired. Both the structure and the function of the ecosystem are recreated. Merely recreating form without the function, or the function in an artificial configuration bearing little resemblance to a natural resource does not constitute restoration. The goal is to emulate nature.

If we got back on the hayride wagon, it would take us to a restoration experiment at Stop #3, another version of what this land might be, what it might mean. It's visible from way off, in big quilted blocks of vivid green against the chalky white. Moving like a field of grass, you can hear the sound of the wind in the willows. This scene might be titled LAND AS MACHINE and be peopled with mannequins of engineers and foresters who are in charge of the machine. They stand before the ravenous jaws of a brush hog and an unending plantation of shrub willows, as thick as the Phragmites and not much more diverse. Their goal is to reestablish structure, and especially function, to a very specific purpose.

Here the intention is to utilize the plants as an engineering solution to water pollution. When rainwater leaches through the waste beds, it picks up high concentrations of salt, alkali, and a host of other compounds that it carries right to the lake. Willows are champions of absorbing water, which they transpire to the atmosphere. The idea is to use the willows as a green sponge, a living machine to intercept the rain before it gets down into the sludge. As an added benefit, the willows can be mown down periodically and used as woody feedstock for biomass fuel digesters. Use of plants in phytoremediation schemes holds promise, but an industrial monoculture of willow, however well-meaning, does not quite meet the standard for true restoration.

This kind of fix is at the core of the mechanistic view of nature, in which land is a machine and humans are the drivers. In this reductionist, materialist paradigm an imposed engineering solution makes sense.

But what if we took the Indigenous worldview? The ecosystem is not a machine, but a community of sovereign beings, subjects rather than objects. What if those beings were the drivers?

We can clamber back on the hay wagon to travel to the next display, only this one is not well marked. It sprawls across the oldest lakeside section of the beds into a scruffy patchwork of vegetation. The restoration ecologists here at Stop #4 are not university scientists or corporate engineers, but the oldest and most effective of land healers. They are the plants themselves, representing the design firm of Mother Nature and Father Time, LLC.

After that momentous Halloween excursion years ago, I felt completely at ease on the waste beds and enjoyed rambling there to watch restoration in action. I never encountered another dead body. But that is part of the problem. It is, of course, dead bodies that build soil, that perpetuate the nutrient cycle that propels the living. The "soil" here is white emptiness.

Here on the waste beds there are expanses without a living thing, but there are also teachers of healing and their names are Birch and Alder, Aster and Plantain, Cattail, Moss, and Switchgrass. On the most barren ground, on the wounds we have inflicted, the plants have not turned their backs on us; instead, they have come.

A few brave trees have become established, mostly cottonwoods and aspens that can tolerate the soil. There are clumps of shrubs, some patches of asters and goldenrod, but mostly a thin scraggly collection of the common roadside weeds. Dandelions, ragweed, chicory, and Queen Anne's lace blown to this spot have made a go of it. Nitrogen-fixing legumes in abundance, and clovers of all kinds, have also come to do their work. That struggling field of green is, to me, a form of peace-making. Plants are the first restoration ecologists. They are using their gifts for healing the land, showing us the way.

Imagine the surprise of the infant plants who emerged from their seed coats to find a waste bed habitat no one in their long botanical lineage had ever experienced. Most died of drought, of salt or exposure, or starved from lack of nutrients, but a select few survived and did their best to carry on. Especially the grasses. When I dig my trowel under a grass patch, the soil is different. The waste below is no longer pure white and slippery, but dark gray and crumbly between my fingers. There are roots all through it. The darkening of the soil is humus mixed in; the waste is being changed. True, a few inches down it is still dense and white, but the surface layer holds promise. The plants are doing their work, rebuilding the nutrient cycle.

If you get down on your knees, you'll see anthills, no bigger than a quarter. The granulated soil the ants have mounded around the hole is as white as snow. Grain by grain, in their tiny mandibles, they are carrying up waste from below and carrying seeds and bits of leaves down into the soil. Shuttling back and forth. The grasses feed the ants with seeds and the ants feed the grasses with soil. They hand off life to one another. They understand their interconnections; they understand that the life of one is dependent on the life of all. Leaf by leaf, root by root, the trees, the berries, the grasses are joining forces, and so there are birds and deer and bugs that have come to join them. And so the world is made.

Gray birches dot the top of the waste bed, arriving on the wind, no doubt, and lodging fortuitously against a gelatinous clot of *Nostoc* algae bubbling in a puddle. Protected in the selfless scum of *Nostoc*, the birch can grow and thrive on its nitrogen inputs. They are now the biggest trees here, but they are not alone. Directly beneath almost every birch are small shrubs. Not just any shrubs, but those that make juicy fruits: pin cherry, honeysuckle, buckthorn, blackberry. These shrubs are largely absent from the bare expanse between birches. This apron of fruit bearers speaks of the birds who passed over the waste beds and stopped to perch on the trees to defecate their load of seeds into the shade of the birch. More fruit drew more birds, who dropped more seeds, who fed the ants, and so it goes. That same pattern of reciprocity is written all over the landscape. That's one of the things I honor about this place. Here you can see beginnings, the small incremental processes by which an ecological community is built.

The beds are greening over. The land knows what to do when we do not. I hope that the waste beds do not disappear entirely, though—we need them to remind us what we are capable of. We have an opportunity to learn from them, to understand ourselves as students of nature, not the masters. The very best scientists are humble enough to listen.

We could name this tableau LAND AS TEACHER, LAND AS HEALER. With plants and natural processes in sole command, the role of land as a renewable source of knowledge and ecological insight becomes apparent. Human damage has created novel ecosystems, and the plants are slowly adapting and showing us the way toward healing the wounds. This is a testament to the ingenuity and wisdom of plants more than to any action of people. I hope we'll have the wisdom to let them continue their work. Restoration is an opportunity for a partnership, for us to help. Our part of the work is not complete.

In just the last few years, the lake has offered signs of hope. As factories have closed and citizens of the watershed build better sewage treatment plants, the waters have responded to that care. The natural resilience of the lake is making its presence known in tiny increments of dissolved oxygen and returning fish. Hydrogeologists have redirected the energies of the mudboils so that their load is lightened. Engineers, scientists, and activists have all applied the gift of human ingenuity on behalf of the water. The water, too, has done its part. With lessened inputs, the lakes and streams seem to be cleaning themselves as the water moves through. In some places, plants are starting to inhabit the bottom. Trout were found once again in the lake and when water quality took an upward turn it was front-page news. A pair of eagles have been spotted on the north shore. The waters have not forgotten their responsibility. The waters are reminding the people that they can use their healing gifts when we will use ours.

The cleansing potential of the water itself is a powerful force, which gives even greater weight to the work that lies ahead. The presence of eagles seems a sign of their faith in the people, too, and yet what will become of them, as they fish from the wounded waters?

The slowly accreting community of weedy species can be a partner in restoration. They are developing ecosystem structure and function, beginning ever so slowly to create ecosystem services such as nutrient cycling, biodiversity, and soil formation. In a natural system, of course, there is no goal other than proliferation of life. In contrast, professional restoration ecologists design their work to move toward the "reference ecosystem," or the predamage, native condition.

The volunteer successional community creating itself on the waste beds is "naturalized," but it is not native. It is unlikely to lead to a plant community that the Onondaga Nation would recognize from their ancestral past. The outcome will not be a native landscape peopled with the plants who lived here when Allied Chemical was only a gleam in the eye of a smokestack. Given the drastic changes produced by industrial contamination, it is probably not possible to recreate cedar swamps and beds of wild rice without some help. We can trust the plants to do their work, but except for windblown volunteers, new species can't get here across highways and acres of industry. Mother Nature and Father Time could use someone to push a wheelbarrow, and a few intrepid beings have volunteered.

The plant communities that will thrive in this environment are the ones that are tolerant of salt and the sodden "soil." It's tough to imagine a reference ecosystem of native species that could survive. But, in presettlement times, there were salt springs around the lake, and they supported one of the rarest of native plant communities, an inland salt marsh. Professor Don Leopold and his students have brought in wheelbarrows full of these missing native plants and conducted planting trials, watching their survival and growth with hopes of playing midwife to the recreation of a salt marsh. I went out to visit with the students, to hear their story and look at the plants. Some were dead, some were hanging on, and some were flourishing.

I headed to where the green seemed the strongest; I caught a whiff of a fragrance that haunts my memory, and then it was gone. I must have imagined it. I stopped to admire a thriving stand of seaside goldenrod and some asters. To witness the regenerative power of the land tells us that there is resilience here, signs of possibility that arise from partnership between the plants and the people. Don's work fulfills the scientific definition of restoration: working toward ecosystem structure, function, and the delivery of ecosystem services. We should make this nascent native meadow the next stop on the hayride, Stop #5, with a sign that says LAND AS RESPONSIBILITY. This work raises the bar for what restoration can mean, to create habitat for our nonhuman relatives.

As hopeful as this tableau of restored vegetation might become, it doesn't feel quite whole. When I visited with the students with shovels in their hands, their pride in the planting was evident. I asked what motivated them in their work, and I heard about "getting adequate data" and "devising a solution" and a "feasible dissertation." No one mentioned love. Maybe they were afraid. I've sat on too many dissertation committees where students were ridiculed for describing the plants they've worked with for five years with so unscientific a term as *beautiful*. The word *love* is unlikely to make an appearance, but I know that it is there.

That familiar fragrance was tugging at my sleeve again. I raised my eyes to meet the brightest green in the place, shiny blades gleaming in the sun, smiling up at me like a long lost friend. There she was—sweetgrass—growing in one of the last places I might ever have expected. But I should have known better. Tentatively sending out rhizomes through the sludge, slender tillers marching bravely away, sweetgrass is a teacher of healing, a symbol of kindness and compassion. She reminded me that it is not the land that has been broken, but our relationship to it.

Restoration is imperative for healing the earth, but reciprocity is imperative for long-lasting, successful restoration. Like other mindful practices, ecological restoration can be viewed as an act of reciprocity in which humans exercise their caregiving responsibility for the ecosystems that sustain them. We restore the land, and the land restores us. As writer Freeman House cautions, "We will continue to need the insights and methodologies of science, but if we allow the practice of restoration to become the exclusive domain of science, we will have lost its greatest promise, which is nothing less than a redefinition of human culture."

We may not be able to restore the Onondaga watershed to its preindustrial condition. The land, plants, animals, and their allies among the human people are making small steps, but ultimately it is the earth that will restore the structure and function, the ecosystem services. We might debate the authenticity of the desired reference ecosystem, but she will decide. We're not in control. What we *are* in control of is our relationship to the earth. Nature herself is a moving target, especially in an era of rapid climate change. Species composition may change, but relationship endures. It is the most authentic facet of the restoration. Here is where our most challenging and most rewarding work lies, in restoring a relationship of respect, responsibility, and reciprocity. And love.

A 1994 statement from the Indigenous Environmental Network puts it best:

> Western science and technology, while appropriate to the present scale of degradation, is a limited conceptual and methodological tool—it is the "head and hands" of restoration implementation. Native spirituality is the 'heart' that guides the head and hands . . . Cultural survival depends on healthy land and a healthy, responsible relationship between humans and the land. The traditional care-giving responsibilities which maintained healthy land need to be expanded to include restoration. Ecological restoration is inseparable from cultural and spiritual restoration, and is inseparable from the spiritual responsibilities of care-giving and world-renewal.

What if we could fashion a restoration plan that grew from understanding multiple meanings of land? Land as sustainer. Land as identity. Land as grocery store and pharmacy. Land as connection to our ancestors. Land as moral obligation. Land as sacred. Land as self.

When I first came to Syracuse as a student, I had a first—and only—date with a local fellow. We were going on a drive and I asked if we could go to fabled Onondaga Lake, which I had never seen. He reluctantly agreed, joking about the city's famous landmark. But when we got there he wouldn't get out of the car. "It stinks too much" he said, as ashamed as if he himself were the source of the foul odor. I'd never met anyone who hated his home before. My friend Catherine grew up here. She tells me that her weekly ride to Sunday school took the family along the lakeshore, past Crucible Steel and Allied Chemical, where even on the Lord's day, black smoke filled the sky and pools of sludge lay on either side of the road. When the preacher talked of fire and brimstone and the sulfurous vents of hell, she was sure he meant Solvay. She thought she drove to church each week through the Valley of Death.

Fear and loathing, our internal Haunted Hayride—the worst parts of our nature are all here on the lakeshore. Despair made people turn away, made them write off Onondaga Lake as a lost cause.

It's true that when you walk on the waste beds you can see the hand of destruction, but you can also see hope in the way a seed lands in a tiny crack and puts down a root and begins to build the soil again. The plants remind me of our neighbors at Onondaga Nation, Native people faced with daunting odds, great hostility, and an environment much changed from the rich land that first sustained them. But the plants and the people survive. Plant people and human people are still here and are still meeting their responsibilities.

Despite numerous legal setbacks, the Onondaga have not turned their backs on the lake; rather, they are the authors of a new approach to healing it, put forward in their "Onondaga Nation Vision for a Clean Onondaga Lake." This dream of restoration follows the ancient teachings of the Thanksgiving Address. Greeting in turn each element of Creation, the declaration offers vision and support for returning the lake to health and with it a mutual healing of lake and people. It is an exemplar of a new holistic approach, called biocultural or reciprocal restoration.

In the Indigenous worldview, a healthy landscape is understood to be whole and generous enough to be able to sustain its partners. It engages land not as a machine but as a community of respected nonhuman persons to whom we humans have a responsibility. Restoration requires renewing the capacity not only for "ecosystem services" but for "cultural services" as well. Renewal of relationships includes water that you can swim in and not be afraid to touch. Restoring relationship means that when the eagles return, it will be safe for them to eat the fish. People want that for themselves, too. Biocultural restoration raises the bar for environmental quality of the reference ecosystem, so that as we care for the land, it can once again care for us.

Restoring land without restoring relationship is an empty exercise. It is relationship that will endure and relationship that will sustain the restored land. Therefore, reconnecting people and the landscape is as essential as reestablishing proper hydrology or cleaning up contaminants. It is medicine for the earth.

One day in late September, while earth-moving machinery dredged contaminated soils on the western shore of Onondaga Lake, another group of earth movers worked on the eastern shore—dancing. I watched their feet as they moved in a circle led by the water drum. Beaded moccasins, tassel-tie loafers, high-top sneakers, flip-flops, and patent-leather pumps all beat against the ground in a ceremonial dance to honor the water. All the participants carried vessels of clean water from their home places; their hopes for Onondaga Lake were held in these vessels. Work boots brought spring water from the high hills, green Converses carried city tap water, and red wooden sandals peeking from below a pink kimono carried sacred water all the way from Mount Fuji to blend that purity into Onondaga Lake. This ceremony is also restoration ecology, the healing of relationship and the stirring of emotion and spirit on behalf of the water. Singers, dancers, and speakers took the stage by the lake to call for restoration. Faithkeeper Oren Lyons, Clan Mother Audrey Shenandoah, and international activist Jane Goodall joined the community in this water communion to celebrate the sacredness of the lake and to renew the covenant between people and the water. There on the shore where the Tree of Peace once stood, we joined to plant another tree in commemoration of peacemaking with the lake. This should be on the restoration tour, too. Stop #6: LAND AS SACRED, LAND AS COMMUNITY.

Naturalist E. O. Wilson writes, "There can be no purpose more inspiring than to begin the age of restoration, reweaving the wondrous diversity of life that still surrounds us." The stories are piling up all around in scraps of land being restored: trout streams reclaimed from siltation, brownfields turned into community gardens, prairies reclaimed from soybeans, wolves howling in their old territories, schoolkids helping salamanders across the road. If your heart isn't raised by the sight of whooping cranes restored to their ancient flyway, you must not have a pulse. It's true that these victories are as small and fragile as origami cranes, but their power moves as inspiration. Your hands itch to pull out invasive species and replant the native flowers. Your finger trembles with a wish to detonate the explosion of an obsolete dam that would restore a salmon run. These are antidotes to the poison of despair.

Joanna Macy speaks of the Great Turning, the "essential adventure of our time; the shift from the Industrial Growth Society to a life-sustaining civilization." Restoration of land and relationship pushes that turning wheel. "Action on behalf of life transforms. Because the relationship between self and the world is reciprocal, it is not a question of first getting enlightened or saved and *then* acting. As we work to heal the earth, the earth heals us."

The last stop on the ride around the lake hasn't been finished yet, but the scene is planned. In this tableau there will be kids swimming, families picnicking. People love this lake and take care of it. It's a place for ceremony and celebration. The Haudenosaunee flag flies alongside the Stars and Stripes. Folks are fishing in the shallows and keeping their catch. Willow trees bend gracefully, their limbs full of birds. An eagle sits at the top of the Tree of Peace. Lakeshore wetlands are rich with muskrats and waterfowl. Native prairies green the lakeshore. The signpost at the scene reads LAND AS HOME.

People of Corn, People of Light

T he story of our relationship to the earth is written more truth-
fully on the land than on the page. It lasts there. The land
remembers what we said and what we did. Stories are among
our most potent tools for restoring the land as well as our relationship
to land. We need to unearth the old stories that live in a place and begin
to create new ones, for we are storymakers, not just storytellers. All stories are connected, new ones woven from the threads of the old. One of
the ancestor stories, that waits for us to listen again with new ears, is the
Mayan story of Creation.

*It is said that in the beginning there was emptiness. The divine beings, the
great thinkers, imagined the world into existence simply by saying its name.
The world was populated with a rich flora and fauna, called into being by
words. But the divine beings were not satisfied. Among the wonderful beings
they had created, none were articulate. They could sing and squawk and growl,
but none had voice to tell the story of their creation nor praise it. So the gods set
about to make humans.*

*The first humans, the gods shaped of mud. But the gods were none too
happy with the result. The people were not beautiful; they were ugly and ill
formed. They could not talk—they could barely walk and certainly could not
dance or sing the praises of the gods. They were so crumbly and clumsy and
inadequate that they could not even reproduce and just melted away in the rain.*

So the gods tried again to make good people who would be givers of respect, givers of praise, providers and nurturers. To this end they carved a man from wood and a woman from the pith of a reed. Oh, these were beautiful people, lithe and strong; they could talk and dance and sing. Clever people, too: they learned to use the other beings, plants and animals, for their own purposes. They made many things, farms and pottery and houses, and nets to catch fish. As a result of their fine bodies and fine minds and hard work, these people reproduced and populated the world, filling it with their numbers.

But after a time the all-seeing gods realized that these people's hearts were empty of compassion and love. They could sing and talk, but their words were without gratitude for the sacred gifts that they had received. These clever people did not know thanks or caring and so endangered the rest of the Creation. The gods wished to end this failed experiment in humanity and so they sent great catastrophes to the world—they sent a flood, and earthquakes, and, most importantly, they loosed the retaliation of the other species. The previously mute trees and fish and clay were given voices for their grief and anger at the disrespect shown them by the humans made of wood. Trees raged against the humans for their sharp axes, the deer for their arrows, and even the pots made of earthen clay rose up in anger for the times they had been carelessly burnt. All of the misused members of Creation rallied together and destroyed the people made of wood in self-defense.

Once again the gods tried to make human beings, but this time purely of light, the sacred energy of the sun. These humans were dazzling to behold, seven times the color of the sun, beautiful, smart, and very, very powerful. They knew so much that they believed they knew everything. Instead of being grateful to the creators for their gifts, they believed themselves to be the gods' equals. The divine beings understood the danger posed by these people made of light and once more arranged for their demise.

And so the gods tried again to fashion humans who would live right in the beautiful world they had created, in respect and gratitude and humility. From two baskets of corn, yellow and white, they ground a fine meal, mixed it with water, and shaped a people made of corn. They were fed on corn liquor and oh these were good people. They could dance and sing and they had words to tell stories and offer up prayers. Their hearts were filled with compassion for the rest of Creation. They were wise enough to be grateful. The gods had learned their *lesson, so to protect the corn people from the overpowering arrogance of their predecessors, the people made of light, they passed a veil before the eyes of the corn people, clouding their vision as breath clouds a mirror. These people of corn are the ones who were respectful and grateful for the world that sustained them—and so they were the people who were sustained upon the earth.* *

Of all the materials, why is it that people of corn would inherit the earth, rather than people of mud or wood or light? Could it be that people made of corn are beings transformed? For what is corn, after all, but light transformed by relationship? Corn owes its existence to all four elements: earth, air, fire, and water. And corn is the product of relationship not only with the physical world, but with people too. The sacred plant of our origin created people, and people created corn, a great agricultural innovation from its teosinthe ancestor. Corn cannot exist without us to sow it and tend its growth; our beings are joined in an obligate symbiosis. From these reciprocal acts of creation arise the elements that were missing from the other attempts to create sustainable humanity: gratitude, and a capacity for reciprocity.

I've read and loved this story as a history of sorts—a recounting of how, in long-ago times just at the edge of knowing, people were made of maize and lived happily ever after. But in many Indigenous ways of knowing, time is not a river, but a lake in which the past, the present, and the future exist. Creation, then, is an ongoing process and the story is not history alone—it is also prophecy. Have we already become people of corn? Or are we still people made of wood? Are we people made of light, in thrall to our own power? Are we not yet transformed by relationship to earth?

Perhaps this story could be a user's manual for understanding how we become people of corn. The Popul Vuh, the Mayan sacred text in which this story is contained, is perceived as more than just a chronicle. As David Suzuki notes in *The Wisdom of the Elders,* the Mayan stories are understood as an *ilbal*—a precious seeing instrument, or lens, with which to view our sacred relationships. He suggests that such stories may

---

* Adapted from oral tradition.

offer us a corrective lens. But while our Indigenous stories are rich in wisdom, and we need to hear them, I do not advocate their wholesale appropriation. As the world changes, an immigrant culture must write its own new stories of relationship to place—a new *ilbal*, but tempered by the wisdom of those who were old on this land long before we came.

So how, then, can science, art, and story give us a new lens to understand the relationship that people made of corn represent? Someone once said that sometimes a fact alone is a poem. Just so, the people of corn are embedded in a beautiful poem, written in the language of chemistry. The first stanza goes like this:

Carbon dioxide plus water combined in the presence of light and chlorophyll in the beautiful membrane-bound machinery of life yields sugar and oxygen.

Photosynthesis, in other words, in which air, light, and water are combined out of nothingness into sweet morsels of sugar—the stuff of redwoods and daffodils and corn. Straw spun to gold, water turned to wine, photosynthesis is the link between the inorganic realm and the living world, making the inanimate live. At the same time it gives us oxygen. Plants give us food and breath.

Here is the second stanza, the same as the first, but recited backward:

Sugar combined with oxygen in the beautiful membrane-bound machinery of life called the mitochondria yields us right back where we began—carbon dioxide and water.

Respiration—the source of energy that lets us farm and dance and speak. The breath of plants gives life to animals and the breath of animals gives life to plants. My breath is your breath, your breath is mine. It's the great poem of give and take, of reciprocity that animates the world. Isn't that a story worth telling? Only when people understand the symbiotic relationships that sustain them can they become people of corn, capable of gratitude and reciprocity.

The very facts of the world *are* a poem. Light is turned to sugar. Salamanders find their way to ancestral ponds following magnetic lines radiating from the earth. The saliva of grazing buffalo causes the grass to grow taller. Tobacco seeds germinate when they smell smoke. Microbes in industrial waste can destroy mercury. Aren't these stories we should all know?

Who is it who holds them? In long-ago times, it was the elders who carried them. In the twenty-first century, it is often scientists who first hear them. The stories of buffalo and salamanders belong to the land, but scientists are one of their translators and carry a large responsibility for conveying their stories to the world.

And yet scientists mostly convey these stories in a language that excludes readers. Conventions for efficiency and precision make reading scientific papers very difficult for the rest of the world, and if the truth be known, for us as well. This has serious consequences for public dialogue about the environment and therefore for real democracy, especially the democracy of all species. For what good is knowing, unless it is coupled with caring? Science can give us knowing, but caring comes from someplace else.

I think it's fair to say that if the Western world has an *ilbal*, it is science. Science lets us see the dance of the chromosomes, the leaves of moss, and the farthest galaxy. But is it a sacred lens like the Popul Vuh? Does science allow us to perceive the sacred in the world, or does it bend light in such a way as to obscure it? A lens that brings the material world into focus but blurs the spiritual is the lens of a people made of wood. It is not more data that we need for our transformation to people of corn, but more wisdom.

While science could be a source of and repository for knowledge, the scientific worldview is all too often an enemy of ecological compassion. It is important in thinking about this lens to separate two ideas that are too often synonymous in the mind of the public: the practice of science and the scientific worldview that it feeds. Science is the process of revealing the world through rational inquiry. The practice of doing real science brings the questioner into an unparalleled intimacy with nature fraught with wonder and creativity as we try to comprehend the mysteries of the more-than-human world. Trying to understand the life of another being or another system so unlike our own is often humbling and, for many scientists, is a deeply spiritual pursuit.

Contrasting with this is the scientific worldview, in which a culture uses the process of interpreting science in a cultural context that uses science and technology to reinforce reductionist, materialist economic and political agendas. I maintain that the destructive lens of the people made of wood is not science itself, but the lens of the scientific worldview, the illusion of dominance and control, the separation of knowledge from responsibility.

I dream of a world guided by a lens of stories rooted in the revelations of science and framed with an Indigenous worldview—stories in which matter and spirit are both given voice.

Scientists are particularly good at learning about the lives of other species. The stories they could tell convey the intrinsic values of the lives of other beings, lives every bit as interesting, maybe more so, as those of *Homo sapiens*. But while scientists are among those who are privy to these other intelligences, many seem to believe that the intelligence they access is only their own. They lack the fundamental ingredient: humility. After the gods experimented with arrogance, they gave the people of corn humility, and it takes humility to learn from other species.

In the Indigenous view, humans are viewed as somewhat lesser beings in the democracy of species. We are referred to as the younger brothers of Creation, so like younger brothers we must learn from our elders. Plants were here first and have had a long time to figure things out. They live both above and below ground and hold the earth in place. Plants know how to make food from light and water. Not only do they feed themselves, but they make enough to sustain the lives of all the rest of us. Plants are providers for the rest of the community and exemplify the virtue of generosity, always offering food. What if Western scientists saw plants as their teachers rather than their subjects? What if they told stories with that lens?

Many Indigenous peoples share the understanding that we are each endowed with a particular gift, a unique ability. Birds to sing and stars to glitter, for instance. It is understood that these gifts have a dual nature, though: a gift is also a responsibility. If the bird's gift is song, then it has a responsibility to greet the day with music. It is the duty of birds to sing and the rest of us receive the song as a gift.

Asking what is our responsibility is perhaps also to ask, What is our gift? And how shall we use it? Stories like the one about the people of corn give us guidance, both to recognize the world as a gift and to think how we might respond. The people of mud and wood and light all lacked gratitude and the sense of reciprocity that flowed from it. It was only the people of corn, people transformed by awareness of their gifts and responsibilities, who were sustained on the earth. Gratitude comes first, but gratitude alone is not enough.

Other beings are known to be especially gifted, with attributes that humans lack. Other beings can fly, see at night, rip open trees with their claws, make maple syrup. What can humans do?

We may not have wings or leaves, but we humans do have words. Language is our gift and our responsibility. I've come to think of writing as an act of reciprocity with the living land. Words to remember old stories, words to tell new ones, stories that bring science and spirit back together to nurture our becoming people made of corn.

Collateral Damage

The headlights throw two beams through the fog from a long way off as the car winds toward us. The rise and fall of the lights has become our signal to dash into the road, grabbing up one soft black body in each hand. The beams appear and disappear in the dips and curves as we shuttle back and forth with flashlight beams speckling the pavement. When we hear the engine we know there is only time for one last run before the car crests the hill and bears down upon us.

Standing on the shoulder, I can see faces as the car draws near, greenish in the dashboard lights, looking right at us as the spray from the tires flies up. Our eyes meet and the brake lights flash red for just a heartbeat, lit up like momentary synapses in the driver's brain. The light telegraphs a hint of thought for fellow humans in the rain on the side of a lonely country road. I'm waiting for them to roll down a window and ask if we need help, but they don't stop. The driver looks back over his shoulder, brake lights dimming as he speeds away. If cars scarcely brake for *Homo sapiens*, what hope can we hold for *Ambystoma maculata*, our other neighbors who travel this road in the night?

Rain beats against my kitchen window in the falling dusk. I can hear geese outside, in low formation over the valley. Winter is letting go. Pausing by the stove with raincoats draped over my arm, I stop to stir a pot of pea soup, sending up clouds of steam that mist over the window. We'll be glad for a warm cup during the night ahead.

The six o'clock news comes on while I am headfirst in the closet, rounding up flashlights. It has begun—bombs are falling on Baghdad tonight. I stop in the middle of the floor, listening, with my hands full of boots, a red pair and a black. Somewhere another woman looks out her window, but the formation of dark shapes in her sky is not a skein of spring geese returning. Skies billowing with smoke, homes alight, sirens wailing. CNN reports the number of sorties and tons of ordnance like box scores in a baseball game. The level of collateral damage, they say, is as yet unknown.

Collateral damage: shielding words to keep us from naming the consequences of a missile gone astray. The words ask us to turn our faces away, as if man-made destruction were an inescapable fact of nature. Collateral damage: measured in overturned soup pots and wailing children. Heavy with helplessness, I turn off the radio and call my family to supper. When the dishes are done, we slip into raincoats then out into the night, driving the back roads to Labrador Hollow.

While it rains bombs on Baghdad, the first rain of spring falls on our valley. Soft and steady, it penetrates the forest floor, melting away the last of the ice crystals beneath the winter-weary blanket of leaves. The splatter and splash is a welcome sound after the long silence of snow. To a salamander beneath a log, the first heavy raindrops must sound like the knuckles of spring knocking hard on the door overhead. After six months of torpor, stiff limbs slowly flex, tails wiggle out of winter immobility, and within minutes, snouts nose upward and legs push away cold earth as the salamanders crawl up into the night. The rain washes away traces of clinging soil and polishes their smooth black skin. The land is waking up, rising to the call of rain.

After we pull off the road and get out of the car, the quiet is stunning in the wake of swishing windshield wipers and the defroster going full tilt. The warm rain on cold earth has raised a ground fog, wrapping around the bare trees. Our voices are muffled in the mist. Our flashlights diffuse into warm halos.

Here in upstate New York, flocks of geese mark the change of seasons, noisily making their way from winter safety to the breeding grounds of spring. Largely unseen, but equally dramatic, is the migration of salamanders from winter burrows to the vernal pools where they will meet their mates. The first warm rain of spring, a soaking rain coinciding with a temperature above forty-two degrees, sets the forest floor to rustling and stirring. En masse they rise from the hidden places, blink at the open air, and start on their way. This outpouring of animals is nearly invisible, unless you happen to be in a swamp on a rainy spring night. Salamanders move when darkness protects them from predators and rain keeps their skin moist. And they move by the thousands, like a herd of sluggish buffalo. Like the buffalo, too, their numbers diminish each year.

Like its nearby cousins, the Finger Lakes, Labrador Pond lies in the bottom of a V-shaped valley flanked by two steep hills left behind by the last glacier. The forested slopes curve around the pond like the sides of a bowl, funneling amphibians from the woods of the entire watershed straight to the water. But their route is interrupted by a road that snakes through the hollow. The pond and surrounding hills are protected as state forest, but the road is a free-for-all.

We walk down the deserted road, scanning our lights back and forth over the pavement. Salamanders aren't the only ones on the move tonight: wood frogs, bullfrogs, green frogs, leopard frogs, and newts also hear the call and begin their annual journey. There are toads, peepers, red efts, and legions of tree frogs all with mating on their minds. The road is a circus of jumps and leaps flashing in and out of our flashlights. My beam catches the glittering gold of an eye. The peeper freezes as I approach and then hops away. Ahead of us, the road is alive with frogs leaping across, two here in my light, three over there, bounding toward the pond. With their prodigious leaps they cross the road in just a few seconds. Not so the heavy-bodied salamanders, who belly their way across the road. Their journey takes about two minutes, and in two minutes anything can happen.

Spotting the lumbering forms among the frogs, we stop and pick them up one after the other, carefully setting them on the other side of the road. We walk back and forth between the passage of cars over the same small stretch, and each time we look there are more—the land seems to be releasing salamanders as numerous as the geese rising off a marsh.

I run my light across the road and the center line reflects bright yellow against the rain-black asphalt. In the corner of my eye, there is something darker than dark, a break in reflection off the pavement that draws my light back to that spot. The shadow resolves into a big spotted salamander, *Ambystoma maculata*, black and yellow like the road. The shape is so primitive, with right-angle limbs jutting from the side and moving with a jerky, mechanical motion across the road, dragging a thick tail in a sinuous side-to-side wave behind it. When it stops in the circle of my light, I reach out to touch its skin, blue-black, like night congealed. The body is splotched with opaque yellow like drops of paint on a wet surface, blurred at the edges. Its wedge-shaped head swings from side to side, blunt snout with eyes so dark they disappear into its face. By its size—about seven inches long—and its swollen sides, I'd guess this is a female. I wonder what it feels like to drag that tender skin—with a smooth, soft belly made for sliding over wet leaves—across the asphalt.

I stoop to pick her up, circling my two fingers just behind her front legs. There is surprisingly little resistance. It's like picking up an overripe banana: my fingertips sink into her body, cold and soft and wet. I gently set her down on the shoulder and wipe my hands on my pants. Without a backward glance, she lunges over the embankment, down to the pond.

The females are the first to arrive. Heavy with eggs, they will slide into the shallows and disappear among the decaying leaves on the bottom. They wait, fecund and sluggish in the cold water, for the males, who will make the same journey down from the hillsides a day or two later.

They come out from under logs and across streams all pointed in the same direction: the pool where they were born. Their route is circuitous because they don't have the ability to climb over obstacles. They follow along the edges of any log or rock until it ends and they are free to go forward, on to the pond. The natal pond may be as much as half a mile from their wintering spot, and yet they locate it unerringly. Salamanders have a guidance system easily as complex as the "smart bombs" winding their way to targets in Iraqi neighborhoods tonight. Without the benefit of satellite or microchip, salamanders navigate by a combination of magnetic and chemical signals that herpetologists are just beginning to understand.

Part of their direction-finding ability relies on a precise reading of the lines in the earth's magnetic field. A small organ in the brain processes magnetic data and guides the salamander to its pond. Though many other ponds and vernal pools lie along the route, they will not stop until they arrive at the birthplace, struggling mightily to get there. Once they are close, homing in salamanders seems to be similar to salmon identifying their home river: they smell their way with a nasal gland on their snouts. Following the earth's magnetic signals gets them to the neighborhood and then scent takes over to guide them home. It's like getting off an airplane and then finding your way to your childhood home by following the ineffable odor of Sunday dinner and your mother's perfume.

On last year's mission to the hollow, my daughter begged to follow the salamanders and see where they were going. We trailed behind by flashlight as the amphibians twined between scarlet stems of red osier and clambered over flattened tussocks of sedge. They stopped far short of the main pond, on the edges of a vernal pool, a small depression in the land that goes unnoticed in summer but reliably fills with snowmelt every spring, making a watery mosaic. Salamanders choose these temporary basins to lay eggs because they are too shallow and short-lived for fish, which would gobble up the salamander larvae, to inhabit. The pool's evanescence is the newborn's protection from fish.

We followed the salamanders to the water's edge, where platelets of ice still clung to the shore. They did not hesitate, but strode purposefully into the water and disappeared. My daughter was disappointed, expecting to see them loitering on the beach or doing belly flops into the pool. She searched the water's surface with her flashlight, wanting to see what happened next, but there were only dappled leaves on the bottom of the pool, patches of light and dark. Nothing to see—until we realized that the patches of light and dark were not leaves at all, but the black and yellow spots of dozens of salamanders. Everywhere the light stopped there were salamanders, the bottom of the pool a blanket of animals. And they were moving, swirling about each other like a room full of dancers. Compared to their ponderous movement on land, they were fleet in the water, swimming as gracefully as seals. One flick of the tail and they were gone from the circle of light.

The glassy surface of the pond was suddenly broken from below, like the upwelling of a surging spring, and the water started to churn as they moved together in a roiling crowd, yellow spots flashing. We stood in amazed witness to their mating ritual, a congress of salamanders. As many as fifty males and females danced and swirled together, a rapturous celebration after a long year of solitary, celibate existence eating bugs under a log. Bubbles rose from the bottom of the pond like champagne.

Unlike most amphibians, *Ambystoma maculata* does not spill its eggs and sperm freely into the water for a frenzy of mass fertilization. The species has evolved a more probable scheme to ensure the meeting of egg and sperm. Males break away from the dancing swarm, take a gulp of air, and swim for the bottom of the pond, where they release a glistening spermatophore—a gelatinous sac of sperm with a stalk to attach it to a twig or a leaf. The females then leave the dance and seek out the quarter-inch sacs, which hover like shiny Mylar balloons bobbing in the water. They draw the spermatophores into an internal cavity where eggs are waiting. Safely inside, the sperm are then released from the sac and fertilize the pearly eggs.

A few days later, each female will lay a mass of one hundred to two hundred eggs in a gelatinous mass. The expectant mother will linger nearby until the eggs hatch, but then she returns, alone, to the woods. The newborn salamanders stay behind in the safety of the pool for several months, metamorphosing until they are capable of life on land. By the time the pool has dried up and forced them out, their gills will be replaced by lungs and they are ready to forage on their own. The juvenile salamanders, or newts, are wanderers who will not return to the pond until they are sexually mature, four to five years later. Salamanders can be long-lived beings. Adults may make the mating migration through a lifetime as long as eighteen years, but only if they can cross the road.

Amphibians are one of the most vulnerable groups on the planet. Subject to habitat loss as wetlands and forests disappear, amphibians are the collateral damage we blindly accept as the cost of development. And because amphibians breathe through their skin, they have little ability to filter out toxins at that moist membrane between animal and atmosphere. Even when their habitats are safe from industry, their atmosphere may not be. Toxins in the air and water, acid rain, heavy metals, and synthetic hormones all end up in the water in which they gestate. Developmental abnormalities like six-legged frogs and twisted salamanders are now found throughout the industrialized world.

Tonight the salamanders' biggest threat is the cars that go speeding by, their occupants unaware of the spectacle that is taking place beneath their tires. From inside the car, listening to late-night radio, you just don't know. But standing on the roadside, you can hear the pop of the body, hear the moment when a glistening being following magnetic trails toward love is reduced to red pulp on the pavement. We try to work faster, but there are so many, and we are so few.

A green Dodge pickup I recognize races by and we stand back on the shoulder. It was one of my neighbors who has a dairy farm just up the road, but he doesn't even see us. I suspect his thoughts are far away tonight, straining toward Baghdad. His son, Mitch, is stationed in Iraq. Mitch is a nice kid, the kind who, with a friendly wave, would always pull his slow tractor off to the roadside to let cars pass safely. I suppose he's driving a tank now. The fate of salamanders crossing the road in his old hometown might seem completely unconnected to the scene he faces.

Tonight, though, when the fog wraps us all in the same cold blanket, the edges seem to blur. The carnage on this dark country road and the broken bodies on the streets of Baghdad do seem connected. Salamanders, children, young farmers in uniform—they are not the enemy or the problem. We have not declared war on these innocents, and yet they die just as surely as if we had. They are all collateral damage. If it is oil that sends the sons to war, and oil that fuels the engines that roar down this hollow, then we are all complicit, soldiers, civilians, and salamanders connected in death by our appetite for oil.

Cold and tired, we stop and pour out a cup of soup from the thermos. Its steam rises to mingle with the fog. We sip quietly and listen to the night. Suddenly I hear voices, but there are no houses nearby. Up around the curve I catch the strobes of other flashlights. I quickly shut off my light and close up the thermos. We back away into shadow and watch as the lights come nearer, a whole line of them. Who would be out on a night like this? Only someone out looking for trouble, and I don't want to be it.

Kids use this road sometimes as a drinking spot, a place to shoot beer cans. I once saw a pair of young men kicking a toad between them like a hacky sack. I shudder to think what brings them here. The lights are closer now, at least a dozen all scattered across the road like a patrol. The beams scan back and forth over the road. As they come closer, the pattern of their lights becomes oddly familiar. It is the very same pattern we've been making all night. And then I hear their voices through the fog.

"Look, here's another one—a female."

"Hey—I got two over here."

"Add three peepers."

Grinning in the dark, I switch on my light again and step out to meet them as they bend and carry the salamanders to safety. We are so glad to see each other and we pump each other's hands as our voices rise in laughter around a virtual campfire made by flashlights. I pour out soup for everybody and we are all momentarily bound together with the giddiness of relief, both to know that the approaching lights are friend and not foe and to recognize that we are not alone in our efforts.

We all introduce ourselves and get a look at the faces under the dripping hoods. Our fellow travelers are students from a herpetology class at the college. They all have clipboards and Rite in the Rain notebooks to record their observations. I feel embarrassed to have assumed that they were troublemakers. Ignorance makes it too easy to jump to conclusions about what we don't understand.

The class is here to study the effects of roads on amphibians. They tell us that frogs and toads take only about fifteen seconds to cross the road and mostly escape the cars. The spotted salamanders average eighty-eight seconds. They may have evaded countless predators, survived the summer drought, endured the winter without freezing, but it all comes down to eighty-eight seconds.

The students' efforts on behalf of *Ambystoma* go beyond roadside rescue. The highway department could install salamander crossings, special culverts that allow the animals to avoid the road, but they're expensive and the authorities need to be convinced of their importance. The class mission tonight is to take a census of the amphibians crossing the road to estimate the total numbers of animals who move from the hills to the pond, and the number who die en route. If they can get adequate data to show that road deaths endanger the viability of this population, then they may be able to persuade the state to take action. There's just one problem. In order to obtain accurate estimates of salamander mortality, they have to count both the animals who make it across the road and those who don't.

It turns out that tallying death is easy: they've developed a system for identifying the species of animal by the size of the blotch it leaves on the road, which is then scraped up to avoid counting it again on the next traverse of the road. Sometimes death occurs even without collision. Salamanders are so soft bodied that merely the pressure wave generated by a passing vehicle can be fatal. The missing number is the denominator of the death equation—the number of animals who *do* make it safely across. How can they take inventory of the successful crossings on a long stretch of road in total darkness?

At widely spaced intervals along the road, drift fences have been installed. A drift fence is simply a length of snow fence about eight feet long, with a foot-high strip of aluminum roof flashing wired like a wall along its base. The salamanders can't wiggle through. Confronting this obstacle, they edge along the drift fence as if it were a log or a rock. They attempt to follow it to its end, slithering along in the darkness, moving by feel of the fence against skin. Until suddenly the ground vanishes and they fall into a buried plastic bucket from which they cannot escape. The students come along every so often and count the animals in the bucket, record the species on their clipboards, and then gently release them on the other side of the fence, on their way to the pond. At night's end, the number of animals caught by the drift fences provides an estimate of the number who safely crossed the road.

These studies may provide the evidence that will save the salamanders, but there is a short-term cost to that long-term benefit. In order to do the research properly, no human intervention is allowed. When a car is coming, the students have to stand back, grit their teeth, and let it happen. Our well-intentioned salamander rescues have in fact biased the experiment tonight, as we decreased the number who normally would have been hit, causing an underestimate in the serious losses that occur. It poses an ethical dilemma for the students. The dead who could have been saved become the collateral damage of the study—a sacrifice that they hope will pay off in future protection for the species.

This roadkill monitoring is the project of James Gibbs, an internationally renowned conservation biologist. He is a leader in conserving Galapagos tortoises and Tanzanian toads—but his concerns are also here in Labrador Hollow. He and his students set up the drift fences, patrol the road, and stay up all night counting. Gibbs confesses that sometimes, on rainy nights when he knows the salamanders are moving—and dying—he can't sleep. He puts on a raincoat and goes out to carry them across. Aldo Leopold had it right: naturalists live in a world of wounds that only they can see.

As night deepens, there are no more headlights twisting down the hollow. By midnight even the slowest salamander can cross in safety, so we trudge back to the car and head for home, driving at a snail's pace until we're out of the hollow lest our own wheels undo our work. We're painfully careful, but I know we are as guilty as anyone.

Driving home through the fog, we hear more war news on the radio. Columns of tanks and Bradley Fighting Vehicles are advancing over the Iraqi countryside, through a sandstorm as dense as the fog that shrouds us here. I wonder what is crushed beneath them as they pass. Cold and tired, I crank up the heater and the car fills with the smell of wet wool. I think back on our night's work and the good people we met.

What is it that drew us to the hollow tonight? What crazy kind of species is it that leaves a warm home on a rainy night to ferry salamanders across a road? It's tempting to call it altruism, but it's not. There is nothing selfless about it. This night heaps rewards on the givers as well as the recipients. We get to be there, to witness this amazing rite, and, for an evening, to enter into relationship with other beings, as different from ourselves as we can imagine.

It has been said that people of the modern world suffer a great sadness, a "species loneliness"—estrangement from the rest of Creation. We have built this isolation with our fear, with our arrogance, and with our homes brightly lit against the night. For a moment as we walked this road, those barriers dissolved and we began to relieve the loneliness and know each other once again.

Salamanders are so very much the "other," cold, slimy creatures verging on repulsive to the warm-blooded *Homo sapiens*. Their startling otherness makes it all the more remarkable that we were here tonight in their defense. Amphibians offer few of the warm fuzzy feelings that fuel our protection of charismatic mammals that look back at us with Bambi's grateful eyes. They bring us face to face with our innate xenophobia, sometimes directed at other species and sometimes directed at our own, whether in this hollow or in deserts halfway around the globe. Being with salamanders gives honor to otherness, offers an antidote to the poison of xenophobia. Each time we rescue slippery, spotted beings we attest to their right to be, to live in the sovereign territory of their own lives.

Carrying salamanders to safety also helps us to remember the covenant of reciprocity, the mutual responsibility that we have for each other. As the perpetrators of the war zone on this road, are we not bound to heal the wounds that we inflict?

The news makes me feel powerless. I can't stop bombs from falling and I can't stop cars from speeding down this road. It is beyond my power. But I can pick up salamanders. For one night I want to clear my name. What is it that draws us to this lonely hollow? Maybe it is love, the same thing that draws the salamanders from under their logs. Or maybe we walked this road tonight in search of absolution.

As the temperature drops, single voices—clear and hollow—replace the keening chorus: the ancient speech of frogs. One word becomes clear, as if spoken in English. "Hear! Hear! Hear! The world is more than your thoughtless commute. We, the collateral, are your wealth, your teachers, your security, your *family*. Your strange hunger for ease should not mean a death sentence for the rest of Creation."

"Hear!" calls a peeper in the headlights.
"Hear!" calls a young man trapped in a tank far from home.
"Hear!" calls a mother whose home is now a burnt-out ruin.

There must be an end to this.

By the time I get home it is late and I cannot sleep, so I walk up the hill to the pond behind my house. Here too the air is ringing with their calls. I want to light a sweetgrass smudge, to wash away the sadness in a cloud of smoke. But the fog is too heavy and the matches just bleed a red streak on the box. As it should be. There should be no washing away tonight; better to wear the grief like a sodden coat.

"Weep! Weep!" calls a toad from the water's edge. And I do. If grief can be a doorway to love, then let us all weep for the world we are breaking apart so we can love it back to wholeness again.

Shkitagen: People of the
Seventh Fire

S
o much depends upon the lighting of this fire, so neatly laid on the cold ground and circled round by stones. A platform of dry maple kindling, a floor of fine twiglets snapped from the underside of a fir, a nest of shredded bark ready for the coal over which broken pine branches are balanced to draw the flame upward. Plenty of fuel, plenty of oxygen. All the elements are in place. But without the spark it is only a pile of dead sticks. So much depends on the spark.

It was a point of pride in my family that we learned to light a fire with a single match. My father was our teacher, along with the woods themselves, and we learned without lessons, by playing and watching and wanting to emulate his comfort in wild places. He patiently showed us how to search out the right materials. Incrementally, we observed the architecture that would feed the flame. He put great store in a fine woodpile and many of our days in the woods were spent felling, hauling, and splitting. "Firewood warms you twice," he would always say as we emerged from the woods hot and sweaty. In the doing of it, we learned to recognize the trees by their bark, by their wood, and by the way they burned for different purposes: pitchy pine for light, beech for a bed of coals, sugar maples to bake pies in the reflector oven.

He never said so directly, but fire making was more than just a woodscraft skill—to build a good fire, a person had to work. There were high standards; no piece of half-rotten birch was permitted in his wood-pile. "Punky," he would say and toss it aside. Knowledge of the flora was a given, as was respectful treatment of the woods, so that you gathered without doing harm. There was always plenty of standing dead wood there for the taking, already dry and seasoned. Only natural materials went into a good fire—no paper or, heaven forbid, gasoline—and green wood was an affront to both aesthetics and ethics. No lighters allowed. We earned high praise for the ideal one-match fire, but plenty of encour-agement if we needed a dozen. And at some point it became natural and easy, no feat at all. I found a secret that always worked for me: to sing to the fire as I touched the match to tinder.

Woven into my dad's fire teachings was appreciation for all the woods gave us and a sense of our responsibility for reciprocity. We never left a camping place without leaving a pile of wood for the next people on the trail. Paying attention, being prepared and patient, and doing it right the first time: the skill and the values were so closely entwined that fire mak-ing became for us an emblem of a certain kind of virtue.

Once we mastered the one-match fire, then came the one-match fire in the rain. And the snow. With the right materials carefully assembled and respect for the ways of air and wood, you could always have a fire. The power of that simple act—with a single match you could make peo-ple feel safe and happy, convert a bunch of sodden individuals into a con-vivial group thinking of stew and songs. It was an amazing gift to carry in your pocket and a serious responsibility to be used well.

Fire building was a vital connection to those who came before. Potawatomi, or more accurately Bodwewadmi in our own language, means People of the Fire. It seemed only right that this was a skill we should master, a gift to share. I began to think that to really understand fire, I needed a bow drill in my hand. Now, I try to make a no-match fire, to conjure a coal in the old way, with bow and drill, a friction fire, rub-bing two sticks together.

Wewene, I say to myself: in a good time, in a good way. There are no shortcuts. It must unfold in the right way, when all the elements are present, mind and body harnessed in unison. When all the tools have been properly made and all the parts united in purpose, it is so easy. But if they're not, it will be futile. Until there is balance and perfect reciprocity between the forces, you can try and fail and try and fail again. I know. And yet, despite the need, you must swallow your sense of urgency, calm your breathing so that the energy goes not to frustration, but to fire.

After we were all grown up and fully fire-competent, my father made sure his grandchildren could also light a one-match fire. At eighty-three, he teaches fire building at our Native youth science camp, sharing the same lessons he gave us. They have a race to have their little blazes burn through a string stretched across the fire circle. One day, after the contest has been won, he sits on a stump poking at the fire. "Did you know," he asks them, "that there are four kinds of fire?" I am expecting his lesson on hardwoods and softwoods, but there is something else on his mind.

"Well, first, of course, there's this campfire you made. You can cook on it, keep warm next to it. It's a good place to sing—and it keeps the coyotes away."

"And toast marshmallows!" pipes up one of the kids.

"You bet. And bake potatoes, make bannock, you can cook most anything on a campfire. Who knows the other kinds of fire?" he asks.

"Forest fires?" one of the students tries tentatively.

"Sure" he says, "what the people used to call Thunderbird fires, forest fires ignited by lightning. Sometimes they'd get put out by the rain, but sometimes they could turn into huge wildfires. They could be so hot they'd destroy everything for miles around. Nobody likes that kind of fire. But our people learned to set fires that were small and in just the right place and time so that they helped rather than hurt. The people set these fires on purpose, to take care of the land—to help the blueberries grow, or to make meadows for deer." He holds up a sheet of birch bark. "In fact, look at all that birch bark you used in your fire. Young paper birches only grow up after fire, so our ancestors burned forests to create clearings for birch." The symmetry of using fire to create fire-building materials was not lost on them. "They needed birch bark so they used their own fire science to create birch forests. Fires help out a lot of plants and animals. We're told that's why the Creator gave people the fire stick—to bring good things to the land. A lot of the time you hear people say that the best thing people can do for nature is to stay away from it and let it be. There are places where that's absolutely true and our people respected that. But we were also given the responsibility to care for land. What people forget is that that means participating—that the natural world relies on us to do good things. You don't show your love and care by putting what you love behind a fence. You have to be involved. You have to contribute to the well-being of the world.

"The land gives us so many gifts; fire is a way we can give back. In modern times, the public thinks fire is only destructive, but they've forgotten, or simply never knew, how people used fire as a creative force. The fire stick was like a paintbrush on the landscape. Touch it here in a small dab and you've made a green meadow for elk; a light scatter there burns off the brush so the oaks make more acorns. Stipple it under the canopy and it thins the stand to prevent catastrophic fire. Draw the fire-brush along the creek and the next spring it's a thick stand of yellow willows. A wash over a grassy meadow turns it blue with camas. To make blueberries, let the paint dry for a few years and repeat. Our people were given the responsibility to use fire to make things beautiful and productive—it was our art and our science."

The birch forests maintained by Indigenous burning were a cornucopia of gifts: bark for canoes, sheathing for wigwams and tools and baskets, scrolls for writing, and, of course, tinder for fires. But these are only the obvious gifts. Both paper birch and yellow birch are hosts to the fungus *Inonotus obliquus*, which erupts through the bark to form sterile conks, a fruiting body that looks like a grainy black tumor the size of a softball. Its surface is cracked and crusted, studded with cinders as if it had been burnt. Known to people of the Siberian birch forests as *chaga*, it is a valued traditional medicine. Our people call it *shkitagen*.

It takes some effort to find a black knob of *shkitagen* and then dislodge it from the tree. But cut open, the body of the conk is banded in glowing shades of gold and bronze, with the texture of spongy wood, all constructed of tiny threads and air-filled pores. Our ancestors discovered a remarkable property of this being, although some say it spoke its own use to us through its burnt exterior and golden heart. *Shkitagen* is a tinder fungus, a firekeeper, and a good friend to the People of the Fire. Once an ember meets *shkitagen* it will not go out but smolders slowly in the fungal matrix, holding its heat. Even the smallest spark, so fleeting and easily lost, will be held and nurtured if it lands on a cube of *shkitagen*. And yet, as forests are felled and fire suppression jeopardizes species that depend upon burned ground, it is getting harder and harder to find.

"Okay—what are the other kinds of fire?" my father asks as he adds a stick to the fire at his feet.

Taiotoreke knows. "Sacred Fire, like for ceremonies."

"Of course," my dad says. "The fires we use to carry prayers, for healing, for sweat lodges. That fire represents our life, the spiritual teachings that we've had from the very beginning. The Sacred Fire is the symbol of life and spirit, so we have special firekeepers to care for them.

"You might not get to be around those other fires very often," he says, "but there's fire you must tend to every day. The hardest one to take care of is the one right here," he says, tapping his finger against his chest. "Your own fire, your spirit. We all carry a piece of that sacred fire within us. We have to honor it and care for it. *You* are the firekeeper."

"Now remember that you're responsible for all those kinds of fire," he reminds them. "That's our job, especially we men. In our way, there is balance between men and women: men are responsible for caring for fire, and women are responsible for water. Those two forces balance each other out. We need both to live. Now, here's something you can't forget about fire," he says.

As he stands before the kids, I hear echoes of the first teachings, when Nanabozho received the same fire teachings from his father that my dad is passing on today, "You must always remember that fire has two sides. Both are very powerful. One side is the force of creation. Fire can be used for good—like on your hearth or in ceremony. Your own heart fire is also a force for good. But that same power can be turned to destruction. Fire can be good for the land, but it can also destroy. Your own fire can be used for ill, too. Human people can never forget to understand and respect both sides of this power. They are far stronger than we are. We must learn to be careful or they can destroy everything that has been created. We have to create balance."

Fire has another meaning for Anishinaabe people as well, corresponding to the eras in the life of our nation. The "fires" refer to the places we have lived and the events and the teachings that surrounded them.

Anishinaabe knowledge keepers—our historians and scholars—carry the narrative of the people from our earliest origin, long before the coming of the offshore people, the *zaaganaash*. They also carry what came after, for our histories are inevitably braided together with our futures. This story is known as the Seventh Fire Prophecy and it has been shared widely by Eddie Benton-Banai and other elders.

The era of the First Fire found Anishinaabe people living in the dawn lands of the Atlantic shore. The people were given powerful spiritual teachings, which they were to follow for the good of the people and the land, for they are one. But a prophet foretold that the Anishinaabe would have to move to the west or else they would be destroyed in the changes that were to come. They were to search until they found the place "where the food grows on the water," and there they would make their new home in safety. The leaders heeded the prophecy and led the nation west along the St. Lawrence River, far inland near what is now Montreal. There they rekindled the flame, carried with them on the journey in bowls of *shkitagen*.

A new teacher arose among the people and counseled them to continue still farther west, where they would camp on the shore of a very big lake. Trusting in the vision, the people followed and the time of the Second Fire began as they made camp on the shores of Lake Huron near what is now Detroit. Soon, though, the Anishinaabe became divided into three groups—the Ojibwe, the Odawa, and the Potawatomi—who took different routes to seek their homes around the Great Lakes. The Potawatomi traveled to the south, from southern Michigan all the way to Wisconsin. As the prophecies foretold, however, the bands were reunited several generations later at Manitoulin Island, forming a union known as the Three Fires Confederacy that remains to this day. In the time of the Third Fire, they found the place foretold in prophecy, "where the food grows on the water," and established their new homelands in the country of wild rice. The people lived well for a long time under the care of maples and birches, sturgeon and beaver, eagle and loon. The spiritual teachings that had guided them kept the people strong and together they flourished in the bosom of their nonhuman relatives.

At the time of the Fourth Fire, the history of another people came to be braided into ours. Two prophets arose among the people, foretelling the coming of the light-skinned people in ships from the east, but their visions differed in what was to follow. The path was not clear, as it cannot be with the future. The first prophet said that if the offshore people, the *zaaganaash*, came in brotherhood, they would bring great knowledge. Combined with Anishinaabe ways of knowing, this would form a great new nation. But the second prophet sounded a warning: He said that what looks like the face of brotherhood might be the face of death. These new people might come with brotherhood, or they might come with greed for the riches of our land. How would we know which face is the true one? If the fish became poisoned and the water unfit to drink, we would know which face they wore. And for their actions the *zaaganaash* came to be known instead as *chimokman*—the long-knife people.

The prophecies described what eventually became history. They warned the people of those who would come among them with black robes and black books, with promises of joy and salvation. The prophets said that if the people turned against their own sacred ways and followed this black-robe path, then the people would suffer for many generations.

Indeed, the burial of our spiritual teachings in the time of the Fifth Fire nearly broke the hoop of the nation. People became separated from their homelands and from each other as they were forced onto reservations. Their children were taken from them to learn the *ʒaaganaash* ways. Forbidden by law to practice their own religion, they nearly lost an ancient worldview. Forbidden to speak their languages, a universe of knowing vanished in a generation. The land was fragmented, the people separated, the old ways blowing away in the wind; even the plants and animals began to turn their faces away from us. The time was foretold when the children would turn away from the elders; people would lose their way and their purpose in life. They prophesied that, in the time of the Sixth Fire, "the cup of life would almost become the cup of grief." And yet, even after all of this, there is something that remains, a coal that has not been extinguished. At the First Fire, so long ago, the people were told that it is their spiritual lives that will keep them strong.

They say that a prophet appeared with a strange and distant light in his eyes. The young man came to the people with the message that in the time of the seventh fire, a new people would emerge with a sacred purpose. It would not be easy for them. They would have to be strong and determined in their work, for they stood at a crossroads.

The ancestors look to them from the flickering light of distant fires. In this time, the young would turn back to the elders for teachings and find that many had nothing to give. The people of the Seventh Fire do not yet walk forward; rather, they are told to turn around and retrace the steps of the ones who brought us here. Their sacred purpose is to walk back along the red road of our ancestors' path and to gather up all the fragments that lay scattered along the trail. Fragments of land, tatters of language, bits of songs, stories, sacred teachings—all that was dropped along the way. Our elders say that we live in the time of the seventh fire. We are the ones the ancestors spoke of, the ones who will bend to the task of putting things back together to rekindle the flames of the sacred fire, to begin the rebirth of a nation.

And so it has come to pass that all over Indian Country there is a movement for revitalization of language and culture growing from the dedicated work of individuals who have the courage to breathe life into ceremonies, gather speakers to reteach the language, plant old seed varieties, restore native landscapes, bring the youth back to the land. The people of the Seventh Fire walk among us. They are using the fire stick of the original teachings to restore health to the people, to help them bloom again and bear fruit.

The Seventh Fire prophecy presents a second vision for the time that is upon us. It tells that all the people of the earth will see that the path ahead is divided. They must make a choice in their path to the future. One of the roads is soft and green with new grass. You could walk barefoot there. The other path is scorched black, hard; the cinders would cut your feet. If the people choose the grassy path, then life will be sustained. But if they choose the cinder path, the damage they have wrought upon the earth will turn against them and bring suffering and death to earth's people.

We do indeed stand at the crossroads. Scientific evidence tells us we are close to the tipping point of climate change, the end of fossil fuels, the beginning of resource depletion. Ecologists estimate that we would need seven planets to sustain the lifeways we have created. And yet those lifeways, lacking balance, justice, and peace, have not brought us contentment. They have brought us the loss of our relatives in a great wave of extinction. Whether or not we want to admit it, we have a choice ahead, a crossroads.

I don't fully comprehend prophecy and its relation to history. But I know that metaphor is a way of telling truth far greater than scientific data. I know that when I close my eyes and envision the crossroads that our elders foresaw, it runs like a movie in my head.

The fork in the road stands atop a hill. To the left the path is soft and green and spangled with dew. You want to go barefoot.

The path to the right is ordinary pavement, deceptively smooth at first, but then it drops out of sight into the hazy distance. Just over the horizon, it is buckled with heat, broken to jagged shards.

In the valleys below the hill, I see the people of the Seventh Fire walking toward the crossroads with all they have gathered. They carry in their bundles the precious seeds for a change of worldview. Not so they can return to some atavistic utopia, but to find the tools that allow us to walk into the future. So much has been forgotten, but it is not lost as long as the land endures and we cultivate people who have the humility and ability to listen and learn. And the people are not alone. All along the path, nonhuman people help. What knowledge the people have forgotten is remembered by the land. The others want to live, too. The path is lined with all the world's people, in all colors of the medicine wheel—red, white, black, yellow—who understand the choice ahead, who share a vision of respect and reciprocity, of fellowship with the more-than-human world. Men with fire, women with water, to reestablish balance, to renew the world. Friends and allies all, they are falling in step, forming a great long line headed for the barefoot path. They are carrying *shkitagen* lanterns, tracing their path in light.

But of course there is another road visible in the landscape, and from the high place I see the rooster tails of dust thrown up as its travelers speed ahead, engines roaring, drunk. They drive fast and blind, not even seeing who they are about to run over, or the good green world they speed through. Bullies swagger along the road with a can of gasoline and a lit torch. I worry who will get to the crossroads first, who will make the choices for us all. I recognize the melted road, the cinder path. I've seen it before.

I remember a night when my five-year-old woke afraid of the thunder. It was only as I held her and came fully awake that I thought to ask why there was thunder in January. Instead of stars, the light outside her window was wobbly orange and the air vibrated with the pulsing of fire.

I dashed to get the baby from her crib and led us all outside wrapped in blankets. It was not the house on fire, but the sky. Waves of heat came billowing across the winter-bare fields, like a desert wind. The darkness was burned away in a massive blaze that filled the horizon. My thoughts raced: a plane crash? nuclear blast? I bundled the girls into the pickup and ran back in for the keys. Thinking only to get them away, to go to the river, to run. I spoke as calmly as I could, in measured tones as if fleeing an inferno in our pajamas was no cause for panic. "Mama? Are you afraid?" asked the small voice at my elbow as I tore down the road. "No, honey. Everything is going to be okay." She was nobody's fool. "Then Mama? Why are you talking so quietly?"

We drove safely to our friends' house ten miles away, knocking on their door for refuge in the middle of the night. The flare was dimmer from their back porch, but still flickering eerily. We put the children to bed with cocoa, poured ourselves a whiskey, and flipped on the news. A natural-gas pipeline had exploded less than a mile from our farm. Evacuations were underway and crews were on the scene.

A few days later, when it was safe, we drove to the site. The hay fields were a crater. Two horse barns were incinerated. The road had melted away and in its absence there was a track of sharp cinders.

I was a climate refugee for just one night, but it was enough. The waves of heat we are feeling now as a result of climate change aren't yet as crushing as the ones that rocked us that night, but they too are out of season. I never thought that night of what I might save from a burning house, but that is the question we all face in a time of climate change. What do you love too much to lose? Who and what will you carry to safety?

I wouldn't lie to my daughter now. I am afraid. As afraid today as I was then, for my children and for the good green world. We cannot comfort ourselves by saying it's going to be okay. We need what's in those bundles. We can't escape by going to the neighbors', and we can't afford to talk quietly.

My family could go home again the next day. But what about the Alaskan towns being swallowed alive by the rising Bering Sea? The Bangladeshi farmer whose fields are flooded? Oil burning in the Gulf? Everywhere you look, you see it coming. Coral reefs lost to warming oceans. Forest fires in Amazonia. The frozen Russian taiga an inferno vaporizing carbon stored there for ten thousand years. These are the fires of the scorched path. Let this not be the seventh fire. I pray we have not already passed the fork in the road.

What does it mean to be the people of the seventh fire, to walk back along the ancestral road and pick up what was left behind? How do we recognize what we should reclaim and what is dangerous refuse? What is truly medicine for the living earth and what is a drug of deception? None of us can recognize every piece, let alone carry it all. We need each other, to take a song, a word, a story, a tool, a ceremony and put it in our bundles. Not for ourselves, but for the ones yet to be born, for all our relations. Collectively, we assemble from the wisdom of the past a vision for the future, a worldview shaped by mutual flourishing.

Our spiritual leaders interpret this prophecy as the choice between the deadly road of materialism that threatens the land and the people, and the soft path of wisdom, respect, and reciprocity that is held in the teachings of the first fire. It is said that if the people choose the green path, then all races will go forward together to light the eighth and final fire of peace and brotherhood, forging the great nation that was foretold long ago.

Supposing we are able to turn from destruction and choose the green path? What will it take to light the eighth fire? I don't know, but our people have a long acquaintance with fire. Perhaps there are lessons in the building of a handmade fire that will help us now, teachings gleaned from the seventh fire. Fires do not make themselves. The earth provides the materials and the laws of thermodynamics. Humans must provide the work and the knowledge and the wisdom to use the power of fire for good. The spark itself is a mystery, but we know that before that fire can be lit, we have to gather the tinder, the thoughts, and the practices that will nurture the flame.

In making a handmade fire, so much depends on the plants, two pieces of cedar, a yielding board, a straight shaft, made for each other, male and female from the same tree. The bow a flexible wand of striped maple, a shapely grip to bear the bowstring twined of dogbane fiber. Stroking back and forth, back and forth, the shaft spinning, feeling its way into the bowl that burns to meet its shape.

So much depends on the body, each joint at the right angle, left arm wrapped around knee and braced at the shin, left leg bent, back stretched, shoulders locked, left forearm bearing down, right arm pushes and pulls in one smooth draw without breaking the plane of the upright shin. So much depends on the architecture, stability in three dimensions and fluidity in the fourth.

So much depends on the motion of the shaft against the board so that movement becomes friction, heat building and building, spinning and spinning the drill down on the bowl, burning its way into a black and shining space so smooth the pressure and heat burn from the wood a fine powder, which gathers together in its need for warmth until it forms into a coal that falls under its own weight through a notch in the board onto the waiting tinder.

So much depends on the tinder, the flyaway bits of cattail fluff, the softened wads of cedar bark rubbed between hands until the fibers are loose and mingled with their own dust, the shreds of yellow birch bark torn like confetti and all formed into a ball like a warbler's nest, a rough loose weave, a nest for a firebird where a coal will be laid, the whole wrapped in a sleeve of birch bark open at the ends for the entrance and exit of air.

Time and again I get to this point, where the heat has built and the fragrant smoke from the burning cedar bowl begins to rise around my face. Almost, I think, almost, and then my hand slips and the spindle goes flying and the coal breaks apart and I'm left with no fire and an aching arm. My struggle with the bow drill is a struggle to achieve reciprocity, to find a way that knowledge, body, mind, and spirit can all be brought into harmony, to harness human gifts to create a gift for the earth. It's not that the tools are lacking—the pieces are all there, but something is missing. *I* do not have it. I hear again the teachings of the seventh fire: turn back along the path and gather up what has been left beside the trail.

And I remember *shkitagen*, the firekeeper fungus, the holder of the spark that cannot be extinguished. I go back to where the wisdom lives, in the woods, and humbly ask for help. I lay down my gift, in return for all that is given, and start again.

So much depends on the spark that is nurtured by *shkitagen* gold and kindled by a song. So much depends on the air, its passage through the tinder nest, strong enough to make it glow, not so strong as to blow it out, breath of wind and not of man, bundle swung back and forth through Creator's breath to make it grow, embracing bark and dust propagating heat on heat, oxygen is fuel for fuel until smoke plumes billow in sweet fragrance, light erupts, and you hold in your hand a fire.

As the seventh fire people walk the path, we should also be looking for *shkitagen*, the ones who hold the spark that cannot be extinguished. We find the firekeepers all along the path and greet them with gratitude and humility that against all odds, they have carried the ember forward, waiting to be breathed into life. In seeking the *shkitagen* of the forest and the *shkitagen* of the spirit, we ask for open eyes and open minds, hearts open enough to embrace our more-than-human kin, a willingness to engage intelligences not our own. We'll need trust in the generosity of the good green earth to provide this gift and trust in human people to reciprocate.

I don't know how the eighth fire will be lit. But I do know we can gather the tinder that will nurture the flame, that we can be *shkitagen* to carry the fire, as it was carried to us. Is this not a holy thing, the kindling of this fire? So much depends on the spark.

Defeating Windigo

In the spring I walk across the meadow toward my medicine woods, where the plants give their gifts with unstinting generosity. It is mine not by deed, but by care. I've come here for decades to be with them, to listen, to learn, and to gather.

The woods are a drift of white trillium where the snow was, but still I feel a chill. The light is somehow different. I cross the ridge where unrecognizable footprints followed mine in last winter's blizzard. I should have known what those tracks meant. Where they were I now find the deep-rutted prints of trucks headed across the field. The flowers are there, as they have been beyond memory, but the trees are gone. My neighbor brought in the loggers over the winter.

There are so many ways to harvest honorably, but he chose otherwise, leaving only diseased beech and a few old hemlocks, worthless to the mill. The trillium, bloodroot, hepatica, bellwort, trout lily, ginger, and wild leeks are all smiling their last into the spring sun, which will burn them out when summer comes to a forest without trees. They trusted that the maples would be there, but the maples are gone. And they trusted me. Next year this will all be brambles—garlic mustard and buckthorn, the invasive species that follow Windigo footprints.

I fear that a world made of gifts cannot coexist with a world made of commodities. I fear that I have no power to protect what I love against the Windigo.

In days of legend, the people were so terrorized by the specter of Windigos that they tried to devise ways of defeating them. Given the rampant destruction wrought by our contemporary Windigo-mind, I wondered if our ancient stories contained some wisdom that might guide us today.

There are stories of banishment that we might emulate, making pariahs of the destroyers and divesting ourselves of complicity with their enterprises. There are stories of attempted drownings, burnings, and assorted murders, but the Windigo always comes back. There are endless tales of brave men on snowshoes, fighting through blizzards to track and kill the Windigo before it preyed again, but the beast almost always slips away in the storm.

Some folks argue that we need do nothing at all—that the unholy coupling of greed and growth and carbon will make the world hot enough to melt the Windigo heart once and for all. Climate change will unequivocally defeat economies that are based on constant taking without giving in return. But before the Windigo dies, it will take so much that we love along with it. We can wait for climate change to turn the world and the Windigo into a puddle of red-tinged meltwater, or we can strap on our snowshoes and track him down.

In our stories, when humans alone could not conquer them, the people called upon their champion, Nanabozho, to be light against darkness, a song against the shriek of the Windigo. Basil Johnston tells the story of an epic battle fought for many days with legions of warriors, led by their hero. There was fierce fighting, many weapons, trickery, and courage as they sought to surround the monster in his lair. But I noticed something in the background of this story different from any Windigo tale I'd ever heard: You can smell flowers. There was no snow, no blizzard; the only ice was in the heart of the Windigo. Nanabozho had chosen to hunt down the monster in the summer. The warriors paddled across ice-free lakes to the island where the Windigo had his summer refuge. The Windigo is most powerful in the Hungry Time, in winter. With the warm breezes his power wanes.

Summer in our language is *niibin*—the time of plenty—and it was in *niibin* that Nanabozho faced down the Windigo and defeated him. Here is the arrow that weakens the monster of overconsumption, a medicine that heals the sickness: its name is plenty. In winter, when scarcity is at its zenith, the Windigo rages beyond control, but when abundance reigns the hunger fades away and with it the power of the monster.

In an essay describing hunter-gatherer peoples with few possessions as the original affluent society, anthropologist Marshall Sahlins reminds us that, "modern capitalist societies, however richly endowed, dedicate themselves to the proposition of scarcity. Inadequacy of economic means is the first principle of the world's wealthiest peoples." The shortage is due not to how much material wealth there actually is, but to the way in which it is exchanged or circulated. The market system artificially creates scarcity by blocking the flow between the source and the consumer. Grain may rot in the warehouse while hungry people starve because they cannot pay for it. The result is famine for some and diseases of excess for others. The very earth that sustains us is being destroyed to fuel injustice. An economy that grants personhood to corporations but denies it to the more-than-human beings: this is a Windigo economy.

What is the alternative? And how do we get there? I don't know for certain, but I believe the answer is contained within our teachings of "One Bowl and One Spoon," which holds that the gifts of the earth are all in one bowl, all to be shared from a single spoon. This is the vision of the economy of the commons, wherein resources fundamental to our well-being, like water and land and forests, are commonly held rather than commodified. Properly managed, the commons approach maintains abundance, not scarcity. These contemporary economic alternatives strongly echo the Indigenous worldview in which the earth exists not as private property, but as a commons, to be tended with respect and reciprocity for the benefit of all.

And yet, while creating an alternative to destructive economic structures is imperative, it is not enough. It is not just changes in policies that we need, but also changes to the heart. Scarcity and plenty are as much qualities of the mind and spirit as they are of the economy. Gratitude plants the seed for abundance.

Each of us comes from people who were once Indigenous. We can reclaim our membership in the cultures of gratitude that formed our old relationships with the living earth. Gratitude is a powerful antidote to Windigo psychosis. A deep awareness of the gifts of the earth and of each other is medicine. The practice of gratitude lets us hear the badgering of marketers as the stomach grumblings of a Windigo. It celebrates cultures of regenerative reciprocity, where wealth is understood to be having enough to share and riches are counted in mutually beneficial relationships. Besides, it makes us happy.

Gratitude for all the earth has given us lends us courage to turn and face the Windigo that stalks us, to refuse to participate in an economy that destroys the beloved earth to line the pockets of the greedy, to demand an economy that is aligned with life, not stacked against it. It's easy to write that, harder to do.

I throw myself on the ground, pounding my fists and grieving the assault on my medicine woods. I don't know how to defeat the monster. I have no arsenal of weapons, no legions of fighters like those who followed Nanabozho into battle. I am not a warrior. I was raised by Strawberries, who even now are budding at my feet. Amid the Violets. And Yarrow. And Asters and Goldenrod that are just emerging, and the blades of Sweetgrass shining in the sun. In that moment, I know that I am not alone. I lie in the meadow surrounded by the legions who do stand with me. I may not know what to do, but they do, giving of their medicine gifts as they always do, to sustain the world. We are not powerless against the Windigo, *they say.* Remember that we already have everything we need. *And so—we conspire.*

When I get to my feet, Nanabozho has appeared beside me, with resolute eyes and a trickster grin. "You have to think like the monster to defeat him," he says. "Like dissolves like." He points with his eyes to a line of dense shrubs at the edge of the woods. "Give him a taste of his own medicine," he says with a smirk. He walks into the gray thicket and laughter overtakes him as he disappears.

I've never gathered buckthorn before; the blue-black berries stain my fingers.

I've tried to stay away from it, but it follows you. It is a rampant invader of disturbed places. It takes over the forest, starving other plants of light and space. Buckthorn also poisons the soil, preventing the growth of any species but itself, creating a floristic desert. You have to acknowledge that it's a winner in the free market, a success story built on efficiency, monopoly, and the creation of scarcity. It is a botanical imperialist, stealing land from the native species.

I gather all summer, sitting with each species that offers itself to the cause, listening and learning its gifts. I've always made teas for colds, salves for skin, but never this. Making medicine is not undertaken lightly. It is a sacred responsibility. The beams in my house are hung with drying plants, shelves filled with jars of roots and leaves. Waiting for winter.

When it comes, I walk the woods in my snowshoes, leaving an unmistakable trail toward home. A braid of sweetgrass hangs by my door. The three shining strands represent the unity of mind, body, and spirit that makes us whole. In the Windigo, the braid is unraveled; that is the disease that drives him to destruction. That braid reminds me that when we braid the hair of Mother Earth we remember all that is given to us and our responsibility to care for those gifts in return. In this way the gifts are sustained and all are fed. No one goes hungry.

Last night, my house was full of food and friends, the laughter and light spilling out on the snow. I thought I saw him pass by the window, gazing in with hunger. But tonight I am alone and the wind is rising.

I heft my cast-iron kettle, the biggest pot I have, onto the stove and set the water to boil. I add to it a good handful of dried berries. And then another. The berries dissolve to a syrupy liquid, blue-black and inky. Remembering Nanabozho's counsel, I say a prayer and empty in the rest of the jar.

Into a second pot I pour a pitcher of purest spring water and onto its surface I scatter a pinch of petals from one jar, bark shreds from another. All carefully chosen, each to its purpose. I add a length of root, a handful of leaves, and a spoonful of berries to the golden tea, tinged with rosy pink. I set it to simmer and sit by the fire to wait.

The snow hisses against the window, the wind moans in the trees. He has come, followed my tracks home just as I knew he would. I put the sweetgrass in my pocket, take a deep breath, and open the door. I'm afraid to do this, but more afraid of what happens if I don't.

He looms above me, wild red eyes blazing against the hoar frost of his face. He bares his yellow fangs and reaches for me with his bony hands. My own hands tremble as I thrust into his bloodstained fingers a cup of scalding buckthorn tea. He slurps it down at once and starts to howl for more—devoured by the pain of emptiness, he always wants more. He pulls the whole iron kettle from me and drinks it in greedy gulps, the syrup freezing to his chin in dripping black icicles. Throwing the empty pot aside, he reaches for me again, but before his fingers can surround my neck he turns from the door and staggers backward out into the snow.

I see him doubled over, overcome with violent retching. The carrion stench of his breath mixes with the reek of shit as the buckthorn loosens his bowels. A small dose of buckthorn is a laxative. A strong dose is a purgative, and a whole kettle, an emetic. It is Windigo nature: he wanted every last drop. So now he is vomiting up coins and coal slurry, clumps of sawdust from my woods, clots of tar sand, and the little bones of birds. He spews Solvay waste, gags on an entire oil slick. When he's done, his stomach continues to heave but all that comes up is the thin liquid of loneliness.

He lies spent in the snow, a stinking carcass, but still dangerous when the hunger rises to fill the new emptiness. I run back in the house for the second pot and carry it to his side, where the snow has melted around him. His eyes are glazed over but I hear his stomach rumble so I hold the cup to his lips. He turns his head away as if it were poison. I take a sip, to reassure him and because he is not the only one who needs it. I feel the medicines standing beside me. And then he drinks, just a sip at a time of the golden-pink tea, tea of Willow to quell the fever of want and Strawberries to mend the heart. With the nourishing broth of the Three Sisters and infused with savory Wild Leeks, the medicines enter his bloodstream: White Pine for unity, justice from Pecans, the humility of Spruce roots. He drinks down the compassion of Witch Hazel, the respect of Cedars, a blessing of Silverbells, all sweetened with the Maple of gratitude. You can't know reciprocity until you know the gift. He is helpless before their power.

His head falls back, leaving the cup still full. He closes his eyes. There is just one more part of the medicine. I am no longer afraid. I sit down beside him on the newly greening grass. "Let me tell you a story," I say as the ice melts away. "She fell like a maple seed, pirouetting from the autumn sky."

Epilogue: Returning the Gift

R ed over green, raspberries bead the thicket on a summer afternoon. The blue jay picking on the other side of this patch has
a beak as red-stained as my fingers, which go to my mouth as
often as to the bowl. I reach under the brambles for a dangling cluster and
there in the dappled shade is a grinning turtle, shin deep in fallen fruit,
stretching his neck up for more. I'll let his berries be. The earth has plenty
and offers us abundance, spreading her gifts over the green: strawberries,
raspberries, blueberries, cherries, currants—that we might fill our bowls.
Niibin, we call summer in Potawatomi, "the time of plenty," and also time
for our tribal gathering, for powwows and ceremony.

Red over green, the blankets spread on the grass beneath the arbor
are piled high with gifts. Basketballs and furled umbrellas, peyote-
stitched key chains and Ziploc bags of wild rice. Everybody lines up to
choose a gift while the hosts stand by, beaming. The teenagers are dispatched to carry choice items to elders seated in the circle, too frail to
navigate the crowd. *Megwech, megwech*—the thank yous circle among
us. Ahead of me a toddler, besotted with abundance, grabs a whole armload. Her mother bends and whispers in her ear. She stands indecisive for
a moment and lays it all back down, save a neon-yellow squirt gun.

And then we dance. The drum begins the giveaway song and everyone joins the circle in regalia of swaying fringe, nodding feathers, rainbow shawls, T-shirts, and jeans. The ground resonates with the fall
of moccasined feet. Each time the song circles around to the honor beats,
we dance in place and raise the gifts above our heads, waving necklaces,

baskets, and stuffed animals, whooping to honor the gifts and the givers. Amid the laughter and the singing, everyone belongs.

This is our traditional giveaway, the *minidewak*, an old ceremony well loved by our people and a frequent feature of powwows. In the outside world, people who are celebrating life events can look forward to receiving presents in their honor. In the Potawatomi way, this expectation is turned upside down. It is the honored one who *gives* the gifts, who piles the blanket high to share good fortune with everyone in the circle.

Often, if the giveaway is small and personal, every gift will be handmade. Sometimes a whole community might work all year long to fashion the presents for guests they do not even know. For a big intertribal gathering with hundreds of people, the blanket is likely to be a blue plastic tarp strewn with gleanings from the discount bins at Walmart. No matter what the gift is, a black ash basket or a pot holder, the sentiment is the same. The ceremonial giveaway is an echo of our oldest teachings.

Generosity is simultaneously a moral and a material imperative, especially among people who live close to the land and know its waves of plenty and scarcity. Where the well-being of one is linked to the well-being of all. Wealth among traditional people is measured by having enough to give away. Hoarding the gift, we become constipated with wealth, bloated with possessions, too heavy to join the dance.

Sometimes there's someone, maybe even a whole family, who doesn't understand and takes too much. They heap up their acquisitions beside their lawn chairs. Maybe they need it. Maybe not. They don't dance, but sit alone, guarding their stuff.

In a culture of gratitude, everyone knows that gifts will follow the circle of reciprocity and flow back to you again. This time you give and next time you receive. Both the honor of giving and the humility of receiving are necessary halves of the equation. The grass in the ring is trodden down in a path from gratitude to reciprocity. We dance in a circle, not in a line.

After the dance, a little boy in a grass dance outfit tosses down his new toy truck, already tired of it. His dad makes him pick it up and then sits him down. A gift is different from something you buy, possessed of meaning outside its material boundaries. You never dishonor the gift. A gift asks something of you. To take care of it. And something more.

I don't know the origin of the giveaway, but I think that we learned it from watching the plants, especially the berries who offer up their gifts all wrapped in red and blue. We may forget the teacher, but our language remembers: our word for the giveaway, *minidewak*, means "they give from the heart." At the word's center lives the word *min*. *Min* is a root word for *gift*, but it is also the word for *berry*. In the poetry of our language, might speaking of *minidewak* remind us to be as the berries?

The berries are always present at our ceremonies. They join us in a wooden bowl. One big bowl and one big spoon, which are passed around the circle, so that each person can taste the sweetness, remember the gifts, and say thank you. They carry the lesson, passed to us by our ancestors, that the generosity of the land comes to us as one bowl, one spoon. We are all fed from the same bowl that Mother Earth has filled for us. It's not just about the berries, but also about the bowl. The gifts of the earth are to be shared, but gifts are not limitless. The generosity of the earth is not an invitation to take it all. Every bowl has a bottom. When it's empty, it's empty. And there is but one spoon, the same size for everyone.

How do we refill the empty bowl? Is gratitude alone enough? Berries teach us otherwise. When berries spread out their giveaway blanket, offering their sweetness to birds and bears and boys alike, the transaction does not end there. Something beyond gratitude is asked of us. The berries trust that we will uphold our end of the bargain and disperse their seeds to new places to grow, which is good for berries and for boys. They remind us that all flourishing is mutual. We need the berries and the berries need us. Their gifts multiply by our care for them, and dwindle from our neglect. We are bound in a covenant of reciprocity, a pact of mutual responsibility to sustain those who sustain us. And so the empty bowl is filled.

Somewhere along the line, though, people have abandoned berry teachings. Instead of sowing richness, we diminish the possibilities for the future at every turn. But the uncertain path to the future could be illuminated by language. In Potawatomi, we speak of the land as *emingoyak:*

that which has been given to us. In English, we speak of the land as "natural resources" or "ecosystem services," as if the lives of other beings were our property. As if the earth were not a bowl of berries, but an open pit mine, and the spoon a gouging shovel.

Imagine that while our neighbors were holding a giveaway, someone broke into their home to take whatever he wanted. We would be outraged at the moral trespass. So it should be for the earth. The earth gives away for free the power of wind and sun and water, but instead we break open the earth to take fossil fuels. Had we taken only that which is given to us, had we reciprocated the gift, we would not have to fear our own atmosphere today.

We are all bound by a covenant of reciprocity: plant breath for animal breath, winter and summer, predator and prey, grass and fire, night and day, living and dying. Water knows this, clouds know this. Soil and rocks know they are dancing in a continuous giveaway of making, unmaking, and making again the earth.

Our elders say that ceremony is the way we can remember to remember. In the dance of the giveaway, remember that the earth is a gift that we must pass on, just as it came to us. When we forget, the dances we'll need will be for mourning. For the passing of polar bears, the silence of cranes, for the death of rivers and the memory of snow.

When I close my eyes and wait for my heartbeat to match the drum, I envision people recognizing, for perhaps the first time, the dazzling gifts of the world, seeing them with new eyes, just as they teeter on the cusp of undoing. Maybe just in time. Or maybe too late. Spread on the grass, green over brown, they will honor at last the giveaway from Mother Earth. Blankets of moss, robes of feathers, baskets of corn, and vials of healing herbs. Silver salmon, agate beaches, sand dunes. Thunderheads and snowdrifts, cords of wood and herds of elk. Tulips. Potatoes. Luna moths and snow geese. And berries. More than anything, I want to hear a great song of thanks rise on the wind. I think that song might save us. And then, as the drum begins, we will dance, wearing regalia in celebration of the living earth: a waving fringe of tallgrass prairie, a whirl of butterfly shawls, with nodding plumes of egrets, jeweled with the glitter of a phosphorescent wave. When the song pauses for the honor beats, we'll hold high our gifts and ululate their praises, a shining fish, a branch of blossoms, and a starlit night.

The moral covenant of reciprocity calls us to honor our responsibilities for all we have been given, for all that we have taken. It's our turn now, long overdue. Let us hold a giveaway for Mother Earth, spread our blankets out for her and pile them high with gifts of our own making. Imagine the books, the paintings, the poems, the clever machines, the compassionate acts, the transcendent ideas, the perfect tools. The fierce defense of all that has been given. Gifts of mind, hands, heart, voice, and vision all offered up on behalf of the earth. Whatever our gift, we are called to give it and to dance for the renewal of the world.

In return for the privilege of breath.

A Note on the Treatment of Plant Names

We accept with nary a thought that the names of people are capitalized. To write "george washington" would be to strip that man of his special status as a human. It would be laughable to write "Mosquito" if it were in reference to a flying insect, but acceptable if we were discussing a brand of boat. Capitalization conveys a certain distinction, the elevated position of humans and their creations in the hierarchy of beings. Biologists have widely adopted the convention of not capitalizing the common names of plants and animals unless they include the name of a human being or an official place name. Thus, the first blossoms of the spring woods are written as bloodroot and the pink star of a California woodland is Kellogg's tiger lily. This seemingly trivial grammatical rulemaking in fact expresses deeply held assumptions about human exceptionalism, that we are somehow different and indeed better than the other species who surround us. Indigenous ways of understanding recognize the personhood of all beings as equally important, not in a hierarchy but a circle. So in this book as in my life, I break with those grammatical blinders to write freely of Maple, Heron, and Wally when I mean a person, human or not; and of maple, heron, and human when I mean a category or concept.

A Note on the Treatment of Indigenous Language

The Potawatomi and Anishinaabe languages are a reflection of the land and the people. They are a living, oral tradition, which had not been written down in their long history until fairly recently. A number of writing systems have emerged to try and capture the language in regularized orthography, but there is no firm agreement on the preeminence of any one among the many variants of a large and living language. Potawatomi elder, fluent speaker, and teacher Stewart King has kindly sorted through my rudimentary use of the language, confirming meanings and advising on consistency in spelling and usage. I am most appreciative for his guidance in my understanding of language and culture. The Fiero system's double vowel orthography for writing the language has been widely adopted by many Anishinaabe speakers. Most Potawatomi, however—known as the "vowel droppers"—do not use Fiero. With respect for speakers and teachers with these different perspectives, I have tried to use the words in the way that they were originally given to me.

A Note on Indigenous Stories

I am a listener and have been listening to stories told around me for longer than I care to admit. I mean to honor my teachers by passing on the stories that they have passed on to me.

We are told that stories are living beings, they grow, they develop, they remember, they change not in their essence, but sometimes in their dress. They are shared and shaped by the land and the culture and the teller, so that one story may be told widely and differently. Sometimes only a fragment is shared, showing just one face of a many faceted story, depending on its purpose. So it is with the stories shared here.

Traditional stories are the collective treasures of a people and can't easily be attributed with a literature citation to an individual source. Many are not to be publicly shared and these I have not included, but many are freely disseminated so that they may do their work in the wider world. For these stories, which exist in many versions, I have chosen to cite a published source as a reference, while acknowledging that the version I share has been enriched by hearing it multiple times in different tellings. For some, I do not know of a published source for a story passed on in the oral tradition. *Chi megwech* to the storytellers.

Sources

Allen, Paula Gunn. *Grandmothers of the Light: A Medicine Woman's Sourcebook*. Boston: Beacon Press, 1991.

Awiakta, Marilou. *Selu: Seeking the Corn-Mother's Wisdom*. Golden: Fulcrum, 1993.

Benton-Banai, Edward. *The Mishomis Book: The Voice of the Ojibway*. Red School House, 1988.

Berkes, Fikret. *Sacred Ecology*, 2nd ed. New York: Routledge, 2008.

Caduto, Michael J. and Joseph Bruchac. *Keepers of Life: Discovering Plants through Native American Stories and Earth Activities for Children*. Golden: Fulcrum, 1995.

Cajete, Gregory. *Look to the Mountain: An Ecology of Indigenous Education*. Asheville: Kivaki Press, 1994.

Hyde, Lewis. *The Gift: Imagination and the Erotic Life of Property*. New York: Random House, 1979.

Johnston, Basil. *The Manitous: The Spiritual World of the Ojibway*. Saint Paul: Minnesota Historical Society, 2001.

LaDuke, Winona. *Recovering the Sacred: The Power of Naming and Claiming*. Cambridge: South End Press, 2005.

Macy, Joanna. *World as Lover, World as Self: Courage for Global Justice and Ecological Renewal*. Berkeley: Parallax Press, 2007.

Moore, Kathleen Dean and Michael P. Nelson, eds. *Moral Ground: Ethical Action for a Planet in Peril*. San Antonio: Trinity University Press, 2011.

Nelson, Melissa K., ed. *Original Instructions: Indigenous Teachings for a Sustainable Future*. Rochester: Bear and Company, 2008.

Porter, Tom. *Kanatsiohareke: Traditional Mohawk Indians Return to Their Ancestral Homeland*. Greenfield Center: Bowman Books, 1998.

Ritzenthaler, R. E. and P. Ritzenthaler. *The Woodland Indians of the Western Great Lakes*. Prospect Heights, IL: Waveland Press, 1983.

Shenandoah, Joanne and Douglas M. George. *Skywoman: Legends of the Iroquois*. Santa Fe: Clear Light Publishers, 1988.

Stewart, Hilary and Bill Reid. *Cedar: Tree of Life to the Northwest Coast Indians*. Douglas and MacIntyre, Ltd., 2003.

Stokes, John and Kanawahienton. *Thanksgiving Address: Greetings to the Natural World*. Six Nations Indian Museum and The Tracking Project, 1993.

Suzuki, David and Peter Knudtson. *Wisdom of the Elders: Sacred Native Stories of Nature*. New York: Bantam Books, 1992.

Treuer, Anton S. *Living Our Language: Ojibwe Tales and Oral Histories: A Bilingual Anthology*. Saint Paul: Minnesota Historical Society, 2001.

Acknowledgments

I owe a debt of gratitude for the lap of my Sitka Spruce grandma, the shelter of White Willow, the Balsam Fir beneath my sleeping bag, and that patch of Blueberry in Katherine's Bay. For the White Pine that sings me to sleep, and the one that woke me up, for the Goldthread tea, for June Strawberries and the Bird on the Wing Orchids, to the Maples that frame my door, for the last Raspberries of fall and the first Leeks of spring, for Cattail, Paper Birch, Spruce root who care for me body and soul and Black Ash who holds my thoughts, for Daffodils and dewy Violets and for Goldenrod and Asters who still leave me breathless.

For the best people I know: my parents Robert *Wasay ankwat* and Patricia *Wawaskonesen* Wall, who have given me lifelong love and encouragement, who carried the spark and fanned the flames, and my daughters Larkin Lee Kimmerer and Linden Lee Lane, for the inspiration of their beings and for their gracious permission to weave their stories into mine. There are not thanks enough for the love with which I have been showered, in which all things are possible. *Megwech kine gego.*

I have been blessed with the guidance of wise and generous teachers who have contributed much to these stories, whether they know it or not. I say *Chi Megwech* to those to whom I have been listening and learning through their teachings and their lived examples, including my Anishinaabe relations Stewart King, Barbara Wall, Wally Meshigaud, Jim Thunder, Justin Neely, Kevin Finney, Big Bear Johnson, Dick Johnson, and the Pigeon Family. *Nya wenha* to my Haudenosaunee neighbors, friends and colleagues Oren Lyons, Irving Powless, Jeanne Shenandoah, Audrey Shenandoah, Freida Jacques, Tom Porter, Dan Longboat, Dave Arquette, Noah Point, Neil Patterson, Bob Stevenson, Theresa Burns, Lionel LaCroix, and Dean George. And to those myriad teachers along the way at conferences, cultural gatherings, fires, and kitchen tables whose names are forgotten, but whose lessons remain: *igwien*. Your words and actions have fallen like seeds on the fertile ground, and my intention is to nurture them with care and respect. I accept full responsibility for the unknowing errors that I will undoubtedly make from my own ignorance.

Writing is a solitary practice, yet we do not write alone. The kinship of a writing community that inspires, supports, and listens deeply is such a gift. Many thanks to Kathleen Dean Moore, Libby Roderick, Charles Goodrich, Alison Hawthorne Deming, Carolyn Servid, Robert Michael Pyle, Jesse Ford, Michael Nelson, Janine Debaise, Nan Gartner, Joyce Homan, Dick Pearson, Bev Adams, Richard Weiskopf, Harsey Leonard, and others who have offered their encouragement and critique. To my friends and family who have kept me going, your warmth is written into every page. I owe special gratitude to my dear students throughout the years who are so frequently my teachers and who give me faith in the future.

Many of these pages were filled during the tender care of writers' residencies at the Blue Mountain Center, The Sitka Center for Art and Ecology, and the Mesa Refuge. They were also inspired by time at the Spring Creek Project and the Long Term Ecological Reflections residency at the H. J. Andrews Experimental Forest. Many thanks to those who make these times of solitude and support possible.

Waewaenen and special thanks are offered to my welcoming hosts at the College of the Menominee Nation: Mike Dockry, Melissa Cook, Jeff Grignon, and the wonderful students there who created an inspiring and motivational environment in which to complete this work.

Special thanks to my editor, Patrick Thomas, for believing in this work and for his care, skill, and patience with me in shepherding these pages from manuscript to book.

ROBIN WALL KIMMERER is a mother, scientist, decorated professor, and enrolled member of the Citizen Potawatomi Nation. Her first book, *Gathering Moss*, was awarded the John Burroughs Medal for outstanding nature writing. Her writings have appeared in *Orion*, *Whole Terrain*, and numerous scientific journals. She lives in Syracuse, New York, where she is a SUNY Distinguished Teaching Professor of Environmental Biology, and the founder and director of the Center for Native Peoples and the Environment.

Interior design & typesetting by Mary Austin Speaker
Typeset in Fournier

Fournier is a typeface created by the Monotype Corporation in 1924, based on types cut in the mid-eighteenth century by Pierre-Simon Fournier, a French typographer. The specific cuts used as a reference for Fournier are referred to as "St Augustin Ordinaire" in Fournier's influential *Manuel Typographique*, published in 1764 in Paris.

milkweed
editions

Founded as a nonprofit organization in 1980,
Milkweed Editions is an independent publisher. Our mission
is to identify, nurture and publish transformative literature,
and build an engaged community around it.

Milkweed Editions is based in Bde Ota (Minneapolis) within
Mni Sota Makoče, the traditional homeland of the Dakota people.
Residing here since time immemorial, Dakota people still call
Mni Sota Makoče home, with four federally recognized Dakota nations
and many more Dakota people residing in what is now the state of
Minnesota. Due to continued legacies of colonization, genocide, and
forced removal, generations of Dakota people remain disenfranchised
from their traditional homeland. Presently, Mni Sota Makoče has
become a refuge and home for many Indigenous nations and peoples,
including seven federally recognized Ojibwe nations. We humbly
encourage readers to reflect upon the historical legacies held
in the lands they occupy.

milkweed.org